Dennis Delaney

SAVING WHALES

"we had all the momentum; we
were riding the crest of a high
and beautiful wave"

Hunter S. Thompson

GO WEST YOUNG MAN

The sun felt good on the back of his neck. He'd been sitting on this exact same spot of sand all night and the sun rising behind him was beginning to defrost his frozen body. As he began to thaw, his vision slowly returned. This time of morning, in Malibu, on a school day, there weren't many people on the beach. But they were on the way. You could feel it. It was going to be one of those perfect Southern California days.

He hadn't traveled an inch from the night before. His gaze firmly fixed on the ocean in front of him. Something caught his eye, a white puff, a spout of water, then a second, and a third. A pod of California Gray whales traveling very close to shore. The whales appeared to slow down and stop right in front of him. They seemed to be basking. Engaged in pure whale pleasure.

The serenity of the scene was abruptly shattered by the largest whale shooting straight up and out of the water, like a missile fired from a submarine. There was a great splash, then nothing, and then eye contact. The greatest whale had surfaced and was staring right into his eyes. Locked in a stare-down. Not a confrontational stare-down mind you, more like a mutual respect and recognition stare-down. After several moments where time stood still, the whale and its entourage slipped below the surface of the water and were not seen again.

He smoothed the sand in front of him, where his

4

feet had dug deep trenches for the past twelve hours. He needed to tidy up. To simulate order. This was his spot, this spot of sand, where he went to 'find himself', to seek clarity; to one day discover the road map out of the jungle. So far, no such luck. Not last year, not last night, not today. Not so fast. His radar detected something. Close by. Intense. He didn't move a muscle or turn his head, but he could tell there was something, someone, right next to him. Invading his space. Feminine. She copied his way of sitting and staring out to sea. He didn't acknowledge her existence.

"How did you do that?" she said.

He continued to ignore her.

"Are you special?"

After everything that had happened over the last forty-eight hours, the last forty-eight months, this was the last thing he needed, this was the last thing he should suffer. Another young woman. Questioning him. Needling him. On his fucking spot!

"Excuse me?" he said without looking at her.

"Do you think you're special?" she fired back.

"No."

"That whale was looking right at you. You two were having a moment there."

Yesterday, his girlfriend, Lucinda, told him that she was leaving him. Moving out of their apartment, their "shitty Hollywood" apartment she said, and moving in with her History professor who lives in the Valley. The same History professor, by the way, that he encouraged her to study with.

Many cheap beer-and-shot combos later, he made

5

his way here, to his spot, under the cover of darkness, to sort it all out.

"I don't have any money," he said.

"What's your name?" she said.

He considered this question for a few conflicted moments. She smelled good and he's always been a sucker for that sort of thing.

"West."

"Wes?"

"No. West. Like in 'Go west young man'."

"I see. I'm Delilah."

Delilah reached out her hand, but he declined and retreated back into awkward silence mode. After a long uncomfortable pause, he blinked.

"Like Samson and Delilah?"

She dropped a flyer in his lap. West cautiously took the flyer and examined it. It was an invitation. The world-renowned environmental group GreenPlanet had opened a new Los Angeles office. They were looking for volunteers. On the opposite side of the flyer, a drawing of a humpback whale caught his eye. It wasn't quite right. Anatomically. The dorsal fin was too far forward. He broke out of his frozen position to look at Delilah, but she was gone.

#

Weston 'West' Walker was not a man with a clear plan. He was not a student in the traditional sense of the word. Rather, he was more a classically trained drifter guided by an intuitive compass. It never occurred to him that committed study might be required to master a subject, win a debate, or rise to

6

the top. Things came relatively easy to him. He was an adept skimmer. A snapshot artist. Oblivious to prep courses, the need for impressive extracurricular activities, and the perfect 'why you should accept me into your hallowed halls' essay, he was still able to open doors and move forward. It was easy for him to catch the wave, hit the down-the-line winner, and get the girl. It would only be later in life that he would uncomfortably, reluctantly, recognize that some doors are more barricaded than others, that some doors were indeed hard to open, not so much as an inch if you didn't have all of the boxes checked, and West never was a box checker.

He was a float down the river and let it take you where it may guy. An adventure awaits around every turn guy. If it feels good, do it. Again and again. During his time at UC Santa Cruz, he took the same astronomy course three times simply because he loved everything about it. It captured his imagination. He treasured the walk from one end of campus, through the redwoods, across the long wooden bridge, amidst the nonchalant wildlife, finally arriving at the gleaming white building that housed the lecture hall. Inside, the lights were off and the stars were splashed across the ceiling. Galaxies and Cosmology. That was the name of the course. For West, it could easily have been named What Does It All Mean? Why Are We Here? Where Do We Go From Here?

Prior to his arrival at the university, it was necessary for him to wrap up the sticky business of his Conscientious Objector status with the U.S. Selective Service Agency. His refusal to serve in the military, in

7

any capacity, as long as the war in Viet Nam raged, required him to sit before the local draft board and plead his case.

It didn't help him that he refused to serve as a medic, that he had long hair, a beard, and an upside-down American flag sewed on the ass of his jeans. It didn't help that he was recognized from photos taken at numerous anti-war protests in the Los Angeles area, and it certainly didn't help that his older brother Wyatt, a fugitive member of the Weather Undergound, was being hunted by law enforcement at that very moment. There had been a bombing and a death. An FBI agent. Wyatt was a suspect. West was seventeen. Still in high school. Wet behind the ears.

The interrogation room at the draft board was exceedingly claustrophobic, quite the opposite of the Galaxies and Cosmology lecture hall. The long rectangular table and dozen chairs took up most of the space. When the chairs were occupied and the door was closed, breathing was strained.

Sitting around the table were men in suits, men in military uniforms, and West. They didn't like him and he didn't like them. Fair enough. Let's do this.

They asked him 'what if' questions. What if armed men broke into your mother's home, were about to murder her, and you could save her by shooting them? Killing them? Would you?

In this particular instance West came prepared. Days before, he had met with the dean of the local law school who tutored him in the art of draft board inquisition. "Don't answer hypotheticals. They're setting a trap."

If he answered yes he would kill to save his mother, off to Viet Nam he would go. If he answered no he would let her die, they would unanimously conclude that he was lying to avoid service; off to Viet Nam he would go. Therefore, he calmly reiterated his opposition to the war and his refusal to participate in any manner.

Why, they wondered, wouldn't he serve as a medic? He wouldn't be made to carry a weapon. Wouldn't have to kill anyone. Right? Wrong. It's a war zone. Carnage is omnipresent. Imminent death for yourself and your comrades is rife. "The best-laid plans of mice and men often go awry." He didn't intend to learn what he would have to do in a situation like that. The outcome didn't bode well. Instead, he offered gladly to serve his time stateside in the Conservation Corps.

That was that. Inquisition adjourned. Soon after, the mailman handed him two letters, one from the draft board explaining that the draft had been suspended. "At this time your service will not be required." The other letter read "congratulations on your admission to the University of California, Santa Cruz." And there you have it. The metaphorical river had swept him away from the carnage toward the carnal and the cerebral carnival. Who needs a plan?

Santa Cruz in the 1970s was a perfect fit for the man without a clear plan. He could read books, walk amongst the redwoods, and think deep thoughts. There was Steamer Lane, Positively Front Street, and the wafting of Acapulco Gold from naked meadow. There were hippie girls, and hippie drugs, and hippie

9

music, the Grateful Dead, Bob Dylan, Janis, Airplane, Hendrix, Coltrane, Miles, and Joni. Let us not forget the drum circles and the stargazing.

One might cross paths with Lawrence Ferlinghetti, Huey Newton, or Angela Davis. Perhaps Greg Bateson, Elliot Aronson, or Adrienne Rich. Maybe Alfred Hitchcock, Chick Corea, or Alan Watts. There was minimal structure, minimal restriction. It was a magical crucible for serendipitous satori. At any moment that same metaphorical river could and would whisk you away to your next adventure. The redwood spirits gently guided you to let go and flow.

And that's exactly what West did. He went with the flow. Similar to his love of Galaxies and Cosmology, he was enthralled by the Great Whales segment of his marine biology class, and he made it a priority to attend that part of the course two more times before he graduated. He couldn't help himself. He loved grand things: canyons, starry skies, vast oceans, burning deserts, the long song, revolutionary ideas, and endless possibilities. The eventual degree was in Anthropology. The education was nomadic.

#

Driving east on Sunset was always depressing for West. Heading away from the ocean usually meant he was heading toward unanswered questions and unresolved headaches.

As he passed by Tower Records, he saw a billboard displaying the upside down call letters of his favorite radio station KWOT. He turned on the radio. Tom Petty was singing 'Restless'. Perfect, he thought.

Up ahead another billboard advertising the Rolling Stones album Some Girls caught his eye and his imagination. He was in no hurry to get back to the apartment. He shuddered to think what was awaiting him. Lucinda made it quite clear last night that she wasn't bluffing. Not this time. Not like times past. Maybe the fact that she was in the middle of boxing things up, of tearing things down, erasing their history, while simultaneously, enthusiastically, reading him the riot act, maybe that's what made him think this time was very different.

Delilah smelled good, sounded dangerous, dreamy, and he could only imagine what she looked like since he refused to look in her direction. Maybe she was one of those faces on the Some Girls billboard? She sounded more beautiful than that. Dark haired.

Turning off the radio, flipping off the ignition, pulling up the handbrake, West stared at the rental truck parked in front of his apartment.

He could see most of his, their, furniture loaded in the back of the truck. The front door to the apartment was wide open. As he reluctantly, painfully, departed his vehicle, Lucinda came flying out the apartment door, heading straight for him. Some guy was standing behind her in the doorway.

"I need you to help Matty put the couch in the van," she said.

His name is Matty? He muttered to himself "I'm not helping anyone named Matty move my fucking couch. Fuck Matty."

He peeked into the van and saw his most coveted possession. He pointed at it like a springer spaniel

11

lasered in on a dead pheasant.

"Really?" "The foosball table?"

Lucinda stared daggers at him. Yes, technically she did buy the table, she bought everything, but she hated every second it was in their apartment. She felt it was childish and took up valuable space.

West shook his head sadly, walked past Matty into his empty apartment and picked up one end of the couch. Matty lifted the opposite end and they carried it out and threw it into the back of the van.

"We had sex multiple times on that couch," he said to Matty. "You'd think she would want a new couch."

Lucinda shook her head disgustedly, went back into the apartment, returning with her shoulder bag and some loose clothes under her arm. As she was passing by West, he grabbed his UC Santa Cruz t-shirt out from under her.

"Lu, I love you."

She looked him straight in the eye.

"Don't say another word. You love you," she said. Then she did an about face, marched to the driver's side of the van, threw herself in, and slammed the door shut.

He watched as the rental truck carrying his foosball table and his girlfriend moved down the street and out of sight. Dejectedly, he made his way to the front door of his, and now only his, apartment and took a long look. There was one lonely old beanbag chair and an old TV on an old TV stand. Besides the scattered debris of moving out, there was nothing else.

He sank down into the beanbag chair and surveyed his empty pad. An elderly calico cat appeared from the bedroom, voiced a less than confident 'Meow' and took his familiar place on West's lap as he had every right to do.

West looked at the cat as fondly as he did his departing foosball table, and as the cat curled up into a ball and went to sleep, the silence was deafening and his emptiness was gut wrenching. He sat there for a long time, hoping for a sign, a satori. Nothing. Then, as he reached into his pants pocket to assess his financial status, he found the flyer, the whale flyer.

The dorsal fin was still too far forward. It smelled like Delilah. He stared at it. The cat was in a deep, deep sleep on his lap. He looked at the flyer, then at the cat, then at his apocalyptic apartment. He closed his eyes, took a few big breaths, and joined his feline companion in some much-needed sleep.

#

When looking at the lights of the city of angels from a place of luxury, from a place high above the struggle, they sparkle, dance, and seduce even more than usual.

It was one of those rare, magically clear L.A. nights, high in the Hollywood hills. West stood alone by the pool, looking out at the city, banishing any and all thoughts of what took place the past twenty-four hours. The doors and windows of the house were open and he couldn't help but hear the party going on inside.

When he had arrived, he didn't knock, just walked in as if it was his place, his party, his friends. Truth is he didn't know a soul, but he did recognize several

13

faces as he made his way to the bar and got himself a drink.

David Crosby was in animated conversation with Jackson Browne. There was that TV star, but he couldn't remember her name. He was pretty sure that he saw a Beach Boy. There were many hoping-to-be-famous mixed in with the never-to-be-famous-but-fashionable. Music was playing on the stereo. 'Fire in the Hole' by Steely Dan.

The whiskey in his hand was superb. Quite the contrast from the night before. This entire surreal moment was indeed the polar opposite of the freezing-on-the-beach night before. Then, his radar lit up, once again. Next to him he felt a familiar, unsettling presence. This time he looked her square in the eye. Delilah Dean was stunning. Flawless. Jaw-droppingly attractive. Dark brown hair, piercing blue eyes, and a self-assuredness that staggered West like an Ali left hook square on the jaw.

"I see you made it," said Delilah.

He stared at her for a few seconds too long.

"You have quite the talent for appearing out of thin air," he replied as casually as it was possible for someone that couldn't breathe.

"Unforgettable view, isn't it?" she said knowing very well what the view was.

"Coincidentally, I happened to be passing by and I remembered the flyer and..."

Delilah didn't let him finish his feeble try at nonchalance. She hooked her arm with his non-drinking arm and pulled him toward the house.

"Come with me. There are people you need to

meet."

As she led him through the house, he couldn't understand why no one, not a single pair of eyeballs, paid her, them, any attention. How was it possible for people not to stare at her? She was mesmerizing. She was a force of nature. Yes, it was Hollywood. Yes, there were a houseful of beautiful, interesting people, but she was different. She was magnetic. She had stage presence. She smelled of patchouli.

The party guests were arranging themselves in a semi-circle, facing a large screen where a film was about to play. In addition to Delilah's scent of patchouli, there was the concomitant wafting of Humboldt Gold. She led West through the dreamy haze to a ruggedly handsome, road-weary warrior who was anxiously looking for a replacement for his empty gin and tonic. Maybe Hunter Mack drank too much. Maybe he didn't drink enough. Maybe he's seen too much. Too much horror. Too much greed, and selfishness, and stupidity. Maybe he just likes to drink.

"Hunter, this is West. Our new whale expert," Delilah said.

"I'm no expert," said West.

"He talks to whales and they talk back to him," Delilah beamed.

Hunter remained silent as he sized up West, who was trying futilely to think of something to say. They both thought 'who is this guy'?

"You know your way around a boat?" said Hunter.

West nodded his head a less than confident 'yes'. Hunter looked hard into West's eyes, gave him a wry smile and slapped him on the shoulder.

"Welcome aboard Wes," said Hunter as he walked away to find a drink and grudgingly face the assembled audience. Delilah yelled after him.

"West! It's West! As in 'Go west young man'," she exclaimed.

She looked at West who was transfixed on Hunter, the very important looking audience, and the oddly exciting scene that was playing out before him. She kissed him on the cheek.

"He likes you," she said.

He touched his cheek where she gave him the kiss, as he watched on the big screen, GreenPlanet activists led by Hunter, do battle with the Japanese whaling fleet in the South Pacific. Maneuvering small rubber Zodiac boats in between the whalers and the fleeing whales, Hunter and his comrades were risking their lives to block the shots of the Japanese whalers. West had never seen anything like this. He was shaken. He was excited.

"Jesus," he said.

"He likes to think so," said Delilah.

#

Opening his eyes was not an easy or pleasant task, but open them he eventually did. The room was dark and confusing. His head was swirling, and his nostrils filled with the smell of hot coffee. His two stockinged feet jutted out from under an unfamiliar down comforter, on an unfamiliar old leather sofa. He was missing his pants. From another room, Delilah's voice boomed out.

"Get in here," she yelled.

16

Moving into an upright seated position, he tried to focus as Delilah barked at him once again.

"C'mon cowboy, get your ass in here," she demanded.

Sans pants, West headed for the room where the voice was coming from. He stopped in her bedroom doorway and assessed the situation. Delilah, wearing boxer shorts and a worn Smith College sweatshirt, cup of coffee in hand, was sitting on her bed patting the vacant space next to her. The room was organized chaos. Clothes strewn everywhere. Stacks of records, books, and magazines. A cello case in the corner. On one wall were many photos of Delilah with assorted people. He recognized, in one of the photos, the prepossessing, well-dressed older man with his arm around her. Supreme Court Justice Thurgood Marshall. Delilah reached out the cup of coffee to him, as one would seduce a puppy with a squeaky toy. He took a quick glance down to make sure his dick was still undercover, and then proceeded to join Delilah on the bed. She handed him the cup of coffee.

"Is that Thurgood?"

Before he had a chance to finish his question, she kissed him long and slow on the mouth. When he came up for air he flailed.

"I, uh, my girlfriend and I," he mumbled.

"Yea, yea, you told me. You slept on the couch. Nothing happened," she said.

Nothing happened? Nothing happened! In the past forty-eight hours everything had happened. Lucinda left him. She stripped him of his purpose, his pride, his false sense of security, and his foosball table. He consumed an ocean of alcohol and inhaled a cloud of doubt. He crossed paths with rock stars, TV stars, and eco-warriors. He spent a night on the beach, and a night on a mysterious woman's couch. He is, at this very moment, seated next to her, in his underwear, on her bed, her patchouli on his skin as Thurgood Marshall watches over them. It appears that she went to Smith College, knows how to play the cello, reads a ton of books, and she gets more and more irresistible by the second. That's not nothing! That's something. When the world is upside down, when this beautiful creature just kissed you without warning, that's not nothing.

#

Delilah Dean was a different animal altogether. Yes, she, too, was from California, but Northern; Berkeley, not Southern; L.A. Yes, she, too, was twenty-five years of age, but a vastly more mature twenty-five than her new project Weston Walker.

She had decided at a very early age that Smith College and New England would be an integral part of her master plan to conquer the known universe. Feeling the strong need to escape the overwhelming influence of her highly charged parents—her father was a high-profile civil rights attorney; her mother a manic community organizer and honorary Black Panther—she declined the offer to attend UC Berkeley and instead made a beeline for the opposite side of the country.

Like most of her fellow Smithees, she entered thinking she would dramatically change the world. Unlike most of her classmates, she had no plans or desires for a husband, children, houses, cars, and club memberships. It never occurred to her, ever, that she wasn't equal to any man. Quite the contrary. That wasn't even a battle that she felt the need to fight. Delilah always came out on top just being Delilah.

She wasn't part of what the old guard Smith establishment referred to as "the lesbian problem." First off, there was no "problem." Second, she wasn't a member of that tribe. Third, she had bigger fish to fry (no pun intended). No, she was preparing for law school and future levers of power.

In her first weekend at Chapin House, she seduced four lads at a local Northampton pub to drop what they were doing and help her move her newly acquired double bed into her room on campus. Up until that time, no student had been allowed to have a double bed in their room, and definitely no male visitors that might be tempted to occupy said bed. Delilah didn't bother to ask. It was 1972 for God's sake. Ms. Magazine was on the newsstand. The winters got cold there.

Delilah became well known on campus. She was a frequent leader of CR groups. Consciousness Raising groups that served as extracurricular education with regards to green issues, race issues, gender issues, peace issues, etc. For a very brief time, she performed with The Deadly Nightshade, a country-folk band popular in the area. She was arrested at Westover Air Force Base protesting the continued bombing in North Viet Nam, and she organized on-campus protests that resulted in suspended classes and occupied offices. She never let herself feel too lonely in her double bed, and she didn't totally restrict it to one gender or the other.

You could find her on Davis Lawn handing out fliers for organizations like Redstockings, VVAW, NOW, ERA America, and Code Pink. She was a top-notch student that excelled while always keeping her 'eye on the future prize.' Confident, energetic, charismatic, and enthusiastic. She fired on all cylinders, crossing out the months on the calendar as they were easily conquered while steaming full speed ahead; all systems 'go', racing toward the finish line unimpeded. Until. Until she wasn't. Until things suddenly changed. Intangibly. Her spirit had inexplicably shapeshifted. Her cage had been violently rattled. Out of the blue.

Watergate? Maybe it was disillusionment and depression as a result of Watergate? Or not. Recently there had been a photo of her parents in the local paper. It was oddly shocking and a bit destabilizing. Could it be repressed parental poison? Can't be sure. Her friend Yolanda King was being harassed and bullied by the more militant schoolmates that favored Malcolm X over her father. How could, why would, anyone attack the daughter of Martin Luther King? Uncle Tom? Martin Luther King?

Delilah became very depressed, very unsure. She didn't know what was happening. Law school? Power broker? Change maker? Now those thoughts made her nauseous. Three of her four years were already in the books. She never had a 'Plan B.' What the fuck? The road ahead became very unclear.

The eventual degree was in Sociology. The education was dramatic.

He didn't sleep well, even though he passed out cold from the large quantity of all things ingested. He couldn't get that film out of his head. A modern day version of David and Goliath and Leviathan. Longhaired, scraggy-bearded, tie-dyed, hippie boys and girls, two thousand miles out at sea, in little rubber boats, intentionally, insanely, dangerously, positioning themselves razor-close to the front of the bows of speeding whaling ships. Using their bodies to block the shots from the harpoon cannons, simultaneously trying to avoid collision with the frantic, fleeing Sperm whales just feet in front of their Zodiacs. When a whale is considered, by a whaler, to be within striking distance, a two hundred and fifty pound harpoon is fired from the bow of the whaling ship into the whale. A steel cable is attached to the harpoon, which is also equipped with an explosive grenade that detonates after entering the whale's body. It is violent. Scary violent. If you happen to be in a Zodiac, a few feet behind the target whale, and harpoons are fired, with steel cables that can cut you in two like a hot knife through butter, your fate is in the hands of Davy Jones. And the aim of the cannoneer. That's what happened to Hunter and his Zodiac partner. The harpoon went flying directly over his ducking head, into the whale in front of them, the taut steel cable slicing down hard on the starboard side of the Zodiac, just missing him by inches. As the whale thrashed violently for its life, the steel cable moved back and forth over the Zodiac, requiring them to repeatedly duck and dive until they were able to steer out of harm's way just as the harpoon grenade exploded in the whales back. Whale blood and guts covered Hunter as he checked to see if he still had all of his human parts intact. The killer boat sped by the Zodiac and fired another harpoon into the same whale. This particular harpoon had an air line attached to it to keep the whale afloat. Blood covered the surface of the water as the Japanese whalers shouted angrily, waving their arms in a threatening way, while simultaneously turning high-pressured fire hoses on them. It was quite a scene and quite a film.

This is what West was reliving in his dreams all night, that and Hunter's low-key but serious remarks to the star-studded audience. It got him jacked and still had him wired. Not to mention his bedmate.

He found a spot to place his coffee cup, ran his hand through the mop of hair on his head, and leaned in to kiss Delilah the way she did him. Before lips could lock, the phone on her bedside table rang and she was on it. She reminded the caller that it was Saturday morning and that he had better have a fucking good reason to be calling. West could hear a muffled voice say "Santa Barbara." Delilah was writing with seriousness on a strategically located pad.

"On the way," she said and hung up the phone.

"Everything okay?" asked West.

"We have to go," she said as she started to get dressed.

"We?" said West.

"Dead whale on the beach. Pants on. Let's go."

Just that quick, West's life was headed in a dramatically new direction. He didn't know it yet. He never saw these things. When it came to his own life he wasn't a 'big picture' guy. He was a 'moment to moment' guy. See the tennis ball, hit the tennis ball. See the wave, surf the wave. Go to college, graduate from college. A twenty-five-year-old, shaggy-haired, surfer slash tennis bum. A very well educated bum, but bum nonetheless. He got lost the day after he was handed his diploma from UC Santa Cruz, and he hasn't found his way out of the jungle yet. Even now, asleep in the passenger seat of Delilah's 1956 T-Bird, headed north to Santa Barbara, it didn't enter his mind or dreams that the woman next to him, and the dead whale awaiting him would change him forever.

Delilah knew. She knew two days ago. Women have this ability to detect the earthquake before the ground shakes. As she pulled off of Pacific Coast Highway, she studied West sleeping. She thought to herself, "this is it, everything changes starting right now."

West felt her hand shaking his shoulder and bolted upright, wide-awake. On the beach, at waters edge, a small group of people had formed a semi-circle around the dead whale. Delilah grabbed her camera and West grabbed notebook, pen, and measuring tape. As they made their way toward the group, Delilah latched onto one of the belt loops in his jeans and let him lead the way.

The whale carcass was massive and mangled. Guts were everywhere. The crowd parted to allow the two of them access to the whale. West began taking measurements while Delilah took photos. A slick-haired, muscle-bound, fratboy was delivering an error-filled lecture to his girlfriend and the bystanders. He lectured to all that would listen that it was a "Gray whale, probably dead from a rare illness. Died from disease or infection, and that it had been dead for quite awhile." His brain-dead girlfriend found the entire experience "so disgusting." Without looking up from his measurements, West publicly declared "It's not a Gray whale."

The fratboy glared at him.

"It most certainly is a Gray whale, surfer boy," he said.

West detested guys like this. Half-wits. He didn't suffer fools gladly. It often got him in trouble.

"Back half of a Blue whale, cut in half, probably by a tanker," said West without looking up.

Delilah and the brain-dead girlfriend could see fratboy's neck muscles twitching as chuckles came from the group of onlookers.

"I'll call NOAA," said Delilah.

"Who's Noah?" whispered the brain dead girlfriend.

"National Oceanic and Atmospheric Administration," said Delilah.

Muscleboy looked at the faces in the crowd, at his girlfriend, at Delilah, at the dead Blue whale, and at the middle section of the bell curve that would always be his home.

"Well get a load of dork surfer boy and his little dork girlfriend," said the frat boy.

West came to an instant halt, stood, turned, and

24

looked straight into fratboy's eyes. The brain-dead girlfriend, in a rare moment of enlightenment, grabbed her boyfriend's arm and led him away. As Delilah and the crowd watched them retreat, West went back to his measurements.

"Let's find out what vessels in the area are big enough to cut a Blue whale in half," he said without looking up.

Some in the group of onlookers started to applaud. West turned and smiled at Delilah, whose eyes were as big as the moon.

"Whatever you need me to do," she said. "Whatever you need me to do."

#

The night before Lucinda and Matty drove away with West's foosball table, his identity, and his self-worth, Lucinda vigorously pointed out to him that she had bigger plans for her life. Grander than playing tennis, surfing, and hanging out with his "drifter friends."

West fruitlessly tried to make the case for his friends being so much more than drifters. They were, well, they were, surfers. Surfers who needed to move around. In search of waves. In search of meaning. In search of life! As you now know, that final argument to the jury didn't succeed. He spent the rest of the night in an appropriate L.A. dive bar, before proceeding to his sacred spot on the beach. As for the tennis part of his defense, he countered that it was quite the noble sport. For the Patrician class. The country club people. Not to mention the fact that that was how he made his

25

income. Tennis paid the bills! Well, helped, somewhat, pay the bills.

Now, there he was. Walking the walk on the private tennis court of Cassandra Eaton, an attractive, fit, pampered woman of forty-something, who's intentionally too small tennis outfit put all of her wares on display. Cassandra sort of liked tennis, and thoroughly liked West. Even though her lesson was at the midway point, she'd had enough, abruptly stopped, and declared "break time."

Visibly out of breath, she was glistening profusely.

"You okay Mrs. Eaton?" asked West.

"You know I hate it when you refer to me as Mrs. Eaton, it's Cassie or you don't get your money. Break time," she said again as she made her way to the umbrella table and proceeded to pour a glass of water down the front of her top. West decided it would be best, at this time, to take in his surroundings and not Cassie's breasts. The Beverly Hills property was majestic. Next to the tennis court was a sparkling, Olympic-size swimming pool, dressing cabana, and a view of the far-off Pacific Ocean. Fantasizing came easy. When he returned his gaze to Cassie, she was in the process of removing her top.

"What exactly are you doing there, Cassie?" said West.

Cassandra said that "it was fucking hot outside" and that she thought it would be a good idea for them to go swimming. When West nervously declined, Cassie, in jog-bra and short-shorts insisted that he show her that western grip again. Before he could protest, she barked at him.

26

"Would you please get over here, take my hands, and show me? Don't be such a fucking pussy," she said.

Oh well. West decides, 'fuck it', I'll give her what she wants. Taking her shoulders into his hands, he whipped her around, and with her back to him, he put his arms around her waist, took her hands into his, and placed them in the correct position on the racquet. As he did this, she backed up against him. His breath was on her neck and she could feel his attention growing. Dropping the racquet, she grabbed his right hand and placed it on her bare midriff. He left it frozen there for a glorious moment before he moved it, with great care, down to the top of her tennis shorts. Unbeknownst to them, Cassie's sixteen-year-old daughter Hadley was on the far side of the pool. She'd been watching them for the last few minutes.

"That's quite the lesson your having," said Hadley. "Hi West, hello mother, you seem to have lost your shirt, mother," said Hadley.

Cassandra snatched up her shirt as Hadley announced that Steven was on the phone. To her mother's great irritation, she had started calling her father by his first name a couple of years ago. For reasons undisclosed, she decided that he was too much of an asshole to be awarded father status. Cassie stormed off the court on her way to the house.

"You leave West alone, he was just leaving," said Cassandra.

"West, you were just leaving," she said to West.

Hadley watched as West packed up his racquets, balls, and miscellaneous tennis accoutrement. She was

27

barefoot, clothed in a new gleaming white Beverly Hills Hotel bathrobe. She, too, thought it a good idea for them to go for a swim.

"Come for a swim with me," she said to West.

"You heard your mother, time for me to go," he replied.

If you had been a witness to this scene, your intuition would have suggested to you that these two had a history. Some, thing. Was it substantial or slight? Hard to say. No pun intended.

Now that Hadley had West's full attention, she walked to the edge of the pool, paused, dropped her robe, and waited for him to realize that she was proudly naked. West's eyes weren't going anywhere as he watched her dive into the pool and come up to greet him at the opposite end. They both examined each other and pondered the possibilities before West grabbed his gear and walked away. On his way out he heard her say, "You know you want to!"

Yes he wanted to. He wanted to with Cassie. He wanted one more time with Lucinda. He unquestionably wants to with Delilah. That's always a thing he wants to do. But. He needs to go home. The cat might appreciate some food, perhaps some life-saving water. He needs to crawl into his own beanbag chair and sleep, perchance to dream. For days. For weeks. Forever. Jesus, Hadley sure looked spectacular.

Somehow it went from Saturday afternoon to Monday morning and West found himself parked outside the GreenPlanet office contemplating the pros and cons of following his gut. He'd caught up on his sleep, but his head was still spinning and his heart was still beating fast. Little did he know that this would be his permanent state for the next three years.

Before he turned the knob on the office door, he took a big, deep breath, ran his hand through his hair, adjusted his dick, then marched forward full steam ahead. It was obvious that the office was in its initial days of operation. There was the main room with a few desks scattered here and there. The desks were accompanied by assorted garage-sale chairs. Several old metal filing cabinets were surrounded by boxes and boxes of GreenPlanet merchandise; general move-in disarray. Two doors led to smaller private offices. A man from the phone company was installing a Telex machine. And there was Delilah. How did he forget how splendid she was? He was spellbound, watching her give furniture arranging instructions to some wide-eyed volunteers.

At the precise moment that the phone guy gave Delilah the thumbs up, indicating that the install mission was successful, the main line rang. The phone installer, beaming proudly, handed Delilah the phone. She confirmed to the caller that it was indeed GreenPlanet, as she grabbed some paper and pen. Intently listening while offering an assortment of "yes," "correct," "I see," "a Blue whale, that's correct," she scribbled away before saying "can you hold for a moment?"

She gestured excitedly for West to come to her. As he made his way through the clutter, she held out the newly activated phone to him and exclaimed "It's NBC. They want to know if we have a statement for them regarding the dead whale. Here, talk to them."

West felt faint. His dizziness jumped up two levels. What the fuck was she doing? In a rapid-fire whisper she said that it was an oil tanker that killed the Blue whale. The other half of the whale was discovered wrapped around the bow of the tanker. West was shaking his head 'no' when she slapped the phone into his hand and gave him a 'DO IT, MOTHER FUCKER' look. He put the phone to his ear.

Delilah, the phone guy, and the volunteers came to a deadly-silent halt. You could hear West's heart pound. He then said this:

"GreenPlanet is currently investigating the tragic death of the Blue whale this past weekend in the waters off the Southern California coast. We're working closely with the National Oceanic and Atmospheric Administration, and the National Marine Fisheries Service to determine if the ship in question violated the very clear regulations put forth by the Marine Mammal Protection Act of 1972. When we conclude our thorough investigation into this matter, we will alert the various members of the press and the public of our findings, and any actions that we may or may not take."

As he was spelling his name, Weston Walker, for the NBC reporter, Delilah handed him a piece of paper. On it was written: Research Director.

West relayed to the reporter that his title was Research Director, thanked him for the call, and agreed to be in touch soon. He hung up the phone and collapsed onto a garage-sale chair. The attentive audience burst into a grand round of applause while Delilah mocked him for his creative assertion of working "closely" with NOAA and National Marine Fisheries. West looked ill.

"I sort of just lied to the press," he confessed.

Delilah looked at everyone including the phone guy and professorially declared:

"It won't be the last time, sweetie, it won't be the last time."

For a brief moment, his dizziness went away, his breathing calmed, and his eyes cleared. A rush of emotion overtook him. The moment rang true, and if the moment rang true maybe he didn't lie. He felt that he could see into the future. He knew everything he said to that reporter would come to pass. Where all of that came from, he had no clue, but it was effortless, like riding a dream wave. Often, you cannot wait for conditions to be perfect, to be true. You just have to paddle hard, get on your feet, and ride for as long as you can. Ride.

Delilah took his hand, lifted him to his feet and proceeded to introduce him to the whale savers and to give him a tour of his new digs. It all felt right. Her hand in his. These people. This place. Research Director.

Hollywood Boulevard continued to get seedier and seedier. The neighborhood was in decline; overrun with rockers, discotheques, drug dealers and users, runaways, Scientologists, and tourists. Everything felt dirty and unsavory except for one shining oasis in the middle of it all called Musso & Frank. The very best place to see and be seen while sealing the seven-figure deal. Power lunch was in full swing for the show-biz elite as well as the mangy crew occupying the Chaplin Booth. Hunter, well into his second martini, was accompanied by Hugh Simon, chief counsel for GreenPlanet International, Kip Asher, his long time friend and fellow eco-warrior, and Will Stone, a Hollywood veteran compadre of Kip. Kip was waving for another round of drinks simultaneously singing the praises of Will. Hunter had hand-picked his old pal to run the new L.A. office, and Kip, hitting the ground running, was introducing Will as his new right-hand man. With Hunter's blessing.

"Needless to say, Will has amazing connections and friends. He knows lot's of powerful people," Kip crowed.

Hunter was tired, and pissy, and didn't like the slick looks of Will. Something was on his mind and it wasn't all of the Hollywood bollocks.

"Start looking for a boat. I want us in the Pacific this summer, saving whales," he said.

Kip was listening to Hunter like a kid in a candy shop hears his mother. He couldn't take his eyes off of the show going on around them. He would point to someone and Will would explain to the table who the particular starlet or power broker was. There were waves of the hand and blown air-kisses. Kip rolled off a list of rock stars that Will knew "very, very well" as drinks continued to obediently appear at their table. This continued on for several more excruciating minutes while Hunter's fuse burned shorter. Finally, he'd had enough.

"Enough! Shut the fuck up! What the hell is the matter with you two?" exploded Hunter. "This is not a fucking game," he said.

During the painful silence that ensued, Hugh took his cue. Hugh Gordon Simon was born and raised in east London. As a child he was indoctrinated into supporting the West Ham FC, however, upon entering adulthood he soon realized the shame and folly of this and switched his allegiance posthaste to the much more respectable Arsenal. Razor sharp, he walked softly but carried a big fucking stick, and he always, always had Hunter's back.

"Hunter and I are headed for Honolulu tomorrow morning to shut down their operation, they will cease to exist by tomorrow night," Hugh sedately announced.

He went on to explain that the European members were quite unhappy with the pirate behavior of the posse running the Hawaiian office. The Europeans didn't appreciate the fact that the money raised in Hawaii via the GreenPlanet name didn't seem to be going for the advertised campaigns. Hunter was more stinging.

"The money we raise is not for the feeding and housing of freeloaders," barked Hunter. "Fuck with me and I'll cut your fucking head off," he concluded with a long, hard stare at Will.

Loud applause broke out, not for Hunter's proclamation, but for the huge Hollywood movie star that had just entered the room. Kip didn't dare turn to look, keeping his eyes glued on Hunter and Hugh as he tried to wrap his brain around their breaking news. Closing down the Hawaiian office, he knew, was 'nui na nuhou' and would cause giant waves throughout the U.S. organization. It also would attract many suspicious and less than friendly eyeballs to the newly created operation in L.A.

Kip reassured Hunter that they were, as always, simpatico. Nothing to fear. He would turn the L.A. office into the jewel in the organizational crown. Hunter downed his third, or was it his fourth martini? as he and Hugh rose to depart.

"We've got a plane to catch. Don't fuck up, boys," he said as he and Hugh stumbled out into the L.A. smog.

An expat American freelance war correspondent for many years, Hunter Mack learned an invaluable, life-saving asset on the front lines of battle. The camera. In particular, the motion-picture camera. More often than not, having cameras rolling saved lots of lives, especially innocent civilians. Burned out on war and death and the resignation of the disgraced President of the United States, Hunter made his way to the picturesque town of Bergen, Norway to visit an old friend and to decompress. It was there in Bergen, on a quiet, meditative walk, where he witnessed Norway's commercial whaling vessels bringing in their catch, and learned of their intent to return shortly to the sea to kill more whales. He was incensed. Overcome with an acute need to stop it from happening, he hired a fishing boat from a sympathetic, whale-loving fisherman who agreed to take him on a chase of the Norwegian whalers. Hunter's Norwegian friend supplied him with an 8mm movie camera and a few rolls of film. Within 48 hours, the whalers were pushing off from the dock, as was the old fishing boat with Hunter on the bow.

The whaling boats didn't need to go far to find whales, many of which traveled close to the coast, and Hunter soon noticed a pod of whales at the very same time that the whale killers did. As the whalers uncovered their harpoon cannons, Hunter was at the wheel of the fishing boat trying to cut across the bow of one of the whaling boats. It was dangerous and unlawful. Unable to speed ahead of the whaling vessel, Hunter gave the wheel to the fishing boat captain, grabbed the movie camera, and started filming the whalers as he yelled at them over and over again to "Stop killing the whales!" Gesturing angrily at Hunter, the whalers took aim and fired a couple of harpoons into a large whale. Hunter had seen a lot of horror in his short life, but this got to him. The up-close witnessing of the killing of the whale was a violent punch to his gut. He filmed as much as he could until the film ran out and they retreated back to Bergen.

He didn't know it at the time, but that was the beginning of GreenPlanet. The film footage was picked up by international media and shown on news programs all over the world. Hunter returned to London with a new fire in his belly, and because of the

great media exposure of his attempt to stop the
whalers, he was approached by many sympathizers
who wished to join his cause. Little did he realize how
big, and influential, and unruly his merry band would
grow.

Now, three years later, GreenPlanet 1978 had
grown to include offices in London, Amsterdam,
Sydney, San Francisco, Seattle, Honolulu, and the
brand new office in Los Angeles.

The organization grew like the annual Southern
California wildfires. Not necessarily a good thing.
Unapproved 'chapters' and 'groups' calling themselves
GreenPlanet were popping up all over the globe,
especially in the United States. Millions and millions of
dollars were contributed by world citizens to support
the efforts of the organization. Not all of that money
was arriving where it was supposed to arrive. Not all of
that money was used for the specific campaigns of the
organization. The San Francisco office had essentially
gone rogue, claiming to be the superpower in the USA,
granting permission they did not have to give, for the
office that was opened in Seattle. The Hawaii office
operated as if the rest of the organization didn't exist,
as if they were the one and only GreenPlanet. Hunter
and the Europeans concluded that it was time to scrub
the decks and take back control of the hijacked ship.

#

Maintaining control would be a challenge for Kip
too, but now that Musso and Frank had pretty much
cleared out, he was much more serene and focussed.

Kip and Will still occupied the Chaplin Booth. Very

little food and very much alcohol had been consumed. Kip was working hard to assuage Will's fear that Hunter hated his guts, while Will was promising to be serious, straight-arrowed, and all business from this minute forward. That didn't last a nanosecond when they were approached by the irresistible young actress Babette Carson who was unaware that Will was no longer a talent agent at William Morris, and that he had departed the agency suddenly, mysteriously, and unceremoniously in the middle of the night. When Will saw that Babette was suggesting a liaison, a strictly professional liaison it goes without saying, he thought it would be cruel to burst her bubble with the discouraging news of his departure from 'the business'.

"Sorry to interrupt, but you're Will Stone," she said with great cleavage.

"Yes, and you are?" queried Will.

"Babette. Carson. We met in Malibu. At Lou's party."

Will had no idea who she was, but he was pretty sure the Lou she was referring to was Lou Graham, lead singer with Foreigner, and his frequent party mate. She said that she desperately needed an agent, a super agent like Will. She was ready to "audition" for him anytime, any place. He took her number. She made him promise that he would call her. He swore an oath that he would indeed "make contact," and she seductively sashayed away from the Chaplin Booth to both of the lad's delight.

"She thinks you're still an agent," whispered Kip.

"Yes she does," said Will.

"Is this what I have to look forward to?" asked Kip.

Will chuckled and waved hello to a leftover starlet across the room as Kip placed two exuberant fingers in the air, his universal communique for two more Cuba Libre's por favor. Lou Graham would have approved.

#

The euphoria of the morning was instantly wiped out when West arrived home to find a note on the kitchen counter from Lucinda-she had returned for the cat as well as the remainder of the cat food. She knew West well enough to know that her rescue mission was merited, if not absolutely necessary. West was floored. Literally. Not only did she kidnap his best friend, but when he went to collapse in the shitty old beanbag chair, it, too, was gone. So there he was, on the front porch, draped over his decrepit wooden deck chair, forlornly staring out at the Capitol Records building a couple of blocks away.

Surrounded by a sea of empty beer bottles, he struggled to hold onto the almost full beer bottle in his left hand, and the two-thirds empty bottle of Jack Daniel's in his right hand. As the sun got low in the sky, the Capitol Records building lit up, a combination of the sun's reflection off of its windows and the many oncoming office lights. The dimming light within West was almost out. His eyes were heavy and his brain was sloshed. When he awoke hours later it was past midnight and a neighbors dog was licking his Jack Daniel's hand. He got himself up straight, tried with much difficulty to determine exactly where he was, and then came up with the brilliant idea of driving over to Delilah's house. Somehow he managed to safely find

38

his way to her street and to park the car without incident in the general proximity of her house. After mistakenly knocking on the front door of two of Delilah's neighbors, he was gruffly pointed in the proper direction where he made his way to her doorbell and what he thought would be his salvation.

There was much pounding and doorbell ringing before Delilah answered the door. Surprised to find a drunken West reeling on her doorstep, she had a look of seriousness that he had not seen before. She didn't invite him in, rather, she joined him on the porch, closing the door most of the way behind her. West tried to kiss her, but she backed away requiring him to use the wall for support. Slurring, he invited himself to spend the night. She declined.

"Can you get home okay, sweetie?" she said.

West slid down the wall with a thud, and from the seat of his pants replied, "I don't live in Texas." Delilah struggled hard and eventually got West to his feet. He tried to make a break for the front door, but she blocked his path and down he went again. Frustrated, she was breathing heavily. From inside the house, the menacing voice of an unseen man was heard.

"You need a hand?" he said.

"No! I can handle this. Go back to bed," said Delilah.

West, hearing this exchange, made it to his feet, paused, saw a different Delilah that he had come to know, violently lurched backwards from the house, and stumbled badly up the street, past his car, into the night. She didn't try to stop him; watching him until he was out of sight. Checking to see if her neighbors were also watching the show, it occurred to her that she was barely clothed under the bright lights of her front porch. Calmly, coolly, she waved at the houses where she assumed that she had an audience, brushed herself off, made an about-face, and escaped back into her house with the menacing voice.

I know what you've been told. How you've been taught to think. You're wrong. Altruism isn't pure. It's not selfless. One joins a cause, a mission, a charity, for all sorts of selfish reasons. We may not be consciously aware of those reasons at the time that we are engaged, but trust me when I tell you, shit's happening. The psychological undercurrent of behavioral motivation is churning away. American Cancer Society? Selfish. Habitat for Humanity? Selfish. Land mine removal? Selfish. There are a zillion causes in which one might choose to enlist, right? You can't join them all, so the choice that is made can tell us much about the individual or the group, as well as the time period. Occupy Wall Street? Bollocks. So, it should come as no surprise that this band of merry misfits were no different. They, too, were chock-full of flaws and contradictions, and alcohol, and drugs, and passion, and courage, and commitment, and deviousness, and debauchery, and self-delusion, and unfounded senses of brilliance, and very selfish needs. Saving whales was a very specific mission, wasn't it? What was that all about? It was quite the upper-middle-class Caucasian cause that provided it's lost children a temporary vehicle to attempt to find a way forward in a world that made less and less sense.

1978 America was in transition. The experimental, activist, socially conscious mid Sixties to mid Seventies was now starting to fade into black. The Viet Nam war was in the rear-view mirror. So was Richard Nixon, the country's first and only President of the United States to resign in disgrace. Earth Day would turn nine years old and Jimmy Carter would be in the second year of a turbulent and frustrating four-year presidency. The golden decade of film was coming to an end at the same time that disco music reared its ugly head, dominating the radio airwaves for what seemed like an eternity.

Unapologetic hedonism replaced social activism as rising unemployment among the young combined with their disillusion of all things political and ideological. This growing malaise became the cauldron that would fuel punk rock. By 1980, when Ronald Reagan was elected President, most of America was on the verge of becoming a full-blown 'Me Generation' that would immerse itself in fame, fortune, fashion, consumerism, vanity, maxed out credit, Wall Street excesses, cocaine, and the onset of AIDS.

1978 to 1980 was a narrow corridor. A cultural 'event horizon' leading to a 1980's black hole. There was no turning back. There was no way out. This was a group of dedicated adventurers who desperately needed to do something 'macro', to rage against the dimming of the light, to make a great splash before it was all over, and nothing makes a bigger splash than the great whales. BUT, the operative words here are 'desperately needed'. Selfish. Trust me.

41

When all else fails. Go surfing.

So Cal Power Station #3 is located on a most excellent point break perfect for escaping terra firma reality and satisfying the immediate needs of those individuals that have more Sex Wax than sex. The utility company denies public access to the beach in front of 'their' power plant, and even though they were very, very determined, they failed in their attempt to claim the ocean as their property too. Motherfuckers.

West and Kimo were in their third straight day of surfing, eating tacos, sleeping on the beach, talking stupid, and surfing some more. It was late in the day, glassy, no waves to speak of, but they were in the water anyway, bobbing on their boards and continuing the same never-ending debate regarding the guitar playing superiority of Ted Nugent versus Eddie Van Halen. As Kimo was feebly trying to demonstrate the Nugent style of playing, West noticed the water around them begin to bubble and churn. Never a good sign. Kimo, also seeing what was happening, clammed up, and signaled for he and West to head for shore, pronto. Before they could assume the paddling position, a scuba diver shot straight up out of the water and nearly knocked West off of his board. The diver, a young guy in his thirties, ripped off his mask, and gasping for air, frantically pleaded for help. His girlfriend was trapped below, stuck to the ocean water intake pipe that the power plant uses to cool the steam generators. She was almost out of air.

The power plant takes in 300,00 to 400,00 gallons of cold seawater per day in order to cool the steam generating turbines, and then the hot water from the turbines is pumped back out into the ocean. The suction of water into the intake pipe is powerful, often killing seals, sea lions, sharks, tons of fish, and anything that gets too close including people.

West and Kimo immediately exited their boards and gave them to the diver to straddle. Grabbing the divers facemask, West placed it on his own face, while he and Kimo, taking in deep breaths, dove below the surface in search of the girl.

The ocean was not deep in this location, but it was murky, making it difficult to see. The farther down they dove, the more turbulent the water became. Kimo was struggling and short of breath, so back to the surface he returned. West, not faring much better, kept going and made it to the girl, who, he could see, was clinging to the side of the intake pipe, fighting with all of her might not to be sucked into the power plant.

He could also see that she was weakening and knew that he, too, was seconds away from running out of air. A surfer with many wipeouts under his belt, he had been the recipient of more than one 'two wave hold downs', teaching him not to panic when out of breath.

He swam to the side of the pipe, careful not to get sucked in himself, and signaled to the girl that he needed air, now! She took a deep breath, removed her mouthpiece, and handed it to him. Gasping, he was able to refill his lungs and return the regulator back to her. As she reached for the regulator, West seized her arm and violently pulled her off of the intake pipe.

Weak from her struggle, she was unable to protest. Returning the regulator to her own mouth, she signaled to West that the airflow was dying. With one arm around her, he pushed off from the intake pipe, and kicking with all of their strength, they headed for the surface.

Out of oxygen and out of time, it seemed an eternity before their heads broke through the surface of the water into life-saving fresh air. Kimo and the diverguy were waiting, floating on the two surfboards, when West and the divergirl surfaced next to them.

Dragging them to the surfboards, Kimo draped the divergirl fully across his board. She see-sawed back and forth from crying to taking huge gulps of air. West, delirious and hyperventilating, fought to regain his breath, and then slow his heartbeat. Bobbing in the water, he gave Kimo the thumbs up, smiled at the divergirl, who he thought was super cute, then took a long look back at the power plant and it's cooling towers pouring plumes of steam into the sky. Breathing heavily, he thought to himself, "bastards".

Back in Hollywood, Delilah pulled her car up in front of West's apartment, jumped out, ran up to the front door and began ringing the doorbell. That didn't work so she tried pounding on the door. Nope. She tried looking in the front window and was instantly depressed by the bleak scene.

She'd spent the past three days calling, apologizing to him on his answering machine, tracking down where he lived and checking hospitals and jails for any trace of him.

Back at the office she'd been raving about him to

Kip and Will. Extolling his "rock star" skills and potential while giving them a detailed play-by-play of his award-winning telephone performance with NBC, and now she was freaking the fuck out that he may be gone, that maybe she blew it, and that it wasn't supposed to play out this way.

Rifling through her bag, she found an old grocery receipt and a pen. On the back of the receipt she wrote: "Call Me" along with her phone number, sticking the receipt into the doorjamb. Her intuition commanded her attention, straightened her, and informed her that all would be okay, not to panic, it's just a "two wave hold down".

As she made her way back to her car, the twinkling lights of the city caught her eye. She was mesmerized, in awe, as if she were standing on the beach, watching a golden sun sink perfectly into the ocean. A wave of calm washed over her.

On the horizon, a powerful, mystical, orange sun sat directly on top of the water. In the darkness, the cooling towers of the power plant had become humbled and diminished for the day. On the water, a lone figure sat on a surfboard bobbing up and down, up and down, on his own hypnotic waves of calm.

West was not out there to ride any waves or save any drowning souls. He was not out there to argue the superiority of Eddie Van Halen. He was out there to let things sink in, to make sense of things. Or not. He was just out there.

By the time West slipped unnoticed into the back of the room, the press conference was underway. The turnout was impressive and the main room of the L A Press Club was full.

Seated at a table front and center were Delilah and Will. Kip was nowhere in sight, as he decided drinks at the Chimney Sweep were a much better option than answering questions from the media. Will, on the hot seat, was a nervous wreck. You would have been a nervous wreck too if you were completely unprepared, ill-versed in everything GreenPlanet, and flipping out because your pal Kip pulled a 'no show', throwing you to the dogs.

After a failed attempt to make it a "just wanted to say hello, happy to be here" presser, Will was sweating, stammering, and stumbling to answer a question from an L A Times reporter about the Blue whale incident the previous week.

"A spokesperson for CALOCO told me they had every right to be in those waters, they broke no laws, they do not anticipate any punitive actions, case closed. Do you believe this to be a violation of the Marine Mammal Protection Act or is it, like they say, case closed?" asked the reporter.

"The Marine Mammal Protection Act?" said Will looking anxiously to Delilah for a life ring. "It is difficult at this time, I cannot say with, it's important to remember," said a drowning Will as a voice from the back of the room came to his rescue.

"It is true that CALOCO has permission to navigate those waters, but they are expected to navigate them responsibly," said West. "This case is not exactly over."

As he walked to the front of the room, Delilah's and Will's hearts were pounding for very different reasons. West introduced himself to the press gaggle as the Research Director for GreenPlanet. He explained that he had spoken at length that morning with a representative of California Oil Company and that they were working out the particulars of a deal that would bring the matter to an amicable end.

"The fact that ships have permission to navigate through whale and other marine mammal breeding grounds does not mean they should be allowed to do so recklessly. If the National Oceanic and Atmospheric Administration fail to impose a speed limit, lawsuits filed under the Marine Mammal Protection Act may be a fruitful option to pursue. I'm not stating here now that CALOCO knowingly violated the law, only, perhaps, that they were too reckless," he continued.

When asked what the deal was, West replied:

"CALOCO will most likely be sending a generous donation to our friends at the Marine Mammal Research Center next week."

After a few more 'who, what, where' questions, the presser broke up and Will was able to breathe normally again. Delilah put her arms around West and held him tight. Will extended a very grateful hand.

"Will Stone. Thanks for the save," said Will.

"West. Walker. Didn't mean to interrupt," he said to Will.

"Sorry I've been out of touch. Needed to sort through some things," he said to Delilah.

He was ecstatic to see Delilah again and to her

hold her in his arms. As for Will, a complete stranger with whom he'd had ten seconds of interaction, he already liked him, trusted him, and looked forward to working with him. What was it about these people that he felt an immediate bond?

Will invited West to join he and Delilah at lunch, which was code word for margaritas, at Lucy's El Adobe, ostensibly to talk strategy and get to know each other. A disappointed Delilah bowed her head when West asked for a rain check promising that he would see them at the office first thing Monday morning. He was "looking forward to meeting the mysterious Kip." As West headed back to his trusty VW, he interpreted his emotional state as serene, centered, not so lost. He was wrong.

#

Roy Black Elk is six feet four inches tall and weighs two hundred twenty pounds. He is bigger than West, stronger than West, older and more mature than West, most of the time a better tennis player than West, the head pro at the club, his former boss and best friend, and at this very moment, in front of a steadily growing crowd, he is getting his ass beat by his younger, laser-focussed pal.

Tennis is a funny thing. If two opponents possess the same skill level, the same strength, and the same level of physical fitness, the victor will almost always be the player whose mind was functioning on a higher plane that day. With no teammates to rely on, you're an independent contractor; a solo artist. It's you and your inner voice carving your path forward.

Roy, as I've said, is stronger than West, but on this day West was 'in the zone'. He had no interfering thoughts, no hesitation. See the ball, hit the ball perfectly, function at an insanely high plateau, crush your best friend, soak in the adoring crowd, and experience the perfect wave of tennis.

It was match point and Roy was about to deliver another monster serve. On a normal day, West's serve return would fail him, and the result would be defeat. Today was not a normal day. He knew that he would rifle that serve down the line to win the match. He saw clearly how it would all play out. He also knew that he would never play better than he had just played. Never again. You can't explain these things, can't alter them, can't fight it. Just go with the flow. Crush it.

He did. It was over. Game, set, match. Roy couldn't believe it. He didn't play bad, quite the opposite, but who was this guy on the other side of the net? He didn't recognize his old friend. He was concerned. Something was different. Wrong? Dark? He couldn't put his finger on it. It was as if West's spirit had shapeshifted. Roy, part Sioux, part Viet Nam vet, knew all about shapeshifting, and his antenna was picking up loud signals from West.

"What was that?" said Roy. "Felt like I was playing Connors out there."

"Lucky," mumbled West.

"No luck; focus. You were focused like a laser beam."

"Been quite a week. Lu left me."

Roy let this sink in for a few moments, never taking his eye off West. He knew Lucinda Parker well

49

and always figured this day would arrive. She had a bigger life plan that involved more than tennis and surfing. He knew West even better, and he knew his pal was bracing for a lecture from his wise old friend.

"Come back to the club. Teach as many lessons as you want," offered Roy.

"I met these people," said West.

"Surfing doesn't pay the rent, old chum."

"I need to do something important with my life," he said looking Roy straight in the eyes.

Roy smiled a supporting smile. He could see the change in West's aura. He knew it was big.

"Rematch next week. Loser buys winner a tank of gas," instructed Roy.

"Deal," said a half-hearted West.

Roy was not a hugger, so he emptied the rest of his water bottle on West's head and walked off toward his van.

"Sorry about Lu."

West was sorry about Lucinda too, but he was exceedingly happy about Delilah. While he was playing the greatest tennis of his life, he had this powerful feeling, as if she was by his side, cheering him on, infusing him with superpowers that made him invincible.

Delilah was feeling no pain herself. While West was feeling infused, she was becoming imbued, with tequila, from many strong margaritas. By the time she and Will arrived back at the office, it was late on a Friday evening and everyone had disappeared.

At first, she thought it was their tequila-soaked brains that stopped she and Will in their tracks when they opened the door to the office, but as the fog lifted it became clear that the scene in front of her was very real. The entire office had been rearranged into a polished war room that had the feel of being up and running for years.

Her desk was now in a power position, adorned with fresh flowers and a bottle of red wine. There were desks for the Research Director, Merchandise Manager, Volunteer Coordinator, the Director of Fund Raising, and the P.R./Media Director. A new white strategy board covered the central wall. The water cooler and telex machine bookended the room. Banners and photos decorated the walls.

As Delilah and Will made their way into the new environment, the door to Kip's office flew open and an army of cheering volunteers poured into the room carrying trays of food, bottles of champagne, a huge whale-decorated cake, plenty of illegal substances both speedy and slow, streamers, and balloons. They were led by Rocky Michaels, merchandise wizard.

Rocky looked like a young Sonny Bono with the big 'Fu Manchu' mustache and a wide beaming smile. He and Delilah adored each other and shared their deepest, darkest secrets, except for his not coming out of the closet and her not running from a violent, abusive husband. Other than that, everything. Delilah knew instantly who had done all of this, and she ran to Rocky to give him a great appreciative hug.

"Do you like it?," said a very proud Rocky.

"It's perfect," cheered Delilah.

Rocky took her by the arm and proceeded to give her the grand tour. Will spotted a pretty, young volunteer and immediately headed in her direction. Guitars appeared, singing began, and champagne flowed.

On Delilah's desk was a note from a volunteer. It read: Congratulations!! CALOCO donating $10,000 to Marine Mammal Research Center.

West wasn't there for the christening; he was back at his spot staring forever out to sea. In his head he was replaying the GreenPlanet film over and over again, but in his version he was cast as the star, not Hunter.

There he was in the Zodiac, in front of the harpoon. Trying to escape the oncoming killer boat, he gets dangerously closer and closer to the fleeing whales in front of him. Trapped between a rock and a hard place, he watches as Japanese crewmembers load a two-hundred-fifty-pound exploding harpoon into the bow's cannon. The whales in front of him are tiring and slowing down. The killer boat at his rear is almost on top of him. The cannon is being pointed directly at the whales, now just a few feet in front of him. He can see the gunman take aim. He can see that he's in the direct line of the impending shot. He wants to scream out, but no sounds are possible. A loud command rings out in Japanese. He looks back at the killer ship just in time to hear the loud explosion and see the flash of the cannon. He instinctively ducks for cover as the harpoon flies by his head, exploding into one of the whales in front of him. The steel cable attached to the harpoon snaps down on his Zodiac like the razor sharp blade of a guillotine, just missing his right arm. Covered in whale blood and guts, trying to hang on tight through the thrashing of the wounded whale, he veers off to the left to escape the steel cable and the oncoming killer boat.

A blast of music from a nearby radio slapped him back into the present moment. The sun was now below the horizon and the semi-darkness made it possible for him to see the lights of a distant oil tanker.

He wondered if that might be the same tanker that killed the Blue whale? He could hear his heartbeat. It was in sync with the waves breaking on the shore. On the sand next to him was a worn and tattered paperback. Lifting the book as if it were a wounded bird, West stared at its faded cover: Prairie Fire-Political Statement of the Weather Underground.

After assiduous examination and distressing ruminations   about his long-lost brother, he eventually returned his gaze to the sea. The sun had disappeared, and with it, he noticed, the oil tanker.

DRINKING WITH MARLON BRANDO

It was high noon on an absolutely beautiful Monday. Not a cloud in the sky and the water was paradise blue. Since it was a workday and a school day there weren't any crowds. It was a perfect day to commune with nature. A perfect day to be at the beach.

If you were at the beach you could bodysurf, play volleyball, or flirt with cute girls. If the waves got your attention, you could grab your board and head out. You could daydream and suntan and listen to music. If you were at the beach.

West thought hard about all of these things as he sat across the cocktail table from Kip. The Chimney Sweep wasn't at the beach; it was in Sherman Oaks, in a mini strip-mall, next to a poisonous Chinese takeout joint. Inside the Chimney Sweep it was dark as night. They were surrounded by woody, rust-colored walls, several empty cocktail tables and booths, and a congregation of black 'pleather' chairs. In the middle of the room was a coal-black, circular, hanging fireplace. The only light in the place emanated from low-watt table lamps and the neon beer signs above the bar. This was Kip's paradise, his nirvana, his 'spot'.

Kip had already downed a couple of Cuba Libres and had his two fingers high in the air to alert the powers that be that another round was required posthaste. Simultaneously, he was explaining to West the life saving, game-changing power of the motion-picture camera.

Kip was the consummate snake charmer. A charismatic,

mop-haired, burned-out rich kid, and the sole heir to the Asher Oil fortune. A lover of mind-altering chemical substances, he was a very well-read college dropout who was at his best when he was one on one. A benevolent manipulator, lost and unhappy, he never fully recovered from the news of Jim Morrison's death.

West's mind had already been blown once when Kip, right off the bat, congratulated him for saving the divergirl's life. West hadn't told anyone and he was immediately thrown off balance to have his personal business become public knowledge.

"Happy that you could meet with me today. I wanted to see for myself who this guy was that Delilah was gushing about," said Kip.

"I've heard a lot about you too," countered West.

"Promise I'll get you out of here before the sun goes down," Kip crowed, his two fingers still in the air.

West snuck a look at the Coors beer clock on the wall and saw that it was just past noon. He knew that sunset was around 7:00 p.m., and he couldn't help but notice that the drinks in front of them were piling up. So much for a beautiful day at the beach.

As he nervously twirled the straw in one of his drinks, the two bare arms of Connie Mae Cotton wrapped around his waist and delivered two more Cuba Libres to their table.

"You're gonna have to drink them drinks faster than that honey, or this little table is gonna be covered in glasses," she said as she brushed her cheek against his.

An irresistible woman in her fifties; Connie was a landmark, a hallmark, and a benchmark. A no-nonsense, flirtatious, seen it and done it all whirlwind. Bartender par excellence; she ran a tight ship, and on occasion mixed fluids with Kip in the liquor room behind the bar.

As she was berating Kip for signaling to her as if she was his "servant slave," he was informing West of Connie's star turn in 'The Treasure of the Sierra Madre' with Humphrey Bogart. An embarrassed West couldn't remember Connie's performance, or anyone else's for that matter, so Kip observed that she was a most remarkable 'fille de joie'. A pleasure girl. A hooker.

Before she sashayed away, Connie smacked Kip across his head and ordered him to send West to the bar for any and all future drinks. She was thinking it might be a good idea to trade in Kip for West. A very good idea. West liked Connie. I mean what's not to like? Seems he was liking everyone these days. These people were fun. And fearless.

As the drinks continued to flow and Kip continued to charm, West forgot about the sand and the waves. He didn't want to go anywhere. They were getting alcoholically deep. Tapping into the cosmic elements that were responsible for their connection.

"Not an accident you're here. You were meant to cross our path," propheted Kip.

"Delilah appeared out of nowhere," sloshed West.

"She was brought to you."

This notion was both disturbing and exciting to West. He couldn't speak.

"If the doors of perception were cleansed,

everything would appear to man as it is, infinite," quoted Kip.

Yes. That's it, isn't it? The past two weeks; Delilah, Kip, Connie, the gallon of rum soaking his brain, these notions, Lucinda, it was all adding up to multiple tears in the fabric of his old self. He found himself hanging upside down, devouring, digesting his old persona.

"I'll help however I can," said West.

"What you are about to embark on will change your life forever," concluded Kip.

West noticed that their glasses were empty. He put two fingers high into the air and waited for the drinks to appear. No luck. Behind the bar, two arms crossed and a stern look on her face, Connie had two more Cuba Libres waiting for them.

"Better get your ass up there, she doesn't like to be kept waiting," said Kip.

The room began to spin as West tried to stand. He had trouble focussing. As he made his way to Connie he noticed, in the darkest, farthest corner of the bar, a large man with his back to them. Had he been there this entire time? How could the back of someone's head look so familiar? He couldn't take his eyes off of him.

When West leaned over to pick up the two drinks, Connie grabbed hold of his wrists and gave him a kiss on the cheek. Giddily he tiptoed his way back to the cocktail table housing Kip. He didn't know why or ask why he was on this ride, or where it was going. He just knew that he didn't want to get off.

Connie had consumed a few adult beverages herself, and she was feeling perfectly comfortably numb. With a handful of quarters, she made her way to the jukebox to play disc jockey and give the boys a show.

Pink Floyd's 'Us and Them' escaped from the bar speakers as Connie commenced a slow, sultry, solo dance. She immediately had the rapt attention of the men, which included the mysterious large man in the corner. The large man and Connie appeared to know each other. West thought that he detected a furtive smile between the two of them.

The large man theatrically rose to his feet, glided across the barroom floor, and extended an outreached hand requesting her permission for "this dance." She took his hand into hers and they danced the most ethereal, beautiful, dangerous 'pas de deux'.

West felt certain that he knew this man, but the rum, the darkness, the unfamiliar terrain, created confusion and fog.

"I feel like I've known all of you for my entire life," whispered West.

"You have my brother. This is the only dance there is," Kip whispered back.

"That man," said West.

"Kurtz. Today's his birthday," said Kip.

As the music came to an end, Connie gave Kurtz a great smack on the ass and headed back to her sanctuary behind the bar. He turned his gaze on West and Kip, momentarily considered his options, then carefully traversed the sawdust to arrive at their table. He was a big man, intimidating, towering over the table. He didn't say a word.

"Happy birthday brother Kurtz," Kip sighed. "Meet

your new best friend. West, this is Marlon."

West was cemented to his seat. His eyes were locked on Marlon's. After an eternal, uncomfortable silence, West extended his hand to him but could not speak.

Two gentle bear paws reached down and took West's face into its hands. Marlon leaned over and gave him a solemn, ceremonial kiss on the forehead, as tears were streaming down West's face. With a genius smile and a pat on West's head, Marlon made his way back to his dark corner of the world, turned his back on the lads, and became invisible once again.

"This is all a dream isn't it?" said a watery-eyed West.

"He gave you his blessing," comforted Kip.

West drained the last drops of his millionth Cuba Libre inspiring Kip to thrust two victorious fingers in the air. Connie's response to Kip's two fingers was a shake of the head, one middle finger, and a hearty laugh out loud.

#

Incense burning. It's supposed to mask the smell of pot, but it doesn't. Sometimes it's supposed to mask the smell of a rat, a grifter, a charlatan, of the hippie persuasion.

Hunter and Hugh were quietly, deliberately, but forcefully laying it all out for Kai. David 'Kai' Klein, GreenPlanet Hawaii's top dog, cult leader, and new-age charlatan. Hugh politely explained that the GreenPlanet name had been revoked, the Hawaiian bank accounts had been frozen, and a cease and desist

59

order was his for the keeping.

Several angry volunteers sat around the trio, on the floor, in a semi-circle. At a nearby desk, a bare-breasted young woman was typing away madly, trying to get down every hostile word.

"We assemble here every day to save our brother whales from extinction," exclaimed an exasperated Kai.

"You assemble here every day to smoke pot, fuck volunteers, and have your ego fed," slammed Hunter.

The volunteers were getting restless; their crash pad was in real jeopardy, and Kai seized upon their angst to lead the revolt.

"You have no right," Kai yelled. "We're not going anywhere."

The volunteers, led by the bare-breasted girl, jumped to their feet and began chanting, "leave our house!" "leave our house!" "leave our house!" Hunter gave Hugh the 'high sign' which was his signal to produce 'the envelope', which he did. As he handed it to Kai he said "Judith Mason. I believe you know her by the name Paisley Peace."

Oh yea. David knew Paisley. Intimately. He knew her for many nights, bent over many different pieces of ugly office furniture, promising her many future days of glory that would never manifest. Good old Paisley. Whatever happened to her?

It appeared that she was back home at her parent's house with his infant child. It appeared that she was underage and had a very angry father. It appeared that her mother kept saying the word statutory, and it appeared that David had lost his balance. Vertigo was his new mistress.

He grabbed onto his chair for stability, until a moment of clarity interrupted his dizziness. Clapping his hands violently, he waved his volunteer army out of the room. When everyone had begrudgingly obeyed and departed, he ignored Hunter and looked mercifully to Hugh.

"You are shut down, Mr. Klein," Hugh announced coldly.

Kai didn't make a sound. His grift was up. So be it. Not a shameful thing to lose a battle with Hunter Mack.

Hunter proudly patted Hugh on the back and surveyed his newly acquired property. The rainbow-colored desks, the giant humpback whale mural on the wall, yoga mats, and sleeping bags. He repo'd David's keys to the castle and escorted him swiftly out the front door which he then locked up tight. Mission accomplished, well done Hugh, now back to the Royal Hawaiian for sunsets and cocktails.

Speaking of sunsets and cocktails, Delilah and Rocky were indulging in their own anxiety medicine in the form of top-shelf margaritas at a window table at the Sunset Grill on an afternoon they wouldn't soon forget.

While West and Kip were liquidly getting to know each other, and Hunter and Hugh were dropping the hammer in Hawaii, Delilah and Rocky were being thrown for a loop. Two loops.

Will had gone to San Pedro to look for a boat. There were no volunteers milling around the office, so it was just Delilah and Rocky when the door opened and in walked bad news. Very bad news.

A tall, dark, menacing man stepped inside like he owned the joint. He closed the door behind him. Poison wearing a dark suit, dark sunglasses, and carrying a bouquet of white roses. He looked right through Rocky and directly at Delilah, who immediately recoiled. Seeing this, Rocky feebly tried to intervene, but the darkman brushed him off his shoulder like so much dead skin.

"Leave now or I'm calling the cops," Delilah said.

"These are for you," said the darkman as he presented the roses to Delilah. When she refused to take them he moved closer and placed them in front of her on her desk. Even though Rocky was shaking in his boots, he moved toward the man who suddenly pivoted and stared him down.

"I need to speak with my wife," he growled. "In private."

Delilah convinced a trembling Rocky to leave them for a few a minutes; said she'd be fine, not to worry, and when he reluctantly left the office she instantly regretted her decision.

The darkman claiming to be her husband informed her that he was going to be staying with her for a while. He asked her for the keys to her house. Evidently, he needed to drop out of sight "until a storm passes." She was having none of it, threatened to have him arrested while throwing the bouquet of white roses in his face. The bad news didn't try to force the house keys from her. Instead, he casually surveyed the office and Delilah's humble desk.

"This is it?" he chuckled. "Doing real good, babe," he said as, less than impressed, he turned his back on her and walked out the door.

In line at the bank, surrounded by the eavesdropping public, Rocky wanted to know all about this drama, right there, right now, in graphic detail.

Delilah noted that in the not-too-distant-past that maybe she had fallen in with a bad crowd. There was this "lost weekend" in Vegas about a year ago and when she woke up she was hitched to cocaine and to the cocaine dealer; that's it in a nutshell.

Oh no. No, no. This was not an acceptable cliche story for Rocky or the woman in line behind them. More, they needed much more.

"It's a classic American horror story," joked Delilah. "Nice girl who enjoys cocaine too much gets mixed up with evil monster."

She said that she did indeed wake up married in Las Vegas, but the real nightmare was yet to come. The very next weekend as a matter of fact. A party at their house. People strewn about drinking, smoking, doing lots of drugs, lap dances, your generic debauchery.

Her new husband had his hands down some chick's pants so she threw an ashtray at his head. He knocked her clear across the room. Her face was bleeding, she was crying, and he escorted the other woman by the hand and off to their bedroom. She dumped him.

It's her intention, her top priority, to get the mistake annulled, but it's complicated, it's a fucking mess. That's why they call it a nightmare. She hadn't seen him until last week. She fucked up. A momentary lapse of reason. Now she has a restraining order and she's convinced he will break into her house and be there if she goes home.

Not only the woman in line behind her, but the entire line of people were hanging on her every horrifying word when Delilah decided to publicly sum things up.

"Sometimes we seek out evil," announced Delilah very loud.

With a shrug of her shoulders she smiled a twisted smile, and when she knew all were looking, demonstrated a grand throat-cutting gesture for all to see.

That was the first loop. The second surprise of the day involved amazement not terror.

She and Rocky departed the bank and headed for a surf shop in Santa Monica to research and price wetsuits. While trying to figure out exactly how wetsuits worked, they overheard two animated surfers telling the story of the rescue of a diver at Power Station 3. The diver had come within seconds of death before she was miraculously saved by one of their surfer pals, and she wasn't the first ocean lover to almost be done in by the pipe.

Kimo was one of those telling the story, who, as you know, was there when it all went down. Delilah and Rocky now became the eavesdroppers. They learned about the ocean intake pipe and the killing of sea life that are sucked into the power plant. They learned of the serious danger to humans that unknowingly get too close to the pipe. They learned that the power company refused to spend the moolah to place a protective cap over the pipe, and they learned the name of the surfer who saved the divergirl.

Walker. West Walker.

What? Who? Delilah was instantly in motion. She introduced herself to the boys, intentionally not informing them of her connection to West. She gave Kimo the GreenPlanet phone number and asked him to please, please, please keep her 'in the loop'–play on words intended–which he lustily agreed to do, and after some additional strategic flirting with Kimo, off she and Rocky went, heads spinning, to seek refuge at the Sunset Grill.

With spectacular ocean view and fresh drinks in hand, Delilah and Rocky were buzzing about the ever surprising West when abruptly another round of drinks appeared in front of them. Before they could say 'what the fuck?', Will, straight from San Pedro, plopped down next to them and the party was on. So, okay, three surprises today. A good time was about to be had by all.

They were all talking at once. Will was excitedly filling them in on his search for a boat and this salty character he met named Shakespeare. Said he and his trawler, the Maggie May, might be the perfect match.

Delilah was loudly and proudly telling Will of West's life-saving heroics, while Rocky was expressing his disappointment in the wetsuits. They were all the same color. Black. He also, a bit later, with the help of mucho tequila, spilled the beans and told Will about the very scary office visit from the darkman.

Delilah wasn't happy. She'd made Rocky promise that he wouldn't do what he just did. Result: party over, for her anyway. She departed; Rocky felt bad, but not too bad, and Will felt concerned; very

65

concerned.

After Delilah left them, Rocky supplied Will with every single darkman detail, and Will commended him for breaking his promise. Delilah's safety, he said, was more important than keeping your word. Okay, back to the hooch.

At the Chimney Sweep, the sun never sets because you never see the sun. No sunsets and cocktails there, just lots and lots of cocktails.

West, barely alive, was now at the bar harassing Connie. Kip was nowhere to be seen. Barfly Janelle was purposely occupying the barstool next to West because she had plans for him. He, however, was getting agitated.

Kip and Marlon had disappeared when he wasn't looking; Connie was now too busy to pay any attention to him, and he was out of money and out of his mind. When Connie told him firmly but sweetly to "go home," he struggled to his feet and laboriously searched for the door.

Janelle seized the moment, placing plenty of money on the bar, she grabbed West by the arm and walked him out the door into the fresh night air.

Outside, the night sky was black, the parking lot was gray, and West was ashen. Janelle, the professional that she was, put a hand down the back of his jeans and grabbed his ass. As a token of his appreciation and his inability to give a fuck, he let her explore for a minute or so before he puked all over the parking lot. Time to go home.

Unfortunately for Delilah, she was afraid that she wouldn't be able to go home, afraid of what she would find.

There she was, driving with caution down her street, headlights off, as she brought the car to a crawling stop in front of her house. She summoned up the courage to have a look.

The front porch lights were on. The living room lights were on. The front bedroom lights were on. She saw an unmistakable silhouette move across her living room. Fuck. Fuck, fuck, fuck. What should I do?, she thought. Who should I go to for help?

It occurred to her that her neighbor Amanda Stiff, in all likelihood, saw him enter her house, or rather break into her house. Amanda sees everything. Makes it her mission to know everything that's going on in the neighborhood. She is the self-appointed mayor of everybody else's business. The poster girl for the Junior League. Always smartly dressed, impeccably made-up, hair perfect, with WASPy worldview ready to preach at the drop of a bonnet.

Delilah was correct. Amanda did encounter the bad news. She was making her daily see-and-be-seen 'mail walk' down her driveway to her mailbox when she saw the darkman on Delilah's front porch. He had a large key ring with two-dozen keys, and was patiently, in full view of the entire world, inserting each key into the front door lock. This was way too curious for Amanda to ignore. Big mistake on her part.

"Can I help you?" inquired Amanda.

Like Rocky, Amanda was invisible to him.

"Are you a friend of Delilah's?" grilled Amanda.

The darkman found the key he was looking for, unlocked the door, and kicked it open.

67

"Excuse me sir, someone is speaking to you," chirped Amanda.

The bad news turned to face his victim. Looked her straight in the eyes, and then up and down.

"Fuck off," growled the darkman.

What? No one speaks to Amanda that way. Her husband has connections. With the city council. With the police!

"What did you say?" said Amanda.

He pondered her question for thirty seconds before he deliberately lowered his sunglasses and gave her a look that would paralyze. Amanda wet her pants, her expensive Junior League pants. For the whole neighborhood to see. He stared at her crotch while the wet spot grew in diameter, laughed, and then returned his eyes to hers.

Falling back into the entrance of her house, Amanda slammed shut the door, frantically locking her many locks. Okay, forget Amanda. She'll be of no help.

Delilah, angry and afraid, flipped on her headlights, revved up the car, and sped off down the street. She was not going home tonight. She was going to sleep on the couch in Kip's office.

West was not going home tonight either. Too big of a mountain to climb. Much easier to stagger across the street to the GreenPlanet office where Kip had a couch that would do just fine. So that he did. That they did.

Inside Kip's office within an office, a topless Janelle was pulling the pants off of a helpless West. She succeeded in stripping him naked, simultaneously pulling her skirt down around her ankles. On top of West she climbed and began the monumental task of trying to get it in.

As she feverishly worked on his firmness factor, he was humming 'How Can You Mend A Broken Heart'. Semi-conscious, he decided to reward her 'hard' work and go along for the ride. At long last, Janelle succeeded in her attempted coupling and let out the world's loudest scream of self-satisfaction. So loud, that if you were just pulling your car into the parking lot, you might hear it.

When Delilah opened the door to the war room, it was completely dark. No lights in Will's office; none in Kip's.

She flicked on the main lights of the war room, crossed to her desk, removed her jacket, and set her belongings down. Ignoring the blinking light on her phone, she turned it upside down and switched off the ringer.

The door to Kip's office was closed but unlocked. Kicking her shoes off and unbuttoning her blouse, she opened his door and headed for the much-desired couch. At the exact frightening moment that she noticed a dark figure lying on the couch, West exhaled a loud animal growl causing her to jump backward and scream out loud.

Terrified, she switched on the light to discover a butt-naked West, passed out and snoring. This, she thought, as her pounding heart slowed down, was the most comforting, reassuring, joyful sight that she could ever see on this or any other night. A rainbow after a dark and stormy day. She turned off the light, crawled onto the couch next to him, wrapped her arms around him, and blissfully waited for sleep to come.

West was dreaming. Underwater.

Under the water, the rays of the sun became dimmer and dimmer as their journey took them deeper and deeper. At an unknown murky depth, a naked man swam sluggishly. Upon closer inspection, West could see that he was the naked man. He was sleep-swimming. His arms were heavy, barely moving. His eyes were open yet he was sound asleep. He was able to breathe under the water. Slow and deliberate.

A school of beautiful neon-green fish surrounded and swam with him for awhile before they darted away. He was joined by three electric-orange sea lions who frolicked about before they, too, vanished. The water became darker as he reached the lower depths. His ability to move forward became harder and harder. Barely moving, he was unaware of an unidentifiable presence behind him. This dark underwater cloud was now almost upon him. He came to a stop, his internal radar detecting something.

As he turned his head to look behind him he was suddenly wrapped in straightjacket-like confinement. Unable to move an inch, his limbs rendered useless, panic overtook him. Suddenly he couldn't breathe. Looking down at his abdomen he saw two giant tentacles crisscrossed around his torso. He tried valiantly to break free but was unable. He was fighting mightily for his life. The water was very dark and turbulent now. Terrorized, out of air, with no fight left in the dog, he acknowledged this as the moment of his death.

"Octopus!" screamed West.

Delilah jumped up from her own deep sleep.

"Octopus! Octopus!" West continued.

Delilah put her arm around him and rubbed the back of his neck until he returned to the conscious world. He sat upright. His heart was pounding.

"I was drowning," he said.

"You were dreaming," comforted Delilah.

"I've seen my own death," he concluded.

She kissed him on his alcoholic puke-lips, rubbed her hand through his oily hair, and then gently lay back down on the couch bringing him with her. In seconds they were both dead to the world.

#

So, where did Kip go when West wasn't looking? Van Nuys? No one intentionally goes to Van Nuys, you say, not even when they're exceedingly drunk. Not true, not true. That's where the Cessna Citation II private jet lives.

It's owner, Killian Patrick Asher Sr., had generously made sure it was ready and available for junior, who, aside from the pilot and copilot was the only passenger on tonight's flight.

Seated in a posh, leather, lap of luxury, Kip sipped on a Cuba Libre and stared out the window.

Safely taxiing away from the hangar, the jet made its turn onto the main runway and paused briefly before throttling up the engines and speeding down the tarmac.

As it effortlessly lifted off the ground, the lights of the Los Angeles metropolitan area exploded into view.

He was able to recognize familiar landmarks like

the Hollywood Sign, the Beverly Hills Hotel, the Santa Monica Pier. What got hold of his complete attention though, was the deceivingly peaceful site of SO CAL Power Station #3, lit up orange and in plain view. A serial killer that went unnoticed. Saluting farewell to his city below, he lowered his window shade, fell backward into his cocoon, and disappeared into the black of the night.

JUST THE FACTS

West and Delilah were sound asleep in each other's arms when the pounding on the office door jolted her awake, reminding her of West's naked presence. The cruel daylight revealed the chaotic nature of the office, and her nose discovered the pungent odor of stale sex, which added up to an additional jolt that suddenly turned the beginning of this day into her own drowning nightmare.

She vaguely remembered walking past some woman in the parking lot late last night. Was she coming from this building? The GreenPlanet office?

Delilah detached herself from West, buttoned herself up, brushed herself off, and opened the office door to find a professionally dressed young woman with a copy of the London Times under one arm and lugging a suitcase with the other. Could this be the woman from the parking lot?

Katherine 'Kate' Blair was a whip-smart, no-nonsense, graduate of St. Anne's College-Oxford with a degree in English Literature. A big-picture thinker, she predetermined long ago how all of this GreenPlanet thing would play out.

She was acutely aware of her superior intelligence, and readily accepted her role as organizational advisor. So the story goes, she was briefly a tutor to underclassman Theresa May before she threw in the towel in utter exasperation.

One of the first warriors recruited by Hunter, she was fiercely loyal to the cause; she was fiercely loyal

73

to Hunter, and quite probably the most valuable player on the squad.

Delilah held the door open but blocked Kate's entry into the office. Behind her, West, who had found his pants, was standing in Kip's doorway shirtless, mop-haired, and nasty.

"Can I help you?" asked a very grouchy Delilah.

"You're Delilah," replied Kate. "I'm Kate, from International. I've been sent to get you people up to speed," she said as she insisted her way past Delilah into the war room.

Delilah had no idea who this woman was, certainly didn't appreciate her brashness, and did she say, "You people?"

Kate deposited her suitcase in the middle of the room, collapsed onto Delilah's desk, and discovered a shirtless West standing in Kip's doorway. Her eyes remained fixed on West.

"Who did you say sent you?" asked Delilah.

"Hunter. International. And you are?" she said to West.

West smiled a big, goofy smile and simply replied "West."

Kate found this to be quite curious. She had specifically been sent by Hunter to prepare a "very promising" chap named West to become Kip's media spokesperson, but surely this could not be him.

"Welcome to L.A." beamed West.

Delilah concluded that she did not like her territory invaded, in more ways than one, that she did not like this woman, that she did not like this day, and that she fucking hated her life. So, fuck you.

74

She concocted a feeble story for Kate. Said they had pulled an all-nighter, working on an important local issue that she wasn't able to discuss at that time. Said they were just leaving to go to their respective homes to rest, freshen up, and return later in the day. Office was closing.

Kate didn't believe a word of it, but no matter. She popped to her feet, grabbed her suitcase, and still looking directly at West, said: "How about a lift to my hotel?"

He took a brief look in Delilah's direction then gave Kate the surfer head nod that indicated 'sure, why not?' Delilah stormed across the room, fetched her things, did some more random storming, flung open the door, slamming it shut on her way out. Kate was fascinated as West pulled his dirty shirt over his dirty head.

"She's quite pretty, isn't she?" said Kate smiling like a boxer standing over her unworthy opponent.

West had never before been embarrassed to drive anyone in his humble VW bug, but Kate had a crippling effect on his self-confidence, even as she was informing him of Hunter's praise.

She'd told him Hunter had heard him speak at the L.A. Press Club and was impressed enough to send her. Told him Hunter got a "good vibe" from him at the party in the Hollywood hills. She told him all of this as she was checking her appearance in the rearview mirror, on their way to the very posh Sunset Marquis Hotel. She didn't strike him as a 'save the whales' type, whatever that might be, and he even told her so, and she was pleased to hear that.

"Kip is the talking head," said West. "I'm the research guy."

"Kip is unable," she said. "You're our man."

When they pulled up to the hotel, West was intimidated by the glitz and glamour. He tried to wave off the doorman to no avail. Kate attempted to put him out of his middle class misery by clarifying that it wasn't she that was paying for the hotel.

An ex-lover, lead singer in a rock band, was picking up the tab. This made him even more insecure. She told him to go home, get a shower, and be back at the office ready to learn. Comprehensive courses in whales, seals, nukes, pollution, and acid rain were about to commence, but all would pale in comparison to media school.

Vacating his embarrassing carriage, she walked toward the hotel staff, all who seemed to know and love her. As he was pulling away from the hotel, he felt the need to know more.

"What's the name of his band?" he yelled out his window.

She yelled back at him, but all he could hear was "Boomtown."

#

Roy was sipping on a can of beer while he occupied the trashy wooden chair on West's front porch. The eviction notice that he found posted on the front door was on his lap. West was surprised to see him as he pulled into the driveway.

"You look good," Roy greeted him sarcastically.

"I see you're training hard for our next match,"

countered West.

He patted Roy on the shoulder, put the key in the door, and invited him to precede him into the apartment. Following close behind, he flicked on the light switch. No lights.

"No way?" he said in denial.

Roy opened the window blinds to let some daylight in, while West opened a dark refrigerator and removed a half-slice of pizza, an old container of Chinese food, and a warm can of Bud. He threw the leftovers in the trashcan and popped open the Bud.

"Cheers," said West.

"This is for you," said Roy as he handed him the eviction notice.

West took a big swig of warm beer, placed the eviction notice in the middle of a bright ray of sunlight, and acknowledged that he held in his hand the proverbial last straw.

Ashamed, he looked at Roy, then back at the notice, then at his sad excuse of a dark apartment. Roy picked up the receiver of the phone and listened for a dial tone. Dead.

"On the bright side, you don't need to contact any of the utility companies," said Roy.

Without uttering a word, West headed into his bedroom and began rummaging through a wrinkled pile of clothes on the floor. He grabbed a blue oxford shirt, a crumpled pair of black pants, and the black socks and shoes that completed the sorry outfit.

On the floor, Roy spied a lonely, unhealthy looking goldfish, in a dirty, depressing fishbowl. While West was searching for his belt, Roy nabbed the fishbowl and snuck a twenty-dollar bill in its place.

"I'm late for a lesson," he said as he and the fish headed for the door.

West found the belt and ran to see Roy out. He saw the fishbowl in his hand but said nothing.

Carefully placing the fish on the passenger seat of his van, Roy started her up, and looked back at West.

"I have a couch reserved in your name," he said.

A defeated West hung his head in shame as his best friend drove away with his dying goldfish. This was, he thought, rock bottom. This was even more tragic and pathetic than watching Lu drive off with his coveted foosball table.

She was so right. As always. He needed to grow the fuck up. He needed to take a long, hard look in the mirror. It couldn't get any worse than this; it couldn't get any more humiliating than this, he concluded, as he turned the front doorknob only to discover that it wouldn't turn, not an inch, not a millimeter. He had locked himself out of his dark, repossessed apartment.

In utter disbelief, in catastrophic defeat, he fell onto the porch chair, dropping his head into his hands. You never can go home.

#

That was exactly what Delilah was thinking when she crept back into her neighborhood. Could she ever go home? Would he still be there? With his friends? Did they destroy her house? Steal her blind?

She parked the car a block away and ninja-like assumed a concealed position across from her house. It wasn't a pretty picture. It was a scary picture.

All of the lights in the house were on and her front door was wide open. There were no cars in the driveway, no unfamiliar cars parked in front of the house, no signs of life inside or out. Amanda's house was tightly shuttered, curtains drawn, no spying eyes to be seen. What should she do? She was afraid to go into her own house. She didn't know what or who would be waiting for her. She also didn't know what was taking place at this exact moment in Runyon Canyon.

The dog's name was Cody and the jogger's name was Colby. He a German Shepard, she an out of work actress. Both of them were halfway up the canyon road.

Cody, in much better shape than Colby, was far up ahead, around the bend in the road. This was the normal state of affairs, and each day when Colby finally turned the corner, Cody was always there waiting for her, tail wagging, resting under the shade of a big tree. Until today. Cody was nowhere in sight.

She tried calling out to him, yelling his name over and over. Still no Cody. Panic set in and she started running up the hill, calling his name, swinging her arms, completely out of breath. She was searching the brush and the bushes, contemplating horrific scenarios, when she heard the barking. She knew that bark. Following the sound to a side of the road that dropped off steeply into a ravine, she saw Cody, far down the hill, barking and circling what appeared to be a body.

The office was electric. Volunteers were scurrying around. Some were arranging chairs to face the large white strategy board, while others were setting up the conference table with notebooks, position papers, and writing tools. A film projector was wheeled in and strategically placed to face the pull-down screen above the board. The Telex machine began to whir and come to life as ticker tape sputtered out.

Kate was in the middle of the room shouting orders and giving directions. She stopped a young volunteer and asked her if she knew how to operate the Telex, to which she received a frightened shake of the head 'no'.

"It's about time you learned. Over there. Sit down and read what comes across the printout. Don't be concerned with the tape. Don't type. Don't touch. Anything important, I want to know immediately. You understand?" barked Kate.

The young volunteer shook her head 'yes', and in a daze started to walk in the wrong direction. Kate gently grabbed her shoulders, turned her around, and sent her off on the proper route.

Rocky emerged from Kip's office with a tall stack of campaign prep-folders he had originally assembled for Kip. He offered them to Kate as tutoring materials for West. Impressed with the depth, clarity, and detail contained in each folder, she gave Rocky a big thank-you hug just as Delilah walked through the door.

Delilah halted abruptly as she witnessed the frenetic hustle and bustle, not to mention General Kate with her arms around a beaming Rocky. When Rocky finally looked her way, he saw a fuming Delilah waving him over to her desk. As they both converged at her desk, Delilah took him by the arm.

"Where's Kip?" she said.

"No one's seen him," he replied.

Again the door flung open as West entered dressed in black pants, black shoes, blue Oxford shirt, and wet slicked-back hair. He waved at Delilah and Rocky and headed their way only to be intercepted by Kate who redirected him to the far end of the conference table.

Sitting him down so that he was facing her, she studied him carefully. Then, like a professional hair stylist, she ran her hands through his wet hair until she got it just right.

"You are not allowed to like her," Delilah said as Rocky was waved over to join West and Kate.

Even though it was before noon, Delilah had already seen enough of this day. Fortunately for her, she didn't find anyone in her house when she gathered up the courage to inspect the premises.

The ashtrays were full, the liquor bottles were dented, the music was blaring, but, all in all, it could have been a lot worse. She had to pay a locksmith a hundred bucks to change the locks, and she needed a couple of stiff drinks to settle her nerves, but most importantly, he wasn't there. She had gotten the impression that he left in a hurry, but who the fuck knows? He was gone; that's all that matters. She still had to worry about tonight. What if he returns? Block it out. For now, concentrate on the present, be here now, and listen to your phone messages.

The Telex machine was making noise like a race car. Paper was flowing and ticker tape was flying. Kate noticed the young volunteer breathing heavy, her eyes full of tears.

"Everything okay over there?" asked Kate.

No words, only a head shake and a wiping away of tears.

Kate pointed to Susan Noble, the volunteer coordinator, who promptly dropped what she was doing and rushed over to the Telex to assume the helm. All eyes were on Susan as she ripped the print-out from the Telex and started reading it to the tribe.

"Halifax, Nova Scotia. Sixteen-hundred hours. Members of GreenPlanet Foundation were arrested today in their attempt to halt the slaughter of more than two-hundred baby Harp seals on the ice floes of northeastern Newfoundland. GreenPlanet member Jean Paul Parent was medevaced to a hospital in Halifax for hypothermia and cardiac arrest. His condition is unknown at this time. After chaining himself to a pile of bloody Harp seal pelts, the ship's captain, seeing this, ordered his men to hoist Jean Paul and the bloody pelts, and dunk them into the frigid Arctic waters. Prior to chaining himself to the seal pelts, Parent was seen covering a baby seal to save it from the slaughter. He was pulled off of the seal by three men, and made to watch as two others clubbed the baby seal in the head, cut its throat, and skinned it alive, ending its life."

The young volunteer was sobbing. Kate knew what was about to happen. The phones were about to blow up. The media were on the way. West wasn't ready. Trial by fire. She dictated an exact response for everyone and anyone who answered the phones.

"We are aware of the situation in Newfoundland

and are preparing a statement to be released to the press and public within the day." "Nothing more, nothing less," she commanded.

The Harp seal notebooks were separated from the stack and placed in front of West. Kate sat on one side of him, Rocky on the other, as an accelerated crash course in the politics and science of seals commenced.

Susan scurried back to her desk, and Delilah remained at hers. The phones lit up. Everyone was talking at once. It was exciting. It was urgent.

Delilah hadn't had the opportunity to inform anyone about the anonymous cryptic message she had just listened to because she was answering call after call about the seal slaughter. Susan waved at her to pick up line three. It was Kimo, West's surfing pal whom she met at the surf shop. He was offering to give her a private surfing lesson. Up close and personal.

She didn't have to think about it for an L.A. minute. She needed to get away from Kate. She needed to get away from West. She needed her own campaign. See ya. She grabbed all of her shit, ignored the ringing phone, waved at Susan as she passed by, and out the door she fled.

Kate and Rocky continued to cram facts and talking points into West's head. Volunteers were putting together media kits and answering phones. Film was loaded onto the projector as the screen was lowered into place. When all was ready, Kate mobilized the troops to take their seats, kill the lights, and roll the film.

The projector kicked into action. The moving

pictures on the screen showed baby Harp seals captured, clubbed, and skinned. The ice was covered in blood. The carnage was horrific. Kate, focussed and composed, lectured as West and the gang somberly watched the slaughter.

While the horror in the dark office was taking place, Delilah was behind the wheel of her 1956 T-Bird, top down, sun shining, and music blasting on the radio. Tan, windblown, Wayfarers on, she was a Southern California goddess flying down the road.

Zipping into the beach parking lot, she pulled up next to Kimo and a half dozen other surfers gathered around a beat up pickup jammed with surfboards and a cooler full of beer. One of the guys handed her a cold beer.

"Anybody know where I can find a surfing instructor?" she flirted as each dude melted in her presence.

The film and lecture were over. A brief respite ensued. Susan was eating an orange when Connor Kilkenny walked in and broke the silence. Tall, dark, handsome, and mustached. He entered the room with a confidence and a swagger. Susan saw the tape recorder and microphone in his hand. The KWOT t-shirt, jeans, and cowboy boots screamed lady-killer. He walked right up to her with a big smile on his face.

"Connor Kilkenny, KWOT news," he announced.

From across the war room, Kate was already on the way. She extended her hand to Connor.

"Are those Tony Lamas?" flirted Kate.

"I do believe they are," laughed Connor.

They both sized each other up on the spot and

came to the exact same conclusion. Smart, confident, attractive. He said that he was hoping for an interview for the six o'clock news. "Canadian seal hunt," he said.

Kate didn't know who he was. She didn't know he was the silver-throated, hysterically-funny, rapidly-rising star of L.A. rock radio. She didn't know the station; she's English for Christ's sake, but West sure did.

KWOT. 94.7 on your fm dial. The best rock station in all the land. Like a shot, West appeared right next to Kate, and before she could utter an introduction, he declared for all to hear, the superiority and badassness of the Mighty KWOT.

Pleasantries were exchanged before it suddenly dawned on West that he was about to be interviewed for the evening news. He got nervous, and it certainly didn't help him when Kate whispered in his ear:

"We're about to see how good you are," she said sounding nervous herself.

As Connor was setting up his tape recorder and sound-checking the microphone, West was shaking and his lips were dry.

He started off okay, got his name and title correct, but when he was asked to explain the purpose of the seal protest, the fresh facts and figures crammed into his head were replaced with raw emotion from watching the film footage.

"Let's not call it a hunt. It's a slaughter. Hunt somehow suggests a fair fight. Infants, babies, clubbed in the head. Their throats cut. Why? Their white pelts bring in big dollars," said an animated West.

It went this way for a few more minutes. Connor

still hadn't heard a fact or a figure and understood that he was dealing with a rookie, so he tried to help him out.

"Canadian Fisheries say that the hunt only lasts a few weeks each year and that it is necessary to harvest and control the Harp seal population."

It was a generous assist but to no avail.

"I don't think that anyone who's seen film footage of the decimation will come to the conclusion that the Canadian government has the best interest of baby Harp seals in mind," answered a distraught West.

He knew he was flopping, and looked to Kate for help. Nothing doing. She had zero intention of throwing him a lifeline. Trial by fire, my friend.

His fellow activists weren't sure what to think. Was this going well or not? Connor wisely decided that it was best to wrap things up, so he teased more to come, signed off, shut off the tape recorder, and looked at West with a bemused smile.

"Thanks, man. That was great," he said handing him his card.

West was drained.

"Call me anytime," said Connor as he patted him on the back.

He looked at Kate with a wide smile, and she forced a smile back at him. Waving to the volunteer audience, he victoriously made his exit. The silence was increasingly uncomfortable until Susan began to lead a polite applause for West. Kate didn't join the others; rather, she turned her back, closing the door to Kip's office behind her.

#

Kate had just finished her call with Hunter when West stormed in and proceeded to pace back and forth, frothing at the mouth. West, she had told Hunter, was a quick study, but he was green and prone to emotion. Hunter instructed her to stick with him and "throw him to wolves." She assured him that the wolves were on the way.

West was boiling over. He didn't sign up for this. Or did he? He was a tennis player! What the fuck did she expect?

"Facts, not feelings," she said. He screamed with great lung capacity that he knew the facts. Facts weren't the problem. The film was very upsetting. Slit throats are very upsetting. People choppered away to the hospital is very upsetting.

"We are not the story," she yelled. "Facts, not feelings!"

West stopped his pacing, turned and faced Kate directly.

"Canada's commercial seal hunt occurs on the ice floes off Canada's East Coast in two areas: The Gulf of St. Lawrence and the 'Front' which is northeast of Newfoundland. Sealing is an offseason activity conducted by a small number of fishermen from Canada's East Coast. They comprise less than one percent of the provincial population. They make a small fraction of their annual incomes from sealing. Hundreds of thousands of seals are killed each year. The Canadian government knowingly allows sealers to exceed their quota of animals killed. In the 1950's and 60's, excessive hunting reduced the Harp seal population by as much as two-thirds. Six years ago scientists were warning that the population could be wiped out if the hunt was not suspended for at least a decade. Seals are killed primarily for their fur, which is used to produce high fashion garments. Most of the pelts are shipped to Norway. For the first seven days of a Harp seals life they have a lemony white coat and are called 'yellow coats'. During the second and third week of their life, they are called 'white coats'. The hair follicles are actually transparent and hollow, but they appear white. This white coat period is when they are most desirable to the sealers. The Canadian government could easily shut down the seal hunt and replace it with economic alternatives if it chose to do so. One solution would be a buyout of the commercial sealing industry. Another solution would be to HAVE A FUCKING HEART!"

"Today hasn't been a total waste," Kate replied. "The wolves are on the way. Better get your ass out there and get ready for round two."

They both felt better. He knew the facts, and now she knew that he knew the facts. Look out world.

Arm around him for all to see, she walked him into the war room that was buzzing once again. A new volunteer was at the Telex machine. Rocky had his merchandise army in full work mode. Protestors, he proclaimed, would need t-shirts! Susan was on the phone madly organizing and recruiting for a protest at the office of the Canadian Consulate in downtown Los Angeles.

During his KWOT interview, West, in a moment of desperation, announced that there would be a massive protest at the end of the week. This came as a big surprise to everyone else, seeing that he made it up on the spot, and it was now Susan's job to make it happen.

As the afternoon progressed, Kate stood watch over West as he fielded a steady stream of calls from the media. Occasionally she would hand signal him or slip him a note to slow down, stay cool, use statistics, and sit up straight. He was doing well. With every interview, he got better. He could feel it now. He knew well this feeling of being on center court with all eyes on him. He was focussed. Back in the zone.

When you're in the middle of a marathon tennis match, playing a five-setter, you can lose track of time. Five sets, five hours. Poof. It was now early evening. West was still seated at his desk chomping on a burger and sipping on an Orange Julius. The army of volunteers were gone for the day, Kate was shuttered in Kip's office, and Susan was still at her desk, overwhelmed with the task of planning and coordinating the ad libbed protest. Her phone rang. It was another call for West.

She transferred the call to him, he took another bite of his burger and he was ready for more action. It was not a reporter this time. The woman on the other end was difficult to hear. She was whispering and there was a lot of background noise. West asked for her name, but she wouldn't give it to him. He waved for Susan to listen in on the call.

The caller said she worked inside SO CAL Power Station #3; she would call back at 11 p.m., and then she was gone. The clock on the wall read 5:40.

As West and Susan hung up their phones, Kate emerged from Kip's office dressed for a night of revelry and rock and roll.

"You lived to fight another day," she said to an eager-for-a-compliment West.

"That's it?" he begged.

"Tomorrow morning, ten sharp," she said heading for the door.

When she got to Susan's desk by the door she raved "Good work today, well done," and out she went leaving West and Susan as the last two remaining warriors on the battlefield.

Susan was a smart cookie. Attractive in a covered up, nerdy kind of way. Although she was someone who looked before she leaped, she often leaped.

She could see that West was wounded. In an attempt to make him feel better, she complimented him on a job well done, and for having "great passion." For the first time, he took a close look at her, acknowledged her existence, and suddenly she appeared quite attractive to him.

"I like you better than Kate," said West.

"I think you like Kate more than you let on," she said.

"No, sorry. I like you better," he insisted.

"What's my name?"

West didn't know her name. He hadn't paid her one second of attention the entire day. In all fairness to him, this day, as well as the day before, had been all consuming, overwhelming, and unsurvivable for most humans. She knew this, so she marched over to him, extended her hand, and introduced herself.

"Susan. Susan Noble." He did a poor job of pretending that he knew her name, all the while hanging on to her hand a bit too long. Attempting to learn more personal information about her, he suggested that she stop working for the day and go home to her boyfriend. Did she have a boyfriend?

Freeing her hand from his, she reminded him that someone went on the radio and told all of Los Angeles that GreenPlanet was staging a big protest in front of the Canadian Consulate and that the improvised statement kind of put a crimp in her plans for the evening.

He felt bad, but not too bad. He also felt the need to be in the office at 11 p.m. to field the call from the mysterious whispering woman, and it sure would be nice if Susan were there too.

It was time for him to run home to see if he still had an apartment. He gave her his solemn promise that he would be back shortly with some pizza and beer. She specified pepperoni. He gave her two thumbs up. On his way out the door, she said in hushed tones "I don't have a boyfriend."

The clock now read 5:59 p.m. One minute before West's big interview would air on KWOT. Susan dashed into Kip's office and turned on the radio on his desk. It was already tuned to KWOT. 'Kashmir' by Led Zeppelin was fading out and the news was about to begin. She plopped down on the couch with baited breath.

#

Delilah also had her ear pressed to the radio. She was back in the beach parking lot, drinking beer with

91

Kimo and her new surfer buds. KWOT was playing on the pickup truck radio when she heard Connor Kilkenny say West's name. Kimo started jumping up and down with excitement when West's voice came booming through the truck's speakers. His exuberance was in marked contrast to earlier in the day when the so-called surfing lesson turned out to be something much different.

Delilah had lied to him. She told him that she was a world-class swimmer, even though she couldn't swim a stroke. She asked that they meet at her "favorite" beach, which just happened to be in the close proximity of Power Station #3. Because he was so eager to put the moves on her, he didn't put two and two together until it was too late.

They had waxed their boards down and were in waist-high water when he detected a slight hesitancy in Delilah. She was petrified but didn't want to blow her cover so she bravely continued to paddle out. When Kimo sped past her on his way to the break, she stopped him cold.

"Wait!" she cried out.

"You okay?" asked Kimo.

"Two things," she said. "One, I can't swim. And two, I want to go over there," she said pointing at Power Station #3.

The light bulb went on in Kimo's dim head. The pipe monster! Idiot! She didn't come to see him, they never come to see him. You gotta give her credit, though; she has big, giant, girl balls.

Delilah reached across her board, latched onto his arm, and batted her dreamy brown eyes at him.

"Let's go before I pussy out," she said.

He reluctantly agreed, not against his better judgment, because he doesn't have better judgment, but because she was irresistible. With one hand on her board, he paddled with his other hand until they reached the churning water near the pipe monster. He pointed below, indicating where the intake pipe was located. A rising swell almost knocked Delilah off of her board, and he could see the terror in her eyes. That's it. Time to get the fuck out of there.

"Show's over," he said. "Let's go."

She stubbornly shook her head 'no' and said: "a little closer, please."

La chica loca.

Now that they were back on terra firma, cold beer in his hand, the both of them still alive, he felt mucho mejor.

Listening to his bro West on the radio was the coolest fucking thing ever. Delilah was also happy to be on solid ground, and she too was listening to her bro West, but she didn't arrive at the exact same conclusion.

Kate poured herself another glass of champagne and asked the limo driver to tune the radio to 94.7. Would the interview play better on the radio than it did in person? Maybe? Probably not.

She listened passively to West's debut while watching the lights of the Sunset Strip come to life. The champagne, she determined, made everything more palatable.

Susan didn't get much couch time. The phones in the office exploded. She couldn't answer them fast enough. The KWOT audience flooded the office with requests for protest information, offers of help, congratulations, and best wishes. They wanted to know where they could send money, buy t-shirts, and how to join the cause?

Women were calling and asking to speak with West. Was he single? People were outraged, passionate, and ready to go to war. It became evident that West's fact-free, emotional interview struck a chord. Los Angeles was fired-up.

West was not fired-up. He was low down. After visiting his dark, empty, eviction-noticed apartment, he got back in his car and drove aimlessly.

Listening to himself on the radio was surreal. His voice was coming out of the car speaker. On KWOT! With Connor Kilkenny! But it wasn't good. It was painfully amateur. Embarrassing. And now he was feeling sorry for himself, in a daze, in his car, hiding from the world in the parking lot of the Toluca Lake Tennis Club.

A loud tapping on his window rudely slapped him back into the painfully present moment. He rolled down his window to discover the whitest guy he's ever seen. White tennis shirt, white shorts, white socks, white shoes, and a white sweater wrapped around his lily-white neck.

He had no idea who this guy was, but Mr. White knew him. Called him West. Introduced himself as Steven. Eaton. Cassie's husband. You know, Cassandra, tennis lessons? Yikes! Yes, West knew Cassandra. He knew his daughter too. He thought to himself, you know, there are still a few hours left in this day; plenty of time for more degrading, debilitating high drama. Let's have it.

No debilitating drama. Quite the contrary. Steven had heard from Roy that West might be looking for a place to live. It just so happened that he had a guesthouse on his property. He traveled a lot, and it wasn't easy for him to keep track of what's going on at home, if you know what I mean?

Seeing that West already knew the lay of the land, knew his wife on a professional teacher-student basis, and would be providing him with a valuable service; spying on his wife and daughter and reporting back to him; maybe they could help each other out? Quid pro quo motherfucker.

West considered this for two seconds and concluded 'beggars can't be choosers'. If one must be removed from their exceedingly depressing dump of an apartment into a luxury guesthouse in the hills of Beverly, in order to assist a fellow human being in his great time of need, so be it. I mean, that's what altruism is all about. Right?

#

I know what you've been thinking. Where's Kip? Where's Will? How does this day end? Good questions. Let's start with Will.

While GreenPlanet activists were being beaten and arrested on the ice floes of Newfoundland, and media madness ensued at the office in L.A., and Delilah was getting up close and personal with the pipe monster, Will was at the Palm, having lunch, mostly drinks, with the biggest soap star in Hollywood, Natalie Singer.

Natalie was going on and on about getting pulled over by this dashing LAPD cop. He didn't pull her over for any wrongdoing; rather, he wanted an autograph and a date! The cop said she was the most beautiful woman in the world, but she told him don't be silly, surely there must be someone more beautiful than she.

Will was staring into his half-empty half-full martini glass, depending on your worldview, pretending to hang on her every word, but his thoughts were elsewhere. He was remembering the last time he lunched at the Palm. Only a couple of months ago he was sitting at a much better table, that one, right over there. He came there directly after a doctor appointment. The doctor had bad news; his heart, his liver, his blood pressure. Apparently, the Hollywood agent life can kill you. Who knew? Doctor told him to change his ways now or die.

Will knew why his blood pressure was sky high. He knew why his heart was failing. It was his proximity to the nightmare, low-life, greed-is-good, evil, ass-licker, zero-redeeming-values, loser, which was his boss.

On that day, just like today, Will was drinking martinis. He drank several come to think of it. Got himself good and sloshed, then headed straight to the office. Not his office.

He took the elevator all the way to the top. When the elevator doors opened, he walked right past Denise, the executive secretary, and into Satan's office. Satan wasn't there. Probably out ruining countless people's lives.

He knew his time was short, in more ways than

one, and that Denise had surely called for security, so he started to smash and destroy everything in sight. Lamps, pictures, expensive paintings, the glass coffee table, the liquor cabinet, everything.

He urgently had to relieve himself from his liquid lunch, and Satan's desk and chair seemed the perfect place to empty his bladder, so he whipped the old boy out and had at it.

Natalie's voice intruded, returning him to the present moment and his very real martini. She was thanking Enzo, their waiter, who had just delivered a bottle of champagne compliments of Mr. O'Neal.

It was always bittersweet for Natalie when she was out power-lunching. Was she famous? Yes. Was she wealthy? Yes. Was she a star? Yes. Was she a movie star? No. Was she taken seriously as an actress? No. As a person? No. Was the grass greener over on table 23? Absolutely. Would Ryan O'Neal ever offer her a part? Not unless she slept with him, and even then she couldn't be sure.

Will recognized her existential pain. He knew she craved respect. He knew, on her own, she could never escape the 'soap actor' label of shame. That's why the lunch. He had a plan.

She could be seen in a whole new light. Become the esteemed center of attention with the serious journalist crowd and the informed public. She could come to the aid of endangered animals and get free, significant, weighty publicity. He also knew that she would look smoking-hot in a GreenPlanet t-shirt.

Tranquil, unemotional, and brutally honest, he laid out the course of action that he thought she should take. Join the cause and get out of soap opera jail. A win for everyone. The deal was sealed.

His approach with Vanessa Gray Reynolds was a bit different. Vanessa was different. A movie star of the highest caliber. A media magnet. A regular on Carson. Always on the covers of the coveted magazines. Talented, passionate, eccentric. Respected.

He knew that he had to put on a show for her, had to bring his 'A' game for her. That's why the Polo Lounge, that's why the theatrics. She sat on the edge of her chair, sipping on a Bellini, her eyes glued to Will.

He was using props. Salt and pepper shakers, a water glass, his gin and tonic, and his hands. Demonstrating how a harpoon boat chases down, then shoots and kills a whale. He was maniacal. The gin from lunch with Natalie combined with his current gin and tonic fueled his performance.

At the most dramatic moment of his demonstration, right when the harpoon canon lets her fly, he violently swung his hand and knocked his g & t into the next county. Vanessa was in the palm of his hand. She could visualize the entire movie in her head.

The waiter brought him a fresh drink, which Will used to stoke the second show of his double bill. The Harp seal slaughter.

I'll let you imagine the pantomime. It was very effective. Vanessa was sold. Count her in. She was ready, willing, and able to lead the troops into battle.

As he drove away from his triumph at the Beverly Hills Hotel, his radio was tuned to, you guessed it, KWOT. He listened with glee as West fired up the always laid-back L.A. audience.

As he passed by his former place of employment, he looked up toward the top of the building, wondering exactly what Satan had thought of his parting gifts? Will's attorney had informed him that they were received with less than the spirit of gratitude. Oh well. Can't please everyone.

Kip, he knew, would be pleased, very pleased. Natalie and Vanessa would be welcomed additions to the GreenPlanet team, and Will would be viewed and appreciated in a whole new light.

So how about Kip?

He flew south of the border, and on this particular day he was occupying a submerged barstool at a hotel pool bar, sipping on margaritas.

Periodically, he would massage the back of his companion's brown neck and shoulders, and stomach, and small of the back, and her breasts too. She didn't mind. She liked it. She was seventeen. They had an arrangement.

Kip hadn't listened to any radio interviews, or recruited any Hollywood stars, or found any eviction notices on his apartment door. He was done with all of that high stress, big city stuff. He had a one-way ticket, two fingers in the air, and a delicious lady-in-waiting to keep him company.

#

By the time West returned to the office with two 'six packs' of beer and a pepperoni pizza under his arm, more than four hours had passed. The office lights were low and Susan was not at her desk. Depositing the pizza and beer on the conference table,

99

he peaked into Kip's office where he found Susan sleeping on the couch.

Selecting the most aromatic slice of pie, he knelt down beside her and waved the pizza back and forth under her nose causing her to blissfully dream of pepperoni pizza. It was an incredible dream. It smelled so real she could almost taste it until she did taste it as West wiped the corner of the slice across her lips. She made sounds of pleasure that got his blood stirring. Without opening an eye she said:

"How many women have their very own celebrity pizza delivery boy?"

"You're the only one I'm aware of," said West.

"Guess what I want?" she teased.

"My autograph?" he parried.

"It starts with the letter beer," she said as she sat up and attacked the pizza slice.

He grabbed the pizza box and the beer and arranged it on the couch between them. She gunned a beer and popped open another one, then pointed at the clock on the wall, silently informing him that two hours had somehow turned into four.

Before he could get an apology or an explanation out of his mouth, she described the madness that followed his radio interview. The phone frenzy was indicative of a big turnout for the protest. There was much work to do. He created this firestorm, so he was going to have to help her put it out.

Immersed in an orgy of pizza and beer, he tried to get her reaction to his interview, but she had no comment, pretending not to hear him. When he started to give his own analysis, she stopped him by giving him a kiss on the cheek. He tried to be cool, but he mistakenly interpreted this kiss as a positive review.

"I'm not girlfriend material," she said with a mouthful of pizza. "I'm attracted to you, and I might sleep with you, but the jury is still out," she continued.

West was speechless and aroused. He couldn't think of anything clever to say.

"You never want a serious relationship?" he floundered.

"I want more beer," she said as she grabbed another and headed for her desk.

He was right on her tail, and before she had a chance to sit, he captured her hand, whirled her around, and pulled her close to him. Slippery slope.

Reaching into his back pocket, he removed a red bandana, and then gently wiped the corner of her mouth. She put her arms around his waist, and the second before he leaned in to kiss her, the door opened and in came a sunburned, hungry, exhausted, Delilah.

West instinctively took a step back, as Susan coolly held her ground. Delilah promptly got the picture, marched over to her desk, threw her shit down, and slammed herself into her chair.

What the fuck was going on there? Last night she found a naked West smelling of bad sex. When she flew the coop this morning, he was looking doe-eyed at the dragon lady as she ran her fingers through his golden locks, and now, less than twenty-four hours later, here he is with his arms around 'what's her name'?

101

"Hey, Dee. It's been quite the day. We were just administering a little hug therapy," he said to the disgust of both of the women.

"Want a hug? You look like you could use one," he said digging the hole deeper.

No, she didn't want a fucking hug. She wanted some of that pizza and beer. Susan was already on it, delivering said items to Delilah at her desk.

"Everybody's working late tonight, eh?" he said lamely.

"Don't act so guilty," admonished Delilah. "You're a free agent."

Yes, technically he was a free agent, he thought, but he was acting guilty because he felt guilty. Maybe he was guilty. How come he didn't know?

Susan, the savvy lass that she was, scooped up a mountain of papers, stuffed them under her arm, and bid them both farewell as she raced for the exit. West watched helplessly as she disappeared out of sight.

The silence was brutal. West noticed Delilah's sunburn. That's nice, he thought. At least someone got some sun today. How was the water? Which beach did you go to? Any waves? I remember when I used to ride waves.

"Why did you run off today?" he stupidly asked.

Delilah was about to explode, but he couldn't keep his mouth shut.

"Some of us had to...", he wasn't allowed to finish.

"I heard you. On the radio. What the fuck was that?" she howled.

It was on. Back and forth. Angry voices growing louder and louder.

She reminded him of how she found him last night. He reminded her of what he'd recently been through. She reminded him of why he was there. He reminded her that he did not have to answer to anyone. He suggested to her that maybe she should do the interviews if she was such an expert. She reminded him that she was the one that rescued him from the beach and brought him into the fold.

Unbeknownst to them, while their battle was raging, a pockmarked man in a bad suit had slipped inside the office and was standing by the door, patiently watching the fireworks. Delilah saw him and flinched.

"Can I help you?" she asked.

The man held out a detective's badge for them to see, and when he stretched his arm forward to show it to them, it also revealed the handgun that he was wearing.

"Detective Moses," he said. "I'm looking for Delilah."

He held a manila envelope containing three 8 x 10 photos. He also possessed a GreenPlanet business card with her name on it.

"I'm hoping you can help me identify the person in these photos," he said as he handed her the envelope and the business card. "This card was in the deceased's pocket."

Remember Cody and Colby? This morning in Runyon Canyon? I know, I know, it seems like years ago, but this story jumps around. These were photos of the body that Cody found. The body was currently in the morgue, and Cody was back at home chewing on a rawhide dog toy.

The detective didn't like the look or the sound of West, and he instructed him to back away and let Delilah examine the photos. She was afraid to look. Afraid because, ashamedly, she wanted it to be a certain person and was afraid it might not be him.

She opened the envelope and examined all three photos without uttering a sound or changing her expression.

"My husband," she said matter of fact.

West, on the other hand, he had some facial expressions going on. Husband? What? Holy fuck! Husband?

The detective asked her to have another look to make sure it was him. It was. She said that they were separated, hadn't been married long and that she had a restraining order against him.

The detective knew all of this already. He knew the deceased man's dossier. He instructed her to come to the downtown police station tomorrow for an interview, then to the morgue to identify the body. She took his card and thanked him as she escorted him out the door.

"Holy fuck!" "You're married?" exclaimed a stunned West.

"Not anymore," she sighed as she dropped into her chair.

Before West could commence with any cross-examination, the phone rang. He looked up at the clock. 11 p.m. Scooping up the phone on his desk he answered: "GreenPlanet, West speaking."

It was her. The mystery woman from PS3. He

signaled for Delilah to listen in on her phone. The woman said it wasn't safe for her to talk. "Three sea lions are dead. Thrown in the dumpsters. I have to go," she said before the line went dead.

Delilah hung up her phone and looked at West.

"P S Three. That's where I was today," she said. "I went there with Kimo."

West was staggered. This left-right combo had him reeling and confused. This day had him down for the count. Nothing more could or should be spoken today.

He collected the remaining beers and walked to the entrance of Kip's office. He peered at Delilah, tears streaming down her face, and extended his hand to her. This was a platonic hand; a let's go collapse in exhaustion hand; a no questions will be asked hand.

She locked the door to the war room and turned out the lights. Finding her way to West, she placed her hand in his.

He flipped on the radio, and they fell onto the couch. A song had just ended and the late-night jock began to speak.

"I don't know about your day. What happened to you on your journey today, but mine was, you know, sometimes, sometimes we have to embrace the mystery. We're not always meant to understand why things happen the way they happen. Sometimes life just kicks our ass. Kicks it hard. Are you following me? Are you with me on this? What a day. Sometimes, my late night friends, we just have to throw up our hands, throw in the towel, and, surrender."

As he finished, music took over. 'Surrender' by Cheap Trick. Then his voice came back, over the music.

"You're listening to KWOT Los Angeles. Just surrender.

NOTHING COMES FROM NOTHING

The rain hadn't let up for days. Not for a split second. The L.A. gods were angrily shattering rainfall records. It looked like every street in the city was flooded. Many traffic lights were out, while others endlessly flashed red. Abandoned cars blocked submerged intersections. A portion of Rod Stewart's face slid off of a billboard on Sunset Boulevard. Laurel Canyon was closed to all non-resident traffic as city laborers worked feverishly to place plastic sheets on the sides of the sliding hills. The Hollywood Sign was crying, while an empty Dodger Stadium had its lights on to assist the ground crew struggling to deploy the infield tarp. To the west, a hard rain continued to pelt a dark, angry, turbulent ocean, and even though it was midday, the darkness required running lights on all ships at sea.

Under the water, it was equally menacing. Even for a California sea lion. Especially if you were a sea lion being tailed by a big scary shark.

The particular sea lion in question had been on the run for awhile, and was showing definite signs of fatigue and vulnerability as the charcoal silhouette of the shark was closing the gap between them. The sea lion was headed for the safety of the shore, or what it determined was the direction of the shore, but just as the shark was about to have sea lion for lunch, they crossed in front of the intake pipe at PS 3, which promptly inhaled the sea lion and deposited it's battered and bloody body into the power plant intake tank located on the beach.

The sea lion, bleeding and weak, swam in futile circles around the intake tank until it couldn't swim anymore. Out of gas, with no rescuers to save it, the animal sank beneath the surface of the water and died.

Late that night, workers at the power plant removed the dead sea lion from the tank, placed it in a thick black plastic bag, threw it into an outside dumpster, and covered it up with literally a ton of dead fish. Business as usual. As they left the scene chatting and arguing about whom the football Rams should pick in the upcoming draft, they passed by an unseen figure hiding in the shadows. Was the deluge finally over they wondered aloud?

It's called a 'heat-treat', short for heat treatment. That's what Norma was explaining to Delilah and Susan at their clandestine meeting at the Chimney Sweep. Not quite certain that Norma was her real name, they were sure that she was the whispering mystery caller from inside PS 3.

Earlier in the week, Delilah succeeded in sweet-talking Fred Lloyd, the PS 3 plant manager, into meeting with she and Susan, on this very day, at the power plant, to discuss the intake pipe. It didn't hurt that last week's protest at the Canadian Consulate had a gigantic, successful, turnout with heavy media coverage.

Delilah passive-aggressively suggested that she didn't see any reason to conduct a protest at the power plant, not at this time, anyway, and Fred anxiously agreed, unaware of the informant phone calls coming from inside the plant. Coming from

108

Norma.

During a heat-treat, Norma explained, they reverse the flow of water from the plant back into the ocean. The water is super hot, and it kills all of the fish, sand sharks, crabs, lobsters, octopus, seals, sea lions, anything, and everything trapped in the intake tank. People too? TBD. Last night's heat-treat was considered a 'partial'. Twenty-five hundred pounds of dead fish. Normally it's twice that much, and normal is once a week.

Norma hated Fred Lloyd. Called him a "gutless sheep" and "a pussy." She said that anytime there's "funny business" going on, he sends her away to do secretarial work! She's a maintenance worker, not a damn secretary. There are only two women maintenance workers in the whole damn joint and she's one of them!

Connie intentionally interrupted the spy meeting because she was dying to know what they were up to, so she delivered three scorpions with their names on them, even if it was before noon.

"Ladies, this is the Chimney Sweep. Excessive drinking required," she announced as she placed the drinks in front of them.

"Compliments of the gentleman," she said walking away and pointing in Marlon's direction.

There was Marlon, sitting alone at his usual dark, shadowy table. He had his back to them, lost in his own imaginary world. The trio didn't recognize him from behind, but they sure did appreciate the scorpions. According to Susan, they were "yum-yummy."

Norma said that Fish and Game, and National Marine Fisheries were in cahoots with the execs at the power plant to keep things quiet.

"Fucking assholes increase the water temperature. They tell us it will make the seals jump into this stupid floating cage they put in the intake tank. All it does is boil the fish, then the seals start to panic, they try to swim back into the pipe and they drown," exclaimed Norma as she threw back her scorpion.

Susan handed her a sheet of paper and a pen so that she could show them where the intake tank and the dumpster were located. Connie could hear them clear across the bar and decided that she couldn't take the suspense any longer.

"What's all this noise you're making over here? Are you three cooking up some trouble?" she begged as she pulled a chair up to the table with her very own scorpion.

Delilah filled her in. She and Susan were on their way to a power plant to investigate the multiple deaths of seals and sea lions. They were going to demand a protective cover be placed over the pipe to prevent any future incidences. They were going to take some undercover photos. They were going to go kick some power plant ass! Connie loved it. She loved these green people. They were crazy. In the very best way.

#

West was headed for a late breakfast of his own. The hostess at Dupar's was showing him to his seat when he heard his full name, Weston Walker, broadcast loudly throughout the restaurant. He knew this voice. It was unmistakable. This voice was often his driving companion, and more recently his interviewer.

At the back of the diner sat Connor Kilkenny waving madly at him to come join him. West was looking around to see who else might be dining with him, because the amount of food on Connor's table was enough for five people. No others. It was just Connor, engulfed in a breakfast orgy.

All eyes were on West as he traversed the diner to Connor's table.

"Hey, man. Breakfast's on me. Have a seat," said Connor slapping the Naugahyde booth with a broad grin.

West took a seat as Connor motioned for Virginia, his favorite Dupar's waitress. She was well aware that she was fifty-five years old, divorced, been through some hard times, worked for minimum wage at a humble diner, and that all of his flirting wasn't real, but she loved him anyway. Everybody there loved him. The whole world loved him.

With pad and pen at the ready, she and Connor traded winks and smiles.

"May I please have three eggs scrambled, bacon, toast, and coffee?" said West.

"Double that, all on one plate. He needs to eat," ordered Connor.

"West, this is my girlfriend, Virginia. She's a keeper." he proudly announced as she walked away giggling and shaking her head.

He congratulated West on the Harp seal demonstration at the Canadian consulate. KWOT had been broadcasting from the scene, as most of those protesting were listeners of the radio station. He also congratulated him for the interviews he did during the protest. It was apparent to him that West had made a big leap forward in his spokesperson skills. This, as you might imagine, was a big ego boost and confidence builder for West.

They attacked their mountain of food, chatting about different rock bands, how the radio station might work hand in hand with GreenPlanet, surfing, tennis, women. Connor asked him about Kate. Wanted to know if she was his girlfriend? West found this curious, not to mention preposterous. Maybe Connor had his eye on her?

"She wants to do you," said Connor nonchalantly. "It's there for the taking," he concluded.

West didn't know what to say to that. Susan had said something similar the other day, but before he could change the subject, two young women were standing at their table. Both of them were making eyes at Connor as they offered up the standard fare. "Can we ask you a question? We know who you are. You're on the radio, right? KWOT. We love that station. That's the greatest station. I'm Carla. This is Sky."

This wasn't Connor's first rodeo. He took a dramatic pause, looked at West with a seriously disturbed look on his face, and then turned his attention back to the women.

"It's not fair", said Connor very solemnly. "Not fair at all."

As soon as they heard his voice, they were Jello.

"What's not fair?" asked a breathless Carla.

"Beautiful and smart," Connor said with amazement. "All the women in the world must hate you two," he said.

Game. Set. Match. He winked at West, and for the first time, the young women noticed another human sitting there. He must be someone too they thought. Maybe he's in a rock band!

"Ladies, this is my pal West. You've heard him on the Mighty KWOT, and you've seen him on TV. Proceed with caution," said Connor with delight.

The two young lasses turned their backs on the guys to have a private moment. When they turned back to the table, Carla handed Connor a slip of paper with their numbers.

"You should call us," she said.

Connor thought this seemed like a reasonable request. He looked to West for a verifying head nod, which West readily supplied, then carefully tucked the slip of paper into the pocket of his western shirt. The girls, giddy, administered kisses to the cheeks of the boys, then sashayed away on cloud nine.

Virginia and her female coworkers were off to the side watching this old familiar show. She passed by the exiting young women and placed the bill on Connor's table.

"Ginny, you know you're the only girl for me," flirted Connor as she melted like butter.

He jumped up, threw a big pile of money on the table, and gave Virginia a grand embrace and a sloppy kiss on the cheek.

"Gotta run, I'm an hour late," he said gesturing for West to stay in his seat and continue eating.

113

"Thanks for breakfast," said West.

Connor bolted for the door, yelling at the top of his lungs.

"Call me. Let's hang out!" he shouted, then he was gone.

West surveyed the room to see if there were any eyeballs on him. He looked down at his eggs, looked over at Virginia, looked at the enormous pile of money on the table, and in a rare moment of clarity, decided more coffee was in order.

#

Hunter and Will were behind closed doors in Will's office. It would be completely understandable if you jumped to the conclusion that this was not a pleasant get together, not a reunion of kindred spirits, not a meeting that you would want to join. Completely understandable, but wrong.

They were, in fact, getting along famously. Events were progressing quite nicely, thank you very much. The Hawaiian operation had been dissolved; its funds transferred into the bank of the L.A. office. The global Harp seal protests, by all accounts, were a huge success. Will's successful recruitment of Vanessa Gray Reynolds and Natalie Singer gave Hunter a huge hard-on, instantly erasing any doubts about Will's monetary value. Money was filling the coffers, and Hunter was about to head north to San Francisco to address the much more complicated mutiny underway up there.

They had just hung up the phone with the mysteriously missing Kip. He called them. From Cabo San Lucas. Drying out. Well, cutting back. Moderation, and all that. Needed to get away. He had heard the news of the passing of their friend Sandy Denny. He took it hard. Not much fight left in the old dog. You know where to find him. Hunter assured Kip that all was well. Take all the time you need. Kate's here and has the bull by the horns. Talk again soon.

While Hunter was chatting up Will, something to do with a celebrity fundraising event, they were interrupted by a booming voice coming from the war room.

"Ahoy in there! Anybody here?" the voice commanded.

Hunter and Will peeked into the war room to find Shakespeare Jones admiring a wall-mounted photo of the London GreenPlanet anti-whaling boat.

"Hundred and eighty foot converted Navy mine-sweeper," said Hunter proudly.

Shakespeare continued to closely examine the photo, keeping his back to them.

"Converted to what?" he snarled. "Without the heavy machinery, she's a cork in the water," he huffed as he turned to face them.

Will couldn't believe his eyes. It was the captain! The very same captain that he encountered when he went boat shopping. The crusty old character he told Delilah and Rocky about.

"Captain!" exclaimed Will. "What are you doing here?"

A Hemingwayesque ships captain, Shakespeare Jones was a former US Navy seaman who served on the USS Yorktown in both the Battle of the Coral Sea and the Battle of Midway. On more than one occasion he narrowly escaped residence in Davy Jones locker, and has ever since reminded himself that he operates on precious borrowed time.

"There's a tide in the affairs of men, which, taken at the flood, leads on to fortune; omitted, all the voyage of their life is bound in shallows and in miseries," quoted Captain Jones.

"On such a full sea are we now afloat, and we must take the current when it serves, or lose our ventures," replied a jubilant Hunter extending his hand in friendship.

Hunter and Shakespeare introduced themselves to each other and traded friendly barbs about becoming old salty dogs that the world had traded in for newer models. Ignoring Will's presence, Shakespeare mentioned that down on the docks he had a GreenPlanet visitor tell him, with a straight face, that they were hoping to set sail this summer to battle Japanese and Russian whalers. Going to drive little rubber boats in front of their harpoon canons. Going to prevent them from killing whales and earning a living. Going to do all of this without arms, without the protection of the United States government, without any experience on the high seas, he said, pointing at Will.

Hunter laughed out loud, and confirmed, yes indeed, that is exactly what they were planning to do. Shakespeare nodded his head in astonishment and disbelief. Hunter, he determined, was a straight shooter, and he now understood that they were indeed serious.

"I hear you're lookin for a boat," he said.

The Maggie May was his pride and joy, and the only good reason to live another day. An old fishing trawler, she might not look pleasing to the eye, but she was strong and tough. Could she handle rough seas? Absolutely. Could she do twenty knots or more? Yessir, she could. Did she have deck space for three or four inflatable Zodiacs? Yep. Could she accommodate a crew of twenty to thirty, which included young women? Hmm. Twenty, no problem. Seeing as these hippie kids all like to sleep on top of each other anyhow, sure why not?

Shakespeare said that he had repaired and refitted every plank and fixture, rebuilt every piece of machinery and retooled each and every engine part. The hull was sound and the rigging was right. She was watertight and ran like a top. Radar and 'ship to shore' were new, and the galley was big enough to feed the troops. Showers were cold, salt-water showers, no curtains for privacy, same goes for the heads. Maybe the girls could take turns standing guard to keep the boys away? Hunter assured him that this was not a problem.

He said she could use some fresh paint, and they were welcome to paint some whales or whatever on her, but absolutely nothing unpatriotic.

Will suggested they all go around the corner to the Chimney Sweep to have a drink, negotiate the details, and arrange for a test drive of the Maggie May. This sounded good to Shakespeare. Hunter thought so too. Time to go have a drink with his new mates, Shakespeare Jones and Will Stone.

As they were exiting out of the office, Will scooped

up a marker, and in large letters wrote on the strategy board: WEST: CHIMNEY SWEEP NOW. He flipped off the lights, locked the door behind him, and out the door they went.

#

West entered a dark, silent, abandoned office, which confused him. He thought he was having a PS 3 meeting with Delilah. Did he lose a day somehow? Was there some sort of emergency? Where was everyone? On the strategy board he read: WEST: CHIMNEY SWEEP NOW. Seriously? The Chimney Sweep? "I just had breakfast," he muttered to himself as he did a '180' and soldiered off to the bar.

In the parking lot, outside of the Chimney Sweep entrance, he could hear loud music and revelry coming from inside the bar. This was unusual midday. Before he could push the door open, it was opened for him by a large man on his way out, wearing a white suit, dark sunglasses, and a big floppy hat that covered much of his face. In the daylight, West didn't recognize Marlon, who whizzed by him, and slipped into a waiting black BMW sedan.

Inside, the joint was jumping. Delilah and Will were dancing. Norma was sitting on Hunter's lap. Hunter! West didn't expect to see Hunter. Holy shit. Susan was straddling the back of some old salty-looking character as he did push-ups, while Connie officially counted them out. He didn't see Kate anywhere, and who knows where Kip was? What he did see was a GreenPlanet party in full swing.

Hunter waved West over to his table, Norma still

118

on his lap.

"Hunter! Great to see you," said West reaching around Norma to shake his hand.

Hunter tried unsuccessfully to introduce Norma, but she had been stung by too many scorpions and was not functioning on a sufficient level to perform the proper introductions.

Connie ran over, threw her arms around West and kissed him smack on the mouth. He had no idea what instigated this midweek, midday bacchanal, but when in Rome, right?

Hunter saw the look in West's eyes, and extinguished the fire before West could switch gears and get a drink in his hand.

"No, no. Sorry, my friend. I have a last minute assignment for you," he said pointing to the chair next to him.

West learned that Norma was the anonymous caller from inside PS 3. He was briefed about the heat treatments and the disposing of dead sea-life in the dumpsters. He was informed that he and Rocky would be replacing the very drunk and disorderly Delilah and Susan in a meeting with Fred Lloyd, the plant manager at PS 3. That meeting was in two hours. He was instructed to get photos, get confessions, and to get going! Vamanos!

On the 405, West and Rocky were going through their checklist. Camera? Check. Bail money? Check. Feed the dog? Check. Scared? Check. Rocky was scared, mucho scared. This mission rattled him more than the visit from Delilah's evil husband.

"It's pretty obvious we're not the women," said a

119

shaky Rocky.

"Deep breath, pal," comforted West.

West pulled the car up to the guard post at the power plant, rolled down his window, and informed the security guard that they were the people from GreenPlanet, and had a meeting with Fred Lloyd.

After several anxious minutes, the gate-arm rose and the guard instructed them where to park the car. Fred was waiting for them outside the building. The quintessential member of Club Mediocrity, Fred was an uninspiring man. He wasn't pleased when he saw two longhaired males instead of Delilah and Susan.

"Who are you two?" bleated Fred. "I agreed to meet with Miss Dean and Miss Noble."

When West departed the Chimney Sweep, Miss Dean and Miss Noble were drunk and dancing on the bar, placing them on the disabled list, requiring he and Rocky to assume their duties.

"Ah, yes. Miss Dean is feeling a bit under the weather, and Miss Noble had a family emergency that required her attendance," explained West.

"Weston Walker and Rocky Michaels at your service," he said extending his hand only to be left hanging.

Fred was vexed. He never liked surprises. He didn't like curve balls. He was a firm believer that one could be and should be in control of the world around them. He didn't want to have this meeting in the first place. He only acquiesced because the trouble makers would be women, confident he could shovel them some bullshit and dispense with them without resistance. He informed West that this was not how they operated and unfortunately, they would not be able to enter the plant without proper clearance.

West knew there was no going back empty-handed. He again apologized for having to substitute for the women, and went on to say that, in all confidence, he and Rocky didn't want to spend much time there, they had much bigger fish to fry, no pun intended. If they could just be given a quick tour, the PR would be good for SO CAL POWER, and they would have done their due diligence. A win-win for everyone.

Fred looked unhappy, maybe because he was considering a change in his plans, maybe because of his sad and depressing life, or both? It didn't help when he spied the camera around Rocky's shoulder and the anxiety on Rocky's face.

"No cameras. No photos allowed inside the plant," barked Fred.

West assured him that they had no intention of taking photographs of anything inside the plant. He was hoping that Fred would agree to a photo of the two of them for distribution to the newspapers. Again, good PR for the both of them.

Fred just happened to be wearing a new tie that day, and the glowing image that he had of his picture in the papers caused him to reconsider.

"Okay, but we have to make this quick," said Fred.

Once inside, West and Rocky were issued visitor identification badges, and all of the men donned hard hats.

Rocky took multiple photos of West and Fred smiling for the camera, shaking hands, and looking very simpatico. Fred was no dummy, well, yes he was, but in any event, he guided them on a carefully selected tour of the plant. He showed them the steam generators, the condenser tubes and giant cooling fans. He proudly presented the blinking lights of the electrical grid representing all of their electricity-receiving customers. He showed them everything but what they came to see, the intake tank on the beach.

When West politely requested to see the tank, Fred got grouchy once again. He told them the tank was being cleaned, and not available for viewing. Told them there was nothing to see there anyway, just a concrete block filled with water. Told them it was time to end the tour, and for them to be on their way.

"We need to see it before we go," West said.

Fred didn't like West; he didn't like Rocky; he didn't like granting this visit; and he certainly didn't like the thought of showing them the intake tank, but he wanted them out of there asap, so he reluctantly motioned for them to follow him outside.

The intake tank sits on the beach. It is a large, rectangular, concrete receptacle that is filled with cold ocean water. The seawater flows through the pipe monster, into and through the intake tank, and into the power plant. A large screen prevents anything, plants, animals, debris, from entering the plant and clogging the system.

The trio were now standing on an observation platform twenty feet above the tank, and West could see for himself that there was no way for a seal or sea lion or human to escape once they got sucked into the tank. They were trapped.

When asked what they do to rescue the marine

mammals, Fred said that it wasn't an issue. In the
twenty years that he'd been there, only three or four
sea lions had come into the tank. West, unbeknownst
to Fred, knew this to be an outright lie. A drunken
Norma told him so. He asked Fred about the rescue
cages, and Fred was taken aback that he knew about
them because they were not public knowledge.

At that unsettling moment, Fred decided, that's it,
tour over, but before he could escort them away, as
they were all looking down into the tank, a bloody and
battered sea lion shot through the intake pipe and into
full view.

"Holy shit! Mr. Lloyd, do you see that?" said a
jacked up West.

Fred Lloyd was dumbstruck.

"Rocky! Camera! Shoot!" blared West.

Rocky started shooting rapid fire. Photos of the
injured sea lion, of the stunned look on Fred's puss, of
West pointing into the tank. He stumbled back two
giant steps when he saw West slip out of his shoes,
and begin to take his shirt off.

"Are you fucking crazy?" screamed Rocky.

Before West could climb the railing of the
observation deck, three men in suits had their arms
around him, and not so gently deposited him on the
ground. Fred tried to make light of the situation as the
boys were speedily escorted off the beach, through the
power plant, out of the building, and into their car.
One of the suits threw West's clothes through the open
car window, as Rocky discretely placed the camera
under the passenger seat. West started the car and
shifted it into reverse.

As the car was backing away from the building, Fred Lloyd yelled after them.

"That never happens," he insisted. "I'm telling you that never happens."

"Right, only three or four times in twenty years!" skewered West.

The exit gate-arm was already up, demanding the long-hairs depart and never fucking come back there again.

West and Rocky were breathing heavily. Their adrenaline was pumping as they drove away from the power plant toward the 405. Jesus. That was crazy. Did that happen?

"Were you going to jump into that tank?," asked Rocky.

"It was a long way down," panted West.

They couldn't wait to get back to the office to tell their story, but they were paranoid. West drove super cautious, under the speed limit, continually checking his rear-view mirror, convinced that any moment they would be surrounded by LAPD, lights flashing and sirens blaring.

After several minutes passed, their heart rates returned to normal, and they realized how silly they were acting. There would be no LAPD drama. For what? They had a good laugh, and a temporary calm came over them as they continued up the 405. Temporary.

#

Rocky was having a meltdown. He was pounding his fists on the interior roof of the car and howling.

"No, no, no, why, why, why?" he moaned.

West was dealing with an eighteen-wheeler in front of him that was misbehaving badly, and he wasn't, at this moment, able to pay Rocky the much-needed attention that was required.

"Easy buddy," said West. "Maybe they won't let the sea lion die."

Rocky was rocking back and forth, cradling the camera in his lap like a dead puppy. He continued to say "no, no, no."

"The camera," said a defeated Rocky.

"What?" asked West.

"No film," whispered Rocky.

West kept his eyes on the road and his mouth shut. A speeding Cadillac cut in front of him. It displayed a bumper sticker that said "Don't Look Back."

A moment was needed for him to process this new twist. Unlike Fred, West was becoming all too familiar with curveballs, and was beginning to learn the benefits of embracing the unforeseen event.

He crossed from the fast lane to the slow lane like a relay runner that just handed off the baton. Off the nearest exit they went, stopping next to the first payphone they could find.

"Quarters," he demanded of Rocky. "I need quarters."

Rocky poured all of his change into the outstretched hand of West, who hopped out of the car and pounced on the payphone.

Connor Kilkenny was just about to go live with his five o'clock KWOT news report. He had West on speakerphone, and was giving him last second instructions. He told him to cover the mouthpiece to reduce any background noise, told him to take his time, told him to standby.

"Five O'clock. Ninety-four point seven K W O T, Los Angeles. Connor Kilkenny here with the late-breaking news and headlines of the day. In the news this hour friends, GreenPlanet has confronted the Department of Water and Power in Redondo Beach at SO CAL Power Station Number Three. They say that numerous Harbor seals and sea lions are being killed by the plants intake water system. Apparently, GreenPlanet had been tipped off about the recurring deaths by an anonymous person from inside the plant. On the phone with me is GreenPlanet's Weston Walker. West, where are you right now?"

West was amped and you could hear the excitement in his voice. As he relayed his version of the events to the rock music tribe, Connor was grinning from ear to ear, rocking back and forth in his chair, taking copious notes. Through a shared window with the DJ studio, the afternoon jock was giving him two thumbs up. West was in the zone.

"Reluctantly they took us outside to the retaining tank, and as they were trying to convince us that this was a rare event, only a couple of seals had been sucked into the plant in twenty years, we're standing there looking into the water and all of a sudden here comes a sea lion, gets sucked right into the plant, right? Right into the tank, and we're standing there watching, and these guys now have nothing to say, what can they possibly say? They start admitting 'oh yes, sharks get sucked in, sunrays get sucked in, tons of fish get sucked in', and there's no way for anything to escape back into the sea. So everything dies. They don't seriously attempt to rescue any marine life because, listen man, they don't care. We've got quite a problem here. We're down here. We've seen it with our own eyes. We're going to try to stop this and we could use your help," said a racing West.

"Why don't they cover the pipe before someone gets killed?" asked Connor.

"Money. They don't want to spend the money."

The phone lines at the radio station exploded. Connor saw the program manager watching and listening through the glass window in the door. She never watched him do the news. He knew they were on to something and tried to keep West going. West was saying how it was going to cost them a hell of lot more if; and then the line went dead. Out of quarters. Interview over.

Connor assured his listeners that KWOT would stay on top of the story. Assured them the phone lines would be open for all of their calls, then effortlessly segued into the rest of the news.

#

Madhouse. All hands were on deck including a score of volunteers, and a steady stream of visitors wanting to say hello, purchase merchandise, and make the scene.

Hunter was on the phone with Hugh in London. Will was leaving messages for Vanessa Gray Reynolds and Natalie Singer. He informed them that a press conference was happening the next day to announce the summer's anti-whaling campaign. Asked if they could they be there?

Kate was directing traffic, and outlining future campaigns on the strategy board: Whales, Harp Seals, Nukes, Toxic Waste Dumping, Grey Wolves, Water Contamination, Intake Pipes. Every sixty seconds she would ask the tribe if anyone had heard from West and Rocky?

Hugh was reporting to Hunter that the San Francisco people were going rogue, exploring trademark infringement as a legal avenue for a coup d'état. Hunter told him to catch the next flight to San Francisco, he would see him there. Delilah was conducting non-stop media interviews, and Susan was on the phone, speaking to a very angry Fred Lloyd.

Amidst all the madness, nobody noticed West and Rocky. They were standing in the middle of the room witnessing the pandemonium that they had created. West waved at Delilah, who dropped what she was doing, made a wild dash across the room, getting an inch from his face.

"Am I your girlfriend or not?" she demanded.

Rocky, hearing this, escaped to his corner of the office, where he was greeted by his motley volunteer crew like a returning war hero.

Before West had time to think of a reply to Delilah's thunderbolt, Kate had hold of his arm and was pulling him toward the conference table.

"Is it true?" she wanted to know. "The sea lion came into the tank as you were standing there?"

"You should have seen old Fred's face," said West.

"Photo's?" asked Kate.

Ugh. Well. West gave her a 'not exactly' look, and she gave him a 'what the fuck does that look mean' look.

"No film in the camera," he said.

Kate paused, considered her reply, looked approvingly at West, aware that the bedlam around them was his doing.

"They don't know that," she said as Susan stole him away to take a call on line three from Connor Kilkenny.

The frenzy carried on for some time, with all of the principals switching partners, energetically getting all of their organizational ducks in a row. And then. It was quiet. Just like that. All at once. It was a jacked-up silence. Everyone was looking for someone to guide them forward.

Hunter climbed up on Delilah's desk and stared down at the crowd.

"Pizza and beer!" exclaimed Hunter to a great roar of approval from the troops.

"And whiskey and beer!" he continued feeling the moment.

"For Harry, England, and Saint George!"

#

In San Francisco, it was a completely different kettle of fish. Pun intended.

The San Francisco office was the first 'true' GreenPlanet operation in the United States. Hawaii had a presence before any of the other entities in the USA, but San Francisco legally organized first.

They incorporated, received permission from International, a.k.a. Hunter, to use the GreenPlanet name, raised funds, opened bank accounts, and conducted successful environmental campaigns.

They controlled the media operations within the United States, which meant that they controlled the message and the money. The San Francisco office steadily gained power and prestige. The United States, after all, offered more wealth, more media attention, more political power, and more opportunities for growth than did Europe or the South Pacific. It also created the perfect conditions for eventual greed and abuse of power.

The city itself was the obvious place to set up shop. It was the liberal, revolutionary, new age, gateway to the Pacific home of endangered whales. It provided the perfect location to take advantage of all that the United States had to offer. Until it didn't. Until there was a new kid in town named Hollywood.

Four hundred miles to the south, the GreenPlanet tribe in Los Angeles was in the midst of an epic eco-warrior day. Here in San Francisco, it was another story altogether.

An emergency meeting was underway. In attendance were representatives not only from San Francisco, but also from GreenPlanet offices in Seattle, and the now-defunct Hawaii office.

A tense discussion was raging with their lawyer David Middling. It involved drafting a letter to the Los Angeles office 'revoking their right to exist', combined with a 'cease and desist' order with regards to raising any money in the name of GreenPlanet. They wanted him to invoke 'the law of prior usage'.

The tribe up north was feeling the pain of losing money, attention, and control, to the upstarts from down south. Their proud anti-whaling ship Gaia, a once upon a time, immaculate, swift sailing, mechanically sound, save the whales vessel, was now decaying and tied up to the dock. They heard rumors that an upcoming 'Save the Whales' voyage would soon leave from Los Angeles with Hunter at the helm.

David Middling was often put in this position. Often required to politely, artfully, explain to them that they had no idea what the hell they were talking about. They had no authority to do any of the things they wanted him to do. He offered them a new shiny object of distraction.

"I'll take a look at trademark infringement," he said knowing full well what bullshit that was.

The unexpected opening of the new L.A. office was a real kick in the pussy to these guys and gals. They had been painstakingly planning the ouster of Hunter, and the secession from their European colleagues. They were on the verge of executing their overthrow plan of action when the Hawaii operation was suddenly, and shockingly shut down, and the new operation in L.A. was suddenly, and shockingly opened. A civil war was brewing.

#

West opened his eyes to find a wet-haired, bathrobe-wearing Delilah staring down at him. She had invited him to sleep in her bed last night, but he respectfully opted instead for the couch. The big press

131

conference was later in the day, and he wanted to make sure that he was well rested. At least that was his excuse.

Yesterday, after an appropriate amount of celebrating with the troops, Hunter and Kate had gone to dinner to discuss her future in light of Kip's absence. She knew why they were dining. Hunter was going to gently twist her arm into staying on board for the unforeseeable future. Which he did. And she will.

Will, rightly so, was feeling on top of the world, and decided that it was the perfect time to fetch the card with Babette Carson's phone number and ring her up. Which he did. Unlike West, he wasn't at all concerned about being well rested for the impending press conference. It goes without saying that Babette was thrilled to hear from him, and with the assistance of expensive champagne, and plenty of stay-up-all-night powder, they partied until the sun came up.

Rocky, as always, was the smart one. He fled to his respectable abode and dove into his bed in search of some much-needed sleep.

"So, am I your girlfriend or not?" Delilah asked as soon as she saw West's open eyes.

West pulled the comforter over his head hoping she wouldn't see him.

"You're not paying enough attention to me," she said.

He sat up and made the universal gesture for coffee. She sat down next to him.

"It's a little too soon for me to jump into the next girlfriend thing," he replied.

"Do you realize how amazing I am?" she asked.

132

"I do," he said. "I definitely do."

She shot back up on her feet and walked toward her bedroom. Stopping in the doorway, her back to him, she paused, then dropped her robe.

"Get your ass in here," she commanded.

#

Delilah discretely had a hold of West's hand as they were standing off to the side of the pressroom waiting for the press conference to begin.

"If we would've had sex last night or this morning, it wouldn't have been the smartest thing to do, at this time, don't you agree?" West whispered.

She silently brushed some invisible lint off of his shirt and combed his hair with her hand.

"It's probably a good thing that Kate is sticking around for awhile longer," West said, changing the subject to the wrong subject. "Hunter thinks it's for the best, and we all know that you'll be back in charge soon," he continued.

The room was filling up. A gaggle of mixed media from television, newspapers and radio assumed their positions. Seated at the press table were Hunter, Vanessa Gray Reynolds, and Natalie Singer. West and Delilah stood off to one side, while Will, Kate, Susan, and Rocky were on the opposite side of the room. Moments ago, not bothering to inform any of her new friends, Vanessa thought it the perfect time to ingest a modest amount of LSD.

Hunter started things off with the announcement of the summer anti-whaling voyage in the Pacific. July 22nd a GreenPlanet crew would push off from the docks in Los Angeles and head due west toward the Hawaiian Islands in search of the Russian whaling fleet.

He made no mention of the boat that would facilitate the voyage–they hadn't taken the Maggie May for a test drive yet, and the Gaia wasn't seaworthy. Gambler that he was, he conducted the entire press conference with his fingers crossed.

The crew, he said, would be comprised of GreenPlanet activists from each of the U.S. offices, as well as the London office. It was their hope and intent to swiftly locate the whalers, and, if necessary, take action to prevent them from killing whales. He emphasized the non-violent nature of the mission. The whalers would only be challenged by using cameras, human shields, and eyewitness journalists. On board for this voyage would be a documentary film crew, a reporter from Rolling Stone magazine, and ship-to-shore radio reports and interviews would be conducted whenever time, weather, and equipment permitted. When asked about possible Russian aggression toward himself and his crew, he downplayed the danger.

"You are referring to last years voyage when my head had a close call with a harpoon," he joked. "That was the Japanese, and we caught them by surprise. The Russians know who we are. They know we're coming for them. I don't expect anything like last year will occur. It should be one big love fest."

The Soviet whaling fleet, he told them, preferred to stay out of the spotlight. In addition to killing whales, their vessels were equipped with sophisticated spy surveillance equipment, and it wasn't uncommon to find them very close to United States territorial waters. GreenPlanet's use of cameras and audio monitoring would, he argued, be the best defense against any Russian notions of aggression.

Switching gears, he redirected the attention of the media to the two famous actresses flanking him on both sides.

"I am thrilled and delighted to be joined today by the biggest star of American daytime television, Natalie Singer, as well as one of the biggest movie stars in the world, Vanessa Gray Reynolds. I'm sure they would be happy to answer any questions you might have for them," said Hunter passing the torch.

An L.A. Times reporter asked the celebrities why they were there, and what roles did they plan on playing within the organization? Natalie politely waited for Vanessa to take the lead, seeing as she was the bigger star, but Vanessa was chemically sidetracked and not quite ready to address the world.

"I've always been an animal person, a nature person. It breaks my heart to see those baby seals clubbed to death, and to know the great whales are being wiped out. Something must be done to help them. In my own small way, I will try to help publicize these atrocities and to raise the necessary funds to combat them," answered a well-coached Natalie.

All eyes turned to Vanessa who appeared to be a million miles away. After several uncomfortable seconds of silence she made eye contact with the reporter.

"If I can use my celebrity standing to attract attention, your necktie is so incredibly beautiful," she replied in awe.

Vanessa became visibly overwhelmed with the beauty of his tie. She reached her hand out to the reporter, who, not sure what to do, removed it from around his neck and handed it to her. Hunter looked to Kate, who punched Will in the arm. Vanessa held the necktie up for the cameras to see.

"The largest living creatures to inhabit the Earth," she solemnly said as if the tie were a great Blue whale. "We cannot allow them to be destroyed," she concluded dramatically.

Hunter seized upon the silence to redirect the media's attention back on him, answering questions about diminishing whale populations, the recent arrests of GreenPlanet members on the ice floes of Newfoundland, and toxic waste dumping in the North Atlantic. A television reporter recognized West standing on the sidelines, and asked if they planned to continue putting pressure on the coastal power plants to cover the ocean intake pipes. West nodded his head 'yes', and gave a big thumbs up, but declined to join the others at the table.

"Thank you all for coming," said Hunter. "It's always a treat when I can escape the rain and fog of London, and enjoy sunshiny days here in L.A."

The press conference came to an end as the members of the media began to break down their equipment and exit the press club. Will darted to Vanessa. He didn't want her to be corralled by any reporters.

"Vanessa, what can I say? We must do dinner when I get back in town," Hunter said as he gathered up his things.

Vanessa, examining the Humpback whale pin on Hunter's jacket, reached out her hand and held it over the pin and his heart until Will came to the rescue and gently escorted her out of the public eye.

Natalie was feeling ignored and invisible. She was waiting for Hunter to offer her the very same dinner invitation.

"Natalie, thanks so much. Appreciate you being on the team, I've got a plane to catch," he said leaving her in the dust. Discouraged and dejected, she sat watched the room empty out and thought to herself "it's not easy being a soap star."

#

Back at headquarters, Kate and Susan were having a private pow-wow behind closed doors in what used to be Kip's office. Kate, preferring to be back home in London, was in semi-denial about Kip's 'temporary' leave of absence. Deep down she knew that he would not return, elevating the importance of grooming one or more of the staff to eventually replace her and set her free. She was sent there by Hunter, specifically to develop West, but she also had her eye on Susan.

"I need you, you need me. We're the smartest people in the room," she said to Susan.

She needed Susan to help "get Delilah on board." Delilah, she could see, was tough, smart, and committed. A valuable asset to the operation. Kate wanted to go into battle with her, not against her, but she also saw in Delilah someone that would not hesitate for very long to oppose and defy her. As for

West, she played her cards closer to the vest.

"He has potential," Kate said.

"He'll do whatever you want him to. I've seen the way he looks at you," said Susan.

"And you, and Delilah, and her, and her, and her," said Kate.

Right on cue, West and Delilah strolled into the war room. Meeting over.

Sorting through his messages, West saw that Connor had called, also Lucinda. Lucinda! What's that all about? He didn't want to know.

Delilah had messages from Marine Mammal Rescue, Rocky, and the very cute pro-surfer Shane Durban. The same Shane Durban that visited her in the office last week, and offered to produce a local surfing contest to benefit GreenPlanet. The very same lad that Delilah decided to back pocket and not tell West about. There was a movie premier on this night, and she had been invited to be his date.

Kate asked West to come into her office to have a chat. She had him leave the door open, this way anyone could watch them if they were inclined to do so, or if their names were Delilah and Susan.

She laughed at all of the stupid things West said, and reciprocated his flirtation. She had him and her audience of two, in her clutches.

Delilah had seen enough. She took another look at the message from Shane. A movie premiere might be just what the doctor ordered.

As soon as Kate saw Delilah exit stage left, she brought her performance to an abrupt end and gathered up her possessions.

"Off I go. Tomorrow morning, bright and early," she said with a wink to Susan, and out she went.

West noticed that Delilah was gone, and Susan noticed that West noticed.

"Delilah took off," she said.

"I can see that," said West getting into a bad mood.

He asked Susan to call Connor for him, and she looked at him as if he were stark raving mad. What? Did he think that she was his bloody secretary? Did he think that she came to the office every day to serve him? Did he think he was above her? Are you fucking kidding me? She ignored him for several minutes before she leveled him.

"Delilah's going to a movie premiere tonight, with some surfer dude named Shane Durban."

Sometimes we don't hear things correctly. Sometimes our brain plays tricks on us and we conjure up horrific thoughts that have no basis in reality.

We might dream that we are drowning, or we might think that we heard Susan say that our potential girlfriend was going on a date with another guy. On a date with one of our idols. Someone better looking, someone with a big future in front of him. Someone named Shane Durban, 1977 pro-surfer of the year.

Now West was looking at Susan as if she were stark raving mad. He was looking at her and hoping with all of his hoping ability that this could not be true, but he could see the unimaginable truth in her eyes. In a daze, he got himself to his feet, found his keys, and limped his way toward the door.

"I'm not your secretary," said Susan.

He shook his head in agreement with her, and pulled open the door.

"Don't forget it," she said delivering the knockout punch.

West was absolutely positive that he would not forget.

#

Hunter was sipping on some expensive rum that was sent to his table by Bill Graham, who was dining with Grace Slick at the other end of the room.

The first time Hunter and Bill met was at this very same restaurant, The Trident, a few years back. Hunter was carousing with the painter George Sumner, whose home slash studio was located there in Sausalito. George insisted that they stop in the Trident as part of their appointed rounds, where they inevitably crossed paths with Bill Graham.

These three were quite the combination. Between them they knew everyone, and, more often than not, were the center of attention. Bill and Hunter immediately liked and respected each other. Both of them were intimidating, demanding, successful, big-picture men. They didn't suffer fools at all.

Tonight, Hunter's dining companions were not as gratifying. Hugh Simon and David Middling, both lawyers, were engaged in a back and forth about the future of the San Francisco office. They, too, had the very same expensive tumblers of rum sitting in front of them, sadly untouched, and sadly unappreciated.

David had agreed to the covert meeting, hoping that he might be able to soften the blow of Hunter's

140

mighty sword, or at least get a clear picture of what was intended. Hunter, on the other hand, figured, why not give David an opportunity to defect? It might make the taking of the hill that much easier.

It didn't take long for Hunter and Hugh to realize that David was not there to defect; he was there to deflect, and defend, and descend. He was there to convince Hunter to step down; to hand over the reigns of power to those more able and relevant, but one must never pull the dragon's tail.

"Hugh, you're English, what Shakespeare character said 'kill all the lawyers'? Shakespeare hated you fuckers too," said an animated Hunter.

"Just the opposite I'm afraid," said an uninsulted Hugh. "He was complimenting the British system of justice by showing the enemies of the king to be lovers of anarchy."

"Where do you come up with that shit? David, where does he come up with that shit?" asked Hunter. "That's almost as crazy as trademark infringement. That's almost as crazy as suggesting that I step down. That's almost as crazy as stealing from me," he concluded as he threw back his glass of rum.

David argued, unsuccessfully, that the GreenPlanet name was not Hunter's to give and take away. He argued that the unilateral closing of the Hawaii office was illegal, as well as a shameful power play. He was outraged at the opening of an office in, of all places, Hollywood! He accused him of "selling out," of redirecting funds that rightfully belonged to the San Franciscans, of an ego out of control for far too long. He accused him of being a "has-been nobody."

141

Hunter switched his empty glass with David's full tumbler of rum, took a slow, delicious sip, and considered David's words.

"So, why are you here?" said Hunter.

"Because they can't win a war against you, and they're not smart enough to realize that," said a checkmated David.

The San Francisco office, he offered, was the jewel in the American crown. The center of power and fundraising. It was the keeper of the spiritual flame. The home of the Gaia. There was history there. The best and the brightest were stationed there. Surely it would be unthinkable to shutter this operation. Perhaps there were restructuring possibilities?

Joan, their magnetic bohemian waitress, put her hand on Hunter's shoulder and asked if all "was beautiful?" Mr. Graham and Ms. Slick, she said, had told her who he was, and she wanted his assurance that everything was perfect.

Hunter looked first to Hugh, then deep into David's lawyer eyes. He hoisted his expensive glass of rum in the direction of Bill and Grace.

"To has-been nobody's," he trumpeted.

\#

The starlit Sausalito night, and the full moon illuminating the San Francisco Bay, could not have been more different than the stormy scene to the south, where the stars were earthbound and wore sunglasses in spite of the absence of the sun.

The red carpet in front of the Samuel Goldwyn Theatre was becoming soaked around the edges. The skies over L.A. had opened once again and the pouring rain was putting a damper on the film premiere of Big Wednesday.

Director John Milius was hustled off the carpet and into the theatre where he could find shelter from the storm. Already come and gone were the films leading men, Jan Michael Vincent, Gary Busy, and William Katt. Surfing champ Gerry Lopez was garnering a lot of attention from the photographers, but not as much as an unknown young woman on the arm of Gerry's main surfing rival Shane Durban.

The flash frenzy was directed primarily at a very willing Delilah, who looked every bit the splendid Hollywood starlet. She felt no need to accommodate the paparazzi with any of her personal information. Rather, she smiled, posed, and waved to the cameras as if she had been doing this her entire life. She pictured West walking by a future newsstand, then screeching to a stop when he inadvertently caught a glimpse of her on the cover of some celebrity magazine. Or, maybe he would be leafing through a surfing magazine and be broadsided by a photo of her with Shane Durban close by her side? That would teach him a lesson. That would get him to pay attention to her.

Shane, wisely aware that he was not the center of the media's attention, had his arm tight around Delilah, pretending to the world that she belonged to him. As the thunder boomed, and the storm grew worse, he threw his jacket over her shoulders, rescued her from the press, and whisked her off into the sanctuary of the theatre.

Meanwhile, West tried to block from his mind that, just a few miles away, Delilah was on the arm of his hero Shane Durban, playing movie star to an adoring press corps. He purposely was not on Wilshire, driving through Beverly Hills, so he wouldn't pass by the scene of the crime. He was driving aimlessly through the seedy sections of Hollywood, looking for a cheap whiskey, beer, and refuge from the storm.

The rain was unrelenting, pelting the roof of his tin can ride. Visibility was poor, but not poor enough to prevent him from recognizing The Frolic Room up ahead. Construction was underway next-door, and under the scaffolding, pimps, prostitutes, and the homeless took cover, took drugs, and took a much-needed timeout from their miserable lives. Perfect, West concluded, The Frolic Room it is.

Drago was behind the bar, as he had been for the past three hundred years. His nickname was 'the brute'. No more explanation needed. Dark, dirty, and reeking of stale beer and cigarettes, both Drago and the bar had known better days. On the jukebox a Wayne Shorter tune, 'Miyako', was playing. At the ugly end of the bar sat the 'prince of darkness'. That's how Drago referred to him. "The prince of darkness," he said.

The prince had also seen better days. He didn't look good, not that anyone in that part of town, drinking in the Frolic Room, looked particularly good. When the Shorter tune ended, the prince painfully slid off his barstool and put more quarters in the jukebox. 'Miyako' again.

West looked at Drago with questioning eyes and

144

pointed at his empty whiskey glass.

"I think the world is coming to an end," West said as Drago refilled his glass paying him zero attention.

On the way back to his barstool, the prince passed by West.

"Jack Daniel's is for pussies," growled the prince.

West turned to look at the prince and disturbingly thought that he knew him from somewhere. How could that be? Impossible.

"Not your hood. I'd like you to leave," said the prince as he hobbled into to the toilet.

Drago gave West the 'it's cool' eye. Don't mind him. That's when he referred to him as "the prince of darkness."

West didn't have any idea what that meant and he didn't care. He just wanted to sit, and drink some whiskey, and reflect on the blur that had become his life. He didn't put two and two together.

The prince gave out a wounded yelp when he made it back onto his barstool, his pants open and wet. He was not happy to discover that West had not followed his direct marching orders.

"You still here, motherfucker?" barked the prince.

West was, indeed, still there, bonding with his holy water.

"You're trying to get real. Trying to appear real. With your stupid fucking glass of Jack Daniel's. You don't know shit," said the prince.

West didn't look up, but that hit a nerve. He agreed with the prince; he didn't know shit. He pointed again at his empty whiskey glass and Drago was kind enough to make it a double. Wayne Shorter continued on the jukebox.

"You're a phony; you're a pretender," the prince summed up perfectly.

Without looking up, West shook his head 'yes' in agreement with the prince of darkness, whom, at that precise moment, he recognized as a disheveled and deteriorated Miles Davis. At the Frolic Room? Busting his balls? No way.

The clock on the Hamm's beer sign read eleven o'clock. West had accepted an invitation to hang with Connor, who was doing a late night DJ stint at the radio station, which was right around the corner.

The best course of action, he decided, would be to have one more. Perhaps the prince might have some final words of wisdom for him? Maybe he would play 'Miyako' again? He threw back his whiskey and waited for Drago to fill her up again. The prince spit in his direction. Perfect.

From 'Miyako' to 'The Girl With The Far Away Eyes'. Surrounded by stacks of vinyl and tape cartridges, Connor sat behind the microphone. By his side, West, sipping a beer, occupied a high-back leather chair. A pleasant, smoky haze filled the booth as Connor did his thing.

"The girl with the, well you know what kind of eyes she gots, far away eyes. That's from the yet to be released album Some Girls by the Rolling Stones. My name is Connor Kilkenny, sitting in tonight for the impossible to sit in for Mary Turner. Before that, we heard 'Cold As Ice', 'Barracuda', and 'Victim of Love'. Now I'll let you decide if that set was thematic or not. I, or I should say we, will be here till two in the a.m.

146

Hanging out with me here in the studio tonight is my pal West Walker from GreenPlanet. So happy to be high, I mean to be here. You're listening to the Mighty Quat, KWOT, Los Angeles."

Connor sat back in his chair, king of the jungle. West handed him another cold beer and reveled in their surroundings.

"So glad you could hang, my friend. I've got a little surprise for you," said Connor waving his hand high in the air.

Into the studio came Carla and Sky, the two girls from Du-Pars. Wearing what one would reasonably conclude as revealing attire, they were ready to party, ready to please.

Connor fired up a fatty and sent it on its way around the circle. All proceeded to get high, then higher. West's consumption of many whiskeys, many beers, and many assaults, combined with the music, the killer pot, the intoxicating and inexplicable circumstances, and the very friendly Carla and Sky, made him ready and willing for any and all possibilities.

Connor put on a long song and gave the ladies the 'high sign'; pun intended. Kneeling in front of the boys, Carla and Sky skillfully unbuttoned each of the lad's jeans, then with aplomb began to service their respective clients. Connor, rocking back and forth, smiled the biggest smile while West tried to remember to breathe.

West was not the only one short of breath. Earlier that evening, a Catalina 30 sailed past the Port Hueneme Power Plant on the Ventura County coast.

147

Little did anyone on board know that fifty feet below their sailboat, in turbulent water, a scuba diver struggled helplessly, pinned against the opening of the power plant intake pipe.

Using all of his might, he was eventually able to pry himself free from the super strong suction of the pipe, but in his attempt to escape to the surface, he was sucked all the way back into the pipe, and for three-quarters of a mile, he traveled at high speed through the narrow ten-foot diameter until he violently smashed into the screen at the end of the retaining tank, breaking his neck. He was killed instantly, his lifeless body stuck to the retaining tank screen. Affixed to the filter screen, the body was surrounded by a school of fish, bunches of seaweed, and random debris.

As Carla and Sky were wrapping things up and the lads were coming back down, in Ventura, a large piece of driftwood shot through the intake pipe, into the tank, slamming straight into the dead diver, dislodging him from the screen.

For a moment, his body was suspended in the water, motionless. The strong flow of incoming ocean water eventually caused the body to rise to the surface, bobbing up and down, to and fro. The rain had stopped. The storm was over. The Sausalito full moon had made its way down south, lighting up the entire west coast of California. It was a magical light. A mystical light. The kind of light that happens when everything in the world is perfect.

POOR, POOR PITIFUL ME

Back when Lucinda and Matty drove off in the rental truck, she had extracted pretty much everything not bolted down. The apartment was left empty except for West's clothes, surfboards, tennis gear, and the eviction notice. This turned out to be a blessing in disguise, allowing him a quick and easy transition from hell to his new living situation in Beverly Hills.

It was a disorienting experience when he arrived at the property just as the sun was coming up. Oh so quiet, he trekked to the back of the main house and found an unlocked front door to the studio guesthouse, his new home.

His clothes he tossed on an expensive dark brown leather couch, and his keys on the thick, cut-glass coffee table that faced an inviting, but dormant fireplace. On a raised platform, a King-sized bed dominated. Through a large window, the Olympic-sized swimming pool, and the adjacent tennis court constituted the lavish view. An antique mirror, on the wall next to the bed, provided him a shocking reflection of his bedraggled state and unhealthy physical appearance. It took him thirty seconds to shed his clothes and embark on what he intended to be the longest hot shower of his life.

When the door to the guesthouse opened, the antique mirror was fogged up from steam. Dressed in skimpy, expensive tennis attire, Cassandra Eaton made a quick survey of the room, heard the shower running, and instantly understood the situation.

It took her no time at all to rid herself of her micro-tennis attire. Slipping unnoticed into the bathroom, she stood naked, watching West through the shower door. When she saw that he had a head and face full of shampoo, she opened the shower door, stepped in, and placed her hands lovingly on his shoulders.

"Want me to do your back?" she whispered.

West jumped out of his skin. Clutching his chest, he sucked in a gallon of hot water. His heart pounded. He knew he was going to die right then and there.

"It's me, Cassie," she teased.

His composure was completely destroyed. His mind blown. He got an erection.

"We don't have a lesson today," he said shaking.

Cassandra reached around his waist and took him into her hand.

"Maybe today I can give you a lesson?" she said.

Still breathing hard, spitting water, and wiping soap out of his eyes, he tried to think of something mature and responsible to say. Nothing doing. He was now the opposite of putty in her hands.

"Clearly, Steven arranged for you to keep an eye on the Eaton women, so here you go. Have a look," she said as she brought him to his knees.

The subconscious mind; think of it as a backup system that autocorrects the conscious mind when necessary. Most of the time. Hopefully.

West's VW bug was traveling down Benedict Canyon Drive, and yes, he was physically behind the wheel, but his brain was a million miles away. His anterior cingulate cortex was driving the car. It wasn't his fault that he had been placed in a hypnotic state, a dream state, an emotional state of fantasy and escapism. He imagined himself driving next to three short-short wearing, jogging, breasts bouncing, high school girls. Farther down the road a beautiful Hollywood starlet, driving a fast car, passes by him on the wrong side of the road and blows him a kiss. Then an old pick up truck is stopped at the light in front of him. In the back are several female domestic workers in uniform. They all seem to be madly in love with him. Now he is driving west on Sunset Blvd. A limousine pulls up next to him, the rear window opens to allow a mysterious, cigarette-smoking woman to lasciviously check him out. As he passes by UCLA he sees dozens of young, attractive coeds waving to him on their way to morning classes. As he continues to subconsciously drive and consciously daydream, his mind is filled with images of beautiful women from all over the globe. Semi-aware that the Pacific Ocean is up ahead, he pulls off the road to check out the surf. Roller-skating young girls cross his path and he imagines them roller-skating naked. On the beach, a young mother breastfeeds her baby, and he fantasizes that he has taken the baby's place. Using his fantasy binoculars he watches a goddess carve up the surf. She has the name 'West' tattooed on her left thigh. He remembers all of his past girlfriends and dreams of all of the future women that he will know. He remembers Cassie, minutes ago, behind him, in the shower, in his new guesthouse, and then abruptly snaps back to conscious reality in the existential nick of time, barely avoiding what would have been an unpleasant coupling with the halted garbage truck in front of him.

#

West floated into the office to find Rocky and Susan glaring angrily at Delilah, and Delilah glaring right back at them. The stand-off looked serious.

"Hey gorgeous girls, and Rocky. How's it going?" he said trying to break the tension.

"We're not girls," snapped Susan.

"We're women," snapped Delilah.

"Big difference, pal," snapped Rocky.

Rocky had just informed Delilah and Susan that he was going to take some time off in order to do volunteer work for those opposing the Briggs Initiative, Proposition Six on the upcoming Fall election ballot.

Susan thought it a terrific idea, Delilah did not. Susan knew what the Briggs Initiative was all about, Delilah did not. Rocky and Susan explained.

John Briggs was a state senator from Orange County. Let me rephrase that, an asshole state senator from Orange County. He was inspired by the success Anita Bryant had in Florida, Oklahoma, and Arkansas when each of those states ruled it permissible to discriminate against gay and lesbian schoolteachers, essentially preventing them from teaching in their schools. Briggs was trying to do the same thing in California. Rocky was not going to stand idly by. He was going to San Francisco, in September, to fight the fight.

Delilah was fed up with all of the undesirable change happening in 'her' office. She didn't like to be abandoned. She did like Rocky. Adored him. Now he's

152

leaving?

"If the planet is destroyed, we won't have any schools or school teachers to discriminate against," she said with extra intense glaring.

Right then, the door to Will's office opened and out he came, arm in arm, with the beautiful blond television star Farrah Fawcett. West froze in place like a rabbit acutely aware of a nearby hawk.

"We were just talking about you," Will said to the star-struck West. "Say hello to Farrah," he teased.

Shaking her hand, the softest hand he had ever held in his life, and looking into her eyes, the most beautiful eyes he had ever seen, he was able to muster up a self-conscious "hello."

"Looks like you and I have a tennis date," Farrah said with a sparkling TV star smile.

Will took great delight and glee in this little exchange, while Delilah, Susan, and Rocky looked on in glaring disdain. As Will walked Farrah out the door, Kate zipped in the door with bagels and doughnuts in hand.

"Morning folks. Let's go. Lots to cover today," she said placing the morning goodies on the conference table.

Everyone took their usual place at the table, which found the dumbfounded West seated between Delilah and Susan. A beaming Will returned and informed everyone that Ms. Fawcett had agreed to headline a celebrity benefit tennis tournament to raise money for this summer's whaling campaign. Farrah and Will would round up the celebrities, and West would recruit the tennis players. West asked if Farrah would need a doubles partner, which produced an audible groan from Delilah.

Kate was at the strategy board listing all of the 'to do' items, and handing out assignments. West and Susan would work on the tennis benefit. Will informed the group that he was meeting with Elliot Irving, personal manager of the rock band Desperados. They would be discussing a possible GreenPlanet benefit concert in Aspen.

Movie star Ann-Margret and her husband Roger Smith were donating a small inflatable boat; it needed to be picked up today. Will reminded Kate that tonight they had a dinner engagement at the Bel-Air mansion of brain surgeon Dr. Zelda Xavier, hopefully resulting in a big donation, and Delilah announced with glee a benefit surfing contest to be held in early June, produced by world surfing champion Shane Durban, with close assistance from herself.

West was blind with jealousy and disbelief. He could feel the entire group waiting for him to react in some juvenile manner. He held his ground.

"Where exactly will this take place?" asked Kate.

"I forget the name. Just north of Malibu," answered Delilah knowing that there was a certain someone at the table who would know.

"Surfrider Beach," mumbled West.

"That's it! You got it! Surfrider Beach!" exclaimed Delilah.

Kate decided that the best course of action for the day would be for Will and West to team up. First, they would go see Mr. Irving, after which they would go collect the inflatable, and West, not she, would accompany Will to dinner at Dr. Xavier's.

Susan passed along a message to Kate. Jackie Speier called from Leo Ryan's office. He'll be in town next week and would like to meet with her. Kate looked puzzled.

"Congressman Ryan. From Northern California. Very pro-environment," said Rocky.

"He and Jim Jeffords just returned from witnessing the Harp seal hunt," instructed Susan. "He wants to help in any way that he can."

"I heard that he's coming to town to investigate that Scientology group," added Delilah.

Kate wrote on the board: KATE MEETING WITH LEO RYAN.

"One problem, though," said Delilah.

Delilah told Kate about the phone call she had received from Karma Parrish of the GreenPlanet office in San Francisco. Karma had reported that they were not pleased that Congressman Ryan had made contact with the L.A. office. The L.A. office, Karma claimed, was illegitimate, and needed to forward any and all future calls to the office in San Francisco or face legal repercussions.

Kate thought about this for a moment, then returned her attention to the board. With verve she swiped the eraser through KATE MEETING WITH LEO RYAN and wrote in its place: KATE FUCKING THRILLED TO MEET WITH LEO RYAN.

When she turned triumphantly to face the table, a very tall, curly-haired, mustachioed man entered the office carrying several coffee cans stuffed with money. The cans were covered with GreenPlanet bumper

155

stickers. He placed the overflowing coffee cans in the middle of the table next to the bagels and doughnuts, and after a quick survey of the office including the motley crew seated around the table, he turned to leave.

"I put donations cans in all of our stores. I hope this helps a bit," he said, and out the door he went.

There was an astonished silence before Rocky whispered something into Delilah's ear that made her laugh. The group looked around at each other before they began to chuckle. West had absolutely no clue what just took place.

"You must be joking," said Will.

"Didn't see that coming," said Delilah.

"Welcome to L.A." Susan said to Kate.

West was a stranger in a strange land. What on Earth was going on here?

"What?" he asked the table. "Who was that guy? What just happened?"

"John Holmes," said Delilah.

All eyes were on West, who had no knowledge of John Holmes.

"Who's John Holmes?" asked West.

John Holmes a.k.a. Johnny Wadd a.k.a. Big John Phallus a.k.a. Long John Holmes a.k.a. Mr. 13 Inch a.k.a. Big Dong on Campus. The biggest penis in porn, the Babe Ruth of adult films.

West had never seen an adult film. Everyone could see that West had never seen an adult film. All were overjoyed.

Kate wrote on the board: WEST-BEHIND THE GREEN DOOR.

The margaritas at Lucy's El Adobe Cafe were lethal. Exactly how a margarita should be. Exactly what West believed he was in need of at this moment in time.

Will had been ushered to the front of the restaurant to take an important phone call, thus leaving West to stare at the celebrity photos on the wall, sip his tequila and lime juice, and find some kind of mischief to keep him entertained.

Seated at the table next to him, a professional looking woman was nursing a club soda and reading an unidentifiable screenplay. The perfect person to entertain him.

"Excuse me?"

He was invisible to her as she continued reading.

"Do you know who John Holmes is?" West asked.

"I have a date with Farrah, and Marlon kissed me on the forehead," he carried on with no success.

"What are you reading?" he persisted with the help of his atomic margarita.

Uncharacteristically, she decided to indulge him. Closing her script, and taking a sip of her water, she looked at him for the first time.

"It's a film script about a nuclear power plant disaster," she said.

"You mean a meltdown?" said West.

She wasn't sure if she was talking to a fool or not, so she questioned him. Does he know anything about nuclear power? Power plants? Meltdowns? Fission? Fusion? Safety issues? Does he know anything about anything?

West dove right in. He works for GreenPlanet, maybe she's heard of them? Nuclear plants are not safe. Not at all. Radiation leaks, targets of attack from our enemies, potential meltdowns, waste disposal. What are we going to do with the fucking radioactive waste?

She asked him why he was so sure about his positions? What if he were wrong?

"What if I'm right?" asked a cocksure West.

She found him mildly interesting, but not enough to continue her indulgence. Fortunately for her, the hostess returned to the table along with Will.

"Ms. Lansing, your car is here," said the hostess.

Will knew who Sherry Lansing was, though they'd never met. He didn't run in crowds that high up on the food chain. He sneaked a peek at the cover page of her script as she was placing it under her arm–The China Syndrome–hmm.

West swayed as Ms. Lansing took her leave, and then returned his attention to his grande margarita.

"Go easy on those," cautioned Will. "We still have mucho to do."

Elliot Irving was too busy to meet with them today. After they finished lunching, it would be straight over to pick up the inflatable at Ann-Marget's house, and then they could chill until dinner in Bel Air.

"Do you think Delilah is, you know, involved, with Shane Durban?" asked West.

Will studied his menu, pretending not to hear him.

"Shane Durban, the best surfer in the world?" West whined.

Will looked up from his menu, and nipped it in the

bud.

"She's your co-worker, not your property, not your girlfriend. Jealousy is a deadly poison. Don't go near it," said Will.

West knew that he was right. Right? But. She could be his girlfriend. Right?

"Besides, trust me, this is not the time that you want to be off the market," Will wisely prophesied. "You should get the enchiladas suizas, they're killer."

#

Will had a surprise for West as they were driving to Ann-Marget's house. Tonight, after their dinner with Dr. Xavier, they were taking a red-eye to Denver, where a private plane would be waiting to whisk them off to Aspen. Elliot Irving would be meeting them in the Aspen Bowl to conduct their talks of a possible Desperados concert. Kip was supposed to go, but we all know what happened with him, so Kate suggested Will take West in his place. He pulled the two tickets out of his jacket pocket and handed them to a wide-eyed West.

The rental truck pulled up to the security gate that guarded the driveway to Ann-Margret's house. A voice came over the intercom asking them to identify themselves, and then the gate crawled open allowing them to proceed up the long, and winding driveway.

A well-dressed, distinguished gentleman was waiting for them in front of an eight-car garage that was the home to a Rolls Royce, a Bentley, a Porsche 911 Targa, a Corvette Stingray, a classic Ford Truck, and a ten foot inflatable Zodiac.

Pointing at the Zodiac, he said nothing to West and Will. A patient man, he waited as West and Will struggled to pick up one end of the Zodiac and load it into the truck. When they finally accomplished their mission and secured the inflatable inside the rental truck, Will waved a 'thank you' in the direction of the gentleman, who, in return, signaled for them to follow him to the front door of the manor house.

Holding the door open with one hand, he gestured for them to enter the house, stopping them in the large foyer at the bottom of a grand spiral staircase.

The three men stood there in uncomfortable silence until they witnessed the dramatic appearance of Ann-Margret at the top of the staircase.

In spite of her casual attire, West and Will stood awestruck in the presence of the most beautiful woman that they had ever laid eyes on. On her way down the stairs, Will tried to think of a proper thank you. West was spellbound. With an outstretched hand, she approached Will.

"A pleasure to meet you. Thank you for your thoughtful donation," said Will.

"I hope you can put it to good use," she said.

She turned to West and could see the 'deer in the headlights' look in his eyes.

"What's your name?" she said to West.

"West," he whispered.

She smiled, looked him in the eyes, and took both of his hands into hers as if she could see his future.

"Good luck. Be careful," she said.

Opening the front door with proper decorum, the gentleman indicated that it was time for them to be on their way. West and Will floated out of the house, climbed into the rental truck, and sat fixed in silence. No words were spoken until they had traveled several blocks away from the house.

"What do you have to say about that?" said Will.

"This day must never end," whispered West.

#

While West was learning to embrace the unknown, Delilah was rebelling against it, and there was no better place to rage against the abyss than the Chimney Sweep. No better place for anyone that is, except Connie, who was once again pelted with unanswerable questions.

What difference does it make what we do in life? From the moment we arrive, we deteriorate. What's the point? What if it's all one big cosmic joke? Why should anyone join a cause? Why should we give a shit? We're all biding our time in the great galactic waiting room. Why should we get attached to things, or to someone?

Ah! There we have it. There it is. Connie, a great and wise bartender, learned long ago to wait. If you listen, and you wait, the occupant of the barstool will eventually tell you what's eating away at them. A few more seconds, a few more sips, and voila! the truth, the whole truth, and nothing but the truth.

"My whole world is fucked up," said a world-weary Delilah.

"I'm all ears, sugar," said Connie.

Susan would have made a great bartender. She, too, was able to see beneath the surface. She, too, was able to wait until just the right moment for the extraction of the truth.

Rocky was about to embark on a new journey; he was about to visit his parents in Bakersfield, and Susan knew the time was right to open the floodgates. To open the closet door.

"So when do think you'll give voice to the unspeakable words?" she said watching him pretend to be immersed in work.

"My guess is that your parents won't be that shocked."

He couldn't hear a word she was saying. He had merchandise to sort out. He didn't have time for such folly. He tried to change the subject to she and West. No such luck.

Susan told him about her sister. How difficult it was for her to tell her parents. How her sister's intense fear morphed into tremendous relief and empowering liberation once she did the deed. She told him of the great burden that was lifted from her sister's shoulders.

"What's that? Did you say something? What do you think of this new Blue whale t-shirt?"

The phone rang. It was Rocky's mother. She never called the office. He made frightened faces at Susan to be interpreted as 'I'm not here, take a message'.

Susan hung up the phone and looked at Rocky who was shaking.

"Chimney Sweep?" she said.

Delilah was still there when they arrived. She and Connie were well oiled and deep into the thicket.

Susan and Rocky dove right in and ordered two scorpions apiece. Seemed like the appropriate thing to do.

Announcing to anyone that would listen, Delilah stated that she offered herself to West and he turned her away! And Connie was saying that he probably did that because he was afraid of falling in love! What kind of bullshit is that?

"So that means he is more likely to sleep with any other woman on the planet than Delilah," said Susan.

"Bingo, sugar," said Connie.

"Because he's attracted to Delilah more than any other woman on the planet," said a proud Rocky.

"Precisely," said a soused Connie.

Susan congratulated Connie for being a genius, which, she was confident, would result in some free drinks for all, which it did, and Rocky's quick consumption of his two scorpions brought him to a place where he found the courage and clarity to make an important announcement to the group.

"I told you all that I was leaving to do Proposition Six volunteer work in September," he said taking center stage. "I'm not," he said to cheers from Delilah. "I'm leaving tomorrow," he said looking at Susan.

"But first, I'm going to Bakersfield, because it's time to speak the unspoken words," he said embracing a teary-eyed Susan.

Delilah looked at Connie with a 'See? I told you the world is a fucking mess' look, while Connie wondered what in God's name was in Bakersfield?

The twins were not in Bakersfield. They were in North Hollywood. The Bakersfield of L.A.

Will and West were standing on the front porch of Natalie Singer's house when they were greeted by her tall, blond, beautiful twin sister Anastasia. This day was going so very well, and Will was feeling in such a grand mood, that he called Anastasia from the truck rental place to arrange a quickie 'meeting' to take care of some "pressing business." Coincidentally, it was advantageous to have West attached at the hip. West could entertain Natalie while Will and Anastasia met in private.

Anastasia handed each of them a glass of champagne and escorted them into the house.

"Natalie's in her bedroom. Come say hello," she said leading the way.

It was the middle of the day, and Natalie was still in bed. Unabashedly, unconcerned, and wearing a revealing negligee, she was sitting up in bed, champagne in one hand, and the next days script in the other. She was watching herself on the TV in front of the bed.

"You even look gorgeous when you're lounging around," said Will cheerfully.

"I'm working, I'll have you know," said Natalie defending her lifestyle.

Will introduced West to the women, and Natalie reminded Will that they had already been introduced at the infamous press conference on acid. West noticed Natalie's empty champagne glass and insisted on refilling it for her.

While he went off in search of more champagne, Will pleaded with Natalie to keep West company while he and Ana attended to some long overdue business. He volunteered West to assist her with her lines for tomorrows taping, and since it didn't appear that she had much choice, she reluctantly agreed.

When West reappeared with champagne bottle in hand, Will and Anastasia were gone. This made him nervous. Did I mention that revealing negligee?

Natalie extended her empty glass to West, who obediently refilled it. He was again at a loss for words. She patted the empty side of the bed next to her.

"Come. Sit here and help me run these lines," she said.

He mumbled something about his dirty clothes due to moving Zodiacs, whatever that meant, and that she probably didn't want him sitting on her bed, whatever that meant, but she did, she did want him to sit on her bed, right next to her, so she could, you know, act.

With nervous stomach, he sat down next to her, and saw, on the TV in front of them, the very same woman that he was inches from. The woman on the TV was passionately kissing some doctor in what looked like a utility closet. It was surreal.

"So, you're an actress, huh?" he said.

Natalie Singer was the single, biggest star of daytime television. Beloved by millions of viewers, she was astonished and delighted that he had no idea who she was. It made him attractive to her. She handed him some pages of her script.

"You read this part here," she said leaning over him, exposing her breasts through her negligee.

165

He started to get an erection.

"You mean out loud?" he said.

"Yes, I think that would be best," she said keeping a straight face.

Before they had a chance to begin, unmistakeable sounds emanated from another part of the house. Will and Anastasia were conducting their meeting for the whole world to hear. Now, he was more than nervous, and she could see that he was more than nervous, so she asked him to do her a huge favor and fetch her robe from the bathroom door. She was getting cold she lied.

West jumped at the chance to get away before he and his erection did something stupid. On the wall in the bathroom was a large black and white photo of a nude Natalie. As he grabbed her robe off the hook on the door, his attention to the photo lingered a bit too long.

"Ana took that photo of me," said Natalie giving him permission to gaze longer.

"Very nice," said West as he exited the bathroom, handing her the robe.

Natalie got out of bed and slipped into her robe. The house was quiet. The business meeting must have adjourned. West didn't know where to look, so he looked at the television. Sex everywhere, he couldn't escape it.

Natalie put him on the spot. She asked him if he thought she was the epitome of shallowness? A silly actress that did nothing meaningful, nothing important. A self-involved, uninformed, soap star?

He assured her that he did not think any of those

things. He thought that she did a bang-up job at the press conference, and he was confident that she would be a great asset to the cause. He told her that she should feel good knowing that she was someone who was willing to take a risk, to stand up and be counted.

Being the great actress that she was, Natalie conjured up two tear-filled eyes and allowed her robe to fall open, instantly reviving West's erection to full strength.

"Could I have a hug?" she asked?

West and his erection didn't need to be hugging semi-naked actresses at this moment in time, or did they? Jesus. Decisions, decisions.

"Just one good hug?" she pleaded.

West trudged her way as if he were walking to the gallows. She threw her arms around him and gave him and his friend a great embrace. As he struggled to find an appropriate place to put his hands, she let her robe fall to the floor. Oh well, why should Will have all of the fun?

"Champagne anyone?" intruded Anastasia holding a newly opened bottle of bubbly.

She and Will were standing in the doorway watching Natalie and West as if they were on the television, at the fictional hospital, in the utility closet, about to get intimate. Life imitates soap imitates life. Maybe another time, eh?

#

Will figured that the Palomino Club would be the ideal place to go after a tryst with the Singer sisters, and before the fancy dinner with Zelda Xavier.

The Valley home of Johnny Cash, Willie Nelson, Buck Owens, Patsy Cline, Tanya Tucker, and so many other country music artists. It was more Bakersfield than Bakersfield.

A soundcheck was in progress. A few crusty old characters were drinking at the weathered bar. Will was communing with a whiskey and a beer. The stool next to him was empty—a whiskey and beer awaiting the missing occupant—until the remarkably beautiful, raven-haired and ruby-lipped Linda Paloma sat down on the vacant barstool, tossed back the whiskey, and sampled the beer.

"Thanks for the drink, stranger," she said to Will as she messed up his perfect hair.

"Didn't you see the 'No Rock Stars' sign outside?" he replied.

He and Linda went way back to when she first arrived in town. Long before she became one of the biggest acts on the planet. She was country before she was rock. He guessed that he might find her here.

West was looking down, zipping up his fly, when he discovered his barstool was occupied. Even though he hadn't had that much to drink, for him, on this extraordinary day, he was now convinced that he was hallucinating. Maybe the bartender slipped him something? For an insane moment, he thought that he was looking at Linda Paloma sitting on his barstool, drinking his beer. Rockstar Linda Paloma, the same Linda Paloma that he had forever been head over heels in lust. Dreamland Linda Paloma.

"See what happens when you leave your drinks unattended?" she said.

"I will never attend to another drink in my life," he said with confidence.

She made up her mind about him right then and there. Will did the introductions as the bartender poured more whiskeys. The three of them chatted about saving whales, being runner-up for 'Record of the Year', and where to find the best Mexican food in L.A. She was then called to the stage. Soundcheck time.

"If you're free Friday night, come see the show, as my guests," she said looking at Will, intentionally ignoring West.

Will said that they were off to Aspen, but should be back in time to see the show. Deal.

"Fabulous Forum," she said. "VIP passes under your name."

Linda walked toward the stage, leaving the boys in her dust.

"It will be so cruel when this dream ends," said West.

#

"Things are not always what they seem; the first appearance deceives many; the intelligence of a few perceives what has been carefully hidden" wrote Phaedrus the fabulist. He might as well have been referring to Dr. Zelda Xavier, and her/his very strange dinner date with West and Will.

This part of the dream couldn't end quick enough for the lads. It was a very good thing that an imminent red-eye flight was on their calendar.

On first arrival at her mansion, they sat in the car

169

for what seemed a very long time, waiting for security to allow them entrance. When the gate finally receded, and they pulled the car forward to the front of the house, the massive front door was wide open, but no one was present to greet them.

Hesitant to enter unannounced, they waited on the covered portico until Zelda appeared and invited them inside. She was simultaneously alluring, mysterious, and seriously creepy. An elegantly dressed, famous brain surgeon in her fifties, she appeared to be the only person that inhabited the colossal property, except for the domestic staff.

An abbreviated tour of the mansion was followed by cocktails and hors d'oeuvres in the great library. West and Will were underdressed and out of place. They were equally ill-equipped to discuss anything brain surgery. They knew nothing of the wine in their hands, nor the caviar on their plates. The first editions on the shelves completely escaped their awareness, as did the gender of their host, and the reason they were there.

At dinner, they sat at a long table, in a dark and intimidating room. The butler religiously attended to their wine glasses, and course after course of never before experienced 'haute cuisine' was served and then removed from the table.

Never once did the topic of saving whales arise. Nothing environmental, nothing political, nothing financial. Zelda did almost all of the talking, as West and Will pretended to be fascinated, and in complete agreement about everything.

With dinner concluded, cognacs in hand, and Zelda

feeling free of her chains, it was decided, by her, that cigars in the billiard room were mandatory. She called it the billiard room. It was a secret room behind a moveable wall.

The room was equipped with a perfectly stocked bar, a billiard table, a massage table, and unsettling metal shackles attached to one of the walls.

Two paintings dominated the room. Salvador Dali's original Three Sphinxes of Bikini adorned the wall opposite of the shackles, and a master replication of Madonna by Edvard Munch covered the wall behind the bar. West and Will, nervous, but determined, and desiring her significant monetary contribution to the cause, pretended that everything was absolutely normal and delightful.

West declined the cigar, which produced a frown from Zelda, but to the rescue came Will who always appreciated an outstanding Cuban, and was able to intelligently discuss them.

The undercurrent in the room was the fear and expectation from the whale boys that at any moment something disturbing, something sexual would occur, requiring a quid pro quo for the moolah.

It never happened. The clock on the wall saved them. The time had come for her guests to depart for LAX. Escorting them to the front door where their car was waiting, Zelda placed a check for ten thousand dollars into Will's hand, thanked them for accepting her invitation, for the absolutely delightful company, and insisted that they schedule another dinner in the near future. The butler led the way to Will's once-upon-a-time nice car where there were final waves of farewell before the boys, relieved and fatigued, drove away into the confusing, unpredictable, lucrative Bel Air night.

It was late. The cabin of the plane was half-filled with sleeping passengers, and completely dark except for the lights above the seats of West and Will. Both were drinking Cuba Libre's. Will was reading Rolling Stone magazine, and an overwhelmed West could not stop thinking about his encounter with Linda Paloma, the softness of Farrah Fawcett's hands, the breasts beneath the negligee of Natalie Singer, and the unimaginable day that he had just lived.

Outside of the airplane, at thirty thousand feet, a full moon reflected off of thick white clouds. West was detached from his body. Without looking in his direction, Will reached over and put a small, round object in West's hand. Popping the pill without pause, West, images of Linda Paloma dancing in his head, succumbed to a deep, peaceful, much needed sleep.

#

On this Thursday morning, Delilah and Susan were the only heartbeats in the office until the door opened and in slithered Jonah Stern and Gary Leech.

Jonah was the top dog and evil genius in the San Francisco office. Early on, he overthrew their first Executive Director by rallying the groundlings to revolt. It was a bloodless coup, one that provided him a permanent position of power. As always, he was dressed in Goodwill clothes from head to toe. He wore prescription aviator glasses without which he was blind to the world. He never smiled, never bathed, never slept, and he could never be trusted.

172

Gary 'worked' out of the Seattle office of GreenPlanet, which one would never think of as an actual office, housing responsible adults, conducting meaningful business. In truth, one would never think of them at all, unless there was a problem, an uprising, or a crime committed.

Gary was wearing the only garments that he owned. The same worn out GreenPlanet tee shirt covered by smelly, dirty, farmer's overalls. He's a fucking idiot plain and simple. And Jonah's friend.

Delilah and Susan got bad vibes, very bad vibes, the minute they laid eyes on them. The two untouchables entered the office as if they owned the joint. They said they were looking for Kip, and commenced with their pre-planned snooping. Jonah pulled the paper from the Telex machine and began to read. Uninvited, Gary entered Kate's office and opened a file cabinet.

"Hey!" yelled Delilah.

Jonah introduced themselves.

"Jonah from the San Francisco office, and Gary from the Seattle office."

"Get out of there right now!" Susan screamed at Gary.

"It's okay," said Jonah. "It's all in the family."

Gary reappeared with two folders containing L.A.'s Articles of Incorporation and some bank statements. Susan, already on her feet and ready for a fight, seized the folders out of Gary's hands, marched them back into Kate's office, and stood sentinel in the doorway.

Jonah sat himself down at the conference table, opened his Dickensian briefcase, and began to set up a workspace. He disclosed that he and Kip went all the way back to the beginning of GreenPlanet. Said that they had a lot of history. Said they were like brothers.

"Kip's a fucking burn-out wasteoid," Gary said as he farted. "We're closing you down. You're not GreenPlanet."

Pointing to the water cooler with incredulity, Gary demanded to know what that thing was doing in their office? Were they spending 'save the whales' money for bottled water?

Delilah had seen and heard enough. She picked up the phone.

"That's it. Time for you to go," she said to Jonah.

Jonah pointed out that this wasn't 'her office'. It belonged to 'the family'. He informed her that he and Gary would be staying right there in the office for a few days, and would require keys, a couple of sleeping bags, and some "walking around money."

Ready to explode, Delilah threatened to call the police. She had recently gotten to know them very well.

Jonah and Gary were unfazed.

"You ever been arrested, Delilah? I have many times," said Jonah. "You ever been arrested, Gary?"

"Fuck yea, a million times," said the moron.

"How about you Susan? You ever been arrested?" Jonah taunted.

"Fuck you asshole," said Susan.

Delilah punched the zero on her phone.

Jonah, showing no concern, returned his papers to his briefcase and vacated his place at the table.

"I need the police, please," said Delilah into the

174

phone.

Jonah gestured for her to hang up the phone, waving at Gary to follow him toward the door. Delilah, seeing that they were about to exit, hung up the phone, and stared them down.

"Gary and I will stop by later to see if Kip made it in," said a smiling Jonah as he and Gary let themselves out and closed the door behind them. Rushing to the door, Susan locked it tight.

"Walking around money?" said Susan.

"Where the fuck is everyone?" Delilah angrily screamed to the gods.

#

West and Will were standing at the base of the breathtaking natural amphitheater that is the Aspen Bowl. Their tour guide was Todd Grant, KSPN program director, DJ, and friend of Elliot Irving. He was outlining the logistics of the Bowl, where the stage was erected for concerts, as well as passing along Mr. Irving's apologies for not being able to meet with them after all. Last minute changes in his plans required him to stay in L.A.

To make up for Elliot's absence, Todd made them a proposition. If they would agree to do a lengthy radio interview about all things GreenPlanet, he would show them the town all expenses paid, and put them up at his house on the mountain. No arm-twisting was required. The boys were all-in.

Since the interviews would be conducted later in the afternoon, they headed for Cooper Street Pier for burgers, beer, and some eight-ball. Aspen, West thought, could be in his future. Maybe later in life, when he had had his fill of surfing, tennis, and running wild; he could go there and bask in the Rocky Mountain beauty?

It was a bright, cold, majestic day as the trio departed Cooper Street Pier, and waltzed down South Mill Street, petting dogs, making eyes at young women, and greeting familiar faces. Todd knew everyone in town. He was wonderfully carefree.

At the radio station, it was a different story. Todd was behind the microphone, at the helm of the broadcast booth, and he was informed, prepared, and ready to deliver an in-depth, no time limit, high quality program for Aspen's sophisticated audience.

All ground was covered. Whales, seals, nukes, acid rain, groundwater poisoning, climate change, offshore oil, pesticides, industrial pollution, hunger, poverty. West, and even Will were firing on all cylinders. They knew their shit. They made an impact.

It was these periodic solid moments that helped counterbalance their flaws, their absence of a clear identity, their unknown raison d'être. Perhaps it was indeed possible to make a contribution, a significant contribution to the forest, while you were simultaneously lost deep within it?

At the conclusion of their interview, on the way out of the station, they stopped for publicity photos, and additional photos were taken with the staff. The sun goes down in an instant in the Rocky Mountains, as does the temperature. On their short walk from the radio station to the J Bar, it got cold.

Upon entering the bar, they discovered three

empty barstools hosting three shots of whiskey. Todd had called ahead and arranged for the bartender to save them places at the bar. Like I said, Todd knew everyone in town and everyone loved Todd. Almost everyone.

Seated at one of the large round tables at the back of the bar was Hunter S. Thompson. He was, in a disgruntled manner, sorting through a big pile of bills, fan mail, newspapers, and magazines. A wide assortment of beverages were in the mix. Rum, red wine, Bloody Marys, Mezcal, and Ouzo. Looking up from his paper mountain, he needed to see who was invading his space. Todd waved an enthusiastic hello to him, and in return, HST mouthed the words 'Fuck You' back at Todd. What is it with guys named Hunter?

Drinks turned into drinks and dinner. Todd notified his guests that a party—held in their honor—was happening a bit later at his house, but before they made their appearance, they still had time to mosey over to the Motherlode to listen to some live music. They weren't there very long before three lovely local gal-pals of Todd joined the party.

Although it was May, there were still plenty of patches of snow on Aspen Mountain. Todd's house was the classic ski house located next to one of the most popular runs on the mountain.

West, howling at the crescent moon, was rolling naked in a deep and fluffy snow patch until he couldn't stand it for one more second. Jumping to his feet, he ran full speed back to the palatial wooden deck that was home to the extra large, party-size hot tub currently occupied by the three, now equally naked, local girls, and an equally naked Will. West let out a yelp of delight as his skin went from frozen to boiling. One of the local girls passed him a lit joint with a twinkle in her eye.

Inside the house, a fire roared in the stone fireplace. Naked, semi-naked, and fully clothed revelers mingled, drank, smoked pot, played music, made out, and consumed a fine variety of pharmaceutical drugs. Todd, camped on one of the living room couches, was playing his guitar to an appreciative audience.

West decided that he, too, needed to join the house party. With towel strategically wrapped around his waist, he walked about the house in search of his long lost clothes.

As he passed by a prepossessing semi-dressed woman who was waiting to use the powder room, she abruptly took him by the hand, pulling him into the opening bathroom door. It wasn't what he thought.

She wanted to know what it would take to be a crewmember on the upcoming whale campaign in the Pacific. How could she get on the boat? She had to be on that boat! She was meant to be on that boat!

Tugging at the towel that he was holding tightly around his waist, she begged him to tell her if there was something, anything she could do? "Absolutely anything," she said.

Spying his clothes under a pile on the bathroom floor, he pointed to his pants and shirt. That's it? Nothing more? Are you sure? Dejected and defeated, she handed him his rags and backed out of the room.

The remainder of the night was quite civilized.

West and Will had several intimate conversations with very informed party guests, covering many, if not all of the topics that they had discussed on the air.

The house grew dark and quiet as the party eventually waned. The fire continued to give off a warm and nurturing glow as people slept on the various couches, while some were in sleeping bags on the floor. All of the beds, in each of the rooms, had multiple occupants. In one of the guest bedrooms, Will was sleeping between two of the hot tub girls from the Motherlode. West didn't sleep. His mind wouldn't allow it. There were too many things for him to figure out.

As the first light of day crept out of the blackness, there he was, alone, standing by the large picture window, taking in the magnificent grandeur that was Aspen Mountain on a Friday spring-morning sunrise. Fuck sleep.

#

Friday morning turned into late Friday afternoon. Delilah and Susan were once again left to hold down the fort. Delilah was not a happy camper for more than one reason. Periodically, throughout the day, she would scream, "Where the fuck is everyone?" Susan would reiterate that Kate took the day off, Rocky went home to Bakersfield, and West and Will's flight was delayed in Denver. Delilah would then yell at Susan, "Don't speak to me like I'm an idiot!"

Delilah demanded to know why West and Will got to go on all of the fun assignments? Why did they get to go to Aspen? Susan reminded her that they were men, and she and Delilah were just lowly women, and in GreenPlanet that's how things worked. Suffice it to say, not a well-received explanation.

"The weekend is an hour away, ergo the Chimney Sweep is an hour away," said Susan trying to soothe the savage beast.

"What if the Manson twins return?" said a worried Delilah. "Those Neanderthals fucking scare me," she said.

Susan reassured her that the door was locked, and the phone number for the police department was front and center. She suggested that Delilah "stay cool."

"This is no way to run an organization!" screamed Delilah at the top of her lungs, just as there was knocking on the office door. Freeze!

Susan gestured for her to stay quiet as she tiptoed to the door to peek through the viewer. No one was visible. With a shrug of the shoulders, she indicated to Delilah that nothing was there.

"Hello? Anyone there? Hello out there," said Susan.

Silence. Delilah retrieved a 'save the seals' protest sign from a corner of the room, and prepared to wield it as a deadly weapon.

On her way to the door, she got her courage up, and signaled for Susan to open the door. Susan, taking the required deep breath, unlocked the door and threw it open wide. Delilah screamed, and just as she screamed, a loud barking sound could be heard as an adult Harbor seal lunged and tried to bite her.

Jumping back away from the seal, the traumatized whale savers allowed it to force its way into the office; the animal was wearing a make-shift collar with a note attached to it. In a test of her resolve and mettle,

180

Susan screwed her courage to the sticking post, and from behind the intruder, snatched the note from the seal's collar. The seal barked again, scaring the shit out of the two women. Susan, shaking, looked at the note, then handed it to Delilah. The note read: THIS IS NOW YOUR PROBLEM.

Delilah looked at the seal, looked at Susan, looked at the clock on the wall, and looked at the sign she held in her hand.

"Where the fuck is everyone?" she said.

#

West and Will were backstage at the Fabulous Forum. VIP guests of Linda Paloma; they were feasting on a lavish spread and mingling with exotic strangers. In the midst of having too much fun, a rather large, longhaired, menacing-looking roadie approached them and pointed an accusing finger at West.

"You. Come with me," commanded the roadie.

West, looking in all directions, was hoping that the scary guy wasn't talking to him. Will, convinced that he wasn't the target of roadie seriousness, patted West on the shoulder, pointed in the roadie's direction, and helped himself to more shrimp cocktail.

"You better do what he says," said Will.

Cowed, and not knowing what he did wrong, a timid West followed the guy out of the VIP room, feebly trying to chat him up, but the roadie remained silent.

Arriving at an unmarked dressing room door, the roadie knocked twice, opening the door before any permission was granted. Inside, was a kimono-wearing

Linda Paloma sitting in front of a make-up table waiting patiently for her delivery. The roadie pointed West into the room, closed the door behind him, and stood guard outside the door.

From inside the arena, sounds of the arriving Forum crowd grew louder and louder. Inside the dressing room, there were also sounds. Furniture knocking into walls, objects crashing to the floor, muffled voices, glass breakage, and other crash, bangs, and squeals.

On stage, while an MC was pumping up the crowd, laughter was coming from inside the dressing room followed by a loud female scream. The roadie didn't flinch. The introduction of the band was moments away now. No more activity could be heard from inside the dressing room. The time had come; the MC was introducing the band.

"Please give a loud Southern California welcome home to Linda Paloma!"

While the crowd was cheering, the various members of the band formed a circle in front of Linda's dressing room door, which swung open with abandon. Out she strutted; dressed, made-up and ready to rock.

As she joined the circle for the pre-show ritual, through the open dressing room door, West could be seen pulling up his pants and pulling himself together. It was 'go time'. Linda and the band charged the stage to a huge roar from the arena crowd. The roadie motioned West to follow him back to the VIP room.

Will, scotch whiskey in hand, was reconnecting with one of his talent agent colleagues when West and the roadie reappeared. Handing Will two tickets—so they could go out front to watch the show if they wanted– the roadie gave West a subtle nod of approval, wiped his hands on his jeans, and took off into the bowels of the Forum. Mission accomplished.

The concert continued for the next two hours. West and Will partook, with great enthusiasm, all of the various backstage perks i.e. drinks, drugs, and beautiful people. No words were spoken with regards to the roadie-escorted visit to Linda Paloma's dressing room. When the show came to an end, a delirious crowd made its grateful way out into the Los Angeles night.

West suggested that Will leave without him. He was, he said, "going to stick around for a while." Bad idea.

Will countered this bad idea with some food for thought. Inglewood, late at night, without a way home, was an obituary waiting to be written, but West was not swayed, he was about to party, and Will saw that there was no use trying to reason with him. Shaking his head in disapproval, he took his leave.

West was feeling good; he was feeling invincible. He eventually found his way to Linda's dressing room where his new pal, the roadie, stood guard. When he tried to enter her room, he was physically stopped. Unruffled, he interpreted this to mean 'wait for her here, she'll be out in a minute'. Okay, not a problem.

Concert-goers continued to file out. Band members passed by, saying their "good nights" to the big man, while Forum cleanup crews surfaced from the lower depths. When the dressing room door finally opened and out popped Linda, West moved two steps toward

183

her only to discover that she was on the arm of some rocker-dude, laughing, cozy, and carrying on. Seeing West waiting with baited breath, she blew him a kiss, scampering past him, out of the Forum, and into a waiting limousine. West was floored.

Crushed, and feeling a tad humiliated in front of his pal the roadie, West threw his hands up in mock defeat and headed for the nearest exit. All of a sudden, he wasn't feeling so good. Alone in an ever-emptying parking lot, late at night, in a rough neighborhood, with no way home, the word regret came into his mind.

With less than great determination, and tail between his legs, he proceeded to slink through the parking lot of the Fabulous Forum. Horns blared in his direction. Voices yelled out of car windows. He interpreted the laughter as aggressive and mean-spirited. There was the sound of a firecracker or a gun or something. It scared him. He was convinced his goose was about to be cooked when, to his great relief, guardian angel Will pulled up next to him, opening the passenger door to his car, and to safety.

For a long time, neither said a word as they headed up the 405 freeway. West was wounded, but had nothing to be embarrassed about. If he took a moment to think about it, which he did, the last seventy-two hours had been a dream. Unimaginable. Like his future. Like all of their futures. He should feel on top of the world. No regrets. No poor, poor, pitiful me. Forward marc

REMEMBER WHAT YOU SEE

More and more the office was run by women. Kip was in Mexico, Hunter was in Europe, and Rocky was in San Francisco. West and Will seemed to be on the road more than they were at the office. Kate, Delilah, and Susan, with the help of mostly female volunteers, made sure the trains ran on time. Today was no different. The triumvirate were at their desks, and every volunteer was female. Zero dudes.

A few weeks had passed since the Aspen trip. West and Will were now winging their way south to hang out with Kip in Cabo San Lucas. Kip had arranged for them to be official observers of a barbless marlin fishing tournament held each Memorial Day Weekend, hosted by oil magnate and hotel owner Hal Davidson. All expenses paid. Muy Bien.

Susan had joined Delilah in her unhappiness at being overlooked by Kate when it came to the glamour assignments, the 'active', 'in the field', assignments.

"We should quit. It's not fair. They'd be lost without us," she said to Delilah who was listening with rapt attention, not to Susan, but to her phone messages.

"You've been here since day one," she continued. "We barely make enough to pay the bills."

Susan could see that something was up. Delilah was taking notes and oozing wickedness. She hung up the phone.

"How long will they be in Mexico?" asked Delilah in a hushed voice.

Susan said that they would be there in an official capacity throughout the entire Memorial Day weekend, but her guess was no less than a week since they would be hanging with Kip. Delilah's eyes sparkled.

"Perfect. Pack your bags. We're going on assignment."

It was a rough flight with heavy turbulence on the way to Cabo. Not that unusual when flying Mexicana. The cause of turbulence, in general, is almost always thermal, sometimes mechanical.

At the obvious times of the year, the desert southwest heats up fast, and convection is the natural byproduct. Almost always, thermals can be avoided if you know what you're doing. If you don't know what you're doing, and you're flying less than impressive airplanes, well, pray that the liquor doesn't run out.

All on board were buckled up tight, including the stewardesses. Will's face was ashen, and his hands were vice-gripped onto his armrests. West was holding Will's Cuba Libre in one hand, and his own empty glass in the other. He tried to get the attention of a stewardess by holding his empty high into the air. Not happening. When that didn't work, he decided that the responsible thing to do was to adopt Will's.

What was going on with Kip? That's what West wanted to know. It didn't seem like he was in a hurry to return to L.A. Was he doing okay? How does he pay for things? Cabo is expensive, isn't it? Is he in some kind of trouble? Hiding from the law?

Will told West about the phone conversation that he and Hunter had with Kip. Said he sounded pretty good. Said he was going to dry out under the Mexican

186

sun. Said he was the son of Kip Asher Sr., and the grandson of Kendal Asher, as in Asher Oil, as in trust fund baby, as in filthy rich, as in family friend of the Davidsons. The oil Davidsons.

West was still confused. He didn't know who the oil Davidsons were. He was happy to learn that Kip was wealthy. It was kind of weird, though. What other weird stuff was he not aware of? He was stoked that they were headed to Cabo.

The plane took another big drop. Passengers screamed, Will hung on for dear life, and West was oblivious, though agitated that he was left holding two empty glasses. When things settled, Will full of fear, briefed West with regards to the notorious runway at Cabo. According to legend, it was a bit too short for their aircraft to comfortably land. "Comfortably" being the operative word. West could care less. He was going on and on about the great Baja surfing spots that he was going to tackle; sharks or no sharks.

"Is there anything that you fear?" said a white-knuckled Will.

West gave this much thought. Why sure there were things that he feared. He was human after all.

"Boredom. Last call. And Delilah," he said without the least bit of embarrassment.

The runway was, indeed, a bit too short, but the pilot managed, as he always did, to slam it down hard, and bring it to a stop before it made it to the edge of the cliff. Anyone that has landed at LaGuardia can relate.

At the hotel, they were greeted by a sculpture of two twin dolphins leaping from the sea, and at the bar, they were greeted by two margarita's leaping from the bartender's hands.

West reluctantly indulged Will's desire to take to the court and hit some tennis balls. It was the last few days of May, and the Mexican sun was scorching hot, not pleasant tennis weather. They hadn't been out there very long before a couple of rich oil guys challenged them to a doubles match.

West hated this kind of thing. Country club guys with expensive clothes, expensive equipment, and the ludicrous notion that they were 'players'.

Will didn't play tennis often. He was a hacker, not a player. West was a player, and an opportunist. This, he calculated, could be worth of few drinks, or a favor or two. He was right. After about an hour under the brutal sun, the money guys suffered humiliating defeat, and everyone made a hasty retreat to the pool and the pool bar. Set 'em up bartender.

At sunset, a noticeably sunburned West and Will watched spouts from Gray whales on the horizon. The hotel guests surrounding them were decked out in preppy evening attire, martinis in hand. Kip walked into the room as one might enter a political fundraiser, waving at various groups at various tables, never stopping until he arrived at West and Will's perch.

They were thrilled to see him. Lots of hugging and hand shaking ensued. Kip threw three fingers in the air and got right to it.

"Nice work at PS 3," he said to West. "Is it true that a diver was killed in Ventura?" he asked.

West filled him in on everything. The lawyer representing the diver's family requested that West testify as an expert witness if it went to trial. The power companies were now under tremendous pressure from the public and some prominent politicians. The legal ramifications could facilitate real change.

A puffy-chested Will laid out all of his successful celebrity fund-raising efforts which included rock bands, movie stars, TV stars, authors, and actors.

"Even a famous surfer," he said as West winced.

Kip pointed across the room to where Hal Davidson was handing out cigars and engraved silver lighters. He knew the lads were less than comfortable. This was not their crowd, their scene. He reassured them that all was cool. Everything would turn out "just fine." Drink up.

The Chimney Sweep crowd was more their crowd if they had a crowd. There were no Gray whales at the Chimney Sweep, but there were scorpions galore. Coincidentally, Delilah, Susan, and Connie happened to be there at this precise moment, in fine fettle.

The whale girls had escaped the office and were flying off on their own covert adventure come morning. Gil was behind the bar on this holiday weekend, so Connie was free to let loose with her trouble-making pals. The always responsible Susan suggested that they 'go easy' on the scorpions, because there was a flight to catch in the morning.

"Sugar, life's not meant to go easy on," instructed Connie.

"Damn straight," said a rebellious Delilah jumping up from her seat, heading straight to the jukebox.

Delilah pumped a bunch of quarters in the

jukebox, played 'La Grange' by ZZ Top, and started to dance. Every guy in the bar stopped what he was doing to watch The Delilah Show. This woman was angry, and when she was angry you couldn't take your eyes off of her.

#

Saturday morning came very early. Delilah and Susan barely made their flight out of LAX–there was no time for showers or breakfasts. Forced to drink crappy, weak coffee on the airplane, they were only able to grab an hour or so of bad sleep.

Standing under a hot Albuquerque sun, they were wounded and waiting for some guy named Luke to pick them up at the airport. He was late, and they started to wonder if he was coming at all. Maybe this wasn't the greatest idea?

On their way back into baggage claim, a battered, rusty Dodge pickup pulled up to the curb. Inside the cab of the truck were three serious looking men. Two longhaired Native Americans, and a clean-cut white guy. Luke, the white guy, stuck his head out the window.

"Delilah? I'm Luke, climb on," he said.

Climb on? Does he mean climb onto the back of the truck bed?

With no help from the men, Susan opened the tailgate. Tossing their bags, the hung-over duo climbed up onto the dirty truck bed as the truck sped away from the airport to New Mexican parts unknown. Their riding-in-the-back-of-a-truck learning curve was expeditious. Step one was finding a reliable place to hold onto so they wouldn't be thrown out of the truck.

Good Zodiac practice. Susan was looking at Delilah with anxiety and a wee bit of aggression. What the fuck?

In a run-down, nondescript house, in an ugly Albuquerque neighborhood, anchored in place by the front door, stood Delilah and Susan.

A dozen people skittered from room to room. No one acknowledged the presence of the two women. Covering the walls were posters of Che Guevara and Crazy Horse. A hand-painted sign read: Man Cannot Own the Land. There were maps of Indian reservation lands and a mix of old and new newspaper and magazine clippings.

Two men were wearing firearms. Several rifles were stacked in an accessible corner. There was little furniture in the house. Delilah and Susan couldn't help but notice that they were the only 'pale faces' in sight.

From another part of the house, Luke reappeared and led them to the kitchen where J T was sitting in front of a large map, a walkie-talkie, and an extra-large cheese pizza. An exceptionally handsome Lakota Sioux Indian with long black hair, steely eyes, and more than a hint of danger, he gave the young women the once over.

Gesturing for them to take a seat, he turned his attention back to the walkie-talkie. FBI were parked down the street. The house was being watched. He could see the look in their worried eyes. Smiling, he pushed the box of pizza in front of them.

"Pizza," he said.

While they were chowing down on cheese pizza, it was spelled out to them. Outside of town; a dangerous

191

armed standoff. American Indian Movement members on one side of the road, and private security forces for the oil companies on the other side. It was about to blow up, and no one on the outside was paying any attention.

Oil companies had illegally moved onto Navajo land. They put up fences, blocked water access, and started drilling holes everywhere, trying to force the tribe to relocate. The Feds were on the side of the oil companies, so the people on the reservation had taken up arms, recruited the help of A I M, and now they were making a last stand to prevent the oil companies from going any further into their territory. GreenPlanet had been asked to come help with the media; to garner national attention; to save lives.

Susan and Delilah exchanged glances of excitement. This was big. This was important. They put down their pizza and rolled up their sleeves. They knew they could help. It was time to go to work.

Splitting up into pairs, Susan and Luke stayed at the house in Albuquerque to work on the press release, while Delilah and J T headed for Sacred Mesa, the front lines of the confrontation.

Thirty-three miles due west, as the crow flies, lies the Canoncito Navajo reservation. A remote section of Pueblo Road became the literal line in the sand. On one side of the road was illegally fenced off land guarded by armed oil company security, and on the opposite side of the road, behind barriers and a makeshift camp, were armed Navajo and American Indian Movement members.

J T was giving Delilah the guided tour. His people

192

were relocated there, he said, because the white man considered the land to be worthless, to be punishment. His people knew this to be false. They knew then as they know now, that the land always provides. Beneath their feet was coal, oil, and uranium.

When the oppressors discovered their mistake, comprehended their own ignorance, they changed the rules. They would take back what they had allocated. Their word, their laws, were hollow, without meaning. They created the Bureau of Indian Affairs to make the illegal land grabs appear legitimate.

"They bought themselves some 'Uncle Tomahawks', put them in decision making positions, and pretended to operate democratically, with the native people's interest in mind. Does this look democratic to you?" he asked Delilah.

J T opened the flap of a small teepee and waited for Delilah to enter. He asked her to remain silent. Inside, an old woman, Winona Fall Leaf, and her granddaughter, Lorelei, were engaged in a healing ritual for a member of the tribe who was ill and dying of cancer. J T and Delilah sat and observed.

Winona and her granddaughter were drenched in sweat, while their patient lay serene and peaceful. As the healing ritual continued, Delilah also became soaked with sweat. She felt dizzy and disoriented. The sounds of the ritual grew louder and louder in her ears. She had difficulty breathing. She began to hallucinate. She saw herself detach from her body, rise up through the teepee, and fly high above the conflict at Sacred Mesa. She rose up and up and up until the ground was invisible and everything faded to black.

The sound of gunshots, and the pain of someone grabbing her by the arm roused her out of her delirium. She wasn't in the teepee. She was in the middle of the road, surrounded by FBI agents with guns drawn. J T had his hands on top of a car and was being frisked. People were scrambling for cover behind vehicles, behind boulders and self-made shelters. Guns were pointed across both sides of the road. It was tense.

Zip ties were used to handcuff J T and Delilah. He yelled out instructions for the tribe to back down; to stay calm. Placed in separate vehicles, Delilah and J T were read their Miranda Rights, and then whisked away surrounded by a convoy.

Back at the house in Albuquerque, Susan was on the phone with a journalist from New York. A newly created television news show called 20/20 was about to premiere. The east coast journalist held in his hands their press release and wanted to know more. As she was filling him in, Luke interrupted her.

"Shots fired," he said. "J T and Delilah. Let's go."

Those words were heard on the other end of the phone in New York City. "We're on our way," the voice said, as Susan dropped the phone and raced out of the house with Luke by her side.

#

On board the forty foot fishing boat Separate Reality, West and Will were the de facto marlin-fishing police. Kip wanted the company of his pals, and Hal Davidson needed reputable monitors that would verify the barbless 'catch and release' nature of their tournament, and West and Will would be crazy to pass up an all expenses paid holiday weekend in Cabo, so the tryst was a win-win-win for everyone involved. Right?

They were assured by Hal, that even though some harm was done, the damage to the marlins was minimal, and on the bright side, the high-profile participants would inspire marlin fishermen the world over to adopt catch-and-release as their modus operandi. If they had any questions or concerns, he would address them immediately. He was on their side.

The lads were stationed on the aft deck as the Separate Reality moved 'full steam ahead' toward the Blue marlin fishing grounds. Sun sparkled off a cobalt blue ocean. The wind in their faces, and the warmth of the sun on their skin felt invigorating and rejuvenating. Dolphins played off the bow of the ship. It was quite the contrast to the gaggle of insanely wealthy oil magnates surrounding them, laughing, drinking, and making mega-deals.

A pod of Gray whales could be seen breaching in the distance. West plucked two ice-cold beers out of a nearby cooler and handed one to Will. The fishing boat slowed to a crawl as the oilmen rushed to the starboard side to witness a magnificent whale shark—larger than the boat they were on—glide serenely by. This was perceived by all on board as a very good omen for the day ahead. It was not.

On the horizon, West and Will had their eyes glued to a fleet of fishing boats that were encircled by scores of frenzied gulls. The activity of the men on those boats was also frenzied. The pursuit of the marlins required the Separate Reality to steer in the exact direction of those same fishing boats, and once the distance between them was sufficiently reduced, all on board could see that it was the Mexican Tuna Fleet in action. Purse-seine nets had been deployed, and hundreds of dolphins struggled in vain to escape captivity. Floating bodies of dead dolphins increasingly replaced the audibly panicked dolphins that were fighting for their lives. No one was doing anything to remedy the situation, certainly not the tuna fishermen. West got belligerent.

"Are we just going to stand here?" he bellowed. "Aren't we going to do something? This is bullshit! This is murder!"

Hal told him to calm the fuck down. They were in Mexican waters. Nothing they could do. He lectured to an apoplectic West that schools of tuna often swim beneath schools of dolphins. When the tuna are captured in the nets, unfortunately, so are the dolphins, and before West could ask, he further clarified: "Release the dolphins, release the tuna. That's not going to happen."

The dolphins continued to thrash, and scream, and drown, and West was out of his mind.

"Can't we do anything?" he screamed at the top of his lungs.

Will put a firm hand on West's shoulder.

"Remember what you see," he said.

It was a completely different scene on the aft deck of the Gaia. Karma Parrish was also counting on people to remember what they saw. Karma was the office manager for the San Francisco operation; an accomplished manipulator, second in command under Jonah Stern, and an unremarkable woman in every other way. If not for GreenPlanet, she most certainly would have been living with her parents in Lodi.

Without the knowledge, consent, and coordination of Hunter and the Europeans, GreenPlanet SF was holding an 'Open House' this Memorial Day weekend to raise money to fund their own summer whale campaign, putting to rest any notion that they were not the number one, legitimate GreenPlanet office in the United States.

The Gaia was freshly painted, gleaming, glowing, and cosmetically ship-shape, never mind the small matter of her unseaworthiness. Visitors streamed up and down the gangplank while volunteers led tours of the ship, sold merchandise, and handed out flyers and info sheets. Television and print media surrounded Karma as she conducted an impromptu press conference. Monitoring from the sidelines were Jonah Stern, Gary Leech, and David Middling.

The members of the press were told that twenty-five crew members from the San Francisco office would set sail on July 4th to hunt down and confront the Japanese whaling fleet in the South Pacific. One very special crewmember spot would be made available to the highest bidder via public auction, with the bidding to begin at ten-thousand dollars.

When asked by the press if they were also participating in the other 'save the whales' campaign leaving from Los Angeles, Karma politely disputed the legitimacy and authority of her unsanctioned tribesmen to the south.

"I'm not aware of any sanctioned GreenPlanet voyage leaving from Los Angeles. Sadly, this happens to all high-profile, successful, rapidly-growing organizations. Impostors begin to pop up. Let me assure you that we are indeed the legitimate USA headquarters of GreenPlanet. Right here in San Francisco. This is where the campaigns are planned, the decisions are made, and the money is raised. If you need any more convincing, you can speak with GreenPlanet legal council David Middling, who happens to be standing right over there," she said pointing in his direction.

David, hearing this outright lie from Karma, and less than happy that she was throwing him under the bus, decided it was time for him to disappear before the press could corral him. He had also had his fill of Jonah, and Gary, and all of the others who ignored his legal advice and disparaged his education. As far as he was concerned, he was finished; they were on their own. Fuck 'em.

\#

The sunset in Cabo was spectacular, but the sashimi in front of West was an insult to injury. Will didn't seem to mind, just the opposite in fact. Both he and Kip were immersed in orgasmic sashimi nirvana, which drove West even madder. When it became clear to him that he would not succeed at getting Kip and

Will on the angry train with him, he got up and stormed out of the room.

"He'll be fine. He saw some pretty fucked-up shit today," said Will as he slid West's plate of sashimi in between himself and Kip.

"I understand, but that's nothing compared to what's coming. How's he going to react in front of a whaling boat closing in on him at twenty-five knots?" asked Kip as he helped himself to the biggest piece of tuna on the plate.

The sunset in Albuquerque was also spectacular, but the smiling, laughing, FBI agent was another insult to injury. Susan and Luke were sitting in the Dodge pickup truck outside the FBI office when the front door opened and out came Delilah. The arresting FBI agent, who was smiling and waving at them, escorted her out the door. Before he retreated back into the building, he was joined by three fellow officers who found the somber circumstances quite hilarious.

Susan pushed open the passenger door and moved next to Luke to make room for Delilah. Luke pulled the truck away from the curb and headed down the street toward the highway. Nothing was said. When the FBI building was out of sight, Delilah sighed a great sigh, and burst into tears.

They were headed out of town. To Santa Fe. Luke had offered, without their knowledge or consent, to share Susan and Delilah with another group, from Colorado, also in need of media assistance. Delilah was stressed. Had she unwittingly opened a Pandora's Box? Suddenly she was feeling very nostalgic about the office in L.A.

The bright moonlight lit up the highway in front of them. Susan put her head on Luke's shoulder and rested her eyes. Delilah became lost in her own thoughts. She saw the reflection of the truck's headlights in the eyes of a dead coyote on the side of the road. She imagined a large black crow circling high above a teepee, her teepee. Inside, Winona Fall Leaf and Lorelei were serenely preparing a dead body for burial. She had visions of West. He was angry. He was missing. She was prescient.

West was angry, and at the moment, he was holed up in his cabana. His buddies, Kip and Will, were dining with Hal Davidson and his billionaire pal Aaron Halston. The oilmen were trying to convince the whale boys that they had more in common than not.

Hal was a close friend of Kip's estranged father Kip Sr. Whenever Hal would cross paths with Kip Jr, he would try to broker a long overdue peace accord between the two.

"Our chef, Claude Renée, is the finest chef on the planet. I stole him from Kip Senior," bragged Hal.

"How is dear old dad?" mocked Kip.

"Your father is a good and wise man. He's made your life quite comfortable," lectured Hal.

"To the oil baron!" snapped Kip.

There was the boisterous sound of men carousing, followed by the breaking of glass. In a back room, John Wayne and Dean Martin were taking the festivities to another level.

"One must never leave Duke and Dino unchaperoned," said Aaron.

Unchaperoned. Where was West wondered Hal?

Was he still out of sorts? This wouldn't do.

Will, hoping to soothe the savage beast, posited that West needed some space to work through what he had witnessed earlier in the day. He promised the oilmen that West would be on board tomorrow, ready to roll.

Hal and Aaron conducted an impromptu private huddle, resulting in Hal waving over his personal waitress. Whispering in her ear, he waited as she took a long pause before nodding in the affirmative.

A bright moon lighted the path from the hotel dining room to the private cabanas on the beach. In the middle of the path, a giant iguana stood sentinel. Two bare female legs carefully stepped over the iguana, which, with disdain, looked up, but refused to move an inch. When Hal's emissary arrived at the door to West's cabana, she paused, straightened herself, and then knocked.

Sitting on the floor, West was carefully studying a captured scorpion inside an overturned drinking glass. He incorrectly figured the knock on the door was Will or Kip, come to fetch him back to the bar.

Upon opening the door, he discovered the young waitress holding a bottle of silver tequila and two glasses. Standing to the side as she entered, he took a wary look around, closing the door behind them.

Standing guard outside was the iguana looking remarkably like Kip. It's eyes barely open; it's brain barely conscious, it tried, and failed, to comprehend the enormity of the vast and incomprehensible universe.

The next morning, West was missing. Will and Hal were on the deck of the Separate Reality, observing the removal of the gangplank, then adjusting to the side to side motion as the boat pulled away from the dock. West was not on board. Hal was not happy. He brought them there to provide convincing cover for his tournament. Do you think he would be associating with them if there was no significant reward? They were the peasant class; the working class. Yes, politics makes strange bedfellows. That's often how business gets done, but both sides have to uphold their end. West was not on board, not to mention the fact that he was making noise about things that needed to be ignored. This was troublesome.

Will and Hal didn't know that West was at Zipper's Beach, in the middle of a sharp drop down, on the face of a perfect ten-foot wave. They didn't know that he had washed his hands of the whole marlin fishing barbarism, that Hal's late night 'gift' was not successfully accommodated. They didn't know that the number of hours surfing would be in direct relation to his level of agitation.

There was plenty of agitation and unhappiness occurring in all quadrants of the GreenPlanet universe. In San Francisco, Hunter and Hugh were Sunday brunching at the Buena Vista Cafe with a disgruntled and defeated David Middling, who was informing them about the revolt that was underway by the enraged and defiant tribes from Seattle and San Francisco.

At Maria's New Mexican Kitchen in Santa Fe, Susan, Luke, and especially Delilah, were in an overall foul mood as they attempted to regroup from the previous day's ordeal while awaiting the arrival of the anti-nuke people from Colorado.

On board the Separate Reality, Hal Davidson was strapped into a 'fighting chair', his fishing rod bent like a banana due to the seriously big and strong marlin on his hook.

He swiveled from side to side as the marlin fought for its life. Two crewmembers were on each side of him, ready to assist him the moment he gave them the sign. Will was snapping photos with one hand, and, more importantly, drinking a frosty beer with the other.

The marlin was agitated too. It flew completely out of the water, before crashing on its side, making a huge saltwater splash. Hal was getting tired, dead dog tired. He slapped away the helping hand of one of his crewmembers. He was determined to win the fight with this fish completely on his own, but the marlin displayed a great surge of energy that was eventually too much for him. He signaled for help. He was seething.

Two crewmen grabbed onto the rod and began to reel in the marlin. All on board were now an attentive audience for the mighty struggle between Hal and his fish. Several times the marlin completely left the water, thrashing wildly, and then going back under, invisible. After several more rounds of struggle, it started to weaken to the point of surrender. An angry Hal dismissed his helpers and took back the reel. Now able to get the weakened marlin to the side of the boat, it was measured, photographed, and, as agreed, released. Out of breath and completely exhausted, he dropped onto one of the boats fixed benches.

"Hope you got plenty of good shots," he gasped at Will. "I want to be on the cover of magazines! Alert the media!" he bellowed.

This is exactly what the people from Colorado were requesting; assistance in alerting the national media about their civil disobedience at the Rocky Flats Nuclear Weapons Facility.

Susan and Luke listened in earnest as they were briefed about the situation at Rocky Flats. Delilah listened with detachment, as she was immersed in the pile of food in front of her, attacking it as if it were her last meal on Earth.

Plutonium triggers were made at the weapons facility, which required the radioactive material to be transported by train into the plant. In no time, the water table became contaminated in and around Jefferson County and parts of Denver. People were dying, and Rockwell was denying.

The plan was to blockade the railroad tracks that led into the plant, preventing the plutonium-carrying trains from delivering their deadly cargo. The civil disobedience would be carried out in waves. When one group of blockaders was arrested, the next wave of protestors would swing into action the very next day. Success required massive public awareness, and that's where the GreenPlanet expertise was needed, and that's why the Coloradoans drove to Santa Fe to meet with them. Gotcha. Add it to the list.

Kip was expert at letting go of his agitation. He simply put two drink fingers in the air and moved on. It didn't hurt that he was sitting poolside with Elliot Irving, and paying great attention to a comely young beauty swimming laps in the pool.

Her name was Chastity. She was on her honeymoon with new husband Brandel. He was exactly as you might imagine someone named Brandel. Stick up his ass, all work and no fun. He was on the phone, at the pool bar, completely ignoring her.

To their delight, she completed her laps in fine form and swam over to the side of the pool where they were lounging. Introducing herself, she confessed to overhearing their conversation. Were they discussing the current Desperados tour? Because Chastity was the biggest Desperados fan in the entire universe. She insisted that no one was a bigger fan. Nobody. Understand? She especially loved and worshipped Lewis, the lead singer and founder of the band. When Kip introduced Elliot as the band's manager, she was beside herself.

"Elliot, do you see Lewis often?" she asked with baited breath.

"Lewis? I was just about to call him. Want me to say hello for you?" Elliot teased.

Chastity melted right there in the pool, and when Elliot upped the ante suggesting that she say hello to him herself, she was a goner.

The cocktail waitress appeared with more umbrella drinks, and Chastity, without hesitation, accepted the invitation to join the party. New husband Brandel was more interested in the stock market than anything happening poolside, so Chastity was left to her own devices. The combination of sizzling Mexican sun, potent rum, and fantasies of Lewis, dissolved any inhibitions that Chastity might have had.

"Yum. This is a pretty delicious drink Elliot. Will you be calling Lewis from your room?" she asked.

A smiling Elliot nodded in the affirmative, as a delirious Chastity waved at a disinterested Brandel. The moment she lowered her arm, the sunburned, salt-covered body of West whizzed past her head and into the pool. Under the water, he swam to the far end of the pool, then back, surfacing right in front of Chastity.

"I'm West. I've come to save you from these banditos," said West.

Kip introduced West and Elliot to each other, and then pointed out the obvious, West was not on the marlin fishing boat. Rather than going down that road, West sank under the water, and swam to the pool bar, surfacing next to Brandel. He ordered a beer for himself and for the stranger next to him. Why not? He wasn't paying for it.

"Stay away from my wife," Brandel said without looking at West. "This is your one and only warning."

The many hours of surfing hadn't completely erased the entirety of West's agitation, and Brandel was the perfect catalyst to complete the job. After a serene moment of reflection, West noticed the untouched margarita sitting in front of Brandel. With mucho gusto he confiscated and downed his neighbors' refreshment in one move. He then let out a war cry for

206

all to hear.

"Tequila and fresh horses for all my men!" yelled West as he and his beer swam back to the waiting bright light that was Lady Chastity.

#

Delilah had been dropped off at a house in Santa Fe to help the Rocky Flats people with campaign literature and press packets. Susan and Luke escaped to the desert to 'transform their spirit', and get the fuck away from Delilah's negative energy.

Inside the expensive, cliché, adobe Santa Fe house, the interior was lavish, hippie, new-age chic. Delilah was seated on a weathered, but plush couch, pretending to read a worn copy of 'The Only Dance There Is' by Ram Dass. Her hosts Fillmore and Jasmine Sorensen were stuffing envelopes and applying postage stamps. Complimenting Delilah on her choice of books, they confessed how important LSD had been in changing their lives for the better.

Delilah was more than ready to get back to L.A. She supported their cause, but she had causes of her own to attend to. There are plenty of bloody causes, eh? When asked by the Sorensen's if she personally would be joining them in blocking the train tracks, she answered with a less than enthusiastic "not sure."

Abruptly halting their envelope duty, Fillmore and Jasmine zipped to the couch, bookending Delilah. Fillmore took a spliff from his shirt pocket, fired her up, took a drag, and handed it to Delilah.

"We can feel your anger," said Jasmine.

Delilah made an unsuccessful effort to convince

them that she was not at all angry.

"We can help you release," said Fillmore as he moved behind the couch and began massaging Delilah's shoulders.

Jasmine took one of Delilah's hands and commenced acupressure. Expressing their deep need and desire for Delilah's expertise, they offered her their solemn pledge that she would soon be free from her agitation.

It was late afternoon in the New Mexican desert, and the sun was low in the sky. In the middle of a man-made rock circle, sat Susan, Luke, and Gervasio El Brujo, who was preparing an organic substance while sharing some spiritual Native American philosophy. It is possible, he suggested, to exist on many levels at once if you open yourself to experiencing the journey to it's fullest. Handing the peyote to Susan and Luke, he motioned for them to ingest it.

"You may become stomach sick. Often this illness is violent. Do not be embarrassed or afraid. If the illness comes, it will also go. You will then transform. This is a personal experience. Be aware of your animal spirit. Lie down now and look to the heavens," he said. "Embrace the unknown."

Susan and Luke were flat on their backs, looking up toward the steel blue sky. Susan's head began to spin. The clouds above whirled around and around. She felt an intense sexual heat that turned into agitation. The contents of her stomach came hurling out. Violent projectile vomiting morphed into a helpless weakened state that brought her to her hands and knees. In a clear pool of her own vomit, she saw her reflection. A magnificent Grey wolf.

As the wolf, she stood alone atop the ridge of a grand canyon. The sinking of the sun, the chill of the air, the endless expanse of the canyon, gave her an overwhelming feeling of euphoria. Her Grey wolf eyesight was sharp and keen. She spied, clear across the canyon, a majestic buffalo; proud, strong, and attractive. As the sun sank into the canyon, a great flood of tears flowed from her eyes. Tears of joy. Tears of transformation.

Naked, on all fours, she was ridden from behind by Luke, the buffalo. El Brujo was gone, as was the sun, and all gave way to an infinity of stars and mystery. Susan, the wolf, let out a loud and joyous howl.

The sounds emanating from the house in Santa Fe were a bit different. Fillmore, naked, behind the leather couch, was massaging a pair of bare female shoulders, making wounded, moaning sounds, as he humped the back couch. Lowering his hands onto bare breasts, he attacked the furniture with even more mortifying aggression.

Delilah, hiding behind a partially closed door, was watching in silent horror. Jasmine and Fillmore then began their own howls of commingling, sending a terrified Delilah running into the new-age night.

#

Inside Elliot Irving's cabana, a naked Chastity was bent over the end of the bed, emitting squeals of honeymoon joy. A naked West had her from behind, driving home a fine 'fuck you' to her day-old husband

209

Brandel, and maybe to Hal Davidson too. At the same time, he was feeling a great debt of gratitude to a particular Desperado named Lewis, who on the phone, with little effort, worked Chastity into an aroused hysteria.

In San Francisco, howls of revolution filled the air. After surreptitiously trailing David Middling to the Buena Vista Cafe earlier in the day, Gary Leech had uncovered a clandestine meeting between David, Hunter, and Hugh.

As he recounted the seditious details of David's betrayal to his unsanitary clan, they counted the money from the holiday weekend haul, strategized where to hide it, how to make more, and how to exact revenge on the traitor lawyer. Casus belli. War was imminent.

War was imminent in Mexico too. Elliot flew away on a Sunday evening plane, while West was giving the lowdown to Kip and Will.

He had made a phone call to one of his professors at UC Santa Cruz. The marine biology professor explained that catch-and-release wasn't much better than catch and keep. Not only does the marlin suffer, but it most likely dies from the struggle as well as the wound. West felt that they had been played. He was defiant.

When Hal Davidson approached the trio at their table, the tension was palpable. Hal didn't wait. He went right at West.

"You're here to do a job. You think this is a big game"? Hal said attacking West.

"I do, yes," answered West.

210

Kip pleaded with Hal to keep calm and join them for a drink. Nuh, uh.

"I think your friends have had enough to drink. Check out time is noon tomorrow," said a seething Hal.

West laughed out loud as Hal stomped away from the table. Knowing who would have the last laugh, Hal kept his powder dry.

#

Delilah was ecstatic that the time had come to return to L.A. They were back at the house in Albuquerque, all four of them. J T had been released by the FBI due to the clear fact that his arrest was unwarranted, pun intended, or as he put it "guilty while being red."

Susan wanted to stay longer. News crews from some of the networks were headed that way, and she thought it would be a good idea to assist Luke, if you know what I mean?

The oil companies got word of the increasing media attention, and as a result, backed off, and temporarily halted their drilling. Delilah correctly surmised that it was best to transfer the spotlight to J T, Luke, and the house of resisters. This was their fight. It should be their faces in front of the cameras.

The return flight to L.A. didn't depart until seven that evening, which meant that she could spend the day strategizing with J T, and Susan had time to 'assist' Luke.

It wasn't even noon yet, and the Mexican sun was already scorching the Earth. West and Kip, surrounded by vagabond luggage, were standing in the hotel lobby. Kip was making every effort to disguise his sadness.

The quick visit by Elliot Irving promised to be fortuitous for GreenPlanet. Both the Desperados and Linda Paloma expressed a willingness to help out when their respective schedules permitted. Kip told West that Elliot "took a liking to him," which he said, was "a rare and a very good thing."

Behind the closed office door belonging to Hal Davidson, loud, combative voices could be heard, steadily increasing in volume and intensity. West looked to Kip for a clue. His eyes asked 'everything okay?'

When the office door finally opened, out came Will, red-faced and sweating.

"We're good to go," he said.

Kip waved over a waiting taxi, and the lads threw their shit in the trunk. After two rounds of bear hugs, West and Will jumped in the back of the cab.

"Thanks for Mexico," said West.

"You coming home soon?" asked Will knowing that he was not.

"Vaya con Dios," Kip said as he formally blessed them with the sign of the cross.

As the taxi pulled away from the hotel, onto the empty highway, a cocktail waitress handed Kip a fresh drink. Raising his non-drink hand high into the air, he formed a farewell peace sign, put his arm around the waitress, and back into the bar he retreated out of necessity.

At the Cabo airport, West and Will were viewing, with much emotion, a Boeing 727 passenger plane with the Mexicana logo on its side, speed down the runway toward the cliff's edge.

The plane began to lift off the tarmac just as it ran out of runway. After a brief dip down, then back up, then wheels up, it was northward toward the United States. It was their flight; the only flight out for the next three days. They weren't on it.

There were five of them. West, Will, Max, Erin, and Cisco. Sitting on a dilapidated concrete slab, under a blazing hot sun, they were in the middle of the Mexican desert with no water and no shade for miles in any direction. Everyone sat atop their luggage, donning some form of head wear to protect them from the midday tropical sun. Cisco was there to see them off and to serve as intermediary.

The four outcasts, at the last minute, had been bumped from the last flight out of Cabo. They were told that a plane would pick them up in two hours, at a desert landing strip, and fly them to La Paz where they could purchase a ticket back to the United States. Take it or leave it. They took it, and now were feeling incredibly naive and stupid.

"We're going to die," said a withering West.

"Don't worry. They said a plane would be here in two hours," said Erin.

"Jesus, Erin. Look around you. No plane is coming to the middle of fucking nowhere!" cried Max.

"You pissed off the big boss," said Cisco.

213

West looked at Will, who was looking down at a lizard crawling over his shoe. Erin immediately looked at Max with knowing daggers in her eyes. Cisco wiped the sweat off of his brow. Everyone had the same light bulb moment.

The big boss. Hal Davidson. Mr. Hal, as Cisco called him. Even though they all had paid tickets in hand for the departing flight, Mr. Hal made a phone call ensuring that they would not get on that plane. After all, he was the most powerful man in Cabo.

West concluded that he was to blame, a result of his open defiance of the oil magnate. He was correct. That certainly played the biggest part in Hal's decision, but Will sealed the deal when he refused to pay the $1975 bar tab that Hal presented to him at the last minute.

West, feverish and giggling, wanted to know if the tab included Kip's drinks? "No," Will said, "It was just the two of us." Manic West was cheering and applauding, feeling the consumption of two-thousand dollars in booze, in and of itself, was a great achievement on their part. A great 'fuck you' to Mr. Hal.

Erin wanted to know what, exactly, it was that they did to deserve banishment?

"Mr. Hal say your husband is a shit dip," said Cisco.

"Dip shit?" asked Erin.

"Si. Dip shit! Dip shit!" exclaimed a beaming Cisco.

As time passed, and the sun was taking its toll, panic set in. Max jumped to his feet and gathered their luggage. Erin protested that she was not going anywhere. It was his fault that they were in this mess, and he could go without her. Cisco was listening with all of his might as he scanned the sky for flying objects. Before any of the others could see or hear anything, he spotted the twin prop DC-3 heading their way.

"Todos se levantan," he said. "Everyone up."

Seemingly out of nowhere, the old plane circled, then landed on the hard desert floor, pulling up next to the sunburned, beleaguered, and bewildered quintet.

With the twin engines running, the rear door of the plane opened, and out jumped a Mexican guy, wearing jeans, cowboy boots, an old, worn-out Aeromexico shirt, and a holstered Colt Forty-Five.

He waved at everyone to hurry up and get on the plane. When all were on board, and all luggage had been thrown into an improvised baggage compartment, the pilot revved up the twin engines to maximum, turned 180 degrees, and taxied back in the direction that it had landed. At top speed, the plane barely got off the ground. Chugging, it climbed with great effort into the sky, heading north, out of sight, supposedly to La Paz. From the desert floor, Cisco, laughing, waved a fond farewell to his outcast shit-dips and his outlaw compadres.

#

West and Will were fried. They had succeeded in their escape from Mexico and were in the process of boarding an evening flight from Albuquerque to Los Angeles.

In La Paz, they were very fortunate to get the last

215

two seats on any plane leaving for the United States. Unable to go directly to L.A., they had no choice; it was either head to Albuquerque and buy another ticket there, or wait two more days in La Paz.

As they located and settled into their seats, voices directly across the aisle spoke to them.

"West?" said Delilah.

"Will?" said Susan.

Delilah and Susan were seated in the same row, across the aisle. They all gave each other confused and exhausted 'what the fuck' looks. West threw four drink fingers in the air, and they immediately rearranged their seating, Delilah switching seats with Will. Let the games begin.

Will, after hearing why his two colleagues were on the plane in Albuquerque, and the dangerous rogue activities they had been engaged in, began to lecture Susan, who was having none of it. She made it very clear that, except for Kate, the GreenPlanet women were not being treated with the respect and the compensation that they deserved. They were valuable to the organization, just as valuable as he and West. It was about time that their service was properly acknowledged. Will knew that she was absolutely correct, and realizing the error of his ways, changed his tune and agreed with Susan. He promised that he would speak with Kate and champion their cause.

A loud Delilah was breaking up with a defensive West. He was demanding to know how he could be dumped if they were never officially together?

"I had a dream that you fucked some girl in Mexico," she said.

"What difference does it make?" he said. "You're dumping me."

"You did fuck some girl in Mexico!" she cried out.

The drinks continued to flow, right along with the animated conversations. Periodically, they played musical chairs in order to have a go at someone else. Eventually, all ran out of steam as they flew exhausted through the night back to the city of angels.

The foursome shared a taxi back to the GreenPlanet office where their individual cars were parked. Everyone was in ruins, and badly in need of sleep.

From the parking lot, they could see that the office lights were on bright. Not a good sign. They also noticed that said parking lot was unusually full for a Memorial Day night, and then they recognized Kate's rental car. "No one goes home just yet," said Will.

Standing in the office doorway, they found a wild scene. Kate was in the middle of the office barking orders to a small platoon of volunteers. Someone they didn't recognize was manning the Telex machine, typing madly away. Phones were lit up, and one of the volunteers was crying. When Kate saw the quartet in the doorway, she threw her hands into the air.

"There you are! Bloody hell, I've been trying to get hold of all of you," she said very relieved to see them all.

The news came fast. The Gaia had been sunk. An explosion. It was deliberate. She was sitting at the bottom of San Francisco Bay. One GreenPlanet member was dead. Gary Leech from Seattle.

Susan replaced the volunteer that was sitting at

her desk; Delilah headed for hers. Will took over the Telex and set about to read all of the news coming out of San Francisco. Kate intercepted West as he was heading to his desk.

"Looks like you got some sun," she said.

"A bit," he replied.

"You ready?" she asked. "We need your 'A' game."

West took another look around at all of the late night Memorial Day mayhem. He understood that this was exactly where he should be, and exactly what he should be doing. Sleep be damned.

FIRE IN THE HOLE

It was high noon. Standing room only. The office was overflowing with reporters, cameramen, and volunteers. Kate, Will, Delilah, and Susan were standing off to the side, next to the strategy board. Connor Kilkenny was at the and center of a media mob that jockeyed for position .

A makeshift podium was set up in front of Kate's doorway where West was addressing the press. Steady and somber, he spelled out the facts as he knew them.

Two limpet mines exploded several minutes apart. The first mine blew a small hole in the mid starboard side of the ship. It caused minor damage but was dramatic enough to scare most of those on board off of the ship. The second mine was deadly, creating a massive hole in the stern. The boat took on water fast. GreenPlanet member Gary Leech didn't make it out.

West said that they were waiting for the official cause of death. He didn't want to speculate, but did so anyway; perhaps it was a combination of the blasts and drowning? Best to wait for the findings of the experts.

When asked by reporters "Who did this?" "Which one of GreenPlanet's adversaries would be so bold?" "Who could pull off such a sophisticated attack?" "Would you say it has all the earmarks of an unfriendly government?" West deflected.

"Gary was a passionate advocate for the proper care and treatment of our Mother Earth. His death was senseless. His death was criminal. Our thoughts and prayers go out to his family. We, too, were his family," said a sincere-faced West making sure not to look in the direction of Delilah and Susan.

He was asked if the Los Angeles whale savers were now concerned about their own safety? Did they still plan to set sail in July? What was the name of their boat? Where was it docked?

Having no good answers for any of these questions, he looked to Kate for an assist. Unfortunately for him, she was no help, leaving him to sink or swim on his own.

Before he had a chance to go under, a booming voice exploded from the back of the room.

"They've got a boat, mister. She's a terror. Nobody sinks her, that's for sure. The Maggie May, that's her name. Shakespeare Jones, that's my name, and I'm her captain, and we set sail end of July, and it's none of your damn business where she sits," announced the always larger than life Shakespeare Jones.

As the cameras swung around in the direction of Captain Jones, West again looked to Kate, who was nodding in agreement with the captain. So there you go. Looks like they have a boat. Looks like it's full steam ahead. Let's hope she is what the captain says she is.

Shakespeare had completely upstaged West, stealing all of his attention from the members of the media, which was just fine with West because he was having a hard time believing his eyes. At the back of the room, in a corner, stood Lucinda. Foosball-table-confiscating, cat-kidnapping, former love of his life, Lucinda. She made eye contact with him, smiling a wounded smile.

After the room had cleared, and the press had departed, West ushered her into Will's office and closed the door. As you might imagine, it was awkward. He was puzzled. Why was she there? Where's Nordqvist? Austin not a utopia? Come back to tell me that you're gone?

"You're a real big shot now, eh?" said Lucinda.

"I've found a purpose," West replied.

"Oh, a purpose, look at you," mocked Lucinda.

West could have engaged in a battle royale, but he wasn't inspired. He half-heartedly wished her well, and said that he needed to get back to work.

"Which one out there is the new girlfriend?" she said.

Five hours of sleep was not enough. The transition from being deposited in the Mexican desert to die, to flying home with a ranting and raving Delilah, to the news of the sunken Gaia and the deceased Leech, to the ex-girlfriend trying to re-enter the mix. Five hours absolutely did not cut it.

He peered at Lucinda, and oddly he didn't recognize her anymore. She was a stranger. She was an alien.

"I need a place to stay," she said.

West's brain exploded. It literally exploded. Pieces of brain were all over Will's floor. He didn't look at her. He didn't say anything. He opened Will's office door ever so gently, stepped out, closed the door on Lucinda ever so gently, and disappeared into the mystic. You can't make this stuff up.

The Gaia? It was resting on the bottom of the bay, and the mood in the San Francisco office was grim. Sleeping bags, blankets, pillows, dirty clothes and debris covered every square inch of space. Stale cigarette and pot smoke polluted the air. The rag-tag inhabitants of the Gaia were now occupying the office. Internal fear and unrest were in the air.

Earlier that morning, Jonah and Kai were paid a visit by FBI Special Agent Don Harbison. According to agent Harbison, the sinking of the Gaia was deliberate. The FBI was positive it wasn't the Russians, and it wasn't the Japanese. They were placing their bets on the French DGSE.

Jonah theorized, correctly, that the French got nervous and reacted to all of the anti-nuclear talk coming out of the Los Angeles office. He asked Harbison if France was about to conduct more atomic bomb tests in the South Pacific, to which Harbison declined to comment.

"That's all you got for us?" said an unappreciative Kai.

"I shouldn't have told you that. Let's face it fella's, your crowd isn't real popular with us either," said Agent Harbison.

"How do we know the FBI didn't do this?" Jonah said with great stupidity.

A very important lesson to learn, as soon as possible in this life, is when to shut the fuck up. Across the board, GreenPlanet people consistently failed in this area.

"What you meant to say was 'how do we know the

222

CIA didn't do this'? You don't. See you, boys," he said walking off and spitting into the water above the submerged Gaia.

Crammed into Jonah's small cubicle–for privacy from the grumbling groundlings–Jonah, Karma, Kai, and Catty were in emergency session. How do they proceed from here? Except for the peasant slaves, none of the San Franciscans were mourning Gary's death. After all, he was a worthless, disgusting, molesting pig of a human being. What mattered was giving the appearance of mourning his demise.

They needed to encourage their supporters and the general public to mourn him and to be outraged at the cause of his death. They needed to use this opportunity to bring in some badly needed cash, and to keep the wolves at bay, specifically Hunter, from exercising a hostile take-over.

Meanwhile, lawyer David Middling seized this unexpected deadly opportunity with an attempt to convince Hunter to hold off on his plan to shutter the San Francisco office. The San Franciscans were financially and spiritually crippled, and ready to make a deal, argued David. Hunter should shut down Seattle instead. Like the Hawaiian office, they would never see it coming.

"The public is going to want to send money to the San Francisco office. They're still high profile. The sinking of the Gaia is international news. No Gaia insurance money will be coming their way because they're idiots, and they let the policy lapse months ago," he said. "Offer the key players coveted spots on the whale voyage. In return, they quash any attempt at revolution, and assist in shutting down the office in Seattle. You get control of the money, shrink the tribe, and regain absolute power in exchange for their fifteen minutes of fame and temporary survival," he concluded with fingers crossed.

Hunter, painful as it was for him to compliment David fucking Middling on anything, agreed. It was brilliant. Now was the perfect time to create a scaled down, controllable, GreenPlanet USA. Seeing that most of the players were already in San Francisco, he would arrange for some hand-picked Los Angeles representatives to join them for a restructuring pow-wow. Soon! While there was still, literally, blood in the water. Bloody brilliant.

#

Kate was waiting for West. As soon as he emerged from Will's office, she reclaimed and rerouted him into her office, congratulating him on an excellent press conference performance. Something was up. Kate doesn't compliment West. She could see that he was ready to drop so this needed to be quick.

"Just finished a chat with Hunter. Going to be a big pow-wow in San Francisco tonight. Representatives from each American office will meet with he and Hugh to discuss a new way forward. A restructuring, if you will," said Kate.

West commenced shadow boxing, assuming incorrectly that she was about to send him to San Francisco tout suite. She was not.

"Will and Delilah are on the way," she said stopping him in his tracks.

"Which brings me to my next bit of news," she continued. "Kip won't be returning. I'm staying on permanently as his replacement."

She waited for the news to sink in, knowing how fond West had become of Kip. He just spent the weekend with him. Kip didn't say anything about this. He seemed to be doing well. West was crushed, confused, and exhausted. He fell onto the couch.

"The past twenty-four hours," he said in defeat. "No sleep. Left to die in the Mexican desert. Delilah hates me. The bad guys sank our boat. Now you're telling me no more Kip?"

Kate asked about the young woman in Will's office. Was there a problem? What did she want? Could she, Kate, be of any assistance? Ah! An ex-girlfriend. Ex as in former? As in no more? Are you sure?

West was sure. Kate told him to go home. Sleep. A lot. Recharge the battery. She needed him to be in fighting shape. There was an upcoming celebrity tennis tournament, and a benefit surfing contest that needed his attention. They had a boat that needed a test drive and a crazy boat captain that needed analysis. Go home. Sleep. Now.

#

West, his eyes barely open, was driving south on Laurel Canyon Blvd. As always, he had the radio on and tuned to 94.7 KWOT. Connor was on the air doing his wildly popular 'Fish Report With A Beat'.

"And finally friends, Huntington Beach reports in with a dozen scrod, an ample supply of ling cod, several needle-nose garfish, a couple of sexy south of the border tuna, if you know what I mean?, a white

225

powder flat-nosed shoveler, and Foxy's favorite, one impressive blue-veined trouser trout. Whoo-ya. So there you have it. That does it for this 'fish report with a beat'. My name is Connor Kilkenny and we are 94.7 KWOT Los Angeles. Whoo-ya to ya."

'Smokin', by the band Boston, came blasting through the speakers as West closed his eyes, chuckled, lost himself in the music, and slammed into the rear end of the stopped car in front of him. Startled and shaken, he stumbled his way to the driver of the other vehicle, a young woman, unruffled, sitting patiently, waiting for him to explain, apologize, and plead guilty.

She gave him the once over, making sure that he wasn't a threat, and then she opened her door and got out. Walking to the back of her car to inspect the damage, she noticed West's GreenPlanet t-shirt. She pointed at it.

"That's a humpback whale," said West.

"Megaptera Novaeangliae. A rorqual," she replied.

"That's exactly right," said a surprised and suddenly attracted West.

He introduced himself. She said her name was Melanie. He started to chat her up.

"This isn't a date, it's a car accident," she said as she inspected the minor damage to her car. She decided to let it go. Getting back into her car, she started it up and leaned out the window.

"How can I get a hold of you?" asked an interested West.

She again pointed at his shirt.

"The pectoral fins are too short," she said as a

matter of fact. "Your car is in shambles."

West watched Melanie drive away. The front end of his little VW bug was indeed in shambles, just like the direction of his life. Would he survive all of this madness? Was Melanie sent to him like Delilah had been? He had great doubt.

The back of the El Camino was full of surfboards when it pulled up in front of the Eaton house. West fell out of the passenger side, reached through the window, shook hands with the driver, and sent the Chevy on its way.

Dragging his worn-out ass through the side gate to the back of the house, he traipsed past the pool and the tennis court on his way to the front door of the guesthouse. With just enough strength remaining, he put the key into the door, pushed it open, ripped off his shirt, headed straight for the unmade bed, fell face down, and immediately passed out.

#

Speeding north, away from the city of angels, was Will's 1963 silver Mercedes Coupe. The brilliant California sunshine reflected and sparkled off of the polished silver paint, requiring the darkest of Wayfarers to shield him from the blinding light.

As if the car had a mind of its own, it weaved in, out, and by the slower moving, law-abiding vehicles. Delilah fished a couple of freezing beers from a cooler between her legs. Handing one to Will, she placed hers on the back of her neck before drinking it down in one go.

She tried, in vain, to talk about West, but Will

didn't want to talk about West. She wondered what they would encounter in San Francisco, and Will knew what they would encounter in San Francisco. Chaos. Hostility. She asked how things went in Mexico? Were there any girls down there? He couldn't recall. She finally decided to give it a rest. It felt good to be flying up the road on the California coast. It felt good to be young, in the middle of a great adventure. It felt good. Right?

#

Rocky was crying. Good tears. Emotional release tears. A large, raucous protest was underway in front of City Hall. Harvey Milk was addressing the crowd about Proposition 6 a.k.a. The Briggs Initiative, and Rocky was in the crowd holding a sign that read: SAVE ANITA BRYANT'S CHILDREN-NO ON 6. He listened hard to every word Harvey had to say.

"I was raised in a straight household, by straight parents, in a straight neighborhood. My friends were heterosexual. Everyone on television was heterosexual. The culture preached to me every day the evils of and horrors of not being heterosexual. My teachers were straight too, I guess. How would I know? They were teaching and I was learning. So, how is it then that I, you, we are different from the others? We didn't choose. We were not influenced or brainwashed or corrupted by teachers with a straight agenda. It just doesn't work that way!" preached Harvey to a great roar from the jubilant crowd.

Rocky looked at all of the people, at his new surroundings, at his newly found place in life, and like

228

Delilah, he felt good. It seemed right. It made sense. For less than a day.

After a long day of protesting, and an equally long evening of barhopping celebrations, Rocky, carrying his protest sign, staggered and stumbled up Polk Street trying to remember where his friend's apartment was located. He was singing and weaving, completely unaware of the three thugs blocking his path. He walked right into the biggest one.

"Watch where you're walking Nancy," he growled at Rocky.

Rocky straightened up and looked him in the eye. Before he had a chance to say anything, three of his ribs were shattered by a vicious blow from a baseball bat wielded by one of the others. He hadn't even hit the ground when the big guy kicked him in the jaw, breaking it. Writhing in pain, blood pouring from his mouth, the third Neanderthal grabbed the protest sign and beat Rocky into unconsciousness.

"Guess I'm gonna have to de-faggot my bat," the big guy said to his laughing friends.

He then pointed at his partner in crime who was removing money from Rocky's pants pockets.

"Put it back. Now. This isn't a fucking robbery; it's a hate crime. What the fuck's wrong with you?"

The money was begrudgingly replaced, like a pillow, under Rocky's bleeding head, and then the three monsters, in no apparent hurry, strolled away down Polk Street, leaving Rocky to expire.

You couldn't tell if he was dead or alive. West, that is. He hadn't moved an inch, still passed out on the bed of the guesthouse. The slightly ajar front door opened wide as sixteen-year old Hadley Eaton peaked her head in to have a look around. Without turning on a light, she could see West asleep and shirtless on the bed.

Closing the door behind her, she made a quick survey of the room, searching for any available contraband. With no drugs or booze in sight, she tried the refrigerator only to find it empty except for one lonely six-pack of beer. Grabbing a beer, then covering it with her shirt to muffle the sound, she popped it open, drank, and pondered.

Up close to the sleeping West, and with the slightest touch, she brushed the back of his neck, moving her finger down the middle of his back. Nothing. He was out cold. Facing him, she unbuttoned her shirt and opened it as if he was watching this private show. Allowing the shirt to fall to the floor, she seductively removed her shorts.

Hadley crawled into bed next to an unsuspecting West and snuggled up next to him. Her eyes open, she waited to see if he would come to life. He didn't. This felt good, though. For a while she could be his girl, in his bed, her skin touching his. Maybe, when he woke up, he would, you know? She closed her eyes and dreamt of what could be.

Kate and Susan were lost in the vast boat jungle known as the Los Angeles Harbor. Late for an appointment with Shakespeare Jones and his beloved Maggie May, they decided to enter a seedy dock bar, The Yardarm, to ask for help.

A better name for The Yardarm would be The Shit Hole. The interior was dark, smelly, and ugly. It was adorned with assorted mismatched tables and chairs, a cheaply made, unappealing wooden bar, with a dozen vinyl bar stools. On the wall above the bar was a plastic twenty-foot replica of a Great White shark. Elsewhere, on the walls, were old life-preservers, photos of ships, an old wooden steering wheel, and a huge rusty anchor. What was once, many years ago, a pool table, was now a fluid-stained, felt-ripped disaster of a pool table.

Three salty dogs, 'The Captain', 'Jimmy', and 'Doctor' sat drinking rotgut liquor and eating Slim Jims. No one was behind the bar when the two women entered. The three men turned to see who was stupid enough to invade their territory.

Kate, in her very proper British accent, inquired if the gentlemen might be able to point them in the correct direction. They were looking for Mr. Jones and the Maggie May.

The old men got a kick out of their cantankerous old friend being referred to as 'Mr. Jones'. Doctor rudely pointed to the door and said the correct direction was "back where you came from." The Captain asked if she was a "red-coat," and said stupid things like "pip-pip," and "cheerio," and called her

231

"Your Majesty." All in all, they were acting like complete asses so Susan tore into them.

"What's your problem, asshole?" she screamed at The Captain. "You got a problem we need to fix?" she directed to Doctor. "Hey, I asked you a question!" she yelled at both of them.

Everyone was startled by her outburst and boldness. Doctor and The Captain stared down into their drinks. Kate, caught off guard, let Susan take the reins, while Jimmy, silent up until now, stepped in to make peace.

"Sorry. No harm meant. Please accept our apologies," he said to the feisty Susan. "You say you're looking for the Maggie May?"

She was not ready to move on.

"They need to apologize to my friend Kate," she said pointing at Doctor and The Captain.

Jimmy, although hesitant, agreed, looking to his compatriots, shaking his head 'yes'. The Captain and Doctor mumbled embarrassed apologies into their highball glasses, and Kate accepted them with grace.

"This ain't no place for women," said The Captain.

"Then maybe you should assist us instead of being rude and mean," Susan fired back.

From that moment forward, everything changed. Doctor and The Captain offered to personally escort them to the Maggie May. Jimmy, who turned out to be the owner, bartender, cook, and dishwasher, suggested that they first have a drink, on him, as a mea culpa.

The old men jumped up and offered the women their seats, and Susan and Kate were savvy enough to

232

accept. Kate told The Captain that he was welcome to refer to her as 'your majesty' any time he wished. Susan complemented Doctor on the beautiful parrot adorning his silk Hawaiian shirt. The rotgut gin-and-tonics even tasted good.

Two drinks and forty-five minutes later, the five of them, joined by Captain Shakespeare Jones, were pulling up the bow lines and pushing the Maggie May away from the dock and out into the harbor. The placid waters of Los Angeles harbor turned into the much more challenging theatre of the blue Pacific. Shakespeare took stock of his new, apprehensive crewmembers.

"She'll only need a couple of hours to show you what she can do!" he proclaimed. "Here we go!"

The Maggie May may look like a worn-out, old, rusty, bucket of bolts, but looks can be deceiving. She's lightning quick and ready for action.

Kate was training at the helm with instructor Shakespeare at her side as the boat raced effortlessly through the choppy seas. The Captain was teaching sailor knots to Susan, while Doctor was manning the radio and radar. Jimmy, below decks, was in the engine room, keeping her humming along. Make no mistake; the Maggie May was ready and able for whatever waited on the horizon. Shakespeare was spot-on. She was an a terror.

If you think about it, the only proper thing to do after a very successful afternoon test driving your new boat, and arriving at the realization that you've also found your ship's captain, was retreat to the Chimney Sweep for some celebratory cocktails. In fact, it was

Kate's idea to do so. No argument from Susan.

Kate was absolutely thrilled and delighted that their new 'save the whales' vessel performed so well. Thrilled, delighted, and relieved. She would pass along the great news to Hunter, knowing that it would give him even greater leverage heading into the all-important showdown in San Francisco. He would be as pleased with her as she was with Susan.

Even though Connie was 'on duty', she jumped at the chance to join Susan and Kate for more than one round of scorpions. Kate, however, would be required to play two-dimensional chess, concurrently conducting two completely different conversations, one with Connie and one with Susan.

Connie wanted to know all about Kate's background. English Literature at St. Ann's College-Oxford sounded very impressive. Had she ever read Lolita, because Connie just loved that book? That girl was just a child, but she knew how to handle herself. What do you mean he died last year? That old lech was a real person? Oh, Nabakov died last year. I see. Nabakov was Russian, right, so why do they call it English literature? Had Kate ever been married? Boyfriend? Kept woman?

At the same time, in Kate's other ear, Susan needed to talk money. Salaries, to be specific. Was Kate receiving a salary? Didn't she think that Delilah and she, too, deserved to be paid? She had bills and rent to pay. The women should be treated with more respect. Equal to the men. Certainly, Kate must agree.

Kate did agree. She had already spoken to Hunter about this very topic and was given the green light to put all of the main players on a salary that would ensure their continued, enthusiastic participation in the organization. That list included Susan and Delilah. Susan was over the moon. More scorpions were in order. It was all coming together. She could feel it.

Kate also informed Susan of her sincere intention to make things good with Delilah. With the impending voyage on the horizon, everyone needed to be simpatico. Everyone needed to be drama free. West? Did you hear that? Drama free.

#

He didn't hear a thing. He was still out cold, sleeping next to a mostly naked sixteen-year-old, and his ex-girlfriend was at the front door of the main house looking for him.

It's not exactly clear as to how Lucinda tracked him down, but she had her ways, and here she was lying to Cassandra, telling her that there was an emergency, and that she had come to fetch West to take him to a dear friend in need. No drama about to happen here.

Cassie took Lucinda around back, to the guesthouse, which was dark and seemingly lifeless. When there was no response to her knock on the door, she opened it and flipped on the light. In the bed, their bottom halves covered by bed sheets, West and Hadley were wrapped in each other's arms, West still in a deep sleep. Cassandra screamed, ripping the bed sheets off of the two sinners.

It's one thing if she, Cassie, slips unnoticed into the guesthouse and has her way with a naked West, but it's quite another, totally unacceptable thing, for her daughter to do the same.

Hadley wasn't at all fazed by the theatrics of her mother. She was beaming. This was kind of fun for her. She loved the fact that her mother and the unknown woman concluded that she and West had, well, you know. It made her feel grown up and desirable.

West, semi-conscious, was making a concerted effort to shake the cobwebs out, and wasn't completely sure that he wasn't dreaming. Lucinda? Cassie? Hadley?

"Hadley Eaton! Get your underage ass out of that bed right now!" screamed Cassandra.

"Don't be so dramatic, mother," said Hadley nonchalantly getting out of bed.

Cassandra smacked West on the side of his head and told him to get up and get out. She told him, as of that moment, he no longer lived there. No more tennis lessons. No more hand jobs in the shower. Get out! It then became crystal clear to him that he was not dreaming.

He tried to explain. He had been in a car accident with a girl named Melanie. He swore nothing had happened with Hadley. At the office, Kate instructed him to go home and get in bed. How did Lucinda know where to find him? Well played. That should set things right.

Cassandra grabbed Hadley by the hair with one hand and Lucinda by the arm with the other hand, and marched them both out of the guesthouse and away from a very dazed and confused and not exactly drama-free West.

Speaking of drama free. The pow-wow in San Francisco was underway. Many utility tables were arranged to create a very large rectangle in the center of the room directly beneath the huge whale balloon.

Seated at the head of the table was Hunter. On his right sat Hugh, and on his left sat David Middling. David had assured Hunter and Hugh that Jonah, Karma, and Catty were on board with the backroom plan to shutter the Seattle operation. He said that they should not be alarmed or concerned if the trio's public behavior was hostile to them. It was all a show.

Jonah and Karma were at the table representing San Francisco; the banished Kai Klein and Sunset represented the defunct Hawaii office; Catty Slur and Jade East were representing Seattle, and Delilah and Will spoke for Los Angeles.

In honor of the late Gary Leech, a seat at the table was offered to a representative of the San Francisco volunteer corps. Paul Preston a.k.a. Paul Revere, a longhaired, disheveled, garlic-eating anarchist had been chosen by the groundlings to represent them.

Two-dozen or more volunteers, canvassers, and freeloaders occupied a designated viewing space away from the principal's table. The tension in the air was palpable. Hunter spoke first.

"In the spirit of ohana, Karma has been kind enough to volunteer to take the minutes of the meeting, therefore she will be afforded extra time to speak if, and when, she feels she needs it. Those at the table that have a vote are the following: Myself

237

and Hugh Simon from International, Jonah from San Francisco, Catty Slur from Seattle, and Delilah Dean from Los Angeles. Kai and Sunset, from the former Hawaii office, have been invited to discuss the issues at hand, but will not be allowed to vote. Jade will not be allowed to vote; Will does not have a vote, and David does not have a vote. He is here to answer any legal questions that we may have. In honor of our friend Gary Leech, Paul Revere has been invited to join our discussions, but he will not have a vote," said Hunter.

At once, voices cried out from the peanut gallery. They demanded that Paul Revere be allowed to vote. They began chanting Gary, Gary, Gary! The strong odor of pot smoke filled the air.

Karma chimed in, accusing Hunter of his real intentions, the closing of the San Francisco office. Jonah moved to disallow the representative from Los Angeles the right to vote. Kai seconded the motion to no avail because he didn't have a vote, so Catty seconded the motion for him, and Hunter blew a fuse.

"Can everybody just settle the fuck down? It's too early for this shit. You've been invited to witness the meeting, not to disrupt it. If this isn't possible we will clear the room. Paul has generously been invited to express your views. He doesn't have a vote. End of discussion. Now, Jonah, that's an improper motion. You cannot take away the Los Angeles vote. Everybody, please, take a big deep breath. We have a lot of ground to cover tonight," Hunter barked.

Paul Revere knew precisely what to do.

"Gary can't take a deep breath. He's dead," said a

very faux emotional Paul.

The peanut gallery went nuts, pun intended. Whooping and hollering, stomping their feet and chanting Gary's name.

Hunter was prepared. He reached down and pulled a starter pistol out of his bag, raised it above his head, and fired. The concussion from the pistol blew to pieces the inflatable whale hanging above their heads.

The entire room fell silent as bits and pieces of plastic whale debris fell onto the table and floor. The whale's head fell directly in front of Paul Revere who paused, then, with much pomp and circumstance, placed it on his own head. The crowd erupted once again. Raising his hand for silence, Paul removed the whale head and placed it in front of him. He then began reading a list of demands on behalf of the peanut gallery.

He demanded the Hawaiian office be reinstated immediately, and their stolen funds returned with interest. He insisted this summer's voyage to save the whales depart from San Francisco, not Los Angeles, with a crew made up only of people from the San Francisco and Seattle offices. He demanded that any and all money from the "illegal" L.A. office be seized and deposited into the San Francisco account, and last but not least, he went after Hunter.

"Hunter Mack, lacking the best interest of the organization, for causing financial and reputational harm to the organization, and for illegally closing and opening offices within the organization, shall step down as Executive Director of GreenPlanet International effective immediately," proclaimed Paul to a raucous, revolutionary ovation.

Hunter raised the starter pistol and everyone braced for another explosion.

"I am GreenPlanet! Who the fuck made it possible for every one of you to be here today? This once humble movement has grown into a self-perpetuating, useless, destructive monster! And you? What do you call yourself? Paul Revere? The real Paul Revere had courage. The real Paul Revere was in the fight. What have you ever done? Not a fucking thing! The people that started this organization are honorable; they sacrificed and put themselves in harm's way. I'm here to clean up this giant fucking mess that you've created. This meeting is over!" bellowed Hunter with the pistol held high above his head.

There was a commotion at the back of the room. People were scattering in all directions as two SFPD officers pushed their way through the pot-smoking group toward Hunter. He didn't know it, but they were looking for Delilah. The police said that a friend of hers was in the hospital. He had asked for her by name.

The police officers questioned Delilah and Will about any possible enemies that Rocky might have? If they knew how to get a hold of his family or nearest relative? If they wanted to go to San Francisco General to see him?

In the ICU waiting room, Delilah and Will were greeted by Dr. Darwin Dunn who informed them that Rocky was sedated and sleeping. He had three broken ribs on the right side, a fractured jaw, and several lacerations and bruises. They found some internal bleeding, but no acute damage to any organs.

Eventually, the doctor said, he'll recover, but he would have many difficult weeks ahead of him. Rocky, he said, was able to tell the doctors and the police that three men beat him. It had all of the earmarks of a hate crime.

Dr. Dunn led Delilah and Will down a hallway to a room directly next to the nurse's station. Rocky was sleeping, hooked up to machines, drip bags, and oxygen. He looked like someone that had just been beaten within an inch of his life. Delilah took his hand, held it for a moment, and then she needed to get the fuck out of there. She badly needed some fresh air.

On the way out of the hospital, the doctor asked her if she could come again tomorrow. It would, he said, be very good for Rocky to see her if she was up to it.

Yes. Absolutely. She would be there tomorrow she promised the doctor who had one other request. Supervisor Milk. His office called and wanted to know if it would be permissible for him to pay Rocky a visit within the next few days? The Supervisor somehow became aware of the beating on Polk Street and wanted to personally check on Rocky.

Delilah shook her head 'yes', and cried like a baby as Will put his arm around her, walked her out of the hospital, and back out into the chilly San Francisco night.

#

June 5th. The sinking of the Gaia happened one week ago, but to everyone sitting around the conference table in L.A. it felt like a lifetime ago.

241

Things were happening fast and furious, and Hunter and Hugh were there to spell things out for the L.A. contingent.

After the failed coup attempt by Paul Revere and the groundlings in San Francisco, there were two very productive days of meetings that resulted in what Hugh referred to as the "suspension" of the Seattle office, ultimately concluding in its permanent closing by the end of the month.

Seattle's finances were frozen, their accounts were notified, and the use of the GreenPlanet name was no longer sanctioned. Sound familiar Hawaii? All done under the auspices of downsizing and streamlining.

Catty Slur had been wise enough to exchange her cooperation in the closing of her office for a coveted place on the upcoming whale voyage. Hunter made a similar, private, backroom deal with Paul Revere. Paul, he promised, would be one of the principle Zodiac drivers if he could persuade the anarchists to give up the fight.

It didn't take much arm-twisting from David to convince Jonah and Karma of the advantages of eliminating another office other than their own. Two offices would temporarily remain, San Francisco and Los Angeles. They both would bring in more money and garner more attention.

The scuttlebutt was to continue the plan, in the very near future, to create GreenPlanet USA. Jonah, with a little help from David, immediately pictured himself as the obvious choice to run the entire American operation. When the time came to vote on the closing of the Seattle office it was almost unanimous. Hunter, Hugh, Jonah, and Catty, all voted 'aye'. Delilah, slyly, as a result of secret chats with Hunter, voted 'nay', and then gave a heartfelt speech on the merits of keeping the Seattle family operation up and running. Will didn't even know that one was coming.

When word of this trickled down to the groundlings, Delilah was suddenly looked upon with new eyes, new respect, and new admiration. Excellent grasshopper.

Hunter had learned that French Intelligence came to believe that GreenPlanet had obtained detailed information about their future nuclear bomb tests in the South Pacific. They falsely surmised that GreenPlanet was planning to expose and disrupt those tests.

"So they sunk a ship that was not seaworthy," said Kate.

"Affirmative," said Hunter.

"Never very good at war, were they?" she chided.

Little did the French know that GreenPlanet did have a seaworthy ship. Very seaworthy. Kate and Susan, with great delight, reported to Hunter about their glowing test drive of the Maggie May.

"She flies like the wind. Twenty-five knots with no problem. The Maggie May might look worn out, but she's solid. Internally a beauty," bragged Susan.

"She could use some fresh paint, a heavy duty cleaning, and a winch to launch the Zodiacs," added Kate. "As for Captain Jones, I'd sail into harm's way with him without hesitation."

West reported on the very successful celebrity

tennis benefit, and Delilah one-upped him with the even more successful pro-surfing benefit. The coffers were being filled, and Will reported that more cash was on the way.

He was about to again wine and dine Vanessa Gray Reynolds and Natalie Singer in order to discuss new plans to raise funds via the show-biz world. Tinsel town, he said, was getting excited about the whale voyage.

"Which brings me to the big news of the day. We're not setting sail in July. You have twenty days. June 25th we depart. We have very reliable information that the Russians should be close and within reach at that time. There's a shit-load of work to do between now and then. I hope you all are ready," announced a very serious Hunter.

He could see the anticipation in their faces. He knew what they were thinking. They wanted to know who among them would be part of the crew? Were they about to go to war?

"Anybody here that doesn't want to go? Don't be afraid to speak up. It's not for everyone. It's not a tropical cruise. Anybody? Well then, you're all going. Except for Kate. She needs to be here with the volunteer corps to run the land operation. Any questions?" Hunter asked the stunned group.

There were no questions. Not then. All of a sudden it was real. And sobering. Delilah was the first to make a move. Pushing her chair back from the table, she was about to retreat back to her desk before Kate stopped her. One last piece of business. Kate needed two volunteers; she had already decided who they would be; West and Delilah.

She needed them to travel to Colorado, come morning, to get arrested at the nuclear weapons facility at Rocky Flats. She needed them to join the blockade of the train tracks. It would help the locals get national media attention. Susan immediately protested.

"Hang on! Not so fast. That's my baby. Delilah and I were the ones that met with the Colorado people. We should be on the front lines for this one. No offense to West, but it should be me going, not him," insisted Susan.

Before Kate could outline why she didn't want two women to go, Delilah interrupted her, saying that she didn't want to go. Delilah agreed that Susan should be there. Susan was trusted and had already developed connections. West, she argued, was a GreenPlanet spokesperson that had national face recognition and was best at communicating the drama to the national television audience. He should go. Delilah didn't want to go.

Kate thought about this for a few moments, checked with Hunter who was smiling like the Cheshire cat, and decided this would be the perfect time to bond with Delilah.

"Brilliant. Agreed. West and Susan it is. Give you and I an opportunity to prepare for the Russians. Off we go people! Twenty days! West, Susan, in my office," exclaimed Kate as all leaped into action.

Kate took Delilah to the Whisky A Go-Go. She knew the members of one of the bands that would later take the stage, and thought it would be a fun way for Delilah and her to let their hair down. Loud, high-energy music was her milieu and she felt most comfortable and confident in that world.

Additionally, she always saw the bigger picture. More often than not, she would know the end of the movie before it played out. She knew how adept Delilah was, and if it was her choice to stick around after the voyage, how important she would be to the organization.

Kate was a veteran of the cause. She knew how it took its toll. She knew the dramatic impact the voyage would have on each and every one of the crew. This was a way for her to gauge Delilah's GreenPlanet lifespan, and to attempt to heal any and all battle scars inflicted on Delilah by herself.

Delilah was, if truth be told, looking forward to this evening out with Kate. Her intuition detected a recent apologetic energy in her, and although an apology from Kate wasn't needed or expected, it would be cool if it happened. She was also feeling a newfound peacefulness. The confirmation earlier in the day that she would be a crewmember on the Maggie May had a positive, sedating effect. This is what she had always wanted. It was her dream to be one of the chosen warriors that would track down the killers of whales and personally stop them from carrying out their mission. Nothing mattered more to her.

"I asked you to join me tonight because I feel I

owe you an apology. It was awful of me to storm into your office as if it were mine. You were managing quite nicely. I hope you can accept my sincere apologies," Kate said.

Before Delilah could say anything, a cocktail waitress placed an expensive bottle of champagne and two champagne flutes in front of them. "Compliments of a secret admirer."

"Oh, no, I was afraid this might happen," said a giggling Kate.

The crowd roared as the band appeared and assumed their positions. One of the band members wave at Kate, who raised her champagne glass back in his direction.

"Let's start over. Right now. New beginning," said a relieved and happy Delilah.

"To saving whales," said Kate.

"To saving whales," echoed Delilah.

They clinked glasses and waved at the boys in the band. Delilah was ecstatic that she wasn't headed off to Colorado to get arrested. Cheers to that.

West, on the other hand, was headed off to Colorado to get arrested, but first, he would enjoy a quiet, cannabis-influenced evening with his old tennis pal, Roy Black Elk.

Since being booted from the luxury Eaton guesthouse, West had been sleeping on Roy and Sabrina's living room couch, where he was presently stretched out after a big pot-laced spaghetti dinner. What would he do without Roy?

"The tennis tournament was a huge success and all because of you mi amigo," said West.

"You've told me that a dozen times in the last two hours. Glad it turned out well. No more guilty thank yous, I'm begging you," said Roy.

"I hope Sabrina didn't leave because I'm here. Don't want to cramp your style," West repeated.

"We've already been through that too. She went home to console her mother for turning fifty," said Roy.

Roy wanted answers. He didn't understand why West was going to Colorado to get arrested. He understood the purpose, the important reason others were taking action, but that's not what he was getting at. He was pressing West for clarity. Why? Why was he doing all of this? All of a sudden? Where did this come from?

West knew his pal well, and if it wasn't for the high he was experiencing, he would have seen sooner what was coming. Roy pulled out a small cigarette case and removed a tightly rolled joint. He handed the joint and a Zippo lighter to West.

"Psychological egoism," said Roy. "Nietzsche says that the altruistic person projects themselves onto the object of their compassion."

West groaned a loud groan, fired up the joint, and inhaled a much-needed drag.

"You hadn't been dumped by Lu for twenty-four hours before you threw yourself into this cause. Your feelings of being mistreated to the point of extinction you projected onto the whales and the planet. You're trying to save yourself. Feel good about yourself."

Roy knew what West was thinking. He didn't conjure up Delilah. Delilah was a very real person that

248

he believes was sent to him.

"There's an old Native American saying," continued Roy. 'Certain things catch your eye, but pursue only those that capture your heart.' I too believe that she was sent to you, but maybe not for the reason you think she was," he finished.

West rolled over on his stomach and pulled the cushion over his head. Roy stood, took the lit joint from the ashtray, and turned out the lights. He was worried. His friend would be in jail tomorrow at this time.

#

West and Susan had tried their best to get eight hours of sleep, but their racing minds wouldn't allow that to happen. After an early morning flight to Denver, they found themselves involved in nervous work with their new colleagues at the Rocky Flats protest headquarters.

The small bare-bones office was crowded with people preparing for the upcoming action at the nuclear weapons facility in nearby Jefferson County. West was on the phone talking to a local reporter, while Susan was addressing the media committee. Daniel Ellsberg was giving a television interview, as volunteers made protest signs, and put together information packets. Alone in the corner sat a grey-bearded Allen Ginsberg, writing a poem about deadly plutonium. The energy in the room was tense, as it always tends to be prior to going into battle.

So, what would the rest of the GreenPlanet world be doing as West and Susan prepared to get hauled off to jail?

A drop-dead-gorgeous Southern California day found Will and Natalie Singer poolside at the Beverly Hilton, brunching on jumbo shrimp salads and fresh-juice Mai Tai's. She was proudly, vainly, showing him a recent magazine cover of herself. He had brought her an assortment of GreenPlanet attire and jewelry, and she expressed her excitement and eagerness to do whatever she could to raise money and help the cause. They laughed and frolicked.

Musso and Frank was where you would find Hunter and Kate. They were at the bar eating appetizers and drinking martinis. Their conversation vacillated between casual, fun, and serious. GreenPlanet USA. Whom did they feel was best suited, for their purposes, to run the show? How would they make sure their handpicked person got the job? Who would replace Kate in Los Angeles? Hunter had one eye on Kate, and the other was continually roaming the room for high profile individuals. He was starting to enjoy this town.

Delilah was face down on a massage table and experiencing perhaps the greatest massage of her young life. She, too, had garnered little sleep. Last night's blow out with Kate found her crawling into bed as the sun was coming up. So much damaging drama had recently happened in such a brief period of time; she had the scars to prove it, but at this exact moment, face down on the magic massage table, she was in a state of spiritual blessedness.

In his parent's den, in the most depressing house in Bakersfield, Rocky, battered and bruised, surrounded by cheesy, old wood-paneled walls, and nasty soiled carpeting, sat staring at a pre-historic black and white television, watching mind-numbing game shows, wishing he were anywhere else on Earth. He gladly, exuberantly, would change places with West, or Susan, or Delilah, or Will, or the mailman if he could, but he couldn't.

At the end of the pier, overlooking the sunken Gaia, stood Jonah, Karma, Catty, Kai, Sunset, and Jade. Catty held an urn filled with the ashes of Gary Leech. There were no words as each looked helplessly toward the others for some kind of emotion, some kind of direction. Catty attempted to sprinkle the ashes over the site of his watery grave, but the ashes wouldn't sprinkle. Frustrated and angry, she threw the whole damn thing in the water, gave it the 'fuck you' finger, and stormed away, leaving the others to pretend that they gave a shit.

Will, with talent-agent skill, had slipped away from Natalie and traversed his way over to the nearby Polo Lounge where he and Vanessa Gray Reynolds sipped champagne cocktails and nibbled on caviar and pâté.

The garden was bustling with the rich and famous, as Will reassured a remorseful Vanessa not to worry. No one at the press conference was aware of her LSD altered state. In fact, he said, she was "brilliant, beautiful, and most effective." He stretched the truth, telling her that Hunter referred to her as the most valuable asset in the organization. Conjuring up movie-star tears, she supplied Will with many grateful 'thank-yous', and allowed the waiter to pour her more champagne.

That's what everyone in California was doing. In

Colorado, although the sun was shining, it was bitter cold. West, Susan, and a dozen other protestors crawled through a hole in the security fence located on a remote part of the nuclear weapons facility. As they made their way across the difficult terrain, Susan nosedived, taking a hard fall, badly spraining an ankle.

Undeterred, with one arm around West, and one foot in the air, she and the others continued on toward the train tracks. Once there, they formed a chilly human blockade in the middle of the tracks.

It didn't take long before the protestors were surrounded by private security forces and Jefferson County Sheriff's officers. West and Susan were handcuffed with zip ties and led away into waiting Sheriff's vans. At the county jail, each member of the arrested group went through booking and then were put into a jail cell.

Alone, on a bare metal bunk, in a jail cell on the women's side of the prison, sat Susan, rubbing her sprained and swollen ankle, patiently waiting for what was coming next. She was fine. On the men's side, West had been separated from the other male protestors. The authorities didn't appreciate the fact that he had crossed state lines to break the law in their county, so they assigned him to a cell occupied by a mentally unstable, dangerous, felon. West was too afraid to sit on his bunk, so he remained upright and afraid, staring at the mumbling felon that shared his jail cell.

His cellmate was agitated. He asked West for cigarettes. West didn't have any. Not a good answer. His wife, he said, gave him no choice; he had to stab her. She had been asking for it for a long time. He wanted to know why West was in jail? Rocky Flats? What the fuck was that?

As West proffered an explanation, his cellmate grew more agitated. "Are you telling me that you intentionally got arrested? That's the most fucking stupid thing I've ever heard. Are you some kind of an asshole? Are you in here to spy on me? Trying to get a confession?"

West swore to him that he was not a spy. He apologized for not having any cigarettes, for not being a smoker. He offered to start smoking right away. "Maybe I could bum a cigarette," said West. The wife-stabber hated his guts.

It goes without saying that West was overjoyed to see the guard that came to take him away to the courthouse. Even when they were putting body chains around him he felt relief. One of the officers—chaining the protestors together—gave them angry, firm, and specific instructions on how to behave on their walk from the jailhouse to the courthouse.

"Keep your mouths shut. Not one fucking word. Stay in line. When you enter the courthouse keep your eyes front. Make no eye contact with anyone in the gallery. Wait for the judge to speak to you. Violate any of these instructions and I'll march your asses right back to jail. Got it!" threatened the officer. They got it. West got it.

The courtroom was packed. When the body-chained blockaders were marched into the room, the crowd went wild. There were cheers, hooting, and loud shouts of encouragement. West searched the room looking for Susan. He didn't see her. He didn't see any of the female protestors.

West and the other males were seated on benches at the front of the courtroom. A Rocky Flats lawyer moved next to West and whispered into his ear. He and Susan were in a different kind of legal pickle from the rest of their blockading associates. A more serious situation. Crossing state lines to commit a crime was often determined to be a felony that resulted in prison. He was instructed to let the legal team speak for him. "Don't say or do anything stupid." Stay strong.

#

Outside the Jefferson County jail, West and Susan huddled together on a cold stone bench. The sky was blue, but the air was frigid. They were shaking, not from the cold mountain air, which felt like freedom, but from the experience of what they had just been through. Susan's ankle was mangled, and her emotions were on the surface.

"Yesterday, when you put your arm around me, to help me walk," she said taking his face into her hands and kissing him.

He wasn't the Rock of Gibralter either.

"It really, really sucked in there," he said. "I hope our ride get's here soon; I want to get as far away from here as possible."

Will had sent a message to them. A car would pick them up and take them back to the Rocky Flats office. Sit tight and be patient. When the black Cadillac limousine pulled into the passenger drop-off and pick-up area, stopping right in front of West and Susan, they paid no attention to it. The driver side door opened, and out hopped the limo driver, who walked around to the passenger side and opened the rear passenger door.

"West? Susan? I'm your ride. Hope you haven't been waiting too long," said the driver.

West and Susan were incredulous. This can't be right. The limo driver held open the door as West got into the car. After assisting Susan, the driver was back behind the wheel as the two jailbirds surveyed their comfortable surroundings.

Pulling away from the curb and onto the road leading away from the county jail, the driver checked on his guests. "The mini-bar has just been restocked. Please help yourself," he said.

Susan didn't hesitate. She opened the door to the mini-bar and discovered cold Coors beers and mini-bottles of gin, vodka, bourbon, scotch, and tequila. Grabbing two beers and two tequilas, she handed one of each to West.

"Will went a bit overboard with the car," said a gobsmacked West.

"Speaking of Will. He wanted me to give you a message. He said, 'congratulations, you both have big giant balls,'" said the limo driver. "The car was not his doing. Mr. Irving sent me," he said.

The limo driver reached back through the partition window and handed Susan an envelope. Inside the envelope she found two VIP backstage passes to Folsom Field in Boulder, Colorado. On top of each ticket were the words: DESPERADOS-1978 USA TOUR.

She and West were floored. The limo driver laughed. His passengers tossed back the tequila and cracked open the beers. Out the window they could see the weapons facility and the train tracks in the distance.

"Would you put your arm around me again?" asked Susan.

With a nod of the head, West put his arm around his brave friend as the jailhouse disappeared behind them. Smiling, she wiped moisture from his eyes and went searching for more tequila. They rode quiet for a few miles, content to sip tequila and look out the window.

"Hey! You want some weed?" the limo driver asked with glee.

Sixty thousand people filled the stadium to capacity. It eventually turned into a beautiful warm and sunny day. Spring fever had a tight grip on all. Beach balls and Frisbees flew through the air. The Desperados were about to take the stage. Backstage, West and Susan made new friends. They drank, ate, smoked, and told their story to all that were interested. Susan made it a point to find West's hand if he started to drift too far away. She needed him next to her.

Strangers stopped by to say congratulations. There were the familiar faces of rock stars, and actors, and politicians. A documentary film crew scrambled to capture it all. Everyone and everything were beautiful. While Susan was holding his hand, and telling their story, yet again, to another new friend, West glanced up to see a magnificent bald eagle circling high above the stadium; unrestrained, unencumbered, out of harm's way. Free to go in any direction. Free as a bird.

BE PREPARED TO BLEED

The time had come. A dozen people, including West, Delilah, Will, and Susan, had gathered around the strategy board to view the posted crew list for the imminent 'save the whales' voyage. On the board it read:

MAGGIE MAY CREW

1)SHAKESPEARE JONES-CAPTAIN

2)HUNTER MACK-CAMPAIGN LEADER

3)MATT LINCOLN-FIRST MATE

4)JIMMY-ENGINE ROOM

5)JONATHAN SHORE-MEDICAL

6)NATASHA BELOV-TRANSLATOR

7)JONAH STERN-RADIO COMMUNICATIONS

8)SUNSET-COOK

9)JADE-COOK

10)SUSAN NOBLE-ZODIAC CAMERA #1

11)KAI KLEIN-SHIP CAMERA #2

12)CATTY SLUR-ZODIAC

13)WEST WALKER-ZODIAC

14)DELILAH DEAN-ZODIAC

15)WILL STONE-ZODIAC

16)PAUL REVERE-ZODIAC

17)ARIANNA MARRA-JOURNALIST-ROLLING STONE

18) KARMA PARRISH-CREW

19) AXEL D'ARTAGNAN-CREW

20) TBD-LONDON

21) TBD-LONDON

The excitement was palpable. West couldn't take his eyes off of his name on the board.

Kate emerged from her office and forthwith began to direct traffic. She instructed the staff to take their seats at the table and asked the volunteer army to stand-by for instructions. Before turning to the whale voyage, she asked West and Susan to report on their experience in Colorado.

Susan obliged with a Cliff Note's rundown of what took place, and what was yet to come. She and West would return to Colorado in several months to stand trial with the others. The blockades were garnering great press, locally and nationally. She reported that the GreenPlanet participation was important, and in her estimation, very successful.

As loud applause and cheering erupted from the volunteer corps, Susan leaned over and kissed West on the cheek. This did not go unnoticed by either Delilah or Kate.

"Tomorrow we move most of our people and operations to the Maggie May docked in L.A. harbor. I know what you're thinking, tomorrow is Saturday. It is not. For the next two weeks, there's no such thing as Saturday or Sunday. Every day is Monday. I'll need a couple of people to be here to answer phones, monitor Telexes, etcetera," said commander Kate as she handed out pagers to West, Delilah, Will, and Susan.

"These are for you four. We've an answering service. You can call twenty-four hours a day. If you're paged, stop what you're doing and answer it. Let me repeat that. Stop what you're doing and answer it. West, call KWOT. Get them excited. Get them involved. Whatever it takes."

She instructed Will to stay on top of Vanessa Gray

259

Reynolds and Natalie Singer, no double entendre intended. Keep harvesting the celebrity connections. Money, money, money.

She introduced Axel D'Artagnan, an artist from San Francisco. He would be painting the whale art on the side of the Maggie May, as well as joining the voyage as a crewmember. He lost no time picking Delilah out of the crowd. His gaze was transfixed on her every move.

Delilah was assigned to lead the group of volunteers that would supply the ship with all of its life sustaining needs, a huge and most important task.

Kate also assigned a new, brainy volunteer, Salinger Jayne Daniels, to monitor the International Whaling Commission (IWC) meetings in London, and periodically report to West, which was perfectly fine with her.

Susan would liaison with the San Francisco and London offices until the boat set sail.

"Okay folks. Let's go. Action!" yelled Kate.

Everyone sprang went into motion. Will to his office; West to his desk. Susan waved at all of the volunteers to follow her. Delilah, on the way to her desk, was intercepted by D'Artagnan.

"I'm D'Artagnan," he said thinking she would be interested.

"Delilah," she said uninterested.

"I'm here to..."

"Paint whales. Welcome," she said walking away.

He followed her to her desk. He had decided that since she was in charge of supplies, would be going to the ship every day, and coincidentally, he, too, would be going to the ship every day, that she would be the perfect person to provide him with transportation. He also made some less-than-appreciated comment about how beautiful she was.

Delilah considered this for exactly one second. She saw the stupid grin on his face, and she also saw West spying on her from afar. She thought to herself: "no matter what costume is worn, all men, everywhere, are fools."

The millisecond that D'Artagnan took the hint and walked away, West darted over to replace him at Delilah's side.

"Hey, you want to go to a party with me tonight?" he invited.

"No," said Delilah.

"Hang on, I haven't told you about it," he pleaded.

Delilah pretended to ignore him. Why is he asking her? He could just take his little jail buddy Susan, and she could kiss him on the cheek all night long.

He told her it was a "release party." I'm sure it is, she thought. No, not that kind of release party. Atlantic Records. Some Girls. Rolling Stones.

"It should be way too much fun. Sex, drugs and rock and roll," said West.

Delilah had no clue what he was talking about, and it didn't matter in any event. She was mad at him. In general. And she had no desire to become unmad.

He complimented her on her looks, and for having great success with the surfing contest. "How's old Shane Durban doing?" he asked to no response. He wanted to know what "The Musketeer" had to say to her just now? Was she as excited to be shipmates as he was? Nothing. He got nothing. She told him to go away. She had too much work to do and not enough time to do it.

"Hollywood Palladium. Ten O'clock. I'll leave your name at the door," he said heading back to his desk.

Delilah looked at him with a 'who the fuck do you think you are?' look. If only this office could be a women only operation, she fantasized.

#

The Hollywood Palladium was the only place to be on this particular Hollywood night. The Palladium had been converted into a large and lavish nightclub. Cocktail tables filled most of the dance floor in front of the stage. Ten bars were strategically situated throughout the room. An enormous replica of the Some Girls album cover hung high above the stage. A VIP area was delineated by velvet ropes and two rather large security men.

Seated at the most important table were Elliot Irving and a bevy of rock stars, movie stars, and models. The place was jumping, and music from the Some Girls album played through a multitude of speakers.

West had managed to find a drink but had yet to locate Connor Kilkenny, his partner in crime for the night. Sauntering his way past the VIP area he could hear Elliot calling his name.

There was arm waving Elliot. West was overjoyed to see him. He hadn't had the opportunity to thank him for Chastity in Mexico and the limousine in Colorado. The Desperados concert experience, he would tell him, was life altering.

With a great big hug, West lifted Elliot off of his feet.

"Boy, do I owe you for the rest of my life," said West.

"Most people eventually do," replied Elliot.

Elliot introduced him to his friends at the VIP table, referring to him as a "GreenPlanet spokesman, and a fearless activist." West recognized each and every famous face, trying his best to appear cool, calm and collected.

"Come join us," said Elliot.

He couldn't. He needed to find Connor. He had agreed to do a live interview for KWOT, and besides, he was pretty sure, if not positive, that he couldn't hold his own at the VIP table. Apologizing to Elliot, he was graciously granted a VIP rain check.

Backing away from the table, he tripped over the velvet rope into the arms of security who, without pause, stood him up straight, spun him around, and sent him off, head spinning, through the hyperactive crowd.

#

Delilah looked sizzling hot. She was clearly dressed for a night on the town. She and Susan were having Mai Tai's at Trader Vic's in Beverly Hills. Susan had insisted that they get together for a drink. She needed to tell Delilah that she and West were not sleeping together. Did she sleep with him in Colorado? Yes. But not sex sleep. Just sleep. They shared a hotel room to save money, slept in the same bed, but nothing else.

Okay?

"I know we seem pretty cozy these days, and yes, we are closer, I mean, we went through a pretty intense experience together, but that's the end of the story."

Delilah was vacillating whether to go to the Some Girls party or not. She was probably going to go, because why waste the sexy attire, right?

"I don't like having strong emotions for someone," said Delilah.

"Then don't," said Susan.

"Our emotions choose us," said Delilah.

"That's a tad too deep for Mai Tai's," said Susan.

The cocktail waitress placed additional fresh Mai Tai's on their table, compliments of two middle-aged men sitting at the bar. The guys were waving 'hello' at them, and Delilah believed that they were the most depressing drinks that she had ever seen.

"Off I go. Thanks for the chat," she said pushing all of the drinks in front of Susan. She walked past the two men at the bar. They were invisible to her, but she looked hot and she knew it.

#

At a cocktail table, in the midst of release party madness, West was concluding his interview with Connor. They were live on-the-air, with a dozen bystanders serving as an enthusiastic 'on location' audience.

"Ace, there you have it. Much more to come as we continue our non-stop coverage of the upcoming GreenPlanet voyage to save the whales. KWOT. Covering the stories that interest our Southern

264

California listeners. For now, live from the Some Girls release party at the Hollywood Palladium, this is Connor Kilkenny for West Walker. Back to you at the station."

Connor shut down his microphone, placed it on the table, and tossed back a shot of bourbon. Glimpsing three young lovely audience members, he invited them to join he and West. They accepted. Laughter, drinking, smoking, and frolicking ensued. The party was officially in full swing.

Now, it's normal, if not expected, to lose track of time and space at rock revelries, and after an unknown lapse of minutes, West noticed that Connor was nowhere in sight. Maybe it was because he, West, and one of the young lovelies were under the table with their hands down each others pants? One couldn't see much when one was under the table.

It turned out that Connor was close by, right around the corner, behind a velvet curtain, pants down around his ankles, receiving, what he would later describe, as a most excellent "Finally-A-Friday blowjob" from one of the other admiring lasses.

At the stage door, Delilah, still looking amazing, was struggling to convince security to allow her entrance to the party.

"West Walker and Connor Kilkenny. They're expecting me," said a testy Delilah.

"Never heard of them," said the doorguy.

"I'm on the fucking list," snarled Delilah.

"Time for you to go away. Don't make me be mean," warned the doorguy.

After thanking, then swiftly departing from their

265

new female friends, West and Connor reconvened and were now belly-up to one of the many happening bars when they were approached, with purpose, by Elliot Irving. On his arm was a chemically altered female rock star that was loved and admired by the entire musical universe. Bella Stevens, more commonly referred to as Bella Donna was one of the biggest rock stars in the world, and she needed–but not necessarily wanted– a ride home.

Elliot was calling in one of his chips. He called on West to "please take Bella home." He wanted to be sure that she didn't take any detours, that she arrived at home safe and sound and tucked in, and no one says "no" to Elliot. A car was waiting. The driver knew where to go.

"Take special care of her," said Elliot as he transferred Bella from his shoulder to West's.

Bella Donna was hanging all over West. His mind was swirling. He looked with big eyes at Connor and Elliot, who were laughing and having a grand old time. Off you go kid.

Outside, Delilah was pacing back and forth trying to figure a way into the Palladium when the stage door opened and out came West with Bella in his arms. The chauffeur, standing at the ready, assisted West in getting Bella into the back of the limo. Delilah was floored, and West was equally floored to see Delilah floored.

"Delilah? You're here," he said.

Delilah remained floored as the chauffeur was pushing West into the back seat with Bella Donna. What exactly was she supposed to say? West powered down the back window.

"This isn't what you might think," he said.

Raising the window back up, the driver power-locked the doors, power-locked the windows, and drove off with West and Bella Donna, leaving in his wake a crushed Delilah alone with the security guy. After a few seconds of embarrassed silence, he opened the stage door wide. She was welcomed to come inside if she was still interested. She wasn't.

#

The week zipped by too fast. There was so much to be done, and the clock was ticking away. Friday, June 16th, on board the Maggie May it's a beehive of activity. People were coming and going. Delilah, arms full of dry goods, was followed by an army of volunteers who carried many, many, many cases of beer, wine, sacks of rice, canned goods, pancake mix, crates of fruits and vegetables, and gallons and gallons of water. They marched past West, who was answering questions from a reporter. Delilah, a woman with a mission, smiled politely at West as she paraded on by.

Strapped into a bosun's chair, hanging off the side of the ship, was Axel D'Artagnan. Two-thirds of the way to finishing a spectacular painting of a Sperm whale on the starboard side of the Maggie May, he was always on the lookout. When he saw Delilah, he blew her a big kiss.

On the bridge, Shakespeare Jones had binoculars in hand, scanning the action beyond the harbor on the choppy waters of the wide-open sea. He watched with fascination and concern as Hunter was training Will

267

and Susan in the treacherous art of open-ocean Zodiac driving.

On the aft deck, First Mate Matt Lincoln barked orders at three volunteers scrubbing the decks, while Delilah and her army of volunteers continued to make endless supply trips back and forth, back and forth.

The morning turned into the afternoon as West replaced Will and Susan in inflatable boat training. With as much force as they could muster, he and Hunter charged the Zodiac through sizable waves in an attempt to determine it's breaking point. As the day ran out, all of the inflatables were brought back on board ship, and the galley was now overflowing with the necessary supplies.

The Sperm whale painting was very close to completion, and the ship's exterior sparkled like a diamond. An exhausted crew were relieved to halt all activity for the day, pausing to watch the sun sink into the blue Pacific. Nine days to go before they set sail.

That evening, The Yardarm was overtaken by the GreenPlanet crew and volunteers. They covered the place in pizza boxes and fast food containers. Some were shooting pool; others listened to music from a boombox substituting for a jukebox. All were drinking anything and everything that Jimmy had behind the bar.

The joint was buzzing with gossip and excitement. West, Hunter, and Shakespeare were at the end of the bar drinking and discussing a problematic outboard engine on one of the Zodiacs. It cut out a couple of times during the afternoon's high-speed trials, and they needed to make sure that it was repaired or replaced before they pushed off next week.

"That thing stalls out in front of a Russian killer boat and it's curtains," said Hunter.

"Those outboard's are too dangerous even when they're running well. Could run out of gas, gas line could detach, propeller could jam, and that pussy outboard could separate from the transom. You using a kill cord?" asked Shakespeare.

Too risky. Hunter explained to West that a kill chord, also known as a "dead man's switch", is a chord attached to the throttle with the other end attached to the helmsman's ankle. If the helmsman goes into the water, the kill cord would shut off the outboard motor. West didn't hear a word he said after "goes into the water."

"And right on your tail, the whaling boat would chop you into little pieces," Shakespeare said.

Across the bar, D'Artagnan had cornered Delilah and was lobbying her to pose for him. He very much desired to paint her. Naked. It would be discreet and private, and he promised that she would feel very safe.

Her answer was a firm "no," but he refused to give up. Taking her by the arms, he gently turned her so that she was looking over her shoulder at him.

"You see? Very subtle, very alluring, you are so beautiful," he persisted.

Out of the corner of one eye, West was watching this show and didn't like what he saw. He excused himself from Hunter and Mr. Jones, proceeding straight for an intervention with D'Artagnan, who had his hands all over Delilah.

"How about tomorrow night?" D'Artagnan was

asking Delilah.

"She's busy tomorrow night," said West maneuvering his way in between them.

Delilah and D'Artagnan looked at him with amused expressions. Delilah didn't require his help, and D'Artagnan wasn't impressed.

"She's having dinner with me tomorrow night," said a puffed up West.

Delilah stepped back to let the two clowns play out the rest of the scene. D'Artagnan wanted no trouble; he only wanted Delilah. He chose to walk away. Perhaps it was the attractive young volunteer standing alone at the bar that made his decision easier? With a bow of his head to Delilah, he waved a theatrical flourish of the hand, and proceeded, without further ado, to his new 'objet d'art' at the bar.

"I'm not having dinner with you tomorrow night or any other night," said a defiant Delilah.

Those were the first words that she had spoken to him since the infamous Bella Donna encounter. He had unsuccessfully attempted, more than once, to explain, but she wasn't interested.

"I was doing a favor for my friend Elliot," he said.

His "friend Elliot." You see, therein lies the problem. She felt that it was her fault; that she created this monster. He was delusional, an ego out of control. He was always referring to people like Connor Kilkenny and Elliot Irving as his "friends." So sad. Heaven help us all if he begins to pretend that Bella Donna is his new friend. Jesus.

The music suddenly stopped. Hunter, standing on a bench, rose above the bar crowd, commanding the room's attention. "Listen up everybody! Stop! Listen up! Gather around here. Gather around. Great work again today. We're getting very close. The rest of the crew will be arriving next week. A journalist from Rolling Stone will be going with us. For those of you that have already claimed your bunks, don't get too comfortable. We will reassign them and may separate the men and the women if there are those that would feel more comfortable with that situation. When our doctor arrives, he will have a look at each one of you to make sure that your health is a positive and not a negative. We're starting to get daily briefings on the location of the Russian whaling fleet. They're getting closer. Looks like our timing could be right on. Any questions about anything? Jimmy, get over here. Captain, stand up. Where's Doctor? There he is. Let's hear it for our hosts, and for Captain Jones and First Mate Lincoln! Without these guys, we're dead in the water!"

The throng was delirious, and cheers exploded with great gusto. Drinks continued to flow and the mood was electric. West put his arm around Delilah. She immediately removed it. Apparently, there was more work to be done here.

#

Friday, June 23rd. Another week was in the books and zero weeks were remaining. It was late in the afternoon, and the crew of the Maggie May were seated on the aft deck listening to Shakespeare Jones deliver a deadly-serious speech about what would soon become reality.

Three prominent faces were missing. On the bridge, Hunter and Kate were addressing a blindsided West, who couldn't believe what he was hearing.

Kate, with luggage in tow, had to depart straightaway for London. Her father was gravely ill. Her flight departed from LAX in two hours.

"I need you to stay behind. I need you here in L.A. for very important reasons. One, I need you to run the media juggernaut that's about to happen. Two, we heard today from the family of the diver that was killed at the Ventura power plant. They need you to testify in court next week. Three, you're the best person to replace Kate," said an expressionless Hunter.

West's eye's welled up. He looked down at the crew listening to last-minute instructions from Shakespeare Jones. He felt nauseous and could barely speak.

"You need me in the Zodiac," he said.

"We've got it covered," said Hunter.

West locked eyes with Kate. Her father was dying, yet she remained strong. He offered to take her to the airport. She could give him instructions on how to handle things at the office. He couldn't look at Hunter for fear of falling apart.

Hunter grabbed a hold of him, threw his arms around him, and squeezed hard. Down on the deck, Delilah and the others could see the drama unfolding above.

The trio exited the bridge to the aft deck. Hunter stopped next to Shakespeare as West and Kate carried her luggage past the crew, down the gangplank, and out of sight. The entire crew sensed the seriousness of the situation.

"So that's it. We sail in forty-four hours. This is serious business ladies and gentlemen. I plan to come home with the same number of people that I started with," Shakespeare finished as all eyes were on Hunter.

"West is taking Kate to the airport. Her father is dying and she has to return to London. West will be staying here in Los Angeles," said Hunter to an audible reaction from the crew.

Delilah filled with conflicting emotion and shock. Paul Revere was delighted. Everyone was buzzing.

"This isn't about any one of us. We do whatever we need to do for the cause," lectured Hunter.

A snickering Paul Revere made an unsavory comment under his breath. Hunter stared him down.

"I hope everyone heard loud and clear what Captain Jones just said. This crew is a team. We all have to be on the same page every minute of every day. You absolutely must have each other's back. Everyone sleeps on board ship tomorrow night. This is your last night to relax. If you were smart, adult, grown-up people, you would get plenty of sleep tonight, but we all know that's not going to happen. No one here later than noon tomorrow! Let me say that again. All hands on deck no later than noon tomorrow. Okay whale savers. Have a lovely evening," he finished.

Everyone was moving in different directions. Hunter corralled Delilah before she could move an inch. He needed to determine her state of mind. Was she okay? Did she feel betrayed? Did she have any questions for him? She did have a question. Why was that asshole Paul Revere part of this crew?

"He's a damn good Zodiac driver," said Hunter.

"He's a fucking asshole," countered Delilah.

"Keep your friends close, and your enemies closer, right?" he said.

Hunter said that fear was a good thing, it helped keep you alive. He promised to keep a protective eye on her, and she laughed out loud, reminding him that he had a tendency to be shot at with big exploding harpoons. Hard to argue with her there. He sent her on her way with specific instructions.

"Go water your plants. Have a drink or two. Have a good cry. Sleep. The adventure of your life begins tomorrow."

She appreciated the good intentions and the wisdom of his instructions, but she had a new mission. Find West. When she burst through the doors of the Chimney Sweep, she found a bustling Friday night crowd, but no West. Both Connie and Gil were behind the bar working their in-the-weeds butts off.

Wading through the alcoholic sea of people, she got Connie's attention and inquired about West. Was he here? Had she seen him? Heard from him? Anything?

Connie pointed to the end of the bar. Susan had gotten there first and had already scoured the place looking for West. No luck. She was camping out with the hope that West might make a late night appearance. Before Delilah could even ask her, Susan shook her head 'no', and handed her a scorpion.

"He's not at the office. I've got people checking the

beach. I don't think he's going to let us find him," said Susan.

"I know," said Delilah.

Connie could see their pained faces. She placed four drinks in front of them, and then, jumping up and down, informed them that she saw them on television!

"Please tell me that you're not going to get on that horrid old boat," said Connie.

"We leave Sunday morning," said Susan.

Not the words Connie wanted to hear. Clutching a bar towel, she wiped away the tears, as Delilah threw back two drinks in two seconds and bid them both adieu. She had to close up her house before morning and the clock was running.

Darting around to the front of the bar, Connie was bawling like a baby. She didn't understand. Why did her girls have to go through with this dangerous thing?

Delilah whispered in her ear. She said, "look after my man while I'm gone." Susan couldn't hear a word, but she knew the message, and since she wasn't going anywhere for at least two or six more drinks, she promised to call Delilah if West was spotted. Okay. That's it then. Off Delilah went. Next up, the blue Pacific.

#

Saturday, June 24th. Media Day was in full swing. On the dock and on the ship, reporters shoved microphones into the many faces that comprised the GreenPlanet crew. Television cameras surrounded Hunter as he talked about the impending campaign and what might be expected. On board ship,

275

photographers snapped photos of Shakespeare Jones and First Mate Lincoln. Connor and West, yes West, were broadcasting live in front of a giant KWOT logo.

Connor, grinning his usual giant grin, tapped West on the shoulder and pointed to the sky above. A vintage biplane was towing a KWOT banner with the words GREENPLANET AND KWOT SAVE THE WHALES.

At the direction of Hunter, the entire crew, including West, assembled on the aft deck to pose for a crew photo. West strategically placed himself next to a stoic Delilah. As the middle of the day turned into afternoon, then into evening, the various media gradually faded away, leaving only the crew and volunteers to say their goodbyes. Hunter gathered everyone together.

"Gather around everyone! Volunteers too! Let's go troops! All right, settle down please. Crew, it's time. As you know, we depart early in the morning. Tonight, after our first crew dinner, we have some pre-departure meetings to conduct, and some last minute checklists to attend to. Before we say goodbye, I would like to recognize the monumental effort and invaluable contribution made by all of the volunteers, family members, and friends over the last several weeks. Truly inspiring. I'm so proud to know each and every one of you. We'll have all of you in our hearts every day until we return. Crew members, please take this moment to thank your incredible whale saving brothers and sisters," said an emotional Hunter.

A massive amount of embracing, moist eyes, handshaking, and gift giving ensued. West was bitterly reminded that he was with the group that was waving farewell. His strength and courage were tested as he shared his best wishes with each of the crewmembers, even Paul Revere. Susan gripped him from behind. She was crying.

She offered to sneak him on board before they pushed off, and he told her to be careful out there. She could see Delilah waiting patiently, unemotionally, for West's attention, and, in deference, took her leave. West smiled a difficult smile.

"If you didn't want to be my Zodiac partner, you should have said so," said Delilah.

West took both of her hands into his and looked straight into her beautiful brown eyes, which filled with tears.

"Sperm whales are family creatures. They can be as large as seventy feet long and weigh as much as fifty thousand pounds. When they are under attack, when their family members are under attack, they will aggressively defend themselves. They won't know who is a friend and who is an enemy. You let Hunter worry about the killer boat, and you keep your eyes on the whales in front of you," he said with all of the strength he could muster.

"Do you realize how amazing I am?" she said not letting go of his shaking hands.

He nodded his head 'yes'. She kissed him, did a confident about-face, and marched away, never looking back in his direction.

West, the volunteers, and the family members were escorted down the gangplank, and off of the ship. He stopped for one last look. Shakespeare, seeing him, sounded the horn, and waved a resigned farewell.

Devastated, destroyed, and gutted, West and the others drifted off into the labyrinth of the Los Angeles harbor, leaving behind their band of brothers and sisters to journey forth on their great voyage.

#

Midnight was swift in its arrival. On board ship, it was quiet and it was dark. There was no moon on this night. Heavy cloud cover made the night sky very dark. The mostly inexperienced crew exuded a weary, nervous, solemn energy.

The necessary meetings had been conducted, and the checklists were checked twice. Several of the crew were asleep, while a few played cards and talked in hushed voices.

Jade was writing in her journal. Jonah was reviewing his whaling data. Delilah and Susan were laying silently awake in their bunks when the unexpected sound of the engines seized their attention. They could hear the unintelligible voices of Shakespeare, Jimmy, and First Mate Lincoln. They could feel the boat move.

With vigilant eyes, Susan looked over at Delilah, and they both jumped out of their bunks and headed for the main deck. Voices of other surprised and animated crewmembers could be heard as they arrived on deck to find their fellow whale savers gathering.

The Maggie May moved with confidence through the harbor, past the many boats in dock. Over the deck speakers, the voice of Captain Jones filled the night air.

"Good morning ladies and gentlemen. It's now just

past midnight. As we exit the calm waters of the harbor our ride will become more turbulent. Unfortunately, according to the weather service, it looks like it's going to be a bit rough for the beginning of our trip. I've never put much stock in seasick pills, but the doc has them if you want them. If you're going to be sick, try to do it over the side of the boat, but please be careful. Bring someone to hold on to you. Don't want anyone going overboard on our first night out. Being sick is no excuse for not performing your assigned duties. You may feel like you're dying, but you're not. So, do your assigned work. You'll feel better in a few days. Here we go. Godspeed," he announced.

As Shakespeare finished his sober message, the Maggie May entered the instantly choppy waters of the open sea. Delilah and Susan grasped onto solid fixtures, onto each other, and vowed to remain calm. It was dark, scary, and turbulent. No turning back now.

#

It had been thirty-six hours since the Maggie May set sail, making it high noon on a meditative Monday. The office was deserted and deathly quiet except for the graveyard ticking of the clock on the wall. Beneath it, hung the rather large calendar for the month of June 1978. Each of the first twenty-four days had been crossed out with a large red X.

Sunday, June 25th was circled with emphatic exclamation marks as if a square on a calendar could have any significance in one's life. Next to the calendar, written on the strategy board, the list of crewmembers names still remained. Line One was silently blinking on all of the desktop phones when West entered.

Sullen and defeated, he closed the door behind him and stood lost, staring at the empty rooms. Not sure where to go or what to do, he eventually moved toward his desk. Passing by the strategy board, he stopped and stared at the list of names. He could see only one: 13) WEST WALKER-ZODIAC. Where's the eraser? Ah! He erased himself from the list of names.

The blank space where his name once was said it perfectly. That's exactly how he felt today. Erased. He took a seat at his desk and stared at the blinking light on his phone. The hypnotic effect it had on him was medicinal; tonic. His plan was to sit this way for the entire day, perhaps for the rest of his life, until he heard someone trying to open the unlocked office door.

After a lengthy and unnecessary struggle, the door opened and the head of Salinger Jayne Daniels cautiously peeked into the office. West didn't speak; he just stared at her as if she were another blinking phone light.

Uninvited by West, a hesitant Salinger entered the office and closed the door behind her.

"Are you thinking?" she said. "People don't think thinking is work, but it is. Probably the most important work that we do. You looked like you were thinking. If you are, thinking, I can come back later."

West understood this to mean that a very angry God had only just begun to punish him for all of his foolish and sinful transgressions.

Salinger crept further into the office and set her belongings down on Susan's desk. Detecting that West might not remember who she was, or be aware that she was asked by Kate to assist him, work side-by-side with him, seeing as he had gotten the boot from the voyage, she reminded West that Kate had assigned her to him, well, not to him, per se, but report to him.

"The IWC meetings? Remember? I waved at you and you waved at me?" she flailed.

West didn't have the emotional stamina to do this. Not today. He nodded his head 'yes' and returned his stare to the comfort of the blinking light on his phone.

Salinger transitioned into work mode. Moving to the Telex machine, she began pouring through the press releases and news stories. West, in an effort to save his own life, as well as hers, rose from his desk and drifted across the office, past Salinger, escaping into the sanctuary of Kate's office.

Got it. No words necessary, Salinger thought to herself, ripping the very lengthy printout from the Telex machine. With a zip in her step, she returned to Susan's desk, which she now proudly claimed as her own, and there she set up camp for a full days work. This was most excellent. This was the beginning of great things.

#

When West opened his eyes, he saw the ugly light fixture on the ceiling of Kate's office. The light wasn't on and the room was getting dark. Stretched out on the couch, and not exactly sure where or who he was, sitting up helped him to remember that he was in

Kate's office, and that he had lain down to take a brief nap.

Returning to consciousness was unpleasant. It felt to him like all of his blood had been drained out of his unattractive, unhealthy, unworthy carcass. He flipped on the light, opened the door, and peered out into the main office. The lights were still on in the now unoccupied room. He remembered that what's-her-name, Salinger, had been there earlier.

Oh his desk was a stack of messages and a note from Salinger, which read: "Hope you did some good thinking. Messages are stacked according to importance. Most important on top. 5 p.m. Salinger, p.s. See you tomorrow!" The clock showed that it was just past 6 p.m.

With zero interest or intention of looking at any fucking messages, and wanting only to return to the land of the unconscious, he ignored the ringing telephone, hoping it would go silent. It would not. He picked up the phone and punched line one.

A ship-to-shore operator located in San Pedro was on the other end. She had a call from motor vessel Maggie May, and wanted to know "would he accept the charges?"

In a daze, West accepted the charges and waited for her to connect him with the Maggie May. The connection was poor. There was an abundance of crackling and white noise. Hunter's voice was barely discernible.

"West, this is Hunter. West, this is Hunter. Can you hear me? Over."

His blood pressure spiked when he heard Hunter's

voice. He yelled into the phone, for an update, for good news, for reassurance, but it became clear that Hunter couldn't understand anything he was saying.

"Will try you again tomorrow. Same time. Nothing to report. Very rough weather. Seasick crew. Out." Hunter said as the line went dead in West's ear.

Rough weather. Seasick crew. It was torture. He should be out there with them. He, too, should be seasick. It wasn't fair. He was angry and felt madness coming on.

In her note, Salinger said that the top message on the stack was the most important, so he glanced down and saw that it was from Connor. He would be at the Hyatt House later tonight. If possible, "come hang out."

The office was as quiet and depressing as a morgue on a holiday weekend. On the strategy board, he saw where he had erased his name from the crew list. How did this happen? It just wasn't fair.

#

The ghost of West was slouched over the Hyatt Hotel bar, nursing a shot and a beer and feeling miserable, unlike the group of people at the back of the bar where a festive party was in full swing.

Champagne corks were popping and white powder was flying up noses, followed by squeals of delight and debauchery. What the fuck could people be so happy about? The world was a horrible place.

A very young-looking female bounded onto the barstool next to him, white powder on the tip of her nose. Going a hundred miles an hour, she sure didn't look old enough to legally be in a bar. She said her name was Morgana, and that he needed to come, right now, and join their party.

She wanted to know if he was on tour? What room was he staying in? She was screaming at her friends Warren and Waddy to bring her more champagne.

With no warning, she plopped her foot in the middle of his lap, causing her mini-skirt to hike up, leaving nothing to the imagination.

"Look at this ankle. I don't know if it's sprained or broken. I can't go to a doctor. No insurance. It's 1978 man! How is it possible, in America, in 1978, that so many people can't go to a freakin doctor! I love your band. You guys are amazing. Wanna go up to your room?" she said as the bartender handed a telephone to West.

It was Connor. He wouldn't be coming to the Hyatt House after all. Last minute change of plans. Morgana was again screaming for more champagne. On the other end of the phone, Connor could hear her voice. He knew that voice, and instructed West to put her on the phone.

"Who is this? Hi! Hey baby, how are you? Yes. Yes. Yes, he is very cute. Uh, huh. I will. Miss you too!" she squeaked as she slid the phone down the bar to the bartender.

Feeling a bit guilty and mischievous, Connor told Morgana that West was about to be a very famous lead singer in a very famous rock band. He also said that he and West were tight pals, and was hoping that she might take good care of him tonight, as a favor to him.

Say no more. She threw her arms around West

and got real, real close. Don't try to play coy with her. She knew a rock star when she saw one, and here he was, in her arms, and she was absolutely going to "take care of him." Where's her fucking champagne?

The next ten days were tough on everyone, except, maybe, for Salinger, who stayed glued to West wherever he roamed in the office. Whether he was on the phone in Kate's office, at his desk writing press releases, tracking the daily location of the Maggie May on a wall-sized map, or reviewing the incoming Telex news, she was right there by his side, just in case he required her immediate assistance. Each day, she would report to him at length about the ongoing IWC meetings in London, hoping to reignite his extinguished passion.

Every evening, West and Hunter would conduct their six o'clock ship-to-shore phone call, Salinger taking notes. The conversations were dejected and dispirited. Hunter was often agitated.

From day one, the weather had been dreary and raining. The seas were rough, the crew was sick, and morale was low. The San Francisco people hated the L.A. people, and the L.A. people hated the San Francisco people. The Seattle and Hawaii people never left their bunks, except to eat and complain. They saw no whales and found no whalers.

Catty Slur had a huge fight with Paul Revere. He'd been negligent in maintaining the outboard motor on their Zodiac, and during open ocean trials, the motor stalled and couldn't be restarted. She was furious. He didn't give a shit. There was serious talk of throwing in the towel and heading for home.

That was during the day. At night, it was even more discouraging. West would alternate between drinking alone at the Chimney Sweep or camping out in Kate's office with little or nothing to do. Occasionally, he and Connor would go to the Sportsman's Lodge or Barney's Beanery to drink beer and flirt with women, but his enthusiasm was less than full mast.

On the Fourth of July, he climbed up Runyon Canyon to watch the fireworks, but clouds turned into rain, and he was completely soaked and mud covered by the time he made it back down to street level.

Two days later he had to borrow Roy's way-too-big-suit and tie. His time to testify on behalf of the drowned diver's family had come, and he wanted to make a respectable showing at the Ventura County courthouse. On his way there, on the 101, he ran out of gas. He was broken, fiscally and spiritually.

All the while, Salinger was more and more free in her attire, and more and more alluring in her appearance. She was confidant and doing great work for the organization. Her happiness showed. She was amazing! Unfortunately for her, she was invisible to the one person that she was trying to impress.

West, on the other hand, had ditched the suit and returned to the same old dirty clothes he'd been wearing for days. He looked like shit. At the end of the bar, a displeased Connie chatted with a patron that she didn't care for, intentionally avoiding West and his never-ending dark cloud.

When the radiant Salinger walked into the bar—a

bar that she had never once frequented–Connie took notice. With laser focus, she witnessed Salinger approach West, tap him on the shoulder, and whisper into his drunk ear. For the very first time, and with the help of adult liquids, he noticed too. Salinger!

Connie watched her lead him by the hand, through the bar and out the door. Lord have mercy. These kids were something else.

In Kate's office, Salinger insisted that West drink another cup of coffee, and there was more to come after that. Like a puppy dog, he followed orders, continually repeating to her how incredible she looked, and if she so desired, this was the perfect time for her to take full advantage of him. She wasn't interested.

She scolded him. He hadn't been there at six o'clock when Hunter called because he was drinking at the Chimney Sweep. Hunter was about to call back and West needed to sober up. It was urgent.

That got his attention. Why? What's wrong? Is Delilah okay? What happened?

Delilah was fine, she said, but she wouldn't tell him anything else. That was Hunter's job.

"I'm a mess," said West.

"Yes, you are," answered Salinger.

"I'm, it's good, that you're not interested, you know, in me," he said.

Salinger stayed mum. She didn't feel the need to reveal in any way, shape, or form any interest in him at this or any future moment. She had just done that dance for the past two weeks. The phone rang. It was Hunter.

For the entire six-hour flight, West stared out the window and replayed Hunter's words over and over and over again. "Salinger has a ticket for you. Morning flight to Honolulu. Get your ass over here. We need a Zodiac driver."

Now, in the Mai Tai Bar of the Royal Hawaiian Hotel, he was sitting around a table with Hunter, Delilah, Will, and Susan. He didn't say anything, but he was thinking that they all looked pretty bad. They thought he looked even worse.

Each took turns giving him the rundown of the disastrous weeks that they had just spent at sea. The weather sucked. Everyone was sick. The North hated the South, the South hated the North. Paul Revere had tried and failed several times to overthrow Hunter, but at this time, he was not considered a credible threat and would remain on the crew.

Catty, Kai, and Sunset quit the campaign and would remain in Honolulu, crashing at a friend's house for the unforeseeable future. Karma flew back to San Francisco to restore order to an office in chaos. They hadn't seen one single whale, but the latest information from Congressman Ryan's office was promising. The Russians were hunting whales, not far from where they were sitting.

West was unbelievably happy to see them; to be there with them. Maybe he might be able to bring them some luck? Right? And they were equally thrilled to see him, too. He was meant to be there. He would inject a much-needed energy and vitality into a battered and beaten crew. At least that was their hope.

West was also excited to be on Oahu for what he thought would be a few days of rest, relaxation, surfing, and reconnecting with Delilah. On his flight over, he had time to think. Maybe he was ready to do the girlfriend thing again?

He remembered that Roy said that Delilah had been sent to him. Kip said the same thing. She had been right there in front of his face this entire time. Maybe he could repair things with her? Start fresh. Grow up.

His excitement was precipitously redirected when Hunter informed the group that they didn't have a few days to enjoy the islands, they had six hours. The Russians were in the neighborhood. The Maggie May would leave at Sunset. "Don't be late," he said jumping up from the table before the bill arrived, winking at West as he ran out of the bar into the hotel lobby.

West wouldn't be late. Believe me. He had already experienced one painful 'bon voyage' to the Maggie May. Never again, he promised himself. Never again.

It was a glorious Hawaiian sunset. The Maggie May was exiting Honolulu Harbor for the open ocean. The entire crew were on the main deck, taking in the breathtaking view.

West was next to his buddy Will. He couldn't help but flash back to the marlin fishing boat, and the witnessing of the dolphin slaughter by the Mexican tuna fleet. What were they headed for now? How would he handle things?

Several boats of various types and sizes formed an escort for the Maggie May. The flotilla flew whale flags and GreenPlanet banners. Supporters waved, cheered, and sounded their horns. There was a renewed sense of purpose and determination amongst the GreenPlanet crew. They could feel it.

As Honolulu faded into the distance, the Maggie May picked up speed and separated from the flotilla, motoring her way into the open ocean, toward the rough waters of the Molokai Channel.

The Molokai Channel was like sailing inside a washing machine. Large, choppy swells, powerful currents, and mighty winds tossed the crew from side to side. Hanging on for dear life was necessary, relaxing impossible.

The sun slipped below the horizon in a flash. Those whale savers that were on deck, beat a hasty retreat inside, bracing themselves for an ugly night ahead. Most of the crew reacquainted themselves with seasickness.

The ship was thrown about as if it were a toy in a bathtub. West was cold, clammy, dizzy, and sick to his stomach. He wanted to sleep, but refused to lie down for fear of an out of control, spinning universe. He sat there on the side of his bunk, drenched in sweat, holding on tight. He swallowed the Dramamine that the doctor had given him. Finally, utterly exhausted, he tied himself into his bunk and slept.

Someone was hitting him. Roughing him up. He was being roused from a short and disturbing sleep by First Mate Lincoln. One of West's assigned jobs, he was just learning, would be to take the helm every morning from 3 a.m. to 10 a.m. For better or worse, in sickness and in health.

Lincoln led him up to the bridge and strapped him to the wheel to prevent him from falling overboard–his tie-line was long enough for him to get to the side of the boat to puke when necessary. He was given instructions on how to keep the ship moving on the proper heading, and how to contact the Captain if there was an emergency.

After a few minutes of observing West at the helm, First Mate Lincoln gave him the seal-of-approval slap on the back, that caused West to vomit all over the bridge. Handing him a mop, Lincoln rechecked his safety harness, handed him a vomit rag, and left him on his own to perform his required duty.

#

The sun was shining and the sea was blue and calm. On the aft deck, West, asleep in a Zodiac, was again sustaining a beating. It was Delilah. She was shaking his leg, and kicking the Zodiac in an attempt to snap him back into consciousness.

Opening his bloodshot eyes, he saw Delilah's shining face, the majestic sky above, the sparkling blue water below, and for the first time in days, he felt much better. He had no idea that he had been out of commission for three days.

"Hey rookie. You going to sleep another day away? It's been three days now. You need to eat. You need to start moving," said Delilah.

What did she mean three days? That can't be right. Can it? Did he miss anything important? He took her hand in his.

"I missed you," he said.

291

"Huh," said Delilah.

"I've been doing a lot of thinking," he continued.

"Huh," said Delilah.

She commanded him to get his ass out of her Zodiac. She was teamed up with Hunter, and West was paired with Paul Revere. His Zodiac was over there, she pointed.

Before he could get his bearings straight, Will and Susan hustled by them, to the rear of the ship. Something was up.

On the bridge, Hunter, Jonah, Shakespeare Jones, and the Russian translator Natasha Belov were listening to voices on the radio. Russian voices. They were close by.

Natasha said that the factory ship was communicating with the whaling boats. They were, she said, "chasing whales." Hunter checked with Captain Jones, who was scanning the horizon with his binoculars. Nothing but ocean.

Will, on the other hand, did see something. He was jumping up and down and pointing at something in the water. Several of the crew flocked to the rear of the deck, including West, Delilah, and Hunter. A dead whale, recently harpooned, was floating on top of the water, a radar beacon next to it.

"Let's get the Zodiacs into the water! West, grab the meter board. Susan, camera! Delilah, let's go. All hands on deck," barked Hunter.

The six Zodiac warriors strapped on life jackets and retrieved two-way radios. Will and Susan were the first to be attached to the winch and lowered into the water so they could begin filming right away.

Next up were West and Paul Revere. West yelled out to Delilah to be careful and keep her eyes forward.

"Let's go Romeo. Don't fuck this up," Paul said.

After they were lowered into the water, Paul revved up the outboard, and without waiting for instructions from Hunter, sped off toward the dead whale.

While Hunter and Delilah were lowered down into the water, Will and Susan followed West and Paul to document the measurement of the dead whale.

West and Paul were almost there. Paul, it seemed, was going to ride straight onto the back of the floating whale.

"Slow up! Slow Up! We don't know if it's dead yet," yelled West.

Laughing a twisted laugh, Paul pulled up next to the whale, reached over, and patted it on its dead head.

West had the meter board in hand, as Will and Susan arrived on the scene. Leaning over the side of his Zodiac, West placed the meter board atop the bobbing whale while Susan captured it all on film.

Hunter and Delilah caught up with their teammates. Wild-eyed and electrified, they could see, speeding toward them, a menacing Russian whaling boat.

"We've got company," shouted Delilah.

On the two-way radio, Shakespeare Jones' voice warned them.

"Russians due west, heading straight at you, over," he alerted them.

"I don't think they like us fucking with their

293

whale," said an animated Susan.

"They're not coming for us. They're chasing whales. This is it. Let's go!" bellowed Hunter.

The three Zodiacs headed straight toward the oncoming killer boat. As they got closer and closer to each other, they could see waterspouts coming from the fleeing whales. Seconds before all converged at the same point, the whales suddenly veered off to the south. This allowed the more agile Zodiacs to speed ahead and position themselves in front of the killer boat.

West and Paul occupied the lead Zodiac. The fearless Paul Revere skillfully maneuvered their Zodiac within a few feet of the bow of the killer boat so he could salute them with his middle finger.

The angry whalers retaliated by turning high-pressured fire hoses on them. Dousing West and Paul, they attempted to blind them, ultimately driving them away.

Will and Susan positioned themselves on the whaling boat's left flank in order to be in the best position to film the confrontation and keep a sharp eye out for additional killer boats. Delilah and Hunter took up the right flank. The fleeing whales again changed direction, which now forced the Zodiacs to speed through increasingly choppy water.

The whale savers were taking a severe beating as their little rubber boats pounded up and down on the turbulent sea. West's right arm continually slammed down on top of the meter board that he was holding next to him. Susan struggled with the heavy film camera, needing to hang onto the hand rope so that she wouldn't fall out of the boat. Delilah, acting as lookout, screamed directions at Hunter in order to avoid the Sperm whales that were inches in front of their Zodiac.

On the bow of the killer boat, Russian harpooners had loaded the canon and were preparing to take a shot at one of the tiring whales. West could see one of the Russian whalers steer the harpoon cannon in the direction of the whale in front of their Zodiac.

"He's getting ready to shoot," West cried out to Paul.

Paul lurched the Zodiac forward, the fluke of the Sperm whale was directly in West's face. It was large. It was surreal. It was terrifying. The killer boat was bearing down on them while the fleeing Sperm whales were directly in front, they couldn't speed up and they couldn't slow down.

The exhausted Sperm whale, in need of air, surfaced right next to their Zodiac, just missing them. It was enormous and dangerous. West screamed out.

"Whale! Whale! Whale!"

The harpoon gunner backed off the trigger for the moment, but the whaling boat continued to bear down on West and Paul, threatening to run over them. This oceanic 'game of chicken' continued for many minutes, over many miles. The Zodiac was getting pushed to its limit, and then came a sound they didn't want to hear. The outboard engine started to sputter.

Paul throttled up all the way, but something was not right. He tried again. No luck. West was screaming at him to veer off.

"Let Hunter and Delilah take it from here."

"Fuck off," howled a crazed Paul Revere.

The engine was sputtering, the Zodiac was losing speed, and Paul seemed to be on a suicide mission.

West couldn't wait any longer. Struggling, he detached his bow harness and lunged to grab the tiller. Paul was not about to allow that to happen. As they fought for control of the tiller, the Zodiac slowed down making it impossible for the killer boat to avoid ramming into them.

Sounding the alarm, the whalers plowed into the rear of the inflatable, it's bow wake tossing the Zodiac and it's two-man crew up into the air and off to the side. West, no longer tied into his harness, was ejected out of the Zodiac, into the choppy water, directly in the path of the whaling boat and it's whirling propellers. Disappearing under the water, he was nowhere to be seen.

Delilah and Hunter, unaware of the battle between West and Paul, had assumed the vacated position in front of the killer boat, continuing to block the harpoons of the Russian whalers.

Will and Susan, very aware of the drama in Zodiac number two, were frantically searching the open ocean for the missing West. Several minutes of agonizing searching seemed like hours until a panicked Susan spotted an orange figure floating in the water.

Will, putting his Zodiac training to the test, pulled up next to West, who was floating on his back, his arms locked around his life jacket, his eyes shut tight. Dragging him, alive, all of his body parts intact, into their Zodiac, Will spotted the damaged Zodiac Number Two up ahead, tossing up and down in an uncaring sea. Susan attended to West as Will maneuvered alongside the incapacitated Zodiac. It was empty. No Paul.

Scanning the ocean in every direction, they saw nothing but water. West flopped his soaked carcass back into his damaged, vacant Zodiac, as Susan got on the two-way radio and called for help.

"Maggie May, do you read me? This is Susan. We have a man overboard. Do you read me? We have a fucking man overboard. Over. Paul is missing. Over," she roared.

Two hundred yards away came the sound of the outboard engine of Delilah and Hunter's Zodiac. West, Will, and Susan screamed and yelled and screamed and yelled until they could see help heading their way. In the distance, the killer boat steamed off in the opposite direction toward its mother ship. The light of day was almost gone.

As you might imagine, Hunter and Delilah were a welcome sight as they reunited with the other inflatables. They were also carrying extra cargo. Slumped in the middle of their Zodiac was a shaking Paul Revere holding a makeshift bandage to his bleeding mouth.

"You missing something?" Hunter casually said to West.

"Nothing I can think of," West deadpanned.

"The hunt's over. At least for today. Everyone okay?" asked a drained and thankful Hunter.

They inspected each other with great relief and great emotion. Three tiny dots in the middle of a vast saltwater universe. There was an eerie calm and quiet.

297

No whales, no whalers, no Maggie May, only ocean.

"You did good today. You saved some whales," said a beaming Hunter.

As the light faded, they pulled the three inflatables close together, tied them with nylon chord, firmly clasped hold of each other, arm in arm, and waited for the Maggie May to pluck them from the sea.

#

All, except for Hunter, had to be harnessed, then hoisted back on board the Maggie May. Battered, bloodied, bruised, and weak, they were deposited on the aft deck like netted fish plucked from the sea.

The doctor examined each of them for broken bones, cuts, contusions, and in the case of Paul Revere, broken teeth. All, he concluded, would be physically okay. It never occurred to anybody that another kind of doctor might be needed. Someone experienced in trauma and horror and spiritual wounds.

Arianna, the writer from Rolling Stone, didn't want to wait for their experiences to be put into perspective. She didn't want any psychic healing to occur before she had a chance to interview all six. No sleeping was allowed before she could ask her questions. As Connor was always fond of saying, "sleep is for the weak."

#

The intention of the GreenPlanet crew was to stick with the Russians for as long as their fuel and supplies would allow; to fight them at every turn, but during the night, the whalers, in a moment of clarity, turned tail and sailed off full speed ahead for the International Date Line and the safety of their own waters. It was decided the next morning that the Maggie May would return to Los Angeles.

Five days of sailing due east and the Maggie May was resting in the shadow of Santa Catalina Island on another super Southern California day.

West and Will, via Zodiac, had just slipped, unnoticed, into a covert location in the L.A. harbor to pick up Connor Kilkenny and bring him back to the Maggie May. Connor would broadcast live from the boat, as it was welcomed home by friends, family, and the media. A large crowd had already gathered.

With great pride, the Maggie May approached, then tied up to the same dock that she had departed from weeks ago. A jubilant welcome-home crowd cheered as she shut her engines down.

On the main deck of the ship, the GreenPlanet crew was embraced by family and friends. Television cameramen, reporters, and photographers were everywhere. Vanessa Gray Reynolds was the object of desire for all of the paparazzi. Natalie Singer was signing autographs and posing with fans. Hunter was mobbed as he was speaking to a print reporter from the L.A. Times and a television crew from NBC.

"We were able to chase them out past the Hawaiian Islands. We saved several pods of whales from the harpoon guns," he said. "What saves the whales is the film footage, the media coverage. We know, when people can see and hear what's going on out there, they'll take action, and it's their actions that will create the necessary change," he continued.

Shakespeare Jones and Jimmy were being embraced by their old pals The Captain and Doctor.

"Never seen anything like that in all my days. It was something else. It was special," said Shakespeare shaking his head in disbelief.

Jimmy yelled out to anyone that was within earshot.

"This boat you're standing on. She's one hell of a boat. Make damn sure you get good pictures of her. This is a hell of a good day to be alive," he announced to the world.

West was surrounded by cameras, microphones, and note takers. He made sure to thank the KWOT staff and listeners, especially Connor. He reported, in detail, the facts and figures that argued powerfully against any rational reason to kill the whales. A British voice inside his head, that sounded very much like Kate, reminded him "he was not the story, just the facts."

Will and Susan were content to watch the show from the sidelines. Handing him a cold beer, she kissed him on the cheek. Clinking beer cans, Will offered up a toast.

"To saving whales," he said.

"To saving whales," Susan replied.

The welcome home celebration gradually lost steam, and all involved eventually wandered off to their next destination; their next adventure; leaving Shakespeare, Jimmy, The Captain, and Doctor alone once again, and very, very relieved to be relaxing on the deck of the magnificent Maggie May.

West and Delilah, duffle bags in hand, stood in the entranceway of Delilah's dark house. They were still feeling the pitch, roll, and yaw of the Maggie May. It would take a while to get their 'land legs' back. The old salts will tell you to keep moving. Go for long walks. Exercise. I'm guessing none of them battled the Russian whaling fleet, strapped into a thirteen-foot inflatable toy boat.

Sans equilibrium, they made their way into the house, turning on lights as needed. An exhausted West turned left, heading for the inviting living room couch, when unexpectedly, Delilah took his arm and redirected him to her bedroom.

She sat him down on the edge of her bed, and then disappeared into the bathroom where he could hear water filling the tub. When she returned, she got him up on his feet and began to undress him, carefully removing the sling that cradled his injured right arm.

When she had a naked West in front of her, she led him into the bathroom, shut off the water, and tested its temperature. Stepping into the tub was like stepping into a new world. The hot, clean, salt-free water on his skin had an alchemic effect. Delilah supported him as he slinked down into the water. She witnessed the relief, the release, and the ecstasy wash over him.

After two minutes of luxuriating with his eyes shut tight, West watched Delilah undress and stand before him. This was, he was most certain, the most bewitching sight that he had ever beheld in his life. Slipping into the tub with him, she felt the same healing water surround her skin. The tough outer shell that she had created to survive her ordeal, began to "melt, thaw, and resolve itself into a dew."

Opposite each other, her eyes locked on his, the realization of what they had just been through hit her hard, and her tears begin to flow.

Grasping a bar of soap, West proceeded to wash one of her hands, one finger at a time, and then the other hand, and then one arm, and then the other. He took her face into his hands and stared into her magnetic, watering eyes. How was it possible that he was here?

Often, when lost in the woods, we're advised to stay put. By the experts, the elders, the wise men. They tell us "don't move, don't panic, stay right where you are, someone will find you, eventually." Hmm. Maybe? Maybe not? Maybe it's best to keep moving? To wander lost? Maybe a bit of panic is not such a bad thing? Existentially? Sure, we could stray further into enemy territory. We could make our situation worse. We could perish. Or, we might find ourselves on a hero's journey? Swept along by powers greater than our understanding? We might find ourselves to be a temporary, necessary, cog in the cosmic wheel? We might find ourselves in the company of the most magical person in the world.

#

The sun felt good on his face as he sat ensconced on the sand looking forever out to sea. Had he spent the past twelve hours in this exact frozen position, on this exact spot of sand? Sure looks like it. He was watching the boats sail by while keeping one protective eye on some kids swimming a tad too far out. He appeared to be looking for something in particular, something special, something bigger than himself. He took his foot and smoothed the sand in front of him. This was his spot; his magical, mystical spot where he often went to find himself, to seek clarity, and to learn his way forward. His radar detected something. Close by. Intense. Feminine. His girlfriend.

Delilah brushed the sand out of West's hair. She copied his way of sitting and staring out to sea. He didn't acknowledge her existence.

"You looking for an old friend?" she asked him.

"I don't have any money," said West.

"Rumor has it, you know how to talk to whales."

"I've spent some time with them," he said.

"Rumor has it that you're special," she said not looking at him.

"That's a terrible rumor."

She handed him a folded piece of paper, put her arm around his waist, and rested her head on his shoulder. They both stared contemplatively out to sea.

Without moving a muscle, he lowered his eyes just enough to sneak a peek at the paper that she had placed in his hand. It was a duplicate of the very same flyer that she had handed him that very first day, when they both knew, whether they will admit it or not, that they had been brought together, on that same spot of sand, to do great things. Maybe even change the world.

<<<<>>>

PART TWO

"mama always told me not to look into the eyes of the sun, but mama that's where the fun is"

The Boss

WHO ARE YOU?

September 1978. Six weeks have come and gone since the Maggie May returned safe and sound to the Ports O' Call Village in San Pedro. August was quiet at the Southern California GreenPlanet office. The high drama of the preceding months, culminating in the confrontation with the Russian whaling fleet on the high seas, was now in the rearview mirror. Hunter fled underground promising to resurface sometime in September. Kate stayed in London; she's back now. Will popped into the office a couple of days a week to check his messages, while Susan and Salinger held down the proverbial fort.

Since they walked down the gangplank of the Maggie May, West and Delilah have been conducting a trial run of the boyfriend/girlfriend thing. It's going okay. Pretty good. Long walks, movies, and farmer's markets. Sex is frequent and passionate. Making up for lost time. During August they took turns going to the office. He on Monday and Wednesday, she on Tuesday and Thursday.

Delilah suggested that West bring his humble possessions to her house. He could keep them there until a decision was made on cohabitating as well as any agreed upon definition of their relationship. He concurred and complied.

It was a much needed six weeks of drama-free living, a necessary recovery period for all, a critical intermission to reflect, heal, and re-prioritize. Serenity and low blood pressure ruled the dog days of August, but now August was also in the rearview mirror. September had arrived and with it a ramping up, and a return to high stakes poker. Once more unto the breach.

Delilah's blood pressure was anything but low on this particular day, on this particular morning. It was still early, most of the day ahead of them, but she was already hopping mad. Standing at the corner of 6th Avenue and 48th street in midtown Manhattan, she was surrounded by an ocean of New Yorkers moving in all directions. West, a hundred paces ahead of her, was heading straight for the Pig and Whistle and his first beer of the day when, as if struck by a tranquilizer dart, he was stopped in his tracks at the sound of Delilah's voice piercing the membrane of the city.

Turning to face her, he could see Delilah, hands on hips, ready to explode. Gradually, carefully, he made his way to back to her to face the music.

"Can we talk about what happened?" said an apoplectic Delilah.

"What? Let's get a beer. Pig and Whistle," West countered.

"We were on live television. The Daybreak Show. Paula Jane interviewed us. Are you aware of that?" she bleated.

"I am," he mumbled as he ran his hand through his mop of hair.

Oh yea, West was aware of that. NBC studio 8G. Paula sat opposite of he and Delilah, a cheesy TV-show coffee table separating them. Paula, whom he found quite fetching, appeared very serious as she asked her questions, as did Delilah with her well-prepared responses. West, on the other hand, behaved as if he were at a lovely cocktail party, smiling, head nodding in agreement to all that was proffered; basking in the warm glow of the studio spotlight. There was one particular moment when Paula pointed to a monitor, which showed film footage of the recent high seas confrontation with the Russian whaling fleet. West watched along with the two women as if he was not a part of the story, learning all of this for the very first time. He sat calm and detached when the trio, and the millions watching at home, witnessed the near ramming of the Zodiac that he and fellow whale-saver Paul Revere occupied. Surreal, he thought, to watch himself fly out of the rubber inflatable and into the churning sea.

Delilah placed a consoling hand on his arm as Paula looked to West for what she hoped would be a very emotional TV-show response. Didn't happen. Instead, West, eyes flirtatiously locked on Paula, was smiling, and seemingly at peace with the entire world. In that moment he was thinking that it might be nice to go have a beer.

"You didn't do anything that we talked about," Delilah continued. "Where was the passion? Where was the urgency?"

"Weird seeing that footage. Not how I remember things," he said shaking his head.

"You almost died out there," wailed Delilah.

West gave her a condescending look that said 'a bit dramatic, don't you think?' which made Delilah even crazier.

"A big fucking boat ran over you!" she screamed at

the top of her lungs.

West, embarrassed, looked around at the many nearby New Yorkers on the move. Not a raised eyebrow in any direction. Unable to move, not even to the Pig and Whistle, his eyes followed Delilah as she stormed off into the mob of humanity and disappeared out of sight.

Here is what West's gut told him. It told him that The Daybreak Show interview went very well. That phones in the L.A. office would blow up when the tape-delayed version played on the west coast. It told him that events were about to escalate. The spotlight was about to get brighter. His intuition, he felt, was something that he could rely on; his memory was not.

Since that dramatic day in July, he has, each and every day, tried and failed to clearly remember the events. What actually happened out there?

He could recall the beginning moments. Measuring the dead whale. Seeing the Russian whaling boats approaching, the kick of adrenaline, the pounding of his heart. Speeding up to block the Russian killer boats from getting off a clean shot.

But that's it. The rest of the movie is blank. He hears what everyone tells him. He knows the tales of each of his fellow warriors. He has seen the still photography, and now the film footage, but it doesn't help. Doesn't work. Blank slate.

But his gut. His gut tells him that he's on borrowed time now. It tells him 'don't look back.' Looking back would not be a good idea. It tells him to go for a walk. Think things over. His gut says, "follow me."

When West walked into the hotel room he could hear the shower running. On the phone by the bed, he could see the red 'message' light blinking. Delilah's clothes were thrown over the back of a chair.

Softly closing the door and putting the lock firmly in place, he made his way to the side of the bed. His first order of business was to get out of the TV clothes. Delilah wouldn't let him wear jeans and a t-shirt for the television interview, and although he was uncomfortable, he didn't protest, a sign that he was wising up a bit.

As he sat on the bedside in his boxers sans everything else, he could hear another sound in addition to the running water. At first, he couldn't identify it. Sounded like a voice calling his name. Wasn't Delilah. Wasn't his gut. Wasn't ominous. Friendly. Like the voice of an angel, if one could know what an angel sounded like. Across the room. It was coming from across the room. He didn't see anything. Not at first. Scanning high and low, he followed the voice... what the...ah! Ahh! The mini-bar! Old friend! I hear you!

West jumped to his feet to answer the call. As he passed by the chair adorned with Delilah's clothes, he grabbed her blouse and put it to his face like a much-needed oxygen mask after a deep dive into the lower depths.

Johnny Walker Black seemed to be the most responsible choice. Appropriate post Daybreak Show libation, don't you think? He grabbed himself one, then thought "Wait, they're mini-bottles for Christ sake.

Take two."

Back to the side of the bed, plastic cup of whiskey in hand, he could hear no more voices, no running water, no angels, only the sound of honking taxicabs twenty floors below on the streets of New York City. The whiskey tasted good. He let it coat his tongue.

The door to the bathroom opened and Delilah, naked, steam rising from squeaky clean skin, stood in the doorway and allowed the foggy backlight to frame her as the goddess that owned West's free will, owned his notion of independence, and any clarity of thought or action he might try to muster.

Nothing was said by either of them. As a prosecutor holding all of the cards might do, Delilah calculatedly moved to West and stood, feet apart, within an inch of his face. He dared not move or take any immediate action. It was clear that she was the director of this play.

Breathe, he thought, as he stared into the naked abyss, into her center of power. Slow your breathing. Good.

Ever so gently, West leaned forward one inch and touched his lips to hers. Just a hint of a kiss, her hair still damp, her legs strong. Zero reaction from Delilah.

Setting aside the whiskey glass, he took both of his hands and wrapped them around her right knee. Just held them there as he rested his forehead on her leg. No one was in a hurry.

Bracing her leg with his left hand, with great care he moved his right hand up the back of her thigh until it wasn't possible to escalate any further. Until her ass was in his hand, and his thumb, his thumb was, in the perfect place.

Delilah didn't move a muscle inside or out as West tenderly guided his thumb up and into her, then silently commanded it to remain oh so still. Delilah showed no outward signs of recognition, but she was wet, and getting wetter, and this contributed to West getting as hard as Chinese algebra. They both held their ground.

Sixty seconds passed. West's erection was still in his control, but his breathing and composure were going downhill. Delilah could detect his weakening condition, and at the exact right moment, right when West was about to explode, his thumb still inside her, she said the following:

"Don't. Look at me. Relax. Look at me. When you focus, when you're not distracted and self-absorbed, you can dazzle. You can change the world. Do great things. But your Kryptonite is the truth. You fear it and it makes you weak. You fear admitting that you almost died out there and that you were afraid. You fear admitting that you have very strong feelings for me, and that just maybe you might have met your equal. You fear success because it's lonely, and it's hard work. Maybe you're just not up to it, right? You fear the responsibility that comes with power, with leadership. Being a fuck-up is easy for you. Going underground is easy. No effort required. I need you to snap out of this. Right now. I need you to get back in the game. You need to focus. You get me?"

Before he could respond, she took a smooth step back, which allowed his thumb to undock from the mother ship. The phone rang. Their eyes were laser-locked on each other.

On the way to answering the phone, Delilah grabbed the plastic glass of whiskey, took a big gulp, and stranded a staggered West, now under her spell more than ever. Who was this woman? What had he gotten himself into? Was he up for this?

He couldn't take his eyes off of her. There she was, naked, the phone to her ear, sipping his whiskey and silently listening to the voice on the other end. Periodically, she would stare in his direction, and he could feel that whomever it was Delilah was listening to, he or she was saying things about him. Was it Kate? Was it Hunter? Was he in hot water? Had his Daybreak Show performance crashed and burned? He was so sure that he had slayed.

Delilah mumbled a couple of "okays," "will do," "I'll tell him," then hung up the phone and did not tell him. West's intuition turned out to be correct. It had been Kate on the other end of the phone. Jet-lagged, and still on London time, she called from the L.A. office to offer congratulations on a "brilliant" Daybreak Show performance. The tape-delayed version had just aired on the west coast and the phones were erupting. Again his gut spoke true. "Spot on" as Kate would say. Delilah, however, would not say. She would keep him in the dark for a while longer. They had some unfinished naked business to attend to, and Kate had a new assignment for him.

#

San Francisco is on the west coast and San Franciscans get The Daybreak Show too. As it happens, the Northern California GreenPlanet cadre of

Jonah Stern, Karma Parrish, Catty Slur, Kai Klein, Jade, Sunset, and attorney David Middling had also watched West and Delilah do their thing. Safe to say, their reactions to what they witnessed was less enthusiastic than Kate's.

Karma concluded that it was a completely "wasted opportunity," "a disaster," "a train wreck." Catty almost puked as she watched, feeling that things couldn't get much worse for the organization or for the whales. She was angry that the L.A. people "made it all about themselves." Sunset and Kai concurred, expressing their deep hatred of the "fucking Hollywood scum." Jade was confused, she didn't understand why Karma thought that it was a disaster. She thought the film made all of them look like heroes.

Attorney Middling suggested that it might be considered a disaster for their office, but not for their comrades to the south.

"People have their checkbooks out as we speak," said Jonah. "Money is about to flow. Lots and lots of money into the L.A. office," he continued. "Time for a fight."

West and Delilah were breathless and swollen, but not from a fight. Checkout time was one o'clock and they needed to get their overwhelmed asses moving. As they threw on some clothes and began the packing of suitcases, Delilah informed West of the change in plans. Kate was sending him upstate, to Niagara Falls, Love Canal to be specific. There was a plane ticket to Buffalo waiting for him at the hotel front desk. A rental car had been arranged for him in Buffalo. He was to meet with the new head of the Love Canal Home

313

Owners Association. Lois Gibbs was her name. His mission was to meet with Lois Gibbs, bear witness to the developing toxic waste crisis, offer encouragement and GreenPlanet support, and become well versed in the facts on the ground. Kate posited–since West was already in the state of New York–that sending him for a quick visit could prove valuable for GreenPlanet down the road. It would also help build West's credentials. And Delilah? Delilah would be returning to L.A. as planned. She had admirably completed her mission in NYC, and the time had come to throw the switch in the L.A. office back on to full power.

As West drove the eighteen miles from the Buffalo airport to his meeting with Lois Gibbs, he had a love canal on his mind, just not the one he was about to see. It tortured him to part ways with Delilah at LaGuardia, and he didn't understand why she wasn't there in the car with him. It also had him off balance that he was again feeling that strongly about a woman. The monologue that she delivered while they were 'attached' had his head spinning.

So, what's this other Love Canal all about? Along with his plane ticket, the concierge in New York also handed him a manila envelope filled with pages that had been faxed to him from Los Angeles. West had never received a 'facsimile' page before. He was gobsmacked. The corporate logo for Xerox was at the top of each page, and the unmistakable signature of Kate was at the bottom. These were his Love Canal briefing papers to be read on the airplane.

Turns out that Love Canal, named after William T. Love, was an actual hell on Earth. A 'model' neighborhood of thirty-six blocks in the city of Niagara Falls that sat atop a toxic waste landfill known to its owners, the Niagara Falls School Board, but unbeknownst to it's poisoned residents. Eight hundred families with four hundred children in school in 1978. Toxic vapors, poison sludge, tainted soil and groundwater. Benzene, chloroform, dioxin, and PCB's. Birth defects, miscarriages, cancer, epilepsy, infections, asthma, leukemia, cleft palates, and nerve disorders. Scores of fifty-five-gallon drums of deadly chemical waste sat directly beneath two schools. It was "a public health time bomb." A fucking nightmare. Mother Nature on the run in the nineteen seventies. A runaway train spewing its deadly cargo.

Enter Lois Gibbs. The twenty-seven-year-old mother of a very sick child. Her five-year-old son developed epilepsy and breathing problems within four months of attending his elementary school built on the toxic waste site. Seizures, asthma, blood disease. She would learn that her home, the schools, the entire neighborhood was a death trap.

Going door to door, talking with her neighbors, asking questions and comparing notes, she gathered the disturbing evidence of many other horror stories. Something had to be done immediately. Necessity is the mother, right? Hence the birth of community organization and activism at Love Canal. Its fearless leader, Lois Gibbs.

The Love Canal Home Owners Association was formed. Not the most revolutionary or threatening name for this group of moms and pops and grandmas and PTA members. Ms. Gibbs would head the

315

association and lead the troops into battle against the local, state, and federal governments. They would take their fight to the NY State Health Department, the EPA, and ultimately the White House.

A force to be reckoned with, she had to learn how to take on Goliath without any training camp. There simply wasn't any time to develop a polish. People were dying.

West could relate. At least regarding the no time to prepare, get thrown into the deep end and learn to swim aspect. When he pulled up in front of the building where the homeowners were headquartered, he saw tables covered with paper plates, paper napkins, condiments, buns, bowls of potato salad, coleslaw, chips and dips, containers of juice, bottles of soda, and water. Four barbeque grills were fired up and captained by more than enough husbands. Burgers, hot dogs, chicken. Love Canal Home Owners Association looked like one big picnic; like the fourth of July.

Inside it was a different scene. The place was buzzing with organized parents and frenetic children. A variety of activities were ongoing; sign making, leaflet folding, phone calling, and roundtable discussions with physicians and lawyers. As he entered the room, West, an obvious outsider, was scooped up by one of the young mothers–she had seen him earlier on The Daybreak Show. Leading him by the arm, she deposited him in front of a hot dog-eating young woman who was overseeing the whole show.

Lois Gibbs was only two years older than West, but her vibe suggested someone much older and wiser.

The young mother introduced him to Ms. Gibbs as "Mr. Walker from GreenPlanet." Mouth full of hot dog, Gibbs shook her head.

"GreenPlanet. Save the whales," said the young mother trying to help.

"No whales around here," said Lois.

"He was on The Daybreak Show this morning," said the young mother dashing off to rescue one of the children about to jump off of a folding chair.

Lois Gibbs gave West the once-over, and then swallowed her last bite of hot dog.

"You hungry? Want a hot dog? Come with me," she said walking away toward the front door.

West grabbed a hot dog bun and squirted some ketchup on it as she speared a dog and plopped it on his bun. She waved for him to follow her.

"I came to observe first hand what is happening here. Maybe help you with exposure. What brought you here?" said West with a mouthful.

The last thing that Love Canal needed was more exposure. They had been chemically over-exposed, but she knew what he meant. What she wanted was a visit by President Carter. She wanted a sanctioned evacuation. She wanted an admission of guilt.

"I'm busy. I don't have time for small talk. Don't mean to be rude. You're

walking through the valley of the shadow of death. This is a community chock full

of birth defects, and poisoned land and water. Cancer resides on every block. My

five year old's school is built on top of a toxic waste dump. I go to a lot of funerals these days."

317

She walked him through the neighborhood, pointing out abandoned houses, fenced off areas, warning signs, toxic waste bubbling out of the ground, dead birds, squirrels, cats, and dogs. Vegetation was dead and dying. Black goo covered basement floors.

Back at LCHA headquarters, she showed him kids with genetic defects, and a crippled young man in a wheelchair. There were photos on the wall of neighbors that had died due to the toxic nature of their hood. It was a war zone. Winter in America, as Gil-Scott Heron sang. No small talk there.

#

West was full of virulent Love Canal images rattling around in his brain when he walked, suitcase in hand, through the door into the GreenPlanet office in Los Angeles. He could see Kate sitting at the head of the conference table leafing through a stack of documents and position papers. Susan was writing in earnest on the strategy board, as Salinger commanded the reception desk. West could see, via the open door of Will's office, Will at his desk going through a pile of photographs. There were a handful of volunteers, unknown to him, coordinating various merchandise items, and there was Delilah. Standing near her desk, listening on the phone, and jotting down notes. It was only twenty-four hours ago that she was also listening on the phone, standing naked, and ready to rumble. He dared not think about that at this moment. Dropping his suitcase with a loud thud, he tried in vain to gain everyone's attention, and then holding his arms out wide as if to say: Hello? Anybody? It's me. West. I'm back from New York.

Nothing. Not a glance in his direction. Weird. Uncomfortable. Okay, what's going on here? he thought to himself as he made his way to his desk where he found a mound of pink 'while you were out' message slips awaiting him.

Plopping down his suitcase for a second time, he grabbed the top pink slip on the heap. Before he had a chance to decipher its contents, the entire gang, except for Delilah, began to wildly applaud and cheer him. Surrounding him at his desk, they whooped and hollered and backslapped. Delilah waited patiently for the welcome committee to calm the fuck down, and then she politely maneuvered her way to West, put her arm around his waist, and whispered into his ear.

"Apparently The Daybreak Show interview went reasonably well."

West looked at her with a Grand Canyon grin. He knew it! He fucking knew it!

"Phones lit up. People called wanting to know where to send checks; how to get involved. Good Morning L.A. called. They want to book you on the show as soon as possible. Don't get a big head, and remember my fucking speech," she said as she led the principals over to the conference table.

This was the first time that West had seen Kate since he dropped her off at LAX to fly home to a dying father. He'll never forget that day. He gave her a big hug.

"Great to see you again. So sorry for your loss," he said.

"No one here gets out alive," she replied in quintessential Kate fashion.

319

"I hope you knocked all of the toxic waste off your trainers before you got on the plane," she said.

West didn't know about 'trainers.' With a worried expression on his face, he looked down at his crotch, causing Kate to laugh out loud, which startled him. He'd never seen Kate laugh out loud. I guess death changes people. He could dig it, seeing that he recently grasped how being on borrowed time changes people, at least he felt that was true in his case.

Another thing that startled him was how great it felt to return to the fray, the whole gang around the conference table, Kate back at the helm. It was exciting. Like the first day of school, only the stakes were higher, and the mistakes were more costly.

West was in the middle of his detailed and disturbing report on Love Canal when the phone refused to stop ringing. Salinger didn't want to, but she jumped up and headed for her desk. As West continued to describe what he bore witness to, what Lois Gibbs had shown him, Salinger's face grew increasingly grim. She hung up the phone and interrupted West.

"It's Hunter. He's been arrested," she said.

Salinger had everyone's rapt attention. Hunter and a half dozen other GreenPlanet activists—including his pal and GreenPlanet legal counsel Hugh Simon—were on Hvalvik Beach in the Faroe Islands. Hunter and five others had been arrested for trying to interfere with the slaughter of thirty-six pilot whales that had been corralled into the shallow water of the bay, dorsal fins severed, spines cut. Hugh was there to protect the protestors, as best he could, from beatings by the locals, and excessive force from the police. A GreenPlanet film crew was on hand to document the events as they occurred.

Hunter and his mates were covered in whale blood and guts. They had waded out into the bay and valiantly attempted to block the fishermen from using their hooks and knives on the whales. Local media were also on hand to talk to Hunter and telecast the confrontation to their respective stations. As he was being hauled off to jail, Hunter yelled to the microphones. "The whale meat and blubber are poison," he screamed. "Mercury, PCB's, DDT, not safe to eat. MAKES NO SENSE," he exclaimed as he was whisked into a police van and driven away with haste. More than a thousand pilot whales were killed each year as a local Faroese food source and the continuation of cultural tradition. Hunter didn't give a good goddamn about their tradition. He was there to show the world. To take a stand. To interfere. Did someone say rest, relaxation, and anonymity?

While Salinger was informing the clan about Hunter's arrest, Susan was up and at the Telex machine, which began making noise at the exact same moment that Salinger answered the phone. Susan was reading the details of the Faroe Island protest as her replacement spoke them. There was other breaking news that she was also absorbing. Stunning news. Involving Paul Revere.

The split second that Salinger finished relaying the Hunter news, Susan grabbed the baton. Waving the paper torn from the Telex, she began reading aloud.

"For Immediate Release: Paul Revere Departs

GreenPlanet to Create New Environmental Organization: 'Sea Pirates' September 7, 1978. Seattle, WA. Sea Pirates, a 501(c) 3 non-profit environmental NGO has been formed to battle those that would inflict harm upon whales, dolphins, and all forms of aquatic life. Our multivariate direct action intervention tactics will not be limited to observation and reporting. If necessary, confrontations will be carried out in physically aggressive and material means. The members and supporters of Sea Pirates understand that time is of the essence. Endangered ocean life need our help NOW. We refuse to diminish our effectiveness by taking marine life-saving options off the table. According to founder Paul Revere 'my time spent as a member of GreenPlanet was important and rewarding. I wish them well and applaud them for their efforts on behalf of the whales, but effort alone is not enough, for me anyway. I demand results. I want victory. For our cause. For the planet. Whatever it takes'. For more information please contact: Axel D'Artagnan. Sea Pirates International. Seattle, WA. 206-636- 6363"

She handed the press release to Kate. Welcome back Kate! Chaos reigns supreme.

"Would love to see the look on Jonah's face right now," said an understated Kate.

Jonah's face was calm and evil. He too, had just read aloud the news of Hunter's arrest to his tribe, as well as the Sea Pirate press release. No dummy, he knew 'tis better to take the bull by the horns.' Some of the groundlings had already jumped ship and were on their way to Seattle to join the pirates. Jonah knew that there would be more; there was discontent in the ranks, had been for quite a while. The Daybreak Show disaster yesterday morning certainly didn't help matters. Kai Klein, standing by his side, continually reminded him of that.

"A bit too much cheering for Paul, don't you think? And how about D'Artagnan going over to the dark side?" asked a nervous Kai.

"There will be more defections, but we'll be okay," Jonah said.

"Is that why you read the press release to them, to show them no fear?"

Jonah gave him a long, uncomfortable, smile.

"Gave me a chance to see each face. Now I know who'll betray me," said a supremely confident Jonah as he wiped a handful of grease out of his unwashed hair.

Kate's hair was freshly washed, rinsed, and repeated. She had West by the arm as she led him into her office, closing the door behind them. Moments before, she had assigned Susan the task of preparing a Faroe Island-Pilot Whale press kit. West would need it when the press came calling.

West was expecting Kate to lavish praise on him for his Daybreak Show performance, and his in-depth Love Canal report. As usual, she caught him off guard.

"Do you think it a good idea for you to be cohabiting with Delilah?" she asked.

Before he could answer, she said, "seems like a bad idea." Before he could respond, she continued, "When the media press you on Paul Revere, don't be diplomatic. Our official response is: 'GreenPlanet is a non-violent organization. We have zero tolerance for reckless, dangerous, self-promotional behavior. Mr. Revere's actions are irresponsible and life-threatening, and there is no place in our organization for that type of individual.'"

"If it weren't for Delilah," said West.

"About the Daybreak Show, continue to let the media be the first to mention that you were almost done in. You talk about saving whales until they talk about you, and then you downplay your almost tragic demise."

Tragic demise? West was staggered, but not as staggered as he would be within the next few seconds. Unable to speak, he turned at the sound of an opening door. No one there. No one visible out in the war room either. And then, from behind the door, emerged a site for staggered eyes. Kip! Kip Asher!

This was a true surprise. No one expected to see Kip walk through that door again, especially not Kate, and yet, there he was in the flesh. There were smiles all around. West was giddy.

"You back in L.A.? How long? You getting back in the game? Man! It's great to see you," said an over-excited West.

Just then, Will poked his head through the door to kidnap Kip and whisk him off to lunch at Musso and Frank. It was announced that all were welcome to join them. Kip was picking up the tab! Count West in, he was in motion, about to drop everything and join the party when Delilah and Kate intervened.

Delilah reminded West that they had plans to lunch at Lucy's El Adobe Café, and then Kate instantly nixed any and all plans, including Delilah's, that involved

West leaving the building. He needed to get up to speed on the Faroe Island incident. Susan would be his tutor. Additionally, Kate had made arrangements for West to debate the Japanese Consul General at UCLA come Monday afternoon. Susan would be his tutor. He and Susan would be holed up in Kate's office, handling calls from the media, as they simultaneously became expert in Japanese culture pertaining to whaling. Susan had orders not to let him out of her sight. Perhaps Delilah "might bring them some food when she returned from lunch?" said Kate.

Before West or Delilah could protest, Salinger informed the group that there was a call on line one; Connor Kilkenny from KWOT radio station wanting to interview West. Game time had arrived.

Delilah, irritated, raced after Kip and Will, and the three of them scampered in the direction of Musso and Frank and giant martinis. Kate, so it seems, also had a lunch date, a clandestine lunch date with, well, we don't know. It was clandestine. That means secret. Sealing West and Susan in her office, she gathered her things, threw her bag over her shoulder, gave a wink and a nod to Salinger, and out the door she went.

Frustrated, West got on the phone with his KWOT pal Connor Kilkenny as Susan pressed the button to activate the speaker. A word about KWOT. In 1978 KWOT was the most listened-to radio station in Los Angeles. Their revolutionary format took L.A. by storm. Diverse, personal, counter-cultural, socially conscious, outrageous, progressive, activist, fearless musical sets chosen by the DJ's with the carte blanche blessing of their badass female program director. Long songs, deep cuts, cool sponsors, and access to the biggest rock stars on the planet, provided the KWOT coterie with unparalleled street cred. Didn't matter who was behind the microphone, opinions were voiced, Cannabis was occasionally inhaled, and a social consciousness was nurtured. Environmental issues, drugs, war, censorship, civil rights, and corporate intrusion were some of the themes that were woven into the musical mix. They fired up their listeners about nukes, Paraquat spraying, sex, drugs, rock and roll, and "the man." Whales, seals, dolphins, and ocean pollution. It was Southern California after all.

West prudently informed Connor that they were on the speakerphone, and that the lovely Susan was by his side. Comprende? Connor understood, and then joked that he wouldn't mention the prostitutes. West shook his head. Susan made a note.

After some brief chitchat, Connor rolled tape and conducted the interview with West for the five and six o'clock news. He and West worked well together. They knew each other's rhythms and proclivities. West had come a long way from that first interview with Connor, not that long ago. The news of Hunter's arrest and the Pilot Whale slaughter would elicit a strong response from the KWOT listeners. The phones at both the radio station and the GreenPlanet office would light up. A good thing for all. They ended their phone call with plans to get together soon, and then were off to their next things.

The next thing for West was one interview after another, after another; Susan by his side, making notes, handing him facts and figures, and providing him encouragement and support. Like he and Connor, Susan and he also worked well together, and although the day was long, it went very well.

So, now that things had slowed down, West couldn't help but think about his comrades-in-arms, and all of the fun that he was denied. Drinking, carousing, scheming, and perhaps the revelation of the next exciting adventure. He felt a rush of something. Adrenalin? Urgency? He and Susan were sitting side-by-side on the couch in Kate's office. Documents, notebooks, and photos were piled high on the coffee table in front of them. Susan was still going strong.

"You are speaking on behalf of the whales. Whales know no nationality. The Japanese cultural argument is immaterial. Got it?" she said to an antsy West.

He shook his head 'yes.' She carried on "The Consul General begrudgingly agreed to," she wasn't able to finish her sentence. West, without thinking, operating on pure impulse, pulled Susan close and kissed her. Her lack of resistance– her willingness– resulted in the kiss being longer than shorter. What?

"And you were doing so well," said Susan as she moved very slightly back from West.

Unable to think of the right thing to say, he could only smile an impetuous smile. The ensuing silence became uncomfortable. Neither of them knew what to say or do. Delilah popped into both of their heads. Conflicted? Confused is probably a good way to describe what they were feeling.

West was about to say something stupid when a timid knocking on Kate's door stopped him cold. The equally timid movement of the door was followed by

327

the circumspect head of Salinger peaking inside. Salinger could see West and Susan sitting close to each other. She could feel the weirdness in the air. Susan tried and failed to subtly inch herself away from West.

"End of my day. I'm going home. You need anything before I go?" said Salinger.

Susan, jumping to her feet, looking guilty as hell, began to collect the mountain of paper on the coffee table. She said that they, too, were done with their day and were headed out. West sat silent and motionless as Salinger and Susan did their "see you tomorrows." Backing her head out the door, Salinger closed it part way and tried to swiftly make her escape. West was now on his feet.

"Wait! I need something," he said throwing open the door and stopping Salinger in her tracks. "I need a drink," he said. "I need a drink, and I think that you two should join me," said West.

Surprisingly, to Susan anyway, Salinger thought that was an excellent idea, and expressed her desire to go to the Chimney Sweep. Where else, right?

"The Chimney Sweep!" trumpeted West. "Susan, don't say a word, you're coming. We worked hard today. Let's get a fucking drink, or ten!"

Susan made eyes with Salinger, who nodded, and gave her the sparkly eyes of approval. Very well then. Game on.

"Do you think Connie is in a scorpion-making mood?" Susan said dumping the load of papers back onto the coffee table. "Sure hope so."

Let's be honest. Scorpions are a pain in the ass to make. Rum, brandy, orange juice, lemon juice, simple sugar, orgeat, and a goddamn sugar rim. The Chimney Sweep was not Trader Vic's. You want a fucking scorpion; go to Trader Vic's. Unless you're one of the GreenPlanet Girls. If you belong to that gang, you can have as many scorpions as your heart desires because Connie loves the GreenPlanet Girls. Adores and worships them, and they her. Besides, it was Connie's fault that the GG's were introduced to the scorpion. During a momentary lapse of clear thinking, back at the beginning of the year, Connie made a round of scorpions for the GG's. She can't remember why she did, but it doesn't matter now, and needless to say, she has become very practiced in the art of the scorpion. So, was she now or would she ever be in a scorpion-making mood? Never. Would she gladly make them for her girls? Always. Was it permissible for other patrons of the bar, when they see the cocktail being served to the GG's, to also partake? No fucking way. Next topic.

Delilah was drinking wine. She never drinks wine, but that's what Connie's sister Stephanie Lynn was drinking, so when in Rome. Probably better for her than whiskey or scorpions. Delilah could take her time and sip the wine, like she did the four martinis at the Musso and Frank lunch.

Stephanie Lynn is Connie's older sister, but only by a year and a half. Fifty-seven years old, gold-dustily attractive, and exotically dressed in a hippie, fortuneteller, witchy-woman kind of way. Earlier, when

Delilah had entered the bar, Stephanie Lynn was sitting alone, white wine in hand, swaying to and fro as she listened to Fleetwood Mac on the jukebox. 'Go Your Own Way.' Delilah hadn't seen her before. She didn't know Connie had a sister. A couple of hours later and they were besties.

Stephanie knew—her witchy radar lit up—as soon as Delilah sat down at the bar, that Delilah was having "man troubles." Before Connie could even introduce them to one and other, Stephanie had already sized her up. She believed that it never works to seek out that special someone. One must embrace the present. One must let all personal desires and needs come to them. Carpe diem, and in this case carpe noctem. When it was meant to be, the right one would walk through the door at the right time. Trust the path. Embrace the mystery. Another glass of wine?

Delilah tried to explain. Said it was complicated. Said she "found him" at the beach. The stars aligned, she said. She confessed to Stephanie something that she hadn't told anyone. That strange day at Smith College; that sudden U-turn. One minute she was advancing full speed ahead, and the next minute paralysis. To this day, she still doesn't understand what happened. Her cage had become perennially rattled. Then, she found him, and yes, another glass of wine couldn't hurt.

When the doors of the bar dramatically flew open— speaking of the right one walking through the door— they saw West, striding like a colossus, with one arm around Susan, and the other around Salinger. His day must have gone well.

"Enter the king," said Delilah.

"And his court," said a wide-eyed Stephanie.

"Synchronicity?" said Delilah.

West, Susan, and Salinger snaked their way through the now-crowded Chimney Sweep to Delilah sitting gloomily at the bar.

"Did you finish all of your chores?" said an alcoholic Delilah.

"Missioned accomplished," West answered with pride.

"He gets a shiny gold star for the day," said Susan who still hadn't let go of West's waist.

Delilah noticed the cuddly sound in Susan's voice, causing her to sit up straight to have a better look. As unobtrusive as possible, Susan slid her arm off of West's person, and then gladly accepted the cocktail that was being handed to her by her heroine Connie.

Connie, the master bartender that she was, handed Susan and Salinger scorpions, and West a whiskey. Most importantly, she had her own cocktail ready to go because you never know when the moment might call for a toast.

"To accomplishing missions!" toasted Connie.

Glasses clinked together, alcohol was ceremoniously sipped, and the messiness of human relationships shifted gears. Stephanie Lynn was one of the glass clinkers, and since she hadn't been introduced as of yet, she took matters into her own hands. She locked eyes with West.

"I'm Stephanie Lynn, Connie's sister. You must be West," she said.

"Guilty as charged. Hi Connie's sister," said West.

"Delilah and I were just having a discussion about complicated men. Are you complicated West?"

"I'm thirsty. Cheers," he said as he moved in to give Delilah a kiss on the cheek.

Delilah stopped him with two fingers, meticulously wiping a glossy substance from the corner of his mouth. Strange, West smelled like patchouli. Not his style. It was Susan's style, however. Susan and Salinger turned to each other pretending to be oblivious to the impending storm clouds that were on the horizon. Salinger wisely signaled Connie for two more scorpions.

Before the West and Delilah show could pick up steam, two hands grabbed West's shoulders from behind. Kip and Will, on West's heels, feeling no pain from their liquid afternoon, naturally gravitated straight to the Chimney Sweep in hopes of finding this exact group of ne'er-do'-wells. Once again, mission accomplished. Kip blew a kiss to a beaming Connie. Over West's shoulders he addressed Delilah.

"We knew you weren't going home," he said to her.

Delilah smiled a guilty smile, and raised a glass in his direction. Will grabbed drinks from Connie, handed one to Kip, then joined Susan and Salinger who were commandeering an about-to-be-vacated table.

"Ladies, do you mind if I kidnap this guy for a bit? I promise to bring him right back," said Kip to Delilah and Stephanie.

West tried to gage Delilah's emotional and physical state. It didn't look good.

"I need to hang with Kip for a few minutes. Do you

mind?" West asked.

"Go. Hang," she said, and she meant it.

Kip took West by the arm and steered him away
from the group. West on the spot flashed back to his
first meeting with Kip. Right there in the Chimney
Sweep. Middle of the day. No one in the bar except he
and Kip, and the strange dark man in the corner, and
Connie behind the bar. He was anxious to describe in
detail what happened after he and Will bid farewell to
Kip in Cabo San Lucas. Dumped in the Mexican desert
to die. At least that's how it seemed to them at the
time. He wanted to know if Kip was back? As in back in
the office, back in the saddle. Would that mean Kate
would be leaving? Did Hunter arrange this? When
could he go to lunch with Kip? He had lots of
questions, but Kip had a different topic for discussion.
About West, not about himself.

Since they last saw each other down at Kip's
Mexican hideout, West–two thousand miles out at sea–
had faced a harpoon cannon pointed at his head. He
had repeatedly ducked and covered as exploding
harpoons were fired all around him. He'd been ejected
from his Zodiac into a rough sea, and in front of a
speeding Russian killer boat that was willfully bearing
down on him. He unavoidably rode atop the backs of
fleeing Sperm Whales, and battered and bruised, he
lived to talk about it. That's what Kip wanted to chat
about.

"You've been through a lot this year," said Kip.

Getting no reply from West, Kip studied him
carefully, and let West squirm.

"What's that thing that they say about borrowed

time?" said Kip.

"Don't know," said West.

With a knowing chuckle, Kip clinked his Cuba Libre glass with West's whiskey glass, and raised two drink fingers in the air.

"Welcome to the inner circle," said Kip.

A funny thing about inner circles; one is simultaneously pleased and disturbed to be a member. West was no different. It was cool, an honor, to be considered simpatico with Kip and maybe even Hunter, but what was often required for membership was disquieting. Haunting would be more apropos. And West was most assuredly haunted. It would be outstanding, he thought, if everyone–especially his inner voice– would shut the fuck up about his time being borrowed. He could deal with, and would deal with his time, and he didn't need anybody else's thoughts or advice, thank you very much. What he needed was another whiskey.

He spied Susan on her way to the jukebox. She made it a point to take the long way, walking by the inner circle boys. She also made sure to make lingering eye contact with West, or that's what he surmised. Was he seeing something that wasn't there? Did her eyes have a different sparkle to them? Could she tell that he was conflicted? Jesus. He did need another whiskey.

West and Kip cut short their one-on-one and began zigzagging their way back to the bar when they saw Kate come bursting through the doors. Maniacal, distraught, wild, worked-up, frenzied, wounded, hair on fire, horrified. She pushed anything and anyone in her path to the side, squeezed in between Delilah and Stephanie, and loudly bawled at Connie. "Three shots of vodka. Please!" Tears filled her eyes.

No questions asked, Connie put four shot glasses on the bar, three for Kate and one for herself. Most of the patrons in the crowded bar also stopped whatever they were doing, and became a curious audience. Now Connie, she's been around the block a few times; she's been through some shit; she knows the difference between real drama and melodrama, and she could see in Kate's face that this was bad. She filled the shot glasses with her best top-shelf vodka, and then raised her shot glass in trepidation. Kate threw back two shots in the same time Connie imbibed her solo shot. Some of the patrons in the back of the bar cheered, thinking it to be a special, celebratory occasion. West and Kip arrived back at the bar, close to Kate. West's thoughts instantly went to Kate's recently deceased father. "What now?" he thought.

Kate, head reeling, legs wobbly, heart breaking, grabbed onto the third shot glass, put it to her lips, then allowed the distilled spirits pour medicinally down her throat. Raising the empty shot glass high above her head, tears in her eyes, she pointed in the direction of the television above the bar. Everyone, and I mean everyone locked eyes on the television.

There, on the screen, was your typical news anchor dude looking serious and talking straight into camera. You couldn't hear anything because the sound was off on the TV, but over his shoulder there was a photo of a disheveled, longhaired, familiar-looking young guy. The Chyron at the bottom of the screen read: Keith Moon August 23,1946—September 8,1978.

Kip, realizing what was happening, moved behind Kate and gently placed his hands on her shoulders. He whispered something in her ear while signaling Connie to please refill the shot glasses. Susan, still at the back of the bar, put some quarters in the jukebox and punched in 'Young Man Blues' from 'The Who: Live at Leeds' 1970 concert. Hearing the music, Connie cranked the jukebox volume to maximum, poured everyone standing at the bar a shot of vodka, and misty-eyed herself, kissed Kate on the forehead, and threw back her shot of booze.

Someone from the crowd shouted "rock and roll will never die!" and the bar erupted. Heedlessly, the crowd returned to revelry, adding dead rock-star conjecture and speculation to the mix. Kate, head down, was drunk.

Four years prior—in the spring of 1974—Kate and Keith were briefly an item. They referred to themselves as "K Squared." Theirs was a short-lived, passionate, burn the candle at both ends affair, but it was doomed as, eventually, all things were with Keith. Kate unfortunately found herself positioned in the line-up after Kim and before Annette. An impossible situation.

Keith John Moon. Considered by many to be the greatest rock drummer on the planet, was a talented, unusual, destructive force of nature. Simultaneously lovable and intolerable, he desperately wanted to make you laugh. He wanted you to like him, and when you did he would blow up your toilet with dynamite. Drum kits were destroyed on stage; televisions were

336

thrown out hotel windows. There were mountains of uppers, downers, and booze. Lots and lots and lots and lots of booze. Kate couldn't keep up with him, and Kate was a seasoned fast-lane pro. She loved him, but she had no choice but to run for her life.

Crazy, but it was just a few weeks ago. He sent flowers to her father's funeral service. They met the following week for tea. He didn't look good. He told her he was trying to get straight on his own terms. He had recently moved to a flat in Mayfair, and convinced a new doctor to prescribe him medication to help him with his alcohol withdrawal demons. He feigned confidence.

The past several weeks were rough on Kate. She had to bury her father, whom she adored. She was again asked to justify to family and friends her life choices, which have always lacked approval, and then she unexpectedly crossed paths with Keith. Dear, sweet, mad Keith. "Moon the Loon." She always knew this day would come; she knew how it would end, dramatically and tragically. She was thinking those exact thoughts, how it would end, as she sat across from him, sipping tea, only days ago.

Kate took the flight out of Heathrow back to the states with a huge sigh of release, relief, and escape, and foolishly allowed herself to believe that her pain was behind her. Excited to be back in L.A.–she went apartment hunting earlier in the day–she was ready for sunshine and positivity. And then this. The news of Keith. And the false gossip across the pond of suicide and heroin overdose. And the familiar feeling of isolation and failure rushing back, and, and, and, and.

She needed her friends. Her new American friends. So she made a mad dash, a dash of madness to the Chimney Sweep, to join with them, to look up at the TV screen, to say goodbye to her mate, to get shitty, to cry on shoulders.

#

Late at night, when a bar has emptied out, leaving one to contemplate the evening, to contemplate the universe, to contemplate one's life up to this exact moment, it's not always a depressing experience. Not always, but mostly. Often, in an empty bar we look back, we look down. Chemically altered, we review our journey, our choices, our failures, and the little remaining cash in our pockets, and when that one perfect song is played, we become overwhelmed.

West sat watching Connie finish her final cleanup duties. He could tell that she was thrashed. Another night of lunacy, and more mileage added to her already impressive accumulation. He thought, "that Connie, she's something else. She's not haunted." When one is haunted by their past, recent or not, and they find themselves the last patron on the proverbial battlefield, alone with their thoughts, and examining their wounds, it doesn't have to be depressing. Right? It might very well provide one with an opportunity for satori, for a sudden epiphany, a way out of the jungle. Perhaps all that is required is a bit of courage to look within. Courage to face the dragon. Or not. "The better part of valor is discretion" eh?

With caution and effort, West rose from the lifeline that was his barstool. He blew Connie a kiss.

"Connie, you're something else," he said.

Connie was something else. She was extraordinary in a blue-collar, full-life-experience kind of way. An irresistible woman in her fifties, born in Katy, Texas, Connie was a landmark, a hallmark, and a benchmark. A no-nonsense, flirtatious, seen it and done it all whirlwind. A bartender par excellence; she ran a tight ship, and on occasion mixed fluids with Kip in the liquor room behind the bar.

In 1947, at the age of twenty-three, she was cast in a small part in 'The Treasure of the Sierra Madre' with Humphrey Bogart. It was a blessing and a curse. Essentially, she was set dressing. Cast as a 'flashy girl'—her "performance" ended up on the cutting room floor—no acting was required. She and a few other young beauties were hired as eye candy for the predominance of the male cast and crew who were sequestered in the burning Mexican desert.

Bogart noticed her—how could he not? She was stunning— and for the duration of the shoot paid her a good deal of attention. Dining, drinking, and vague allusions about her acting future with his new production company; there was sufficient 'grab-ass' between them to confuse a young woman who was in way over her head. He was a forty-seven-year-old international movie star, and his current movie star wife just happened to be the same age as Connie. He knew all about twenty-three-year-olds.

Connie fell in love, but when the martini shot was completed, and Huston called it a wrap, Bogie was nowhere to be found. De repente desaparecido. Show's over. Heartbroken.

For the remainder of her twenties and most of her thirties, Connie tried and failed to do the 'couples thing.' It wasn't meant for her. Too independent, too adventurous, she needed to be the captain of a ship in a world where women were oppressed, repressed, and restrained. In her forties, when she accidentally stumbled into bartending, she miraculously found her milieu.

The bartender is always in complete and total charge–or should be. There is no democracy in a bar. The bartender commands respect, and if you deserve it, returns respect. The bar is a microcosm of the world, the bartender its ringmaster, and Connie was born to run this circus. She's been at the helm of the Chimney Sweep for a dozen years. An icon.

With a sigh, she watched West go, then judiciously closed and locked the Chimney Sweep doors. The parking lot was empty; well, there were two cars and Connie's Vespa. West's VW bug was parked next to a faded Econoline van. The street traffic was almost non-existent. West was foggy. When exactly did Delilah leave? He couldn't recall. Oh, right, the GG's ran off to another bar. Delilah, Susan, Salinger, Stephanie Lynn, and yes Kate, too. Connie was bummed. She wanted to go, but alas, someone had to be the adult in the room.

West was fumbling for his keys when his brain started to play tricks on him. For a split second, he thought he saw the parking lights of the Econoline van flash on and off. He stared at it, waiting to see if it would happen again or confirm his growing belief that he was gradually going mad. Nothing but darkness and quiet. He noticed his rapid heartbeat, and took a deep breath to steady himself. With car keys in hand, he warily proceeded to his car. Six steps taken and there it was again. On and off. He saw it for sure this time. Stopping on a dime, he thought about retreating back into the Chimney Sweep, but he had heard the door lock behind him and knew Connie would be in the back of the bar counting the day's take.

Again the lights flashed on and off. West maintained his 'deer in the headlights' stance. What should he do? What would you do? Carpe noctem, he decided, and pointedly walked straight toward the van. Show no fear.

Tinted windows. The driver's side and passenger's side had tinted windows. The tinted window of the driver's side lowered, and a voice from inside the van said "West." West halted ten feet from the van. He could see the dark outline of head and shoulders in the driver's seat.

"Hello little brother," said the driver.

What? West squinted his eyes hard. Did he say little brother? That can't be right.

"Been a long time," said the voice. West knew that voice.

"Wyatt?" asked West.

"Get in," said the voice as the passenger door was flung open.

Wyatt Walker was four years older than his brother West. Twenty-nine going on forty-nine. Hardened by life, he looked dangerous and unpredictable. They hadn't seen each other for many years.

"Get in," Wyatt repeated.

341

West, numb, made his way around to the passenger side, hopped up into the van, and took a long look at his brother Wyatt, who already had the vehicle in motion.

"You going to turn on the headlights? Where we going?" said West.

Wyatt flicked on the headlights as the van deliberately pulled out of the Chimney Sweep parking lot onto Woodman Avenue. He turned to West and gave him a big ghost-like smile. The Walker boys back together again. How about that? The van proceeded up the ramp onto the 101 and remained in the slow lane. Neither Walker boy noticed the dark, unmarked car that had been parked on the street, and that was now following a strategic distance behind them. Oblivious to the world around them, they were nervous and mesmerized at the sight of each other. What a trip, man.

Late night eventually turns into the next morning, and feeling no pain eventually turns into the hangover from hell; the Friday morning hangover from hell.

West was trying to find his bearings, trying to put two and two together. He grappled with fragments of memory; driving west on the 101, passing out in the car, falling into some kind of bed, being shaken awake by Wyatt. Now he was seated at a retro fifties Formica table with hot, black coffee in hand, watching Wyatt move scrambled eggs from a cast iron skillet to two plates adorned with white toast and butter. Wyatt then began to pour ketchup over both plates of eggs. The same thing he always did when they were teenagers. Wyatt knew West didn't want ketchup on his eggs, and didn't care that West didn't want ketchup on his eggs. He was older, and he loved ketchup on his eggs, and decided it was the best and only way to eat eggs, so West didn't get a vote. But that was then, when they lived at home with their parents. That was a dozen years ago. This was not home. Where exactly were they?

It looked to West like a doublewide trailer circa 1965. West could smell salt air. The ocean was close by. On a nearby stack of mail he, could read HOWARD ROARK 264 PARADISE COVE RD, MALIBU, CA, 90265.

Paradise Cove trailer park. West knew this place. He'd been to a couple of surf parties up here on the cliff overlooking the Pacific. Howard Roark? The Fountainhead? Ayn Rand? Wyatt Walker a.k.a. Howard Roark? Function began to return to his addled brain. Is this where his brother lives? For how long? Was he calling himself Howard Roark? West's brain hurt.

Wyatt slid a plate of ketchup eggs in front of West and sat down across from him.

"Eat," commanded Wyatt.

West had a better idea. Rising, he limped his way to the avocado-colored refrigerator, opened her up and stared inside.

"No beer," said Wyatt. "Sit down and eat."

West scanned the countertops, and then tried to envision what might be behind the closed cabinet doors.

"No booze. I don't drink," said Wyatt in a patient older sibling voice. "Eat."

West glumly returned to his seat and stared into his red eggs.

343

"That's so wrong," West said. "Ketchup eggs are not the hair of the dog. What do you mean, you don't drink?"

Wyatt grabbed the plate of eggs in front of West and dumped it on top of his already bare plate. He stared at West in silence as he started in on the second helping. Suddenly, West had a lot of questions for brother Wyatt. Were they in Malibu? Is this where he lives? Who is Howard Roark? You? How long have you lived here? Do you live alone? Does mom know where you are? Where have you been hiding all these years? Are you a Weatherman? Did you know those people that were killed in the pipe-bomb explosion? Were they friends of yours? What the fuck were you thinking?

Wyatt finished his second plate of eggs and toast, washed it all down with a cup of coffee, and pushed his chair away from the table. He didn't like to be questioned, but what else could he expect? He'd been on the lam for years, in hiding for years. Certainly, there would be questions. He knew that. He understood that. But that didn't mean that answers would be supplied for all in the inquisition. Some topics were best unanswered.

Weathermen—a radical, militant, left-wing organization—was formed in 1969 on the campus of the University of Michigan; the very same University of Michigan where Wyatt Walker was a student at the time. A restless philosophy major with many of his own unanswered questions, Wyatt was also studying political philosophy, which included the writings and tenets of Karl Marx and Vladimir Lenin. It didn't take him long to become a close follower of the on-campus organization SDS (Students for a Democratic Society); the anti-war, anti-imperialism, black power, socialist movement, that would prove to be the crucible for the birth of the Weather Underground.

Originally they were called Weatherman, which begat the Weathermen, which begat the Weather Underground. "You don't need a weatherman to know which way the wind blows," sang Bob Dylan in his masterpiece 'Subterranean Homesick Blues,' the inspiration behind the naming of the organization that advocated the disruption and destruction of U.S. imperialistic endeavors across the globe.

The Weathermen grew from an intellectual, collegiate, community-organizing operation to the eventual declaration of war against the United States government. Like all political enterprises, there were factions. The loudest voices in the room were preaching violent actions; the necessity for urban guerillas, protests, property destruction, riots, bank robberies, and bombs. Those voices of violent revolution drowned out the voices of white middle-class pacifism. Bombs and mayhem would win out.

Sophomore Wyatt understood that the workers of the world, the oppressed majority, were indeed the creators of the wealth in the world. Empires were built on their backs. The "educational" system was designed to create and perpetuate a workforce, not an enlightened people. He came to believe in the equitable distribution of wealth. He came to believe that equitable distribution was not possible at the ballot box. He came to believe that revolution resulting

345

in overthrow was the only way. He became a Weatherman.

That was nine years ago. He's been 'underground' for eight years, since 1970. He's missed birthdays, holidays, and graduations. His mother was hospitalized for a cancer operation. A childhood friend was killed in the battle of Khe Sahn in Viet Nam. His high school girlfriend got married to his 'best' friend. He wasn't there for his father's funeral. He was a revolutionary. Was a revolutionary. Past tense. As in not anymore. As in rearview mirror. As in about to turn himself into the authorities.

"I've been here a few years," Wyatt said nonchalantly. "The less you know, the better."

West got up on his feet, blood boiling.

"Few years? The less I know?" West repeated in exasperation.

"You were away at college. It wasn't safe for me to come out of hiding."

"Did it ever occur to you that you have a mother who is literally worried sick about you?" bellowed West as he knocked the plates and coffee cups off of the table. Wyatt calmly watched as West paced back and forth across the kitchen floor.

"What happened? Who are you? Howard Roark? Mom, dad, and I were questioned! By the FBI! At our house! What the fuck is the matter with you?"

"Spare me the lecture, little brother. Sit down," said Wyatt with authority.

West did not sit down. He glared down at his older brother.

"I said sit down."

West pounced. Grabbing Wyatt by his shirt collar, he pulled him out of his seat and into a headlock.

"You didn't even attend your own father's funeral," cried West as he wrestled to keep control of the stronger Wyatt.

"I couldn't," gasped Wyatt.

West threw Wyatt against the stove and grabbed the hot skillet.

"You didn't show because you knew you killed him. You broke his heart and he died. You killed your own father!"

West swung the skillet at Wyatt's head. Consequences were not considered. Animal rage had taken over. A rage buried deep within. Wyatt, with one swift and expert move, broke the headlock, avoided the oncoming skillet, and delivered his own debilitating blow to the solar plexus. West crumpled to the floor, writhing in pain, gasping for air, sobbing uncontrollably all at the same time.

"Get up," said Wyatt as West curled into a fetal position. "Get up. We don't have much time."

With two hands Wyatt grasped his younger brother, and with little effort picked him up and slammed him into his chair. Grabbing West's chin, he forced him to look him in the eye.

"I'm going to turn myself in," said Wyatt.

West's teary eyes got big. He was about to speak, but then thought better of it.

"I'm tired of running. Tired of hiding. Those days are over. I didn't kill anybody, didn't bomb anybody. I robbed a bank. The organization needed funds. It was what it was. They can't let me off scot-free. I'll have to do some time."

In 1973, the government dropped charges against most, but not all, of the Weather Underground fugitives. They had no choice. The FBI had conducted a secret operation that they called COINTELPRO. Counter Intelligence Program. An illegal surveillance program that entailed electronic surveillance, mail tampering, and intimidation tactics involving the family and friends of the wanted individuals. Stolen documents were uncovered exposing their secret operation. Said documents were released to the press and public. It cost the head honcho at the FBI his job. It also made impotent any legal actions against most of the Weathermen, not to mention the fact that the government did not want to reveal intelligence-gathering methods and sources that would happen during trial. For the past five years, more and more Weathermen had surfaced and turned themselves in to face less serious charges or no infractions at all. Wyatt was correct, he would have to do some time. Bank robbers do time. How much time remained to be determined.

Wyatt removed a set of keys from his pants pocket. He put them on the table in front of West.

"Keys to the house and the van. Take care of the place for me while I'm away. Will you do that for me?" asked Wyatt?

"How do I know anything you say is true?" said West.

"We don't have much time. I phoned the FBI. You need to pull your shit together. Now."

"Why? Why did you do it?" West said staring at the

keys on the table.

"Why did you almost get yourself killed trying to protect whales," replied Wyatt in a taunting voice that surprised West.

"I know what you've been doing. I've kept a close eye on you," continued Wyatt.

West's emotions were twisted in knots. His big brother had been keeping tabs on him. Apparently cared enough to "keep a close eye on him," and there they were, in the same room, after all of these years, Wyatt not dead. Did he say that he phoned the FBI?

From his other pants pocket Wyatt took five hundred dollars and handed it to West. He took a last look around the trailer, and a quick glance out the window. He gestured for West to get on his feet. "It's go time. I'm taking you back to your car," he said knowing what was waiting for them outside the front door. West, emotionally and physically battered and bruised, stood, stuffed the money and keys into his pants, and looked to his brother for guidance.

"There are many things that I'm not proud of; that I am ashamed of. I caused pain and anguish to you and mom and dad. I was there. At the funeral. A safe distance away. It turns out so was the FBI. I almost got caught. I'm sorry."

Wyatt put his arm around West, gave him a sturdy hug, and then led him to the front door. Before he reached for the door handle, he put both of his arms up into surrender mode, and nodded for West to do the same. West, horrified, wobbled, and then complied.

The Walker boys, arms up, opened the front door

of the doublewide and stepped out into the brilliant Malibu sunshine where they were greeted by a dozen armed FBI agents crouched in a semi-circle, guns drawn and pointed in their direction. Wyatt, finally, was no longer on the run.

#

It was late Friday afternoon when West made it back to the Chimney Sweep parking lot to retrieve his car. He used some of the five hundred dollars that Wyatt had given him to take a taxi from the FBI office. It was hard for him to comprehend that he had been in this parking lot less than twenty-four hours ago; that Keith Moon was dead; that Kip was back in L.A.; that the always in control Kate was a drunken mess; that he and Susan had made out; that Delilah had no idea where he was; and that his brother Wyatt was in jail.

The FBI asked him a hundred questions for which he had no answers. They informed him that he would be "watched closely." They told him "he could run, but could not hide." They released him from custody. His freedom and the weekend were staring him in the face.

As he rummaged through his pockets for his car keys—he now had two sets of keys—he could see out of the corner of one eye, Connie Mae Cotton, standing in the doorway, hands on hips, watching him like a mother hen.

"Someone had an interesting night," said Connie.

West didn't turn to face her; instead he gave her a backward wave of the hand and opened the car door.

"Everything okay sugar? I've got a drink inside

with your name on it," she said.

He gave her the 'thumbs up' as he got into the car, and turned the key in the ignition. Pulling his car up next her, he rolled the driver side window down.

"Mind doing me a favor? Will you call Delilah at the office for me? Tell her you saw me. Tell her nothing bad happened. I have to go do something," he asked.

"Sure you don't want that drink? You're welcome to use my phone, no charge," said Connie desperately wanting to learn about West's late night adventure, knowing a couple of drinks would loosen his tongue.

No deal. Not tonight. West waved a fond farewell out the car window, turned onto Woodman Avenue, just as he and Wyatt had done the night before, and headed off for parts unknown, leaving Connie to her imagination and another Chimney Sweep night.

Up the street from the Chimney Sweep, the GreenPlanet office was quieting down for the impending weekend. Delilah was on the phone with Connie while Salinger was tidying up her desktop pretending not to eavesdrop. As Delilah hung up the phone, Kate emerged from her office looking dog-tired and overwhelmed.

"Any word on West?" Kate asked Delilah.

Delilah repeated to Kate and Salinger what Connie had just told her. West was alive but bedraggled. According to West "nothing bad happened," whatever that means. He said that he had "to go do something," whatever that means. Kate unconvincingly tried to reassure Delilah that all would be okay between the two of them. Not to worry. She was more anxious about West's upcoming debate on Monday with the

351

Japanese Consul General. She wouldn't be there to guide him and hold his hand. She was off to London to attend Keith Moon's funeral.

"You have your tickets?" queried Salinger.

"Got em," said Kate rifling through her bag. "Another flight to London, another funeral. Phone me. Let me know how everything goes. Sorry I have to run off again; back in the office on Thursday."

"I still can't get over the fact that you were friends with Keith Moon," said a starry-eyed Salinger.

"Yes, well. Not sure 'friends' is an accurate characterization. Off I go. Keep an eye on Kip. I haven't yet figured out what he's up to. Ciao."

Kate bounded out the door in eager anticipation of nestling into her first class seat and her first glass of champagne. Salinger could see the need for a drink in Kate's eyes, and she, too, thought that wasn't a bad idea seeing it was Friday evening, and the GreenPlanet world was crazier than ever.

"Let's go have a drink and see Connie," said Salinger.

"No drinking for me tonight. Going to finish up here and drag my tired ass home," replied a defeated Delilah.

"That's the adult thing to do."

"Yea."

"He probably went surfing."

"Yea."

"He's fine."

"Yea."

Salinger gave Delilah a 'see you Monday hug,' gathered her things, and out the door she went. My guess is the Chimney Sweep. It was deathly quiet. Delilah hated when the office morphed into a tomb. Nothing could be heard except the inner voice. Nothing good ever happened when she was alone with that voice. She refused to look in the direction of any telephone.

Suddenly, waves of anxiety washed over her. She felt light headed. She needed to get out of there. Collecting her belongings, she beat a path to the exit. Making the deep dive into her backpack, she had difficulty locating the office keys. Panic set in. Where the fuck are the keys? Where are they? Fuck!

She rescued the keys just as the Telex machine started to hum, then clack, then frenetically type and spit out what she surmised would be some dark and unwelcome news. Unable to move, she watched the devil machine to see how much paper it spewed out. If it's short, she's out of there, see ya. If it's long. Please God, don't make it be long. It was long. The Telex paper reached the office floor before everything once again turned silent. Delilah felt ill. The clock on the wall showed 6:00 p.m. The keys in her hand felt like a twenty-pound weight. Fuck everyone.

She pushed opened the door, toggled off the lights, and fled into the safety of the hallway. The sound of keys locking the door from the outside could be heard. Then silence. Stillness. Tranquility. Then keys. Then the door violently opening. Then Delilah storming back into the office. She threw her shit down on Salinger's desk, stomped over to the Telex machine, seized the paper by the throat, ripped it from the printer, took a deep breath, and glared at the

353

communique.

Her eyes went from the paper in her hand to the empty office back to the paper. She read it a second and third time just to be sure. Like molasses, she oozed her way back to Salinger's desk, respectfully picked up her stuff, brushed off the lights, ever so gently closed the door behind her, and vanished.

#

When West sauntered through the entrance to the bar, everyone who laid eyes on him were caught by surprise. Certainly, this was an unexpected visit. Unexpected and welcome. It was as if time stood still. There was Doctor sitting at one end of the bar struggling with a crossword puzzle, drinking cheap rum. The Captain, at the opposite end of the bar, was head down and asleep. Seated at one of the less than stable tables, Jimmy and Shakespeare Jones were arguing about the baseball teams playing on the barely functional bar TV. Fenway Park's Boston Red Sox were hosting their hated rivals, the New York Yankees. Jimmy hated the Yankees, and the deep wounds from last years World Series against his beloved Dodgers were still fresh. A diehard Dodger fan–since they arrived in Los Angeles twenty years ago–he was crushed when the despised Yankees celebrated yet another championship on the field at Dodger Stadium. And now, here was Shakespeare Jones suggesting the possibility of the Yankees erasing a fourteen game deficit to once again become American League champions. Outrage! Blasphemy! Who is it that just walked through the door? No way!

West was given a warm greeting by all. His self-appointed mission was to seek out and reconnect with Mr. Jones, the captain of the Maggie May; the man who, weeks ago, led the rag-tag GreenPlanet whale savers into and out of harm's way; the man West looked to as a mentor and an adviser. His first stop was down the docks where the Maggie May anchored. When he didn't find Shakespeare on his boat, West knowingly made his way here, to The Yard Arm, the nastiest and most depressing bar west of the Rio Grande. Unless you were family. Unless you had a history with the place.

Shakespeare Jones, fifty-eight serious years old, looked more dashing and tormented with each passing year. A tough-as-nails former US Navy seaman who served on the aircraft carrier USS Yorktown, he narrowly escaped Davy Jones locker in both the battle of the Coral Sea, and a month later in the battle of Midway. He doesn't suffer fools lightly and since leaving the military has always felt that he was on borrowed time. Hmm, that sounds familiar. He loves his fishing trawler 'Maggie May' more than anything on Earth. When he speaks, which isn't often, people listen. GreenPlanet's people, courage, and cause captured his imagination. Little did he know that thirty-six years after his high seas pas de deux with death, he would volunteer to sail into harm's way once again. This time with a bunch of unskilled, undisciplined, and unruly "kids." He was thrilled to see West walk into the bar.

After a drink and some Yard Arm gossip, West twisted the arm of Shakespeare, successfully convincing his idol to take him out for a much-needed excursion on the Maggie May. In the pilothouse, West watched as Captain Jones went through a pre-departure checklist. Fuel levels, navigation charts, weather conditions, radar functionality, radio chatter. This was a life that West could see himself living. On the water, salt air in his lungs, wide open spaces, and the wind in his face. And maybe a whiskey or two.

Jimmy and Doctor were below decks, making sure all was right with the engines. The old Captain stayed behind to keep an eye on the Yard Arm.

"You don't look so good," said Shakespeare without looking at West.

"I'm fine," said an unconvincing West.

"And that girl of yours?"

"Who, Delilah?"

Shakespeare looked up from his clipboard. He gave West a 'don't try to bullshit me' look.

"I seen you on TV," he mumbled.

"How did I look?"

"Like you liked being on TV," said Shakespeare.

Shakespeare aggressively, impatiently pointed to the lines that secured the Maggie May to the dock. West knew that drill all too well and leaped into action. Lines were released and orders were given for Jimmy to set her in motion. As the Maggie May navigated the calm waters of the harbor, heading for open ocean, West monitored the radar, and Shakespeare Jones manned the helm.

"You and me are members of the same club now."

"Yea?" said West.

"On borrowed time club. Me on the Yorktown, you

on the Maggie May."

"Never thought about that."

"Sure you have. Impossible not to. Everything changed for you that day."

"I wasn't in a real battle like you were."

"You were in harm's way, and harm almost did you in," said Captain Jones as the Maggie May hit open water. West was conflicted. He did and did not want to have this conversation, but it occurred to him that maybe that's why he headed to Los Angeles harbor to seek out Captain Jones. Not maybe. That is why.

"You feel lost, not sure who you are, between persons. Not who you used to be. Not who you're supposed to be. You have some choppy waters to navigate before you safely make it into port," schooled Shakespeare.

West stuck his head out the port side bull's-eye of the pilothouse and let the salt air smack him in the face.

"When will you tell me what happened on the Yorktown?"

Shakespeare turned up the volume on the ship's radio.

"Now that we're in the same club, don't I get to know what happened out there?"

Shakespeare couldn't, wouldn't hear him. He made a hard right and steered the Maggie May north, up the coast.

"Nothing? Not a word?" said West.

"Look behind you!" bellowed Captain Jones.

Startled, West whirled about. What was it? Was he supposed to be paying attention to something concerning the operation of the ship? What?

"Have you noticed that shadow following you?" said the captain.

West felt like a fool. It made him angry. Why the games? Why the innuendo? Why couldn't the captain just tell him that everything would be okay? He glared at Shakespeare, waiting for an answer.

"We come into this life with sealed orders," replied the captain.

What? West gave up. He threw his hands in the air, shook his head, and laughed out loud.

"Maggie May is running better than ever," said West.

"She knows her purpose," Shakespeare proudly proclaimed as he kicked her into a higher gear, and let her fly.

#

What was the rest of the gang doing? At this moment? While he was on a sunset sail up the California coast? That's what West was mulling, cold beer in hand, salt spray in his face. Delilah? Kip? Kate? Wonder what good old Connor is up too? What about Hunter?

Turns out Hunter was on the phone with Kip. Hunter was located outside the jailhouse in Hvalvik Beach, Faroe Islands, and Kip was located at Kate's desk in the GreenPlanet office. Will was there too. He had commandeered what was formerly Kip's couch, and was in the middle of rolling a big fatty on the coffee table.

"Hugh and I are on the way back to London," said

a barely audible Hunter.

"Kate is also headed that way," said Kip.

"She is? Why?"

"You haven't heard?" asked a surprised Kip.

"Heard what? My accommodations have been humble."

Kip did not want to be the bearer of this news. He knew that Hunter would worry about Kate's well being.

"Keith Moon. Overdosed. Services on Wednesday at Golders Green," Kip announced reluctantly. There was a long silence. Kip wasn't sure if the line went dead. He waited.

"My god. Let Kate know that I will see her there. At the funeral," said a shaken Hunter.

"Will do," said Kip taking the lighted joint handed to him by Will.

"The world is spinning out of control Kippy," were the last words spoken before the weak connection to the other side of the world did indeed die. Kip hung up the phone, took a long drag off the joint, and passed it back to his pal Will who was waving at someone or something in the outer war room.

Two young women entered Kate's office within the office. They came armed with booze, pills, marching powder, and mischief in their eyes. Will swapped the lit joint for a slug of tequila. Kip's 'special friend' cleared some desk space to carve out four lines of cocaine, and while she was doing that, the other lovely lass requested "music please."

Kip was ready to serve and be served. He turned on the radio, always tuned to KWOT, and turned it up loud just in time for "the news" with Connor Kilkenny who, live on the air, was partaking in his very own marijuana cigarette. Hmm. Apparently, the meticulous newsman that he was, he had spent most of the afternoon in the company of the spokesman for NORML–the National Organization for the Reform of Marijuana Laws. Connor was interviewing him and one of their attorneys regarding the latest dust-up between NORML and the U.S. government.

NORML was calling for the immediate end of the American funding of paraquat spraying in Mexico. Paraquat, a deadly herbicide, was being sprayed on illegal marijuana fields in Mexico as part of the ridiculous "war on drugs" conducted jointly by the U.S. government and Mexico. The D.E.A. was warning Americans that a sizeable portion of the poisoned pot was being confiscated at the border, but not all. If anyone in the United States were unfortunate enough to ingest even the slightest amount of paraquat they could suffer serious lung damage, possibly ending in death.

Last night, late night DJ–the 'L.A. Lonesome Cowboy'–had fired up the KWOT troops by 'suggesting' they call the White House to protest and demand an end to the poisonous spraying. The KWOT audience were no strangers to the companionship and kindness of Senior Cannabis, and the cowboy's passion combined with the tribe's enthusiasm resulted in the overloading of the White House switchboard, closing it down.

Connor, feeling fine, was in the middle of an unforgettable newscast.

"I've been informed, though I don't if it's true or

not, that there might be some KWOT listeners out there that partake, every now and then, in the recreational marijuana arena. Whoo-ya. I've also heard a rumor that you, I mean they, might have been responsible for the shutting down of the White House switchboard last night. Can I just say whoo-ya to ya?"

As Connor was riffing to all of Southern California, his partner in crime, The Burner Mary Turner was about to seize the musical reins of the KWOT control board. She without question wanted in on this.

"So there you have it. Right now it's 78 degrees in downtown Los Angeles, and strangely enough its 78 degrees right here at Metromedia Square in good old Hollyweed. I'm, uh, who am I? Oh, yes, I'm the news guy and that's the news on this 'Finally a Friday,' and so I gives to you The Burner, Mary Turner."

"Hey pal," said a giddy Burner Turner.

"Hey Burner."

"You were a bit late today. Were you hanging out with those guys from NORML again?"

"Why yes I was," said a very high Connor.

"Do you know where you are? Do you know who I am?" she teased.

Connor was rocking back and forth, giggling, and forgetting that he was still on the air.

"Do you know who you are?" she said laughing.

"Me? Well, yes. I'm... Paraquat. Paraquat Kilkenny."

And there it was. The christening. Connor Kilkenny became Paraquat Kilkenny. Turner was beside herself with glee. She cued up 'Who Are You' by The Who.

"I'd wish you a happy weekend, but I think you've

361

already got a head start on me pal. My name is Mary Turner, and he is 'Paraquat' Kilkenny, and you are listening to the best damn radio station in all the land. 94.7 KWOT. Los Angeles. Whoo-ya!

Throughout all of this radio frivolity, Kip had relocated to the more comfortable couch, and plopped down next to Will. Their two engaging visitors now occupied their laps and their undivided attention. It was Friday evening and the sky was the limit.

The sky was also the temporary home to Hunter, Hugh, and Kate. Lifting off from the Faroe Islands, Hugh had a death grip on his armrest as Hunter looked out his window at the carnage below. The cove was blood red, dead whales bobbing in the water as their killers toiled to haul them to shore. Hunter knew they couldn't be saved. Not yesterday. Not today. He was playing the long game, and glad to be returning to London.

Kate was thirty thousand feet over the Grand Canyon, two glasses of champagne successfully completed. Unlike Hunter, she was not glad to be returning to the London she had departed only days before. In light of recent gut-punching events, she was feeling somewhat less British, and dare she admit a bit American? Champagne please.

Remember Love Canal? Lois Gibbs? On this Friday night, Lois was standing in the street in front of her house watching as her neighbors were packing up and vacating their poisoned homes. Windows were boarded up and moving trucks were feverishly being loaded as if in anticipation of an oncoming hurricane or tornado or world war. With a heaviness in her heart, and a sinking feeling in her gut, she bore witness in abject horror.

The sun wasn't close to setting in Seattle where Paul Revere and his cult of worshippers stood on the dock and gazed up in awe at their new acquisition the Threshold Guardian, a two hundred and forty foot converted Norwegian fireboat. She's fast, she's agile, she's evil. She's soon to be the weapon of whale warriors that will abide by no rules, and recognize no laws. Hanging over the side of the ship, in a boson's chair, was Axel D'Artagnan; painting the finishing touches on his new masterpiece. Under fearsome skull and crossbones, he painted the words SEA PIRATES.

Axel and Paul Revere and a bunch of the cult were, as you know, former members of the GreenPlanet operation in San Francisco. Until the insurrection, until the uprising. Now, the office in San Francisco was quieter, more secretive, more two-timing and self-serving, if that was possible. On this 'skies the limit' Friday evening, the cavernous former warehouse was deserted and growing dark. Muffled sounds could be heard coming from one of the rainbow-colored, partitioned offices. Jonah was crouching outside a particular office door, and through a crack, was straining hard to spy on what was going on inside. He had to continually wipe his thick eyeglasses, and readjust his deformed and painful body position. He looked like the slimy character on the cover of the Jethro Tull album Aqualung. Through the crack, he watched as Karma, undressed, was fondling Jade, who simultaneously was kissing Karma's neck. He was breathing hard and getting harder. Karma sensed they had an audience. She knew Jonah was watching because he was always watching. Putting her left hand down Jade's pants, she lifted her right hand in the direction of Jonah, and gave him 'the finger.' Fuck you Jonah, you fucking nightmare human being.

And that takes us back down to L.A. and Delilah. When we last saw her, she, too, was taking flight. Trying to beat a hasty retreat from the never-ending rising tide of drama that had taken a toll on her spirit and her health. All that she wanted to do was go home, close the window shades, pour herself a glass of wine, and hide from the world until Monday. But there she was in the Pacific Palisades, standing in front of the Chumash Elementary School, where a large and boisterous crowd had gathered along the street in front of the school.

Parents, teachers, and children were waving protest signs that read: 'Protect Our School,' 'Not In My Neighborhood,' 'CALOCO GO AWAY,' 'Oil Is Poison,' 'No Drilling.' In the middle of a gaggle of news reporters and television crews stood Delilah. Serious and animated, pointing at the school, then at the ground, a ream of paper in her hands, she was effortlessly reeling off facts and statistics regarding the harm that would come from an oil drilling operation in the neighborhood, next to this school. She was focussed and in total command of the situation.

Prior to this scenario, when Delilah was valiantly trying to escape from the office, the Telex machine had spit out a communique from Jonah in San Francisco. He had sent it down to L.A. just before embarking on his evening Peeping Tom mission. The elementary school parents in Pacific Palisades, not knowing how to get in touch with GreenPlanet in L.A., had phoned the Northern California office that morning, and requested expert advice and assistance about how to effectively address the media during the impending evening protest.

Jonah, conjuring a perfect opportunity to sabotage his despised colleagues to the south, promised the callers that he would promptly send "his people" in Los Angeles to join them in their campaign, but he waited to inform the L.A. people until the end of the day, and instead of a phone call, he sent the Telex knowing full well that the weekend was minutes away, calculating that his illegitimate tribe members to the south would be less than enthusiastic and able. When Delilah read the communique from Jonah, she understood what he had done, and she knew what she had to do.

Between the time that she ripped the printer paper from the Telex machine, surmised that Jonah had set them up for a PR disaster, gathered that no other GreenPlanet comrade was available to assist her, and her eventual arrival at Chumash Elementary School, she was able to calm herself, reassess her priorities, and erase the immediate past from her mind.

She made it to the school fifteen minutes before the press and the police arrived. Greeted with an anxious heroes welcome by parents, teachers, and property owners, she bravely consented to speak to the media on their behalf. A half a dozen people simultaneously got her up to speed as they filled her arms with documents and photos, and her head with facts and figures.

365

During the ad hoc press conference, members of the press informed Delilah that the oil company claimed there were sixty million barrels of oil directly beneath the very street that they were occupying. Sixty million badly needed barrels of oil. They pointed out that Los Angeles currently had numerous oil derricks actively pumping away. Two of them right next to Beverly Hills High School. They asked her why this proposed drilling site would pose a greater threat?

The questions came fast and furious, and Delilah handled each and every one. Making her final statement about the importance of children over profits, she directed their attention to the derrick-free ocean behind them. A magical view. The sun was sitting delicately on the surface of the water. All paying attention could see the silhouette of a ship as it moved across the setting sun. She recognized it immediately. She had an intimate relationship with that boat. She knew who was on that boat.

Soon after, the protest wound down, and the press and police took their leave. Delilah received many pats on the back, and sincere 'thank yous,' and before returning to her car, and ultimately escaping to her hideout from humanity, she took one last look at the familiar ship sailing into the sunset.

In the pilothouse was West. Steering her steady as she goes, never happier. Sitting behind him was Jimmy and Doctor drinking rum and playing cards, oblivious to the world. On the starboard deck stood Shakespeare Jones, thinking, observing, and feeling the nuances of the Maggie May as she glided her way back to the safety of Los Angeles harbor. His eyes were locked on

West. He was trying to gage him, trying to foresee his future. With unease and disquiet, he was staring down at the lurking shadow directly behind his young friend.

SLEEP NO MORE

Dharma Blue. That's what she called herself. Suntanned, barefoot, sun-damaged brown hair, Wayfarers, short-shorts, and a Hawaiian Tropic t-shirt tied at the waist. Twenty years of age. No fear.

She waited until she saw Delilah's car drive away, and then approached the doublewide across the way from her own. The front door was open.

"Hey in there? Are you naked? I'm coming in," announced Dharma.

She found West standing at a kitchen sink full of dirty dishes. He was holding a cast iron skillet encrusted with old scrambled egg remnants.

"Hi. I'm Dharma. I waited for your girlfriend to go."

"West. I don't have a girlfriend," said world-weary West.

"I live across the way. You going to be living here?"

"Yea."

"What happened to the other guy? Heard he was arrested."

"Yea."

Dharma took a quick peek at the surroundings noticing the fingerprint powder stains on the walls, the police tape, and the general chaos and debris. She decided to conduct her own tour of the trailer; inspecting each of the rooms. West watched her every move. Why, he wondered, did he say that he didn't have a girlfriend? Freudian slip?

Dharma strolled into the kitchen, stood a foot away

from West, looked him up and down, and arrived at a conclusion. He was safe.

"West, do you surf?" she asked.

A grand smile from West was met with an even grander smile from Dharma. They stood there beaming brightly at each other. New Malibu neighbors.

Prior to the appearance of Ms. Blue, West and Delilah had arrived, in separate cars, for their post-FBI-raid inspection of the Malibu Cove trailer that Wyatt had left in brother West's care. Five days had passed since Wyatt and West had been taken into custody, and finally, last night, Tuesday night, West received a call from one of the arresting agents informing him that the trailer and the Econoline van were no longer part of a crime scene, and that he was free to assume the property.

Both he and Delilah were relieved to get the call. The past two days and nights had been uncomfortable. In the aftermath of Wyatt's arrest, West, as you know, ran off to Shakespeare Jones and the Maggie May, and Delilah was snookered into a spur-of-the-moment ad hoc battle with the California Oil Company. West, with Shakespeare's blessing, stayed aboard ship for the weekend; scrubbing, scraping, polishing, watching sunsets, and temporarily avoiding the inevitable reunion with Delilah.

Delilah, on the other hand, was pleased to have the house to herself for the weekend. She, too, wasn't all that eager to resume cohabitation. Her intuition was sounding a 'what's going on between West and Susan?' alarm, and she was at the furthest end of her GreenPlanet rope. Hiding from the world for forty-eight

369

hours was just what she needed.

When West arrived at the office Monday morning, his first order of business was to gather the troops and tell them the story of his brother Wyatt, the Weather Underground connection, the FBI arrest, and his soon-to-be new digs in Malibu, all of this occurring since he had last seen them Friday night. He correctly assumed that gossip was in full bloom, and thus wanted to nip things in the bud and move forward as soon as possible. The night before, from the Maggie May phone, he had briefly spelled out to Delilah all of the above, not the least of which was Wyatt's trailer that was now in his custody. He was thrown by her unflustered reception of the news of his moving out. She almost seemed pleased.

Monday and Tuesday, for each of them, was an out-of-body experience. They worked at the office together, went to dinner together, slept in the same bed together–slept being the operative word–breakfasted together, did couple's things together, and waited for the call. Wednesday morning–this morning–they took separate cars, and drove to Malibu Cove to assess the situation.

West didn't have a memory of anything in the trailer. He remembered scrambled eggs, the cast-iron skillet, and the Howard Roark mail. When he entered with Delilah it was, as if, for the first time.

Outside a brilliant sun was shining. Inside it was dark and musty, dominated by the smell of a million stale cigarettes. Delilah opened window shades and windows. Police tape, fingerprint smudges, overflowing ashtrays, and take-out food containers comingled.

Kitchen cabinet doors were left open, revealing a stockpile of canned goods, instant coffee, rice, crackers, and an abundance of cheap booze. Whiskey, tequila, gin, rum, and a dozen mini-bottles of Kahlua were an unexpected find. Scores of books and magazines were piled high in several locations on the floor. On the stove was the dirty skillet with the remnants of the scrambled eggs.

West was staring at the cabinet full of liquor bottles and remembering that Wyatt had said that he didn't drink. The stacks of books caught Delilah's attention. She selected two paperbacks: Elliot's The Waste Land, and Abbey's Monkey Wrench Gang.

"Can I take these?" she said politely, tucking them under her arm.

"Take whatever you want. He said he didn't drink," said West.

Brushing cigarette ashes off of her selected reading material, she said "Did he say he didn't smoke?"

West had the iron skillet in his hand, wielding it like a hammer.

"I almost killed him with this."

"You're not a good cook," said Delilah heading for the door. "I have to go."

West didn't want her to go. He was feeling regret and remorse.

"The place has potential," she offered with sincerity.

"Will you be back? Will you come stay with me?" he asked fearing the answer.

"My students await. 'A.M. Los Angeles' tomorrow

371

morning. I'll be watching," said Delilah with a wave of the hand as she slipped out the front door, carefully stepping over the crime scene tape.

West heard her '56 T-Bird start up, and then drive off down the hill. Placing the egg-encrusted skillet back in the sink full of dirty dishes, he leaned against the kitchen counter to brace himself for the oncoming depression. How did he get here? What was his future? Who was pulling the strings? How many times would he ask himself these questions? "Darkness, darkness, be my pillow." And then, out of the dharma blue, a savior came knocking.

#

Delilah was on her way to Santa Monica City College to give a talk and show the students film footage of the recent GreenPlanet confrontation with the Russian whalers. Kate asked, and she agreed to do the college circuit for a while, but her heart wasn't into it. Her thoughts, like West's, were on her purpose and her road ahead. West, except for the television interview tomorrow morning, was taking the rest of the week off in order to deal with his unexpected family responsibilities. Kate would be back from London tonight, and then in the office tomorrow morning. Kip was back in town, and he and Will were up to something dubious. Everyone appeared to have a focus. Everyone appeared to have clarity.

Delilah was always surprised at the attendance for GreenPlanet lectures. The audience grew with each talk. The lecture hall on this day at SMCC was standing room only. At the conclusion of her presentation, she fielded questions from the student audience.

"At this point in time, what are the odds of extinction?" a student asked Delilah who immediately thought of she and West.

"Hard to say. Overall, things are getting worse, not better."

Another student asked "Are you going out there again next summer?"

"Yes, if we have to."

"You're very brave," said the awestruck student.

Delilah heard some guy say "she's very hot too." Three guys, standing off to the side, were laughing and being idiots. Their timing, she thought, could not be worse for them. This was not a good day to be an unevolved male that foolishly pulled the tiger's tail. Silently staring in their direction, she waited for the entire audience to look their way.

"What did you say?" said Delilah staring down the biggest clown.

"I said, you are hot too," he said laughing with his buddies.

Delilah scooped up a sheet of notepaper and drew an arch with a felt pen. She held it up for all to see.

"See this? What do you see here, Einstein?" asked Delilah.

These guys never did like pop quizzes.

"Nothing sweetheart. Just a lonely white piece of paper with a line on it."

"Take another look. Look real hard," said Delilah.

The three morons and the audience began to squirm, but Delilah wasn't about to take them off the hook. After a long uncomfortable silence:

373

"That's your future. You and your idiot buddies. Not a pretty picture, is it?"

"Not as pretty as you," he said with much less confidence and no supporting laughter from his pals.

"Let me be the first to publicly welcome you to the left side of the bell curve, your permanent home away from home," Delilah said in conclusion as she gathered together her papers, took one last look at her wincing audience, raised a defiant middle finger to the sky, and exited stage left. Revolution was in the air.

Seaspray was also in the air, and that meant offshore winds, and that meant get your ass and your surfboard in the water because the waves were not going to wait all day. Fortunately for West, he always had a stick in his car, so when Dharma encouraged him to go surfing with her, it was a fait accompli.

Not only was Dharma super cute, she was a rad surfer. West was outmatched and outdone. Her prowess was simultaneously a turn-on and a large slice of humble pie for him. Who was this girl with the beach brown hair?

After a couple of hours, blissfully exhausted and surfed out, they dragged their tired asses out of the water, and collapsed next to each other on the sand. It's possible that there was a noticeable sexual energy.

"Damn girl, you kicked my ass out there."

"It's not a contest," said Dharma as she ran her fingers through her wet hair. "You had some good rides," she said.

"You should go pro," said a starry-eyed West.

"Interesting thought," said a deadpan Dharma wiping salt off of her chest and arms.

West gaped at her as he toiled to return his breathing to normal. Did he know her from somewhere? She reminded him of someone, but he couldn't place her. She certainly had skills. Wait a minute! Wait one mother-fucking minute. June. Women's Pro finals. Margo Oberg versus the girl that called herself Blue. Holy fucking shit!

"I saw you!" exclaimed a mind-blown West. "You almost took down Margo Oberg. You were awesome!" he said losing all composure.

"Are," said Dharma.

"What?"

"Are. You said "were awesome," should of said "are awesome." Would you kindly rub some lotion on my back? Please."

That did it. The last degree of cool, calm, and collected melted into a vast wet spot in the sand.

"Will you marry me?" implored the puppy dog as he fumbled for the lotion.

Dharma chuckled, laid out , and let the puppy dog wag his tail. Game, set, match.

#

Thursday morning September 14th. Kate was back from London, and happily back in the saddle a.k.a. her desk. Salinger, Susan, and Delilah were seated on the couch in her private office. It was much too early for the volunteers, and Will and Kip would not be coming in until after their lunch with movie star Vanessa Gray Reynolds. It was just the women. Kate brought coffee and donuts for all. The television was on and tuned to morning show A.M. Los Angeles where West was the

375

center of attention.

He looked good. Well rested, tan, fit, and professional. His interviewer and co-host of the show was a thirty-year-old rising television star named Sarah. She was polished, experienced, and always in total command of the situation. After the usual introduction, brief history of GreenPlanet, and a rehash of the summer voyage to save the whales from Russian harpoons, she arrived at the meat and potatoes. The human-interest drama that fuels talk show television.

"Your rubber boat, the one you were riding in," she said.

"Zodiac," said West.

"Right. Your Zodiac. You were essentially run over by a whaling boat and almost killed. Are you now able to talk about that?" she said as she placed her hand therapeutically on his arm.

West remembered Kate's words and took a serious, reflective, dramatic pause before speaking. He placed a hand on top of Sarah's.

"This is not about me or any individual in GreenPlanet. It's big picture stuff. It's saving the planet stuff. As you can see, here I am, all's well, delighted that you've invited me on your show to talk about something so important and so urgent."

There was a sparkle in her eye when she removed her hand from his. She was thrilled that they were both using the same playbook. He was thinking about his audience. Delilah, Kate, Susan, Salinger, and maybe Dharma too.

"You're up against a mighty adversary. Will you

ultimately succeed?" she asked with faux concern.

He took a shorter dramatic pause this time, smiled, and looked straight into the camera.

"Absolutely."

Back at the GreenPlanet office, the four women were in complete agreement with what they had just witnessed. It was good. The boy did good. Kate was already out of her seat and headed to the war room.

"Brilliant. Bloody brilliant. Five seconds ladies," pronounced a giddy Kate.

Before Kate finished counting down, four, three, two, one, Delilah, Susan, and Salinger were at their desks when the phones came alive.

They couldn't take the calls fast enough. The answering service was required to handle the overflow, and by overflow I mean money. Donations, new memberships, offers of goods and services, and the public outpouring, this momentary passion, wasn't solely happening in Los Angeles. The phones were also ringing in San Francisco. Karma, Catty, Jade, and Sunset were dazed and confused as they fielded early morning calls from Angelinos that mistakenly called the Northern California office. The northerners didn't skip a beat in rerouting as much money from Southern California as they possibly could.

"Yes, you can send your donation here. It all goes into the same pot. Mr. Walker? Yes, I'll see that he gets your message," said an unscrupulous Karma.

"No. We're not able to watch programs that are local to Los Angeles. You did? You are? Let me get your address and we'll send you membership materials right away," steered Catty.

377

"The office in Southern California is one of our chapters. That's correct. We're the main office, the headquarters. You certainly can! You have our address? My name is Sunset. Right. You can send your membership fee to me and I'll see to it personally," said a conniving Sunset.

"He doesn't like to talk about it. I'm sure you can understand. He said that? No, no, I'm not surprised. That's very generous of you. Thank you and tell your friends," said Jade as she excitedly sealed another deal.

The morning chaos shook Jonah into consciousness. He watched the money pour in from Los Angeles with a detached curiosity. He fucking hated Hollywood, hated the press, and hated television. He pretended to hate money, but he coveted his position of power, and his alternative lifestyle. A thought occurred to him. Maybe he should get a videotape of that show? See what West was saying, doing. Maybe money wasn't so bad? If it was headed his way.

The hubbub died down within two hours. That's usually how those things work. People get swept up in the moment and take action. 'Impulse buying' is the term of art.

In Los Angeles, Salinger was back at her reception desk sorting through all of the unanswered phone messages. Delilah had taken her leave and was headed south to Orange Coast College to give yet another GreenPlanet presentation. Lord help any asshole guys that might inadvertently cross her path. Susan and Kate were still huddled together in Kate's office.

Kate was all business as Susan tried to get her to talk about the Keith Moon funeral. She had seen Kate on television standing between Eric Clapton and Charlie Watts, and keenly needed to know much more about that scenario. Perhaps later, at the Chimney Sweep, under the influence of scorpions.

Kate wanted to know "what happened with the Japanese Consul General?" There was supposed to be a debate. It didn't happen. Why? Was West at fault? Was he not prepared? Did they need to do damage control? Explain please.

Not West's fault at all, according to Susan. He was very prepared and ready to go. Some last-minute mysterious emergency was cited as the reason for the cancellation by the Japanese consulate. Salinger had tried in vain to get them to reschedule with no luck. Looked a lot like cold feet.

Kate instructed Susan to try again to reschedule. If they balked, an aggressive media campaign would be implemented to persuade them otherwise. She was very pleased to hear that West was on top of his game. Now, on to much bigger business.

While in London, Kate met with Hunter Mack and Hugh Simon, who had just concluded a series of meetings with representatives from GreenPlanet International. After spirited discussion and much-needed venting, a new master plan had been formulated and agreed upon, and Susan was about to play a very big role. GreenPlanet America. One American corporation under the umbrella and oversight of the international body. One. Not four, not three, not

379

two. One American entity.

In order for that to smoothly transpire with the least amount of collateral damage and financial pain, there would have to be a coming together, a peace treaty, amongst the American offices. In particular, San Francisco and Los Angeles. San Francisco and the surrounding Bay Area were too important, logistically and financially, to jettison, and Susan was considered the best person to help facilitate the plan.

"I saw Hunter while I was in London," Kate began. "He wants us to arrange a meeting with the San Francisco people. He wants us to succeed in establishing a friendly rapport. Says it would be best if we went to them."

"West is taking the rest of the week off to get his living situation in order. Delilah is out on the college circuit this week."

"We want you to go. We think you are the best person to successfully negotiate a peace treaty and future merger," Kate said.

"Merger?"

"There's a new plan for a GreenPlanet America. One American GreenPlanet under the control of the international organization."

"Wow. How?" said Susan.

"We want you to go up there and make nice with them. Find common ground. You became familiar with some of them on the voyage. You've been on the high seas, arrested at Rocky Flats. You're smart and well spoken. You're female. That, I gather, is a big deal in San Francisco. Find an issue. Chat them up. You can even give them the impression that you're jumping ship in L.A. and would like to throw in with them."

"When?"

"No later than tomorrow, but today would be better," said Kate.

Susan was floored. She didn't know what to think. It sounded equally enticing and horrific. Tomorrow? Today? San Francisco? Tomorrow? Right then, an issue she had been reading about popped into her head. Toxic waste dumping near the Farallon Islands. That could be the perfect campaign to work on while operating as a mole in San Francisco. She started to get excited.

At that moment, Salinger walked in with an armful of mail. She was about to drop her bundle on Kate's desk and scoot when she noticed the 'I've just seen a ghost' look on Susan's face. Before Salinger could start asking probing questions, Kate spied a large brown envelope in the stack of mail. It was addressed to West. The sender was Atlantic Records. She snatched it up and began to open it to the obvious discomfort of Susan and Salinger.

"The package is for GreenPlanet. Happens to have West's name on it too. Any questions or concerns ladies?" Kate asked.

No questions or concerns. She removed an LP and a personal note that she read aloud.

"West, enclosed is the new YES album. You might be able to make use of the song 'Don't Kill the Whale.' Please be my guest at the 'Tormato' release party this Wednesday 9/20. Bring whomever."

Kate looked at Susan and Salinger with an 'in the catbird seat' look.

381

"Off to lunch you go whale savers," said a delighted Kate. "Take an extra half-hour. I insist."

#

Musso and Frank wasn't in the lunch budget for Susan and Salinger, but it most certainly was for Kip, Will, and Vanessa Gray Reynolds. As always, seated in their favorite Chaplin Booth, the champagne was flowing and the place was jumping

Even though it had been months since the 'press conference on acid' Vanessa was still feeling embarrassment and guilt for her reckless choice. She felt that she had let everyone down, and was no longer a desirable celebrity asset. She couldn't have been more incorrect.

The high-profile campaign in question was the Canadian Harp seal slaughter that took place each year on the ice floes of Newfoundland. Will and Kip didn't ask her to lunch to convince her to do public service announcements or to proudly wear GreenPlanet attire whenever possible–although that would be most excellent if she did. No, they were there to persuade her to be one of a handful of activists that would travel to Newfoundland and confront the seal killers. They were going for the brass ring.

"So, what do you think?" asked Will.

"By all means I want to go, and I'll let the agency know not to consider me for any film projects during that time, but," Vanessa paused.

"What is it?"

"I'm surprised that you're still interested in me," she confessed.

"We adore you. Why wouldn't we be interested?" asked Kip.

"My embarrassing press conference performance. It was a disaster," she said.

Kip didn't know what she was talking about. Will hadn't briefed him on any dicey issues regarding the press conference. What might she have done that was potentially problematic? Will was finding Vanessa's contrition charming and very harvestable. He was about to go for the kill when an ill-timed middle-aged gentleman appeared at their table with pen and paper in hand. Without skipping a beat, Vanessa took the pen and paper, signed her autograph, and returned it to the guy with a devastating smile.

" I mistakenly ingested, well, maybe not mistakenly, a small amount of LSD," said a soft-voiced, mortified Vanessa.

"You were tripping on acid during the press conference?" asked a delighted Kip.

Will was laughing out loud as Vanessa described a reporter that was in attendance that day–who apparently had some experience with psychedelics himself–trying to get her to cop to the deed. The reporter had corralled her when the Maggie May returned to Los Angeles, and she was waiting on the dock as part of the welcome-home crowd. She denied, denied, denied, and eventually escaped his clutches, but since then had been scouring the supermarket tabloids for any hallucinogenic stories about her.

"Far out, man. That's like the old days. That's fucking beautiful," said Kip.

"Vanessa, it's not a problem. You were terrific at

383

the press conference. You're going with us to Newfoundland, and that's that," said Will waving at some show-biz power brokers at another table.

The deal was sealed. Vanessa Gray Reynolds, star of the big and small screens, soon would be the star of the ice floes of Newfoundland. She was tremendously relieved and newly excited, but there was just this one small thing that needed to be resolved. She delivered a concerned-actress look to Will and Kip. What?

"How tricky do you think it will be to, you know, travel there, carrying a little contraband?" she asked with all sincerity.

Kip and Will didn't dare look at each other. They were having the time of their lives. Kip thrust three drink fingers into the air, and Will playfully pondered Vanessa's question as she raised her champagne glass in salute to her many admiring Musso and Frank fans. Hooray for Hollywood.

#

Now that West's television interview responsibility had been triumphantly met, and he didn't have to be back at the office until Monday, and he hadn't seen his best friend for ages, it was time to put on the tennis attire.

Roy Black Elk is six feet four inches tall, and two hundred twenty pounds. Thirty-something years old, he is a bigger, stronger, and better tennis player than West. The club pro at the Toluca Lake Tennis Club, he was West's former employer, and his best friend. They hadn't seen each other for some time. Since their last get-together, West had gotten himself arrested in

Colorado, run over by a Russian whaling vessel, schooled at the Love Canal toxic waste site, interviewed on television and radio several times, adopted by new 'girlfriend' Delilah, seduced by a respectable amount of alcohol and drugs, ultimately deteriorating into a less than fit athletic condition. His second-class wave riding wasn't enough of a humbling–yesterday, Dharma kicked his ass in the water– so today, his best pal Roy would pound him into senselessness on the tennis court.

Once again they found themselves on center court for all to see, but unlike their last battle, there was no appreciative crowd gathering to cheer them on. Roy was running West from corner to corner, up and back, toying with him mercilessly. West, breathing hard, was covered in sweat, hitting balls into the bottom of the net, continually bending over for breath that was nowhere to be found, and generally sucking. Should you feel like an old man at twenty-five? How does one go downhill this fast? Just say no, kids. Roy finally decided to stop the slaughter.

"Ready to wave the white flag?"

"Feels good to be back on the court. I've missed this," said a gasping West.

"Doesn't look like it feels good."

"I've missed you; I've missed tennis. Hey! I went surfing yesterday," West proclaimed.

Roy could see that his friend had changed, was changing, and was struggling against an existential riptide. But that's what metamorphosis is, right? The transformation out of one skin into another. When caught in a rip current, don't fight it. Swim parallel to the shore. Roy knew that he would have to wait until West was able to swim to safety.

"Whenever you're ready, there are classes to be taught," said Roy.

"Perfect segue. I've been thinking seriously about that. No shit, I have. I'm teaching a private lesson in an hour. Cassandra Eaton," said West.

West had relayed to Roy the whole story about Cassandra surprising him in the shower, then later– with his ex-girlfriend Lucinda at her side– finding he and sixteen-year-old Hadley in bed together, and then evicting him from the guesthouse in Beverly Hills. The guesthouse arrangement, by the way, that Roy brokered between West and Stephen Eaton, Cassandra's husband and Hadley's stepfather. Roy knew the whole sordid tale. This casual announcement of a tennis lesson involving Cassie Eaton was an instant eyebrow raiser.

"As I recall, that relationship came to a fiery end," said Roy.

"Muy fiery, but she called the office. Said all is forgiven and she's willing to pay double."

"You think this is a wise decision?"

"No."

"But you're going anyway."

"Yes."

"What about the husband and the daughter?"

"I need the money."

Do you see? The riptide? The potential drowning? Roy repeated his offer to take him back as a tennis instructor. "Whenever you're ready." He dangled the idea of a road trip to "get away from the madness." He

386

bit his tongue, saying not a word about his concern and worry for his old pal. As was their post tennis match tradition, he poured his bottle of water over West's head, told him to "stay out of trouble," and then headed off in a completely opposite and much healthier direction.

Within minutes, West was standing in front of the Eaton house, tennis bag in hand, undergoing a sudden wave of apprehension. Maybe this wasn't such a good idea after all. He should have heeded Roy's warning. On the front door there was a note. For him. WEST. PLEASE COME INSIDE AND MAKE YOURSELF AT HOME. BE RIGHT BACK. CASSIE. This wasn't good. This was scary. The smart thing would be an about-face, get back in the car, throw it reverse, and get the hell out of Dodge. But he needed the money.

Nervously, he looked from side to side. He looked behind him. Were there any neighbors? Was there anyone watching? What if he was pegged for a burglar? His hand found the doorknob. Turning it effortlessly, the door opened right up. Two steps inside he called out "Hey there? Anybody home? Mrs. Eaton? Anybody?"

The house was as quiet as a graveyard. He stood there, not knowing what to do. On a wall in the foyer there was a family photo of the Eaton's. Stephen, Cassandra, and Hadley were standing in the snow, in front of a mountain lodge, dressed in expensive ski apparel. They looked miserable. West dropped his bag to get a closer look just as a voice rang out from an upstairs room.

"West? Is that you West?"

387

He jumped back from the photo, his heart pounding in his chest. Motherfucker! It was Cassie, Cassandra. Why was she here? I mean, why was she upstairs? She left a note. "Be right back."

"West, Come up here please. I need your help," commanded Cassie.

"I'll meet you on the tennis court," said West.

"Would you please come help me move this dresser? Get your ass up here!" she demanded.

West wanted to turn and run. Somehow he had forgotten the blunt force of her entitlement, and her fearless means to an end. How do we forget these things? Against his once upon a time better judgment he gradually made his way up the stairs and stopped at the top. There were several doors, each partially closed. Cassandra's voice guided him. "I'm in here," she said.

An eerie serenity came over West. Just like that. It was as if his fear respectfully took its leave, allowing he and Cassie to have their privacy. His heart rate and breathing returned to normal. He floated toward the room with the voice, confident that he would slay the dragon.

Peering through the partially open door, no person, no Cassandra could be seen. Without concern, and out of body, he entered the room, the door, like a flash, closing behind him. There stood Cassandra wearing nothing but her daughter Hadley's white Beverly Hills Hotel bathrobe.

"Look at you. Just as delicious as I remember," said Cassandra.

"You don't look like you're ready for a tennis

lesson, Cassie. Maybe I should go and come back later," said West with no intention of going anywhere.

"No tennis lesson today," she said.

"My friend Roy told me this was a bad idea."

"He was wrong."

"What is it you want?" said West.

"Undress for me," she said loosening the belt on her robe, allowing it to open slightly.

"Are you trying to seduce me Mrs. Robinson?"

"I'm hiring you to do a job. Your money is there on the table. Depending on how you perform, this could be a regular arrangement. Undress for me."

There was, indeed, an impressive amount of money laid out in neat stacks on the bedside table. West flipped off his tennis shoes, and then, taking his time, his shirt. He gestured to Cassandra to open her robe. She did. Walking toward her his tennis shorts and undershorts fell down around his ankles. Kicking them away, he stood dick-naked facing her.

"I think you'll be satisfied with my services, Cassie. The 'Better Business Bureau' has awarded me a rating of A-Plus."

Newton's First Law of Motion states: 'An object at rest stays at rest, and an object in motion stays in motion with the same speed and in the same direction unless acted upon by an unbalanced force.' With lightning quickness, tantamount to whipping a tablecloth from under a four-course mise en place table, West deftly disrobed the dragon before she knew what hit her, and threw her over his shoulder, depositing her soundly on the bed. The two of them went at it like there was no Stephen, no Hadley, no

Delilah. A battle royale between two dragons that would, two hours later, end in a draw, and a mercenary pocket full of cash for West.

#

West had moved a chunk of the Cassie cash from the pockets of his tennis shorts to the pockets of his suit pants. His new suit pants.

A few weeks back, Kate had Delilah take all of his vital measurements, passed them along to an English tailor friend of hers, and the finished result was a custom tailored suit specifically for West. For occasions exactly like the one they were now in attendance.

After he had showered off the dragon sex, he morphed into a West that wasn't familiar to him, not that having sex with an older woman for money was familiar. A jacket and tie West. A combed hair, pocket full of money West. It felt both gross and curiously attractive.

A mansion in the hills of Beverly, owned by a good friend of Kyle Asher, Kip's grandfather, Kip Sr.'s father, and the principal shareholder in the Asher Oil Company, was the setting for the evening's black-tie gathering.

Grandfather Asher, it turns out, became a whale lover late in life, and was tickled pink that grandson Kip was a notorious whale saver. He was throwing this bash to put some money in the GreenPlanet coffer, and, no less important, to implement a détente between the oil boys and the environmentalists. So, there, for all to see, was oil magnate Hal Davidson–the same Hal Davidson that arranged for Will and West to be banished into the Mexican desert as punishment for their insubordination–lighting Will's Cuban cigar, and handing him an impressive bank note made out to GreenPlanet.

Kate and West were at the back of the room sipping champagne and watching the elite meet.

"Don't often get a chance to see oil tycoons and the liberal riff-raff in the same room," said Kate.

"I'm trying to believe my lying eyes. Will and Hal Davidson playing nice," said the dapper West. "I still haven't recovered from being left for dead in the Mexican desert."

"Grandpa elucidated to the oilmen that it was financially wise to have us on their side," said Kate.

"Or in their back pockets," said West.

"Go. Work the room. Put on the charm."

"I'm not Delilah, and where is she?" he asked wishing she could see him in his new duds.

"On her way to a radio chat show later tonight."

"I think you've got our roles reversed," he said.

"No, I haven't. How's your new home coming along? All settled in?"

"Let's just say it's been a busy two days."

West watched as Will smoked cigars and schmoozed with Hal Davidson and some of the other planet polluters. On the other side of the room he could see Kip laughing with Grandpa Asher. He felt off-balance again. Not himself, whoever that was. Kate flagged down a waiter and had him refresh their champagne glasses. She was enjoying her proximity to the dressed up version of West.

"One more thing. You're mine tomorrow night,"

she said.

West looked at her with questioning eyes.

"We're attending a record release party. A dignitary at Atlantic Records has requested our presence."

"Record release parties can be quite memorable," said West.

"So I hear."

"You and me, huh. Is this a date?"

"Relax cowboy."

Kate waved at Kip and Grandpa Asher. West emptied his champagne glass. It had been a surreal two days, or more like nine months. His thoughts went to Delilah. Surveying his surroundings, he wondered if it was safe for him to swim to shore.

#

Delilah had, on this same day, returned from a drama-free presentation down south at Orange Coast College, took a necessary cat nap, paid some overdue bills, hid the more painful ones under a pile of paper on her kitchen table, met Salinger for a margarita-laced dinner at El Coyote Café, and was currently stationed in front of a microphone as the guest of Michael Benner on his late night talk show 'Impact.' It was the wee hours of the morning, and the phone lines in the studio were enthusiastically blinking.

"One forty a. m. You're listening to 'Impact.' My name is Michael Benner. My guest tonight is Delilah Dean from the activist environmental organization GreenPlanet. We still have her for another twenty minutes or so and we'll try to get to as many of you,

392

and answer as many of your questions as we possibly can. You're on 'Impact,' good morning."

"Right, hi, my name is Marco. Calling from Inglewood. My question for Delilah, well my impression, not just my impression, lot's of other people's too. How do you respond to criticism that saving whales, and environmentalism in general, is pretty much a white thing, an upper class, upper-middle-class-class white thing? College students that have the time and money to sail around the ocean and go to protests, etcetera, etcetera. Is saving whales the most important issue for people to tackle?"

Delilah was loving everything about this late-night radio experience. The tough questions, the sycophantic praise, even the crazy ravings. She could see herself doing this full-time. It felt right.

"People? I don't know about people. For me? It's something I'm passionate about. My colleagues and I are passionate about many issues. At present, we're deeply involved in this," she answered.

"Curious to know how many black faces are part of your organization?" asked Marco.

"I can't think of one."

"That's what I'm saying."

"Our door is open to everyone. All you have to do is walk on in."

"In my neighborhood we have more pressing matters. More life and death matters. You probably don't know who Adolph Lyons is? A couple of years ago this cat was..."

"Almost killed by an LAPD officer who stopped him for a bad tail light. He's black. He was profiled. The

LAPD officer put him in a chokehold for no reason. Almost killed him. There have been several other similar cases in Los Angeles since then. It's an issue that's on Justice Marshall's radar," Delilah said cutting him off.

"And how the hell would a nice white girl like you, know what's on Thurgood Marshall's radar?" Marco parried.

"Pretty sure you can't see my skin color on your radio. He's an old acquaintance who still happily takes my calls. Our door is always open," said Delilah.

"Thanks for your call Marco," said an intervening Michael Benner. "If I can interject here. That was a great exchange. I view the members of GreenPlanet operating in the tradition of Dr. King. You're conducting civil disobedience on the high seas. Willing to risk jail and risk your lives. You choose action over rhetoric. Standing for something instead of simply opposing something. Most importantly in a non-violent way."

Delilah mouthed the words 'Thank You' to Michael who nodded his head in the affirmative. The last call of the night was from a woman in Hermosa Beach. Guinevere was her name. Talking to animals was her game.

She wanted to know if Delilah communicated with the whales, as in talk to the whales. Maybe, she wondered, did Delilah, like herself, talk to plants and other animals? How about UFO's?

Guinevere kept journals of her conversations with all of the above, she said. She referred to herself as a 'psychic zoologist,' admitted to having sexual dreams about whales and dolphins, and was curious if Delilah did too? She confessed to having a "huge crush" on Michael, who was not a whale. She absolutely "loved" his voice.

Delilah, in a momentary truce with the world, leaned back in her chair, and imagined a life behind the microphone. What if, all this time, she had recruited West to do a job that she was perfectly suited to do? Or at least as suited to do. What if this is where her road was leading her?

She couldn't help but chuckle. Late night chats, she was discovering, was her niche. She hadn't given West a thought all day. It felt good. This whole communications thing. This whole independent woman thing. Go figure.

#

Susan chose not to wait for the next day. While everyone else ran off to lunch, she ran home, packed her bags, left a note for her roommate, gassed up her car, and headed north to San Francisco. Taking Pacific Coast Highway allowed her to stop at the Esalen Institute for the night. Under a bright moonlight, she soaked in hot tubs, gazed at stars, and hoped that she would have the right stuff to facilitate a coming together of the two GreenPlanet tribes. San Francisco or bust.

It was now noon on Friday, and there she was sitting across from Karma and Catty. They were surprised and intrigued by their Southern California visitor. What exactly was going on here?

Susan had phoned Karma from the road to let

them know of her arrival. She alluded to the possibility that she might be interested in working in the more "estrogen friendly" San Francisco office. She said that she had an idea for a campaign that she wished to pitch to them. It was enough to pique their curiosity.

"So how's things in L A? What are you working on?" asked a suspicious Catty.

"Like I said to Karma on the phone, we have a lot going on down there, but I'm afraid the males get assigned most of the juicy campaigns. My intuition tells me it's more girl-friendly up here. The toxic waste dumping grounds around the Farallon Islands is something I'd like to take on, and I was thinking that it might be the perfect joint campaign for our two offices," Susan said.

"What do you know about it?" asked Karma.

"Containers of nuclear waste are leaking near the Farallon Islands. The Atomic Energy Commission and U.S. Navy dumped over forty-seven thousand steel drums in the waters around the islands. Radioactive waste is jeopardizing a major city. Big issue, something we should be making a lot of noise about."

Karma and Catty exchanged unsure glances. Susan seemed sincere. The Farallons were an issue that they, too, had on their radar, but could they trust someone from the phony Hollywood office? It was a question that remained to be answered. On the other hand, it might be very beneficial to have, in their ranks, someone with insider knowledge of the renegade operation to the south, and an additional female never hurt. They would need to hear and see more.

"We think it's important to have a mutual respect

and working relationship between the two offices. Even though we in San Francisco are the true GreenPlanet and have been so from the beginning, we think the Los Angeles branch could prove to be a valuable sub-member of the tribe," said Karma.

"We're all fighting for the same cause, right?" said Catty with faux enthusiasm. "And we women, especially, have to stick together."

"Right on," answered Susan.

"So, why don't you stick around here and take over the Farallon campaign? I'll hook you up with Jade. She can show you around. Set you up with a workspace. Be your campaign partner if you want," offered Karma.

"Yes? That would be amazing. I would love that."

"How will your L A colleagues feel about this?" asked Karma.

"I think they'll be fine. I mean, they may have to answer their own phones for a while, but."

"Speaking of answering phones, we would love to view a tape of West's interview on that morning show. Can you get that for us?" asked Catty.

"We fielded quite a lot of calls yesterday morning. The callers were very enthusiastic. Has he matured since we saw him on the summer voyage?" Karma asked.

Susan knew what they were doing. She couldn't fault them. Expected it. She would be surprised and suspicious if hey didn't test her. She knew that this was only the beginning, and it would take time and patience and more political savvy on her part.

"Hmm. Matured? Let's just say that he's feeling

more and more comfortable in his own skin. I'll see if I can get you a copy of the interview. He was very good," she said.

Karma looked to Catty who gave her the batting eyes of approval.

"Welcome to the real GreenPlanet," said Karma.

Later that afternoon, when Susan found a chance to slip off on her own, she phoned the L.A. office to give her first report. Kate placed her on speakerphone so that Delilah could listen and take notes.

As Susan filled them in on the meeting, Kate listened between the lines. The good news was that Susan had easily succeeded in getting a foot in the door. Maybe too easily? On the one hand, it was good to have a mole in the S.F. office, on the other hand, Susan sounded a tiny bit too excited.

Why did they want a videotape of West's interview? Where would Susan be staying? Had Jonah reared his ugly, evil head yet? Would they use the Farallon campaign as an inducement for Susan to work as a double agent? What would Hunter think?

Susan promised to report back soon and off she ran to meet up with her new tribe. Kate turned her attention to Delilah.

"Thoughts?" said Kate.

"She sounds excited to be there," said Delilah.

"She does, doesn't she?"

"Can I throw something into the mix? A parallel campaign. A caller last
night was asking me about barges off the California coast that carry toxic waste, sometimes nuclear waste. Maybe I could look into that and

perhaps connect it to the Farallon Island campaign?"

That was not exactly what Kate was trying to get at. Maybe she was hearing trouble that was not there?

"Intriguing. We could connect the dots with ocean garbage dumping, and potential nuclear reactor wastewater contamination," said Kate.

After departing the aforementioned black-tie party, Kate had made it a point to tune in to the last hour of the radio talk show starring Delilah. She was impressed with Delilah's performance and professionalism. She was also aware of Delilah's less than enthusiastic participation on the college lecture circuit, and she was looking for a way to reward Delilah and keep her engaged and simpatico.

"I caught the end of your radio show. Well played. Would you like to do more?" asked Kate.

"Very much," said Delilah.

"Brilliant. The toes of West will be stepped on."

"He's got ten toes," said Delilah.

"There you have it. Toxic waste barges are all yours, and I'll put you in the line-up for more interviews. Anything else? Life treating you kindly?"

"I'm good," said Delilah.

"We need to make another date for drinks soon," Kate suggested.

"I'd like that."

"Never dull around here, is it?" said Kate.

#

They were inside one of the Sunset Gower Studios. Prior to arriving they made a stop at Roscoe's House of Chicken and Waffles, paid their respects to Herb

Hudson, and loaded up on Hollywood's version of soul food as preparation for a long night of drinking and other extracurricular activities. West and Kate, whiskeys in hand, were standing at one of the many bars that surrounded the perimeter of the soundstage. Led Zeppelin had been in rehearsal the night before, and the studio required a full day of reconstruction into the present 'party central' to celebrate the release of Tormato, the latest endeavor by the illustrious prog-rock group Yes. The place was full of suits, models, rock stars, wannabe rock stars, celebs, wannabe celebs, and the required amount of power brokers and beautiful people. Kate looked smashing. She looked like she belonged there. West was excited, and in his excitement had already thrown back a whiskey or two. The music was loud and they had to strain to hear each other. As his less than impressive self-control was increasingly lowered by whiskey and whirlwind, West repeatedly told Kate how great she looked. She looked "hot," "amazing," "smokin." Yes she did. No argument there. That was part of the game plan.

She changed the subject to Delilah. West was told that Delilah would be doing more media. More "in front of the microphone and camera stuff." He was told that it would be good for them to have a female voice and face as a contrast and complement to his mug. Also, Delilah could relieve West of the burden he carried as sole spokesman.

Burden? West didn't feel burdened. Au contraire. He was on a roll. Kicking ass and taking names. It wasn't necessary for Delilah to help out. He was sure that she wouldn't feel comfortable with the spotlight on her. Too stressful. When was this decided?

"That's not necessary. Where is Delilah? Is she coming?" asked West.

"No. She said album release parties have not been kind to her."

"I'm never ever getting off the hook for that one."

"No, you're not," said Kate as she brushed a bit of hair off of his forehead.

"So, it's just the two of us then?"

"And four hundred others."

An expensive suit-wearing record executive named Ash approached Kate and gave her a big hug and kiss on the cheek. He completely ignored West, as Kate responded with cool detachment.

"Kate. You look stunning as always," said Ash, his hand still on Kate's arm.

"Do I know you?" said Kate.

"You know everyone. Don't Kill the Whale. That track is my gift to you. You're welcome."

"I think you have mistaken me for someone else," said Kate.

"Ha! Wakeman heard you were here. Sent me to find you and bring you backstage. He's single now, you know?"

"As you can see I'm taken", she said as she put her hand in West's crotch and kissed him on the mouth.

"He wants to see you. You know where to find us. You look better than ever. You left the Irishman?"

"What did you say your name was?" said Kate with her arm around West.

Ash laughed and wandered off into the crowd while

401

West was still trying to regain his composure from Kate's manhandling and affection.

"If you need to use me as a shield or anything tonight, it's, you know, okay by me," said West.

"That's why you're here," she said as she slugged down her whiskey in one gulp, and patted West on the head.

They had a good location. Didn't need to move. It was in close proximity to one of the bars that was captained by a bartender that couldn't resist giving Kate all of the free drinks that she wanted. Bathrooms were within sight, and it was also strategically located close to an exit for when and if they needed to make a quick get-away.

Strategically content, they let the beautiful people come to them. Kate introduced West to everyone, and like the A & R guy had said, she knew everyone. Eddie Van Halen, Rick Ocasek, Joan Jett, Joan Collins, Joan Didion, John Belushi, Kris Kristofferson, David Geffen, Ian Anderson, Greg Lake, Robby Krieger, everyone. She received non-stop condolences as Keith Moon's name was bandied about. Debates raged over who was the greatest rock drummer of all time. Moon? Bonham? Baker? Starr? How about Peart? Don't forget Mason. Lunches were arranged and phone numbers were exchanged and contraband was distributed. When there finally was a lull in the action, West suggested he and Kate go pay their respects to the Atlantic Records table.

"Maybe we should say hello to our hosts," said an increasingly altered West.

Kate grabbed him by the belt on his jeans. "No.

Come with me," she said as she whisked him away toward their escape exit door.

West's 1970 red VW Bug sat purring in front of a secluded house high up in the hills of Hollywood. Before he could shut the engine down, turn the lights off, put the handbrake on, and run to the other side of the car, Kate had disappeared into the house and left the front door open.

As he entered the house he could hear a muffled male voice. Closing the door behind him, he made his way into a magnificently lavish and lascivious living room with huge windows overlooking a sparkling Los Angeles cityscape. The male voice was now recognizable. Even in his alcoholic haze West knew this voice well. The L.A. Lonesome Cowboy, Jim Ladd, was coming through the stereo speakers loud and clear. West listened closely as he stood looking out over the shimmering city below.

"Can you feel it? It's one of those restless nights in Los Angeles. One of those nobody's going to sleep, looking for trouble nights. The good kind of trouble if you know what I mean? Don't try to resist. You can't escape nights like tonight. Don't want to. It's why we live in this city. Something happens here. Something strange and wondrous and wild. My name is Jim Ladd, and you're listening to 94.7 KWOT. Hang on people. It's one of those Hollywood nights."

Cue the music. 'Hollywood Nights' by Bob Seger and the Silver Bullet Band came blaring through the floor speakers. West turned around to find Kate seated on the chocolate leather sofa with two champagne flutes full of bubbly in front of her on the expensive

403

glass coffee table. She was meticulously dividing up four lines of pharmaceutical grade cocaine. Patting the empty place next to her, she enticed West to join her on the sofa. He readily complied. Applying the de rigueur ceremony and ritual, they took turns snorting their respective lines of coke. West was wild-eyed. His world was upside-down. He long ago had lost all control or understanding of who he was or why he was. He looked longingly at Kate.

"Okay surfer boy. Show me what you got."

Before he could make his move, Kate latched on to him and pulled him on top of her. Time stood still. So much happened; everything happened in the blink of an eye, and yet time stood still.

Have you ever dreamed you were flying? Levitating high above the earth? The groundlings watching in awe and bewilderment? Worshipping you and how you're able to do anything. Soar, glide, barrel rolls, upside-down, effortlessly, flawlessly. More cocaine, more champagne, uppers, downers, weed, whip cream, off of naked body parts, whiskey, tongues, fluids, exhaustion, heart palpitations, wet fingers, Zeppelin, Floyd, Sabbath, Zevon, daylight.

In a king sized bed, in an unfamiliar bedroom, a very disoriented, disheveled, and naked West opened one eye, and then the other. The other side of the bed was vacant, but someone had been there. Dripping out of bed onto bruised knees and a wet floor, he tried to get his bearings. He found his way out of the bedroom, through the party room, and into the kitchen. There he discovered a conspicuous note on the counter near the coffee pot. His name was in big, bold, felt pen letters:

WEST. GO HOME. HAVE A NICE WEEKEND. SEE YOU MONDAY. LOCK THE FRONT DOOR.

Pouring himself a cup of coffee, he surveyed the battlefield in front of him. His clothes were on the floor in front of the leather sofa in the living room. On top of the coffee table were empty champagne glasses, a gilded mirror with razor blade and cocaine residue, unopened condoms, and a half bottle of scotch that occupied no place in his memory. Looking down he could see that he was red and swollen. Painfully returning to the scene of the crime, he fingered the cocaine remnants and rubbed it into his gums. It was quiet, no Jim Ladd coming through the speakers, no Kate coming in his ear. Only his inner voice.

"The note said GO HOME. Where is that? The doublewide in Malibu? I wonder what Dharma's up to? Oh, man. Delilah. Jesus. Amazing, I don't feel as bad as I should. Physically I mean. I don't feel physically as bad as I should. But Delilah. I suck. I'm a total asshole. I didn't mean for this to happen. At least I didn't make a play for Kate. Did I? Oh, Kate. Fuck. This changes everything. I think she might be in love with me. Maybe I'm in love with her? Last night was mind-blowing. What's going to happen? What am I going to do? Fuck. Fuck. Fuck. Fuck. Fuck. Fuck. Fuck. Fuck."

Inside his car, he found an article of female clothing. He didn't even know what purpose it had, or where it was to be worn. He was a stinking mess. At least the gas tank was half full, or half empty depending on your worldview. The little red bug, she started right up, rolled right out of the driveway, carefully down the very steep street, out of the

405

Hollywood Hills, and back to the Pacific ocean where she belonged.

It was Saturday noonish when he walked through the front door of his new life. His sincere intention was to clean up the chaos that was once his brother Wyatt's hideout, and now his oceanside home. Dump the ashtrays, dispose of the take-out containers, get the books, newspapers, and records off of the floor, empty out and disinfect the refrigerator, remove the bed sheets, tackle the bathroom, open the windows, and let fresh air and sunshine take over.

He didn't do any of this. He was in no condition. He barely made it to the bed where he fell face first, fully clothed, and didn't stir for fifteen hours. It was the wee hours of Sunday morning when he eventually regained consciousness, struggled to remember where exactly he was, and found his way to the bathroom to take a long overdue piss.

When he turned the water on to take a shower, a brownish liquid poured for a couple of minutes before the water turned clear. The hot water, soap, and fifteen hours of sleep were rejuvenating. At least physically. As the suspect water poured over him, temporarily washing away his transgressions, he tried to wrap his mind around recent events.

Before he was "discovered" on the beach by Delilah, he had never lived or desired a fast-lane life. He was a monogamously dependable boyfriend with a college degree and intentions of doing something responsible with his life. He was in good physical condition. Sure, he liked to drink beer and whiskey, smoke a little pot now and then, eat junk food more than he should, watch bad TV, spend too much time with his surfing and tennis buddies instead of his girlfriend, but nothing earth-shatteringly irresponsible. But. There was always this thing; this feeling; a shadow, a cloud, an unintelligible voice.

That evening when Lucinda informed him that they were done; that same night that he spent on the beach staring out to sea, waiting for a sign, an instruction; followed by the not so coincidental appearance of Delilah had pointed him in the direction of this conflicted, wee-hours-of-the-morning moment.

West was not happy with himself, and then again, he was. He was accomplishing things that he felt good about. He was growing. He was, perhaps, in the middle of a hero's journey, but smack in the middle where perspective did not live and darkness did. More and more these days he felt like someone taken for a ride. A pawn whose choices were being made for him. It was unsettling. It was thrilling. It was crippling. It was all a mystery.

He was hungry, but it was three a.m. and he was afraid to consider any of the food in his less-than-sanitary kitchen. Maybe Wyatt had some canned food? With bath towel secured around his waist, West rummaged through a kitchen cabinet, and found a can of chili that he reckoned was safe to eat.

It hit the life-affirming spot. His innards hadn't ingested anything non-lethal since the chicken and waffles at Roscoe's, and he savored every bite. On the table was the stack of mail that was addressed to

407

Wyatt's alias Howard Roark. In the pile there was an envelope from GreenPlanet. He was all too familiar with that piece of mail. Opening it, he removed the new member documents and the welcome letter with Susan's signature. Wyatt a.k.a. Howard had become a card-carrying member of GreenPlanet. How about that? I'll be damned.

West wondered if the money Wyatt sent to GreenPlanet was, well, where did it come from? No matter. Don't think about it. Don't think about anything. Go back to bed. Get up with the sun. Get your house in order. Don't think.

Sunday came and went. West made real progress in getting his new place ship shape, though one day's work was not nearly enough to do it right. As best as he was able, he erased from his mind Kate and Delilah, Delilah and Kate. He vowed to consider his neighbor Dharma a surfing pal and nothing more. No additional women for him at this time. Maybe it would be best not to be involved with any women at all? That would make life a lot simpler and drama free. Right?

Before entering Monday morning traffic, he called the office to check in with Kate. Hopefully, it would be a relatively normal day that would not require his 'A' game or any game at all. Salinger was on the receiving end when he called, and he wasn't able to speak three words before she went ballistic.

He was learning from a very loud Salinger that he was "fucking scum," a "grade A asshole," a "selfish, mean, inconsiderate, ingrate," a "fucking loser." Kate had informed Salinger that she had drinks, well, a drink, with Delilah the previous night. Told Delilah everything. She confessed to Delilah that she and West had gotten wasted, went back to her place, had gotten more wasted, had unintentional meaningless sex, and that she was so, so, so very sorry, "it won't ever happen again." Delilah, the classy person that she was, remained calm and collected, thanked Kate for her honesty and the drink, and departed for parts unknown. Kate, feeling terrible, was in her office—not taking any calls—and was considering a permanent return to London, and "it's all your fault!" Before West could utter a word of reply, Salinger violently hung up on him. "Fuck you asshole!"

Salinger Jayne Daniels was the third and youngest child of John 'Jack' and Jane Daniels. Not to be cruel, but she was a mistake. An unplanned house guest. Her two older twin sisters Franny and Zoe had only come into this world the year before, and with the unexpected arrival of Salinger came high stress and strain for her parents. Two English professors that had met at an academic conference in Berkeley, their love of *The Catcher in the Rye* led to their love of each other. When the unexpected one arrived, the lovers of literature didn't think that Holden was the right name for a girl. Initially, they decided on Jane, but after further deliberation fabricated the much groovier name Salinger. Additionally, Jane Daniels came up with the brilliant idea of choosing Jayne, as in Jayne Mansfield, for the child's middle name—the couple had recently seen the film *Kiss Them For Me* and Jayne Mansfield was fresh in their brains—this created a backward homage. J.D. Salinger became Salinger J.D.

Why, exactly, Salinger was so upset with West only

she knew for sure. She might have only just turned twenty-one, but she was wise for her age. She had notched her own one-night stands–two to be precise– and was not puritanical by any means, but this pushed her buttons. Maybe her expectations or perceptions with regards to West had been dashed? Maybe her fondness and admiration for Delilah was cause for her outrage? Maybe an ugly experience in her past was reincarnated? Maybe it went deeper? Maybe the Daniels clan simply don't like surprises? I don't know, but she was pissed.

When West burst through the door, Salinger wasn't quick enough to block his path. Into Kate's office he flew, slamming the door behind him.

"What the fuck is the matter with you?" screamed West.

"She wasn't that upset," said Kate.

"Well I'm upset. Big time upset," said West pacing back and forth.

"That's to be expected."

"What you did was downright cruel. Mean, evil, and cruel. What the fuck is your problem?"

"You've already asked that. Sit. I told you that I didn't think it a good idea for you two to be a couple while working for the cause."

"Who the fuck are you? For your information, Delilah and I are not a couple, don't live together, and it's none of your God damn business."

"The sexual tensions in the office had to be put down. We've important campaigns approaching and cannot afford to be distracted. Friday night took care of the problem."

"What exactly did you say to her?"

"I told her that we got very drunk and high, that we had sex, that it was meaningless, and that it would never happen again."

"Jesus."

"She handled it well as I knew she would."

"Are you saying that what happened Friday night, what did Delilah say?"

"She'll be fine. It's for the best. Trust me."

"Everything that happened was part of a plan? It wasn't, you didn't enjoy it? Never happening again?"

"You get distracted easily. Now you've experienced Delilah and me, and Susan is safely away in San Francisco, and none of us will have anything to do with you in that arena anymore, and now you can concentrate on your work and become the superstar you're meant to be."

"For fuck's sake. You are one sick human being. What about Salinger? Aren't you worried about her?"

"I believe she is sufficiently repulsed by your actions that she won't be an issue. You can ask her if you want. Right now, time for you to go. I've important work to do today and you have a phone call to return from the FBI. Out you go."

"You may not have enjoyed Friday night, but."

West waited for a reply that didn't come. Battered, wounded, and humiliated he exited into the main office and toward the door. Salinger buried her head in the papers on her desk and did not acknowledge his existence. As he passed by her desk he said: "You're right. Sorry."

Outside, he couldn't remember where he parked

411

his car. He didn't know where he was going. Home? Bar? Delilah? His car was in the parking lot where it was always parked. After discovering his ride, he checked his pockets for his keys, hopped in, hit his head on the door opening, and then sat and stared through the windshield into oblivion. On the seat next to him was Kate's mystery garment. He sat there immobile, his state of mind fragile, swirling. What had he done? What had happened? Was it all his fault?

Now that I think of it, my telling of this part of the story is not exactly accurate. The whole scene in Kate's office was much shorter, and should be looked at in a different light. Here's how it actually went down: West stormed into Kate's office and screamed "What the fuck is the matter with you?" Kate was sitting with her head down, which gave West pause, and an opportunity to settle down. After a minute and a half of silence, Kate said "I told her that we got very drunk and high, that we had sex, that it was meaningless, and that it would never happen again."

"Jesus," said West.

And that was that. No other words were spoken. They looked each other in the eyes for a good two minutes before West retreated into the war room and exited past Salinger.

All of the other stuff, the sexual tensions in the office, he and Delilah shouldn't be a couple, the whole night was an evil, mean plan executed by Kate, she didn't feel anything for West, it was all for the best, all of that stuff was in his head, was racing through his mind while he was sitting and staring out the windshield of his car. Did he misinterpret the entire

412

night? Was it all a drug-induced dream? Was he losing his mind? Drive. West. Toward the beach and his spot. It was the only thing that made sense.

Delilah, meanwhile, had gone south, to L.A. harbor, to seek out Shakespeare Jones and the old salts. For some inexplicable reason, she had received the news of Kate and West's wild night with restraint and resignation. She felt somewhat bad for Kate. She could see how difficult it was for her to confess. I mean, Kate had just gone through two difficult deaths, her father, and Keith Moon, and she did say that it was "meaningless." Shit happens.

As for West, well, that was a bit stickier. She had been weighing the future of she and West for a while. Now that he would be living in Malibu she would be unencumbered, independent, with more options on the table. She didn't like the wounded feeling of seeing Susan or others cozy up to him. She felt that she was becoming weaker because of her attachment to him. Perhaps this was a blessing in disguise?

Delilah found the motley crew at, where else, The Yardarm. Seated around the only table with four sound legs were Shakespeare Jones, The Captain, Doctor, and Jimmy. On the table, poker chips and playing cards were carefully guarded by cocktails made of cheap booze. The four salty dogs were surprised and delighted that the lovely Delilah had unexpectedly brightened up their den of iniquity, but what was going on? It was only last week that West surprised them with his visit.

After hugs and greetings, Delilah was invited to join the game if she felt "up to it." It didn't take long before most of the poker chips were in her possession, and the old boys were looking for excuses.

"This is embarrassing fella's. We're not spose to lose to a girl," whined The Captain.

"We're not losing Captain, just letting Delilah here borrow some of our chips for a while. Polite thing to do. Lets her think she's equal to us men," said Doc.

"Yea, well, she's going to be borrowing the shirt off of your back if you don't get your shit together and quick," countered Jimmy.

"Beginner's luck boys. Beginner's luck, said Delilah as she corralled the chips in a nice pile in front of her.

Shakespeare, as always, was suspicious of yet another surprise visit. Last weeks visit with West still troubled him.

"It sure is good to see you sweetie. Real good. First West, now you come to visit, but I don't think you came all the way down here to hang out with four old goats, did you?"

"You're the old goat," said Doc.

"I do have something I want to talk to you about," she said.

He knew it. He figured she wanted to talk to him in private. Maybe it had something to do with West and his dark shadow. He was about to suggest they go somewhere private when Delilah continued.

"I'd like to hear what you all know about maritime ships and barges carrying toxic waste materials. Nuclear, industrial, and just garbage in general. Who? What? Where they are loaded? When do they usually leave port? The route they take. Whatever you can tell me," she said.

Well, the old goats didn't see that coming. Speechless, they looked to each other for direction. The discomfort was evident on each face. Shakespeare fidgeted in his seat, but remained silent.

"I know what you're thinking. Dangerous territory for a girl, but you know I'm going to investigate this with or without your help. Do you guys know anything about this? You're holding back on me. I can see it in your eyes. That's why all these chips are sitting in front of me. All of you, you're no good at bluffing. C'mon. What do you know? Time to spill the beans," she said staring down each one of them.

Yea, they knew what most men down at the docks knew about this unspoken topic. Not just dangerous territory for a girl, but for anyone foolish enough to go poking their nose where it doesn't belong. The military was involved, specifically the Navy. The private sector was also involved. Shakespeare had even been approached a few years back regarding use of the Maggie May.

Delilah told them what she knew, and of rumors that she had heard. For years naval vessels around the world hauled thousands of barrels of nuclear waste and toxic waste out to sea, and dumped them where they calculated that it would be safe. She filled them in on Susan's new project regarding the Farallon Islands dumping grounds. She asked them about the hiring of private vessels like the Maggie May. Her understanding was that radioactive waste was supposed to be dumped in a minimum of six thousand feet of water in designated locations out beyond the continental shelf. She heard whispers that some private boats under contract dumped their radioactive cargo close to the shore. They were either too lazy to travel the distance required, or unwilling to use the fuel to navigate that distance, or didn't give a shit, or all of the above. She wanted to know how close to the California coast sailed the ships carrying radioactive material? How safe or unsafe was the toxic cargo in transport? Could they put her in touch with anybody in the know? Had they personally witnessed toxic dumping?

She didn't dare inquire if any of her new friends had ever participated in the ocean dumping of toxic waste. Her intuition led her to strongly believe that they had not. But the look on their faces. Grim seems to be a fair word choice.

Shakespeare nodded his head as if to say "yes, there are things that we can tell you." The Captain shrugged his bony shoulders in acquiescence; Jimmy fled to the bar to make more drinks, and Doctor heaved a great sigh at the sheer madness that was the world. What were they about to tell her?

#

West found his way to the beach, but was much too restless to sit on the sand and stare into space. He needed guidance. He needed counseling. He needed Kip.

After hearing West's muddled and frantic telephone account of the events of Friday night, Kip suggested that the best medicine would be for West, Will, and himself to "hit the town" because "three heads and three bottles are better than one." Tonight, however, would not include the Chimney Sweep, which was just

416

fine with West because he wasn't ready to face the wrath of Connie, and feared the possibility that Delilah might also be present. Kip devised a plan. Drinks at the Riot House followed by drinks at the Rainbow Bar followed by drinks at the Whisky followed by a late night surprise. Done.

Kip and Will didn't find West's one-wild night-stand story all that dramatic or concerning; they considered it normal, even healthy Hollywood behavior. They also weren't worried about Delilah. She was a big girl, smart, wise, and self-confident. She would survive this bump in the road much easier than their young pal West. Kate, as Kip was well aware, was a veteran of the rock and roll lifestyle. Not only would she be completely unscathed by this night of revelry, but there was a very good chance that her intention was exactly that which unfolded. West was a different story. He was rattled.

While becoming chemically altered at the Riot House, West was reminded of Connor's friend Morgana, and his weaknesses with her in that hotel on that night only a couple of months ago. He began to have thoughts that suggested a recurring pattern was underway.

At the Rainbow, he started feeling better, or perhaps comfortably numb. Will introduced him to Alice Cooper and Lemmy Kilmister. Kip introduced him to Mario Maglieri, who insisted they accompany him next door to the Roxy for a "sip and a snort." At the Whisky, a comely young lass took an interest in West, and also took him out to the parking lot for a puff and a tug. Kip's blueprint, it seemed, was going according

417

to plan. By the time they got to the Tropicana Motel, West was delirious.

There was a party going on poolside. Rockers, groupies, motel residents, drifters, and crashers were making quite the scene. West, Kip, and Will were seated at a table with three eager women, and a scary looking guy in the process of arranging several lines of cocaine on a slab of broken bathroom mirror. The scary guy handed West a rolled up hundred dollar bill under a watchful eye.

Not sure which line of coke he should choose, he looked for help from the woman with her hand in his crotch. Hmm, let's see. Where is the fattest, longest, most expensive line? Ah! There it is. With all eyes on him, West snorted his line with a flourish, kissed the fair damsel, and triumphantly handed the rolled up C-note to Will.

"Kate is right, you know? It's for the best," said Kip.

Shaking his head in agreement with Kip, Will snorted his line and passed the rolled up bill to his amigo.

"Delilah is special," said West.

With her hand still in his crotch, his female sidekick squeezed his dick as she said "I can be special too."

Enough with the touchy-feely. The scary looking guy pounded his fist hard on the table three times, which inspired Will to hand him three one hundred dollar bills. West's brain was now hurtling out of control as his young companion had her tongue down his throat.

"It's for the best," repeated Kip.

"For the best," agreed Will.

West uncoupled himself from the wench while somehow managing to get to his feet. Not knowing where he was or why he was, he hot-footed it in the direction of salvation. Running as fast as the cocaine would take him, off into the unmerciful L.A. night he vamoosed.

There are blanks in this part of the story that I cannot fill. How did West make it back to his car? Where was his car? Did he grab a taxi? In L.A.? Was he scooped up on Sunset Boulevard by some strangers or fellow revelers? Did he walk? In L.A.? Did he call someone? Connor? LAPD? I simply do not know the answers to any of these questions. Sorry.

I can tell you this: he found his car; he made the brilliant decision to drive his car, and the even more impressive decision to drive his car fast—how fast can a VW bug go? He made the decision to escape the city limits; to fly away until he could fly no more.

On an empty desert highway, West was behind the wheel of his unable to go too fast car. VW Bug-eyed and wired, he made use of every lane available as he hurtled into the California night. How much gas was in the tank? He never checked. What highway was he on? He never checked. Did he have any money on him? Didn't check. Was that an eighteen-wheeler headed straight for him? Wasn't sure. Is this how it all ends?

Swerving hard right, West saw nothing but a cloud of dust and dirt, and then darkness. His car had come to an abrupt stop, the engine still running. He had not heard any eighteen-wheeler air horn blasts. No blinding eighteen-wheeler headlights. No screeching of

419

tires or grinding metal. No sounds of anything at all.

His heartbeat felt somewhat normal. Not bad for someone with one and a half grams of cocaine in their blood. After a measured assessment of the situation he arrived at the conclusion that he had not died. Had there been an eighteen-wheeler that caused him to veer off the highway? He had no idea.

When the dust cloud settled he found that his vehicle was sitting in the parking lot of a roadhouse, inches away from a brand-spanking-new Ford truck with a bumper sticker that said: EAT-FUCK-SKYDIVE. Checking his pants pockets he was overjoyed to discover cash money. A one hundred dollar bill! Where did that come from?

The name of the joint was The Elephants Graveyard Bar and Grill. West was sitting at the end of a very old, long, damaged, wooden bar drinking cheap whiskey and voraciously consuming free beer nuts from a nasty, unsanitary wooden bowl. A dozen heavy drinking, decaying life forms were spread throughout, some watching and listening to a country singer and her two sidekicks up on a rickety wooden platform meant to be a stage. Four bar stools away from West was a guy in uniform—Air Force wings among the various patches—with his head down on the bar. The bartender was nowhere in sight, and the Air Force guy was not moving a muscle. West tried to get his attention.

"You doing alright there? Don't mean to bother you, but a little proof of life please."

Nothing. No signs of life, and no one in the joint seemed to give a shit. West grabbed his drink and the bowl of beer nuts, and moved down next to the man in uniform. He looked hard to see if he could detect any breathing. Unsure, he was about to poke him in the shoulder when the guy lifted his head and ogled West. Turns out he was an officer. About thirty years old. USAF.

"You look like a Desperado," said the officer.

"I'm mostly a law-abiding citizen," said West.

"Not that kind of desperado. Long hair, bushy mustache, skinny, rock band type. You know, like the Desperados."

"I wish, but alas no. You want a drink? Where are we anyway?" asked West.

"In a load of trouble is where we are. You don't know the half of it. A shit load of trouble somewhere between Baker and Barstow."

The bartender returned from the abyss, and happy to see the fly-boy's head off of the bar, he placed a couple of whiskeys and two cold Buds in front of them. West put the C-note on the bar.

"What kind of trouble? Let me have it," West said.

"Classified. Can't, sure as hell can't tell some fucking hippie kid what almost happened. That's for damn sure."

"You fly jets?"

"I do not. Jets don't fly under the ground. I'm in a lot of trouble, son."

West decided to drop the questions. The cocaine was wearing off, the whiskey was kicking in, and he didn't want any trouble.

"You have no idea," said the drunken officer. "End of the world bad. Third near launch this year. Training

421

tape activated. Mistaken for the real thing. Everyone scrambled. Waiting for a 'stand down' command that never came. Less than a minute to go. One of the top brass, he had a gut feeling and he called it off at the last second. Can't talk about it."

West put his whiskey glass down and sat up straight. Did he say "third near launch"?

"I'm responsible for the tape. I almost blew to smithereens the whole damn world. Less than a minute."

"You're not supposed to be here, are you?" asked West.

"A couple of months ago. President Carter? His suit went off to the dry cleaners. In one of the inside pockets. All of the launch codes. People don't realize. If they did, they'd get their houses in order. They'd do something meaningful with their day. I gotta go."

The Air Force officer struggled to his feet, wiped his hands on his pants, and shook his head at West. His nametag said MARLOWE.

"Don't tell anyone," he said as he staggered toward the exit and out of sight.

West was a lot more sober now, at least for the next ten minutes. The flyboy had said "somewhere between Baker and Barstow." He tried hard to picture a map with Baker and Barstow, but he was too fucked up to accomplish that mission. He was, however, clear-headed enough to notice the untouched whiskeys and beers in front of him, but before he could claim ownership of all four, the female singer of country tunes took over the vacated bar stool next to him, and presumably the vacated drinks.

"Mind if I sit here?" she said. West figured that she was about his age, maybe a few years older.

"I ain't livin long like this," said West.

"Is that a yes?" she asked as she sat down and took a sip of beer.

"I ain't livin long like this, that's a Emmylou Harris song. You kind of remind me of her," he flirted.

"She recorded it. Rodney Crowell, he wrote it. Saw you talking to that guy. Looked serious."

"I'm West. My Name is West."

"Like in 'go west young man'?"

"Exactly like that," said a smiling West.

"I'm Rose."

"Short for Rosemary?" he said clinking glasses with her.

"Not saying one way or the other."

"Rose? You know what I believe? I believe it's very important to make the most out of every day of our lives," he said having learned nothing in the past ninety-six hours.

"This day's not over yet," said Rose.

"I guess you're right."

"You going to buy me a drink?" asked Rose as she emptied her whiskey glass.

Somewhere between Baker and Barstow, somewhere between darkness and light, somewhere between altruism and utter selfishness, West put two drink fingers in the air.

"Yes Rose, yes I am."

When Rose dropped West off at the parking lot of the Elephant's Graveyard it was empty except for his humble little German car. Facing west, he sat quietly, the morning sun rising in the sky behind him, throwing a Vermeer-esque light on the solitary scene. Far out on the western horizon, he could see a dark cloud rising from the desert floor.

Slouching down in the driver's seat, West stared contentedly at the black mass. Change was in the air, and was coming his way. He turned the key in the ignition. The engine started up with no delay. Looking at the gas gage he could see that there wasn't much gas in the tank. Close to zero. He looked around. This wasn't Mexico. No plane would suddenly appear in the sky. Nobody would be coming to rescue him. Bolting upright in his seat, he released the handbrake, threw her into gear, spun her wheels, and limped onto the highway. "Drive," he said to himself. "Drive this little toy car as fast as you can go, right at that oncoming dark cloud. Drive motherfucker."

\#

The last two weeks of September were surprisingly mellow and drama free in the GreenPlanet world. West took over the college lecture circuit from Delilah who was immersed in her toxic waste dumping investigations. He had tried, in vain, to speak with her about the fabled night in the Hollywood hills, but Delilah required no explanation nor did she desire one. They crossed paths at the office on a regular basis, and nothing further was mentioned. It essentially became muddy water under the bridge.

Kate was great. All was smooth sailing between her and Delilah, between her and West, between her and everyone. She also did not speak of 'the night' with anyone. Nothing to be said. Every now and then, she and West exchanged a glance that might be interpreted as 'knowing.' Her father, Keith, and London were in the rearview mirror. She was relaxed and focussed on the successful execution of the secret plan for a GreenPlanet America.

West spent these two weeks getting his literal house in order. Floors and walls were scrubbed, trash was tossed, blinds were cleaned, books were shelved, food was replaced, booze was inventoried, bedding became trash, the Post Office was notified, and drinking and drugs took a hiatus.

He and Dharma went surfing—and only surfing—a couple of times; he played tennis with Roy once, and he informed Cassandra Eaton that there would be no more "private lessons." His intention was to walk the straight and narrow until he could reassess; until he could make amends.

During the first week in October, he turned in a tour de force performance at the rescheduled debate with the Japanese Consul General. His Japanese opponent was so rattled and upset with the UCLA moderator for allowing West to use various poster-size photos of Japanese whalers that were killing and processing whales, that he respectfully bowed to the audience, then abruptly walked off the stage, leaving West to humbly accept moral victory.

On Tuesday, October 10th, he was one part of an official honor bestowed upon the GreenPlanet organization by the mayor of Los Angeles. On the steps in front of City Hall, under a bright blue October sky, West, Delilah, Will, Kip, Salinger, and Kate were photographed with the mayor and several city councilmen. Kate was holding an official plaque that read: GREENPLANET DAY. The city of Los Angeles had honored them with the 'keys to the city,' and recognized their efforts to save the whales and protect the environment. Not bad for a rag-tag group that had not been in town that long.

Connor Kilkenny energetically reappeared on the scene. He and West got together for a Rams game on the Sportsman's Lodge television. A week later, Connor and West attended game six of the World Series between the Yankees and the Dodgers. Sadly, they watched the Yankees celebrate yet another championship on Dodger soil.

Everything was good. October was good. West and Delilah went to lunch a couple of times. She stopped by his pad once to drop off some left-behind clothes and ended up staying for dinner. It was nice. Salinger stopped despising him. Kip and Will took a 'time out' from leading him unto temptation, and twice he filled in as tennis instructor for Roy. All was good. October was good, and then came November. The water got choppy in November. November 16th to be precise.

It was a Thursday afternoon. West was about to run off for the day when the phone rang. It was Susan calling from San Francisco. She had some "troubling news." After many hours of deliberation, the jury in the Rocky Flats nuclear trial had arrived at two verdicts. "Guilty of trespassing, and not guilty of obstructing a public passageway." The decision, she said, would be immediately appealed, and the lawyers explained to her that the December sentencing date would likely be pushed back to a later date in the spring, but as of this moment, West and Susan were guilty of trespassing on a United States nuclear weapons facility. Maximum penalty six months in jail and a monetary fine.

If you remember, West and Susan traveled to Golden, Colorado in the spring of 1978 to assist with national media coverage of the protests by the local anti-nuclear and health organizations that were demanding closure of the nuclear plant, a weapons facility that produced the plutonium triggers necessary for atomic weapons to annihilate the planet. Deadly weapons aside, the plant was responsible for the continuing radioactive contamination of the surrounding soil and water. People were dying from cancer. The duo from GreenPlanet–the day before Mother's Day–joined with a dozen others in blocking the train tracks that led into the plant. Their mission: prevent the trains carrying deadly plutonium from entering the facility. All were arrested, sent before the court, and then released to await trial. This past summer, while West and Susan were tangling with the Russian whaling fleet, hundreds more protestors were arrested on the tracks at the Golden, Colorado facility. The court in Jefferson County strategically decided to break the trials up into small groups of protestors, and today was the first verdict to come down. Guilty of trespassing.

West was just starting to feel stable ground under his feet. He had grown cautiously optimistic that the tide had turned. Better days were ahead. Yes, this was unfortunate, even nerve-racking news, but not the end of the world, right? I mean, first of all, he hadn't been sentenced to anything. Yet. And it might all work out fine during the appeals process, right? And today all was well, the sun was out, the sky was blue. Before the phone rang, he was about to run off to the beach, take in a sunset, stick a toe in the water. Now, it seemed a better idea to drop into the Chimney Sweep for a quick one, or two at most. Tomorrow was Friday, and then the weekend! Nothing bad happens on the weekend.

Leo Joseph Ryan, Jr. was a fifty-three-year-old congressman from California's 11th district, commonly referred to as the East Bay. He was a good man; a man of principle. A questioner of authority, a seeker of truth, he was always ready to lend a helping hand. Leo wasn't a member of the U.S. Congress for long–a little less than six years–but he made a noticeable impact while there. Prison reform, oversight of the CIA, and he was a sympathetic environmentalist. He traveled to the ice floes of Newfoundland to witness the Harp seal slaughter, and he became a valued friend of several environmental organizations including GreenPlanet.

West had never met the congressman, but he hoped that one day soon he would have a chance to thank him for his invaluable whale-saving assistance. Congressman Ryan–his office– was a secret source that provided GreenPlanet with real-time location coordinates for the Russian whaling fleet, which made it much easier for the Maggie May to sail in the correct confrontational direction. It's a big fucking ocean out there. Needle in a haystack kind of scenario. Having the U.S. government tell you where the bad guys were located was a huge assist. Sadly, tragically, West's hoped-for meeting would never occur.

The Monday before Thanksgiving–November 20th– West sauntered into the office delighted that it would be a short week of work. Things had slowed down as a result of the pending holiday, and his mind was on surfing and hanging out on the beach.

Salinger was at her command post, as usual, but she was not in typical work mode. Her eyes were moist and she was staring at nothing in particular. When West bid her a cheery "good morning,' she replied with a meek "hey."

The door to Kate's office was open and the television was turned on, which was a rare occurrence at that time of the day. Kate's face was buried in the middle section of the L.A. Times revealing the headline on the front cover: 400 DEAD IN GUYANA. Something was up, but West didn't understand.

Sound from Kate's television could be heard throughout the main room. A newsman was reporting that less than forty-eight hours prior, in the jungles of Guyana, at a place called Jonestown, just east of the Venezuelan border, more than four hundred people were killed via suicide and murder–the final number was over nine hundred. Leo Ryan was murdered. He had traveled there to investigate the increasing reports of Americans being held against their will, as well as ongoing human rights violations perpetrated by the cult leader Jim Jones. Leo's congressional assistant Jackie Speier was with him. She was badly wounded.

West knew that name. He once heard Susan speak with Jackie on the phone. But did he hear the television correctly? Congressman Ryan? Was murdered? A man that he had never met, and still, it was a punch to the gut. The mood in the office was restrained and subdued.

As the others arrived—Will, Kip, Delilah, and a handful of volunteers—their environmental mission felt oddly diminished; demoted. The world had gone to a darker place. The picture was out of focus. For the moment, their altruism was a house of cards built on shaky ground.

The remainder of the day passed with minimum chitchat. Susan called to say hello. The night before she had marched through the streets of San Francisco in an all-woman event called Take Back The Night. It was "empowering," she said. At days end, most of the group went to the Chimney Sweep for one or two dispirited spirits. West joined the group, but made sure to limit his intake to one drink. Delilah informed West of a Thanksgiving dinner invitation by local American Indian Movement activists. It would take place in Santa Monica, she would be attending, and did he want to accompany her?

Susan's phone call reminded West of their GreenPlanet friend Rocky who was savagely beaten after attending a Harvey Milk rally in San Francisco. Rocky's sole offense was being gay in 1978. Delilah had recently told him of the late night radio caller who had questioned her about "more important" causes. Shouldn't saving whales be lower down on the list of things to fight for? People first? He was also acutely reminded of Delilah and Susan's dramatic experience on the Navajo reservation last spring, as they joined members of the American Indian Movement in a dangerous battle with oil companies and the FBI. He thought about Lois Gibbs and Love Canal. He thought about the radioactive contamination of the Rocky Flats area near Denver, and his guilty verdict. People first? The Thanksgiving dinner invitation intrigued him. Yes. Yes he did want to accompany her.

Thursday, November 23rd, and West and Delilah were the only 'pale faces' in a high school gym full of Native American families. Long tables were topped with platters of venison, lobster, fish, wildfowl, Doritos, clams and oysters, Oreo cookies, corn, tortilla chips, cheese puffs, squash, fresh bread, maple syrup, and Hostess cupcakes. Soft drinks and tea were plentiful, but there was no alcohol on this day. Thanksgiving wasn't a day of celebration, not for these folks. Hung on the walls were three jumbo banners: NATIONAL DAY OF MOURNING; AMERICAN INDIAN MOVEMENT; and THE LONGEST WALK. The adults were zealously helping themselves to food and drink. They mingled and mixed while the kids ran rampant. West and Delilah were made to feel welcome as they shared food, and listened to the stories and viewpoints of their native hosts.

Buffy Sainte-Marie was there to perform songs from her recent album *Sweet America.* Between songs she spoke about the struggles of indigenous people; about war and peace, and broken treaties; about the importance of the American Indian Movement. She spoke about the land and the water and Mother Earth. She acknowledged Delilah and West, and expressed her gratitude for the whale-saving efforts of

431

GreenPlanet.

A Native American comedian did twenty minutes of stand-up. He joked about being referred to as Indians. Said nobody he knew was from India. He joked about being discovered. He didn't know that he was lost. There were many jokes about Thanksgiving dinner. What was the deal with turkey, stuffing, and pumpkin pie? He said "don't blame that on us." There were jokes, painful jokes, about the portrayal of Native Americans on television and in movies. There were jokes about the history books.

West was deeply affected. This was, he thought, "the greatest Thanksgiving dinner that I have ever known." He took Delilah's hand into his and held it appreciatively. He vowed to himself to learn about the true history of his fellow Americans. He remembered seeing a book on Roy's coffee table; *Bury My Heart At Wounded Knee;* he would borrow it and read it. Again he considered "people first?"

The drive back to Delilah's house was nice. The streets of Los Angeles were quiet and serene, as were West and Delilah. This time it was a silence of contentment, not awkwardness, as if the seas had turned to glass after a prolonged and turbulent storm. When West pulled up in front of her house, Delilah had a question.

"Will we ever find it?" she asked softly.

"It?" asked West.

"What we're all looking for. All of us lost GreenPlanet children."

"Yes," answered West confidently.

"When?"

"Monday," he joked.

"Until then?" she asked.

"Holiday weekend. Eat, drink, and be merry."

Delilah gave West a kiss on the cheek, hopped out of his sad little car, and waved farewell until Monday. Driving toward the ocean on Santa Monica Boulevard, he turned on the radio that was always tuned to KWOT. Neil Young's high-pitched voice oozed through the speaker:

"Look at Mother Nature on the run in the nineteen seventies.

I was lying in a burned out basement with the full moon in my eyes.

I was hoping for replacement when the sun burst thru the sky.

There was a band playing in my head and I felt like getting high.

I was thinking about what a friend had said, I was hoping it was a lie.

Thinking about what a friend had said, I was hoping it was a lie."

#

It was gray and cloudy over the holiday weekend with no surfable waves. West hung out in the doublewide reading books, listening to music, and catching up on sleep. He thought about visiting his brother Wyatt in prison, but Wyatt instructed him not to come. He spent an afternoon with his mother, failing to explain why he hadn't achieved anything respectable in his life. Overall, he kept a low profile and a forward gaze.

433

When he arrived at the office Monday morning, Delilah reminded him of his promise that today would be the day that all unanswered questions would be answered. Ah, yes, he remembered, and made a piggyback promise to "get back to her."

The previous Monday was like a bad dream. The news of the Jonestown massacre, in particular, Leo Ryan's murder, was surreal. It had taken West the entire week to sort of let it go. Mondays, in general, made him nervous. He didn't like Mondays. If you remember, it was a Monday when he learned of Kate's confession to Delilah. He concluded that Mondays brought unwanted, unpleasant surprises. So, throughout the morning his internal radar was on red alert. For what? Who knew? There was just this feeling.

By midday the world had not come to an end. Taking his lunch break, he went across the street to the Orange Julius to get a burger. The overcast sky had turned into sunshine, and his apprehension began to melt away along with the dark clouds. Thankfully Monday was behaving itself. And then he returned to the office, and nobody was there. It was the middle of the day, and nobody was there. The lights were on. The phone lines were blinking. The humans were missing. Hello bad feeling. On his desk was a note from Delilah: "Everyone at the Chimney Sweep."

Upon entering the bar, West saw Delilah, Kate, Salinger, Will, Kip, Connie, and her sister Stephanie. All were staring up at the television above the bar. Indistinguishable from his aversion to Mondays, West also didn't like it when people were staring at the

434

television. Last time everyone stared at the Chimney Sweep television Keith Moon was dead, and West's world concurrently spun out of control.

On the television screen, a visibly shaken woman in her mid-forties was talking straight into camera. Dianne Feinstein. She was the President of the San Francisco Board of Supervisors, and was surrounded by a frantic press contingent and a stunned group of onlookers. Below her image a chyron read: MAYOR MOSCONE AND SUPERVISOR HARVEY MILK ASSASSINATED. The live shot morphed into a split screen showing an underground City Hall garage. A handcuffed white man in his thirties was in the custody of police. Everyone watched as he was escorted out of an unmarked car and whisked into a waiting elevator.

"Susan was there," Delilah said to West as he arrived by her side.

"Who? Where?"

"Susan. She was in the halls of City Hall, on her way to a meeting about the Farallon Island's. She heard the shots ring out. The guy with the gun ran past her. She called us. She's okay."

"Darkness at the break of noon, shadows even the silver spoon." More Monday darkness. Only two days before, San Franciscans had buried Congressman Ryan. The city was still in mourning. The city was still in shock. Now the Mayor and Supervisor Milk were shot to death in their offices at point blank range. Murdered in cold blood. That same Harvey Milk that had made it a point to visit Rocky in the hospital after his hate crime beating was now dead on the floor. Three degrees of separation. The entirety of mankind; three

435

degrees of separation. So much for Monday behaving itself. So much for the moratorium on drinking. People first?

The whale savers felt the need to stay huddled together at the Chimney Sweep. No more work on this day, rather, they drank some drinks, ate some grub, and somberly watched the televised candlelight march that began on the corner of Castro and Market streets in San Francisco. Thousands of people gathered, crying, hugging, singing. Joan Baez sang Amazing Grace. The city reeled. 1978 was screaming bloody murder.

#

With the help of Shakespeare Jones and the boys, Delilah had pried the lid off of Pandora's Box, and shockingly discovered a repository of toxic waste dumping misdeeds. The Marine Protection, Research, and Sanctuaries Act of 1972 (MPRSA) was enacted to put an end to all of the illegal, irresponsible, and reprehensible toxic waste poisoning of the world's oceans, rivers, and lakes. Thirteen countries were guilty of brazen, prolific, decades-old polluting. Russia, United Kingdom, United States, Belgium, and Japan being the biggest offenders.

Six years had passed since the enactment of the international law, but not much had changed. A witch's brew of deadly poisons continued to be dumped into the oceans of the world. Petroleum products, heavy metals, municipal sewage sludge, spent nuclear fuel rods, chemicals from mills, high-level radioactive wastes, biological warfare agents, synthetic materials, medical waste, industrial waste, and animal waste. Energy and power companies clandestinely hired private boats to haul radioactive waste out to sea in the dark of night. Shakespeare knew some boat owners who participated, who needed the money, and said that the money was very good. Up and down the coast of California, so close to shore, they moved their deadly cargo.

Delilah would use the month of December to sort it all out, and to create a report from which a GreenPlanet campaign could evolve. She and Susan would then coordinate their individual projects into one comprehensive Pacific campaign to expose and ultimately eliminate the toxic danger, and to prosecute any and all guilty perpetrators. It was exciting, it was urgent, and it was necessary. She didn't realize that this would be the perfect endeavor for a newly formed GreenPlanet America.

December found West and Delilah playing nice. They spent more time together with the occasional sleepover, but no talk about "getting serious." On the few occasions that they engaged in sexual behavior, it was less passionate, more cautious, and less vulnerable. Like married-couple sex. West was loving his Malibu digs. Living oceanside, and living solo was a magic elixir, and good for his soul. He even adapted to the longish drive from ocean to GreenPlanet office and back. The Sunset Boulevard billboards teased him: 'Universal Pictures presents THE DEER HUNTER starring Robert De Niro.' 'Bill Graham presents GRATEFUL DEAD-UCLA DECEMBER 30.' 'THINK PINK - HUSTLER MAGAZINE.' 'ROD STEWART-BLONDE'S HAVE

MORE FUN.' 'DARKNESS ON THE EDGE OF TOWN-
BRUCE SPRINGSTEEN.'

Delilah was content to go with the December flow.
She, too, was basking in solo habitation. In the back of
her mind, she detected the slightest hint of a horizon,
and the faintest light at the end of a long, dark tunnel.
For the moment, anxiety and fear had left the building.
She was hopeful. For her, it was always rejuvenating
to see the final day of the year approach. Like the
finish line of a challenging marathon. She and West
would spend the Christmas holiday together, and then
humbly put this year behind them.

On Christmas morning Delilah was sitting up in bed
as West, wearing a Santa hat and not much else,
entered with a bottle of champagne, a bouquet of
roses, and a breakfast tray fit for a queen. He impishly
placed the champagne and vase of flowers on her
dresser, so that he could, with much pomp and
circumstance, situate the breakfast tray perfectly
across her lap. Back to the champagne he ran, pouring
each of them a celebratory glass, and then climbing in
bed next to her, they clinked glasses, sipped
champagne, and agreed to resolutely block out the
rest of the world until 1979.

Except for New Years Eve. The last day of the year
was a Sunday. The GreenPlanet gang had assembled
for a raucous celebration at the Chimney Sweep the
night before, and Delilah had zero intention of leaving
her house that night. West, however, had plans. Radio
station KWOT was presenting a New Years Eve concert
at the Santa Monica Civic Auditorium. Tom Petty and
the Heartbreakers would be ringing in the new year,

438

and Connor Kilkenny had invited West to join him backstage for way too much fun. West was all in.

The marquee in Santa Monica proudly announced: KWOT PRESENTS TOM PETTY AND THE HEARTBREAKERS- HAPPY NEW YEAR. Backstage West and Connor were laughing so hard they could barely breathe. Not sure if it was the great pot they were smoking, or if life was just way too fun at the moment, it didn't matter. They were happy to be on the ride. A familiar looking longhaired rocker dude passed by and handed West a dented bottle of Jack Daniels. Too high to place name with face, he accepted the whiskey with a nod and a wink. Ten feet away, the bravest of a duo of female fans, let's call her Janie, asked Connor for his autograph, on her tits please. He happily obliged by signing West's name, and invited them to be their backstage party pals. After taking a big slug of whiskey for himself, West passed the bottle to Janie's friend, let's call her Chloe, who giddily accepted and chugged her own chug. The party was now officially on as Tom and the lads took the stage and rocked the house past midnight. Happy New Year!

New Years morning of 1979 was very cold and very dark. In the wee hours, on Colorado Boulevard in Pasadena, the various media outlets covering the Rose Parade had staked out their territory, set up their positions, and retreated to the warm and cozy shelter of their vehicles. Amidst the television station tents, and the print and magazine photographer tents, stood a chastened canopy covering a utility table with a handful of folding chairs. A 'KWOT' banner was attached to the canopy. West, Connor, Janie, and

439

Chloe huddled under the canopy, drank a wide variety of booze, consumed a necessary amount of cocaine, and noticeably disturbed the peace. It was Connor's assignment on this cold January morning to do live reports from the Rose Parade in the only way Connor knew how to do these things, with irreverence, and out of control.

In an attempt to keep warm and keep the party going, West was making out with Chloe, while Connor and Janie were holding court with excited passersby. Playing music loud and periodically doing 'live' pre-dawn broadcasts for KWOT, no one at the KWOT tent gave a shit about the upcoming parade. By the time the sun had come up, and the Rose Parade was underway. West, Connor, Janie, and Chloe were nowhere in sight.

It was just after three o'clock in the afternoon on New Year's Day. West and Chloe were snuggled in her bed sound asleep. Connor and Janie were lounging in a bathtub full of water and soap bubbles in the bathroom of the girls' very nice Studio City apartment. As Janie cuddled close to Connor, the water in the tub started to slosh around, and it wasn't due to foreplay. There was a rumbling sound. In Chloe's bedroom, the bed was moving, and a crashing noise could be heard coming from the kitchen. A big splash of water smacked Janie in the face and she screamed.

All four miscreants simultaneously sensed that they were experiencing an earthquake. The Malibu earthquake of 1979. New Year's Day. Connor found the whole thing hilarious. Butt-naked and soaking wet, he abandoned Janie, ran into Chloe's bedroom, and jumped into bed with West and Chloe. It felt as if the apartment building would crumble into a mound of Studio City dust. The perfect cure for a drug and alcohol hangover. As the earthquake came to an end, a terrified and abandoned Janie, dripping wet and naked, escaped the bathtub and sprinted to the doorway of Chloe's bedroom. Shaking and furious, she threw Connor's clothes at him and pointed to the front door unable to speak. Scrambling into their duds, West and Connor thanked the girls for a great night, suggested the four of them get together soon to do it again, and then high-tailed it out of Studio City in search of the perfect after-quake bar. 1979 had arrived in literal rock-n-roll fashion. "Hey, hey, my, my, rock and roll can never die."

DEEP CUTS

February 2nd was Ground Hog Day in America. Punxsutawney Phil saw his shadow, predicting six more weeks of winter, and Sid Vicious died of a heroin overdose, predicting no more weeks of John Simon Ritchie. The day before Ground Hog's Day, SV had been released on bail from Rikers after two months of incarceration and detox for smashing Patti Smith's brother in the head with a bottle. He was also the prime suspect in the death of his girlfriend Nancy Spungen.

Sid and Nancy needed heroin as much, if not more, than they needed each other. More. They needed it more. Whenever there was a lack of smack, they got testy. They were never far away from violent behavior on a good day, but when they were jonesing it was a surety. Back in October, remember 'October was good'? Well, it wasn't that good for Nancy who was found stabbed to death in their Chelsea Hotel room; also not that great for Sid who was arrested for her murder. He was out on bail in December when he broke a beer bottle on Todd Smith's face. On February 1st they let him loose again, and like a shot from a cannon he went straight for the heroin. Farewell Sid. Give our best to Nancy.

It was a Friday, and the GreenPlanet cadre were in fine fettle. Not only were the usual suspects seated around the conference table, but today they were joined by their beloved missing colleagues Susan and Rocky, who had traveled down from San Francisco to make the group whole once again, even if for one day.

"Happy Groundhog Day my strange American friends," Kate began.

"Did you see your shadow this morning?" West asked Kate.

"Unfortunately the shadow I saw this morning was not mine."

"Valley News left a message. They want to know what our position is on the handling of groundhogs. Cruel or acceptable?" said Salinger.

"They can't be serious."

"Our position? There is no winter in Southern California," offered Delilah.

"Does California even have groundhogs?" asked Susan.

"There's a band called Groundhogs," said Will.

"Okay people! Focus please. Thank you," snapped Kate.

The visit by Susan and Rocky was not one dimensional. There was a tactical, strategic reason for their joint appearance. Susan had successfully infiltrated the operation to the north, and Rocky was about to do the same. He had offered his merchandising skills–that he'd implemented so masterfully in Los Angeles–to the San Francisco office, and they happily agreed to bring him into the fold. Now there were two moles embedded in San Francisco. Both Susan and Rocky reported what they perceived as a slight shift by the women in the northern California office. They said that the females were more open-minded than the men when it came to working with the L.A. contingent. Kate received the news with guarded optimism.

An emotional Rocky informed the gang that the three thugs that had nearly killed him months ago had been tracked down by SFPD and arrested. He also told them of the hospital visits from Harvey Milk, and described the mood in San Francisco as purposeful, saying "since Harvey's murder, people are more committed and determined than ever."

"I assume that you've heard the news," said Kate.

"Sid Vicious died this morning," said Will.

"What? Oh Lord"

"Overdose. Twenty-two years old."

"Who?" asked West.

"No, Sex Pistols," said Salinger.

"Silence! Never mind the bollocks. Sorry to hear about Mr. Vicious, but we've business to attend to," commanded Kate.

"God save the queen!" said Will.

The news that Kate was referring to was the beginning of the 1979 Canadian Harp seal hunt. Due to a change in climate, the hunt was moved up a few weeks early, and all GreenPlanet offices needed to prepare. Hunter had decided that West and Delilah should be included in the confrontation group that would travel to Newfoundland. He also wanted movie star Vanessa Gray Reynolds to go if she was willing and able. Will confirmed that she was indeed on board and eager to be on the team.

"VGR is ready to roll, and not just a joint. She wants to be on the team," said Will.

"Brilliant. Hunter has big plans for her. She'll be the star attraction."

"I think she's very familiar with that territory."

"Will, darling. You, naturally, will hold Ms. Reynolds hand every second of the way until she leaves for Newfoundland."

"Somebody has to do it."

"Also time to bring more celebrities into the fold. Make it your top priority."

Kate asked Delilah and Susan to find some time before Susan's return to San Francisco to compare notes on their respective toxic waste projects. A written report would be lovely, thank you very much. Susan also needed to meet with West and the lawyers to discuss their Rocky Flats situation. Their arrests last spring at the nuclear weapons facility became problematic due to the crossing of state lines. It was important for them to get their wounded ducks in a row prior to the upcoming trial in May. West looked at Susan and smiled a fearful smile as she returned his look with a wink and a shrug of the shoulders. He turned his attention to Delilah, who mouthed the words New Found Land. Holy shit. They were going to Newfoundland. He was going to Newfoundland.

"Okay people. To your battle stations. And watch out for those bloody groundhogs," trumpeted Kate.

Before heading to the ice floes of Canada, West and Delilah continued to carry out their Southern California duties. West performed college lectures and private screenings of the 'save the whales' film. Delilah continued to investigate maritime toxic waste dumping, and she also handled a few media interviews when West wasn't available. They went to dinner on Valentine's Day, and again on the first of March–the one year anniversary of their germinal, life-changing meeting at the beach–and now, with only days to go before they would fly north-east to meet up with their Harp seal comrades-in-arms, they were undergoing last-minute briefings, assembling their cold weather gear, and attempting to find the necessary nerves of steel, and strength of mind that would be required to cope with the looming course of events. Delilah looked inward. West called Kip.

#

It was just past noon on a beautiful March day. Beautiful if you were outside in the fresh air. Inside the Chimney Sweep, it was dark and stale, and the music on the jukebox was on low volume. West and Kip, the only patrons in the bar, were sitting at a cocktail table with Cuba Libre's in full progress. Kip, patiently and politely, listened as West filled him in on his recent stages of evolution; the reformation of his brother Wyatt's Malibu trailer; the redefining of his relationship with Delilah, the rededication to his GreenPlanet mission, and his sincere repentance for being a flawed altruist.

He expressed concern to Kip about his "on borrowed time" status, as Shakespeare Jones called it. Was he playing with fire by placing himself in harm's way yet again? Should he reconsider his decision to accept the assignment? Words of wisdom from Kip would be greatly appreciated.

"Quite a year that you've had," Kip said serenely sipping on his Cuba Libre. "You are about to cross a critical threshold where a fire-breathing dragon awaits.

446

Captain Jones was right about being on borrowed time. As dramatic as that day was for you, it was just the beginning. Bigger challenges draw near."

"Who exactly am I borrowing this time from?" asked West.

"Maybe borrowed isn't the best way to view it. I prefer bonus time. Here's the thing. I don't think you realize. You're not aware, are you? You're being watched. All the time. By lots of people. Everyone's watching and wondering how it will all turn out. Will you climb to great heights, or will you fall to your death. Everyone in our office. In the San Francisco office. In London. Hunter. Your wise old friend Captain Jones. The FBI. The media. The women. Lot's of people. Are watching. You don't see it, do you?"

West felt unbalanced. Kip had this effect on him. He caught a glimpse of Connie winking at him from behind the bar. Out of nowhere, he noticed Marlon sitting in his usual dark corner. Had he been there all along? Blowing kisses, Marlon was blowing kisses at him.

"Do you trust me?" Kip queried.

"Yes, I do," answered West.

Kip removed something, an eyedropper and a small vile, from a pocket. In a deliberate, measured manner, he unscrewed the top to the vile, withdrew liquid into the dropper, and reached across the table depositing two drops into West's cocktail.

"Drink," he said.

West watched as the drops disappeared into the blackness of his Cuba Libre. He didn't dare question his friend. Instead, he looked into the eyes of Kip, and

447

again at the winking Connie and the air-kissing Marlon.

"The only dance there is," said West as he raised his glass to the Chimney Sweep god, and drank.

"Why do you get up in the morning?" asked Kip.

"Same reason as the rest of us. We're saving whales. Fighting for the planet."

"Think so?"

"Isn't that why you get up in the morning?"

"GreenPlanet is our current pathway, but we're here to slay dragons."

"Okay."

"You think you'll be doing this ten years from now? Five?"

"Impossible to see the future," said West feeling a bit spacey.

They continued their abstract chatter for a while before time stopped. West was inside and outside of his body. He remembered a recurring dream. He was fifteen. He and his friends were body surfing at Zuma on a rough day. He wasn't paying attention, wasn't respecting the sea. A large wave knocked him down and then held him under. Frightened, he fought hard for the surface. When his head finally poked through to fresh air, he was terrified and bewildered. He didn't see his friends, didn't have the strength to swim, and felt himself going under again. Panic caused him to flail, gasp, and take in water. He was drowning. He was helpless. And then he felt his feet touch sand. Dumbfounded, he stood up in waist-high water. His friends were laughing on the beach. All this time he had believed that it was a bad dream, but it wasn't. He could now see that it was real. It was a dragon.

"Are dragons headed my way?" he asked as he watched with detachment the jukebox morph into a dragon.

"We're surrounded by them," said Kip.

Like magic, Marlon was standing next to their table. He extended his hand to West pulling him out of his chair and onto the open space in front of the dragon jukebox. The music was louder now; 'Dogs' by Pink Floyd. Connie and Kip joined them in a dream-state group hug. West was soaring. Looking deep into Connie's eyes, he kissed her for an eternity as they danced a supernatural slow dance. Out of the corner of one eye, West could see the dragon jukebox watching him so very closely. Everyone was watching just like Kip said. The dragon snorted, exhaling attention-grabbing fire before shape-shifting into a loaded harpoon gun aimed directly at West and Connie. Pushing her out of harm's way, he used himself as a shield between the deadly weapon and his dear friends. "Over my dead body," he thought. And then, just as suddenly, the harpoon gun reincarnated back into the terrifying fire-breathing dragon that West was expected to slay. Frozen with fear, he tried to move his feet. He felt for the sand. He looked to see if he was in waste-deep water. He searched, but did not see his laughing friends, did not see Kip, or Connie, or Marlon. Taking three deep breaths, he paused, and then ran straight toward the dragon and into oblivion. There was a loud explosive noise. Everything went black, and that's the last thing he remembered, except for the realization that it was not a dream. It was real. Always had been.

It was a cold, foggy, gray, turbulent, late afternoon in the Gulf of St. Lawrence. Twenty foot swells violently tossed the Port aux Basques ferry up and down and back and forth as it stubbornly made its way across the mostly frozen gulf from Nova Scotia to Newfoundland. The GreenPlanet activists were the only passengers crazy enough to ride the ferry on this day. They were fifty miles from either shore with no turning back. Fifty nautical miles before they would reach the safety of Channel Port aux Basques. On a normal weather day, these final fifty miles would take about three hours. Today, in this weather, probably double the time, double the chance of disaster.

Seated around a king size, bolted down commissary table were Hunter Mack and Hugh Simon from London, West and Delilah from Los Angeles, Karma Parrish from San Francisco, movie star Vanessa Gray Reynolds, cameraman Jim Dunn, and Parisian photographer Margaux des Jardin. On the table before them was a large map of the Newfoundland- Labrador coast. As the ferryboat continued to pound up and down, Hunter was explaining their plan of attack. The boat slammed down hard.

"This is bloody ridiculous Hunter. We're the only bloody fools on board this death ship. You know I can't swim," cried Hugh.

"Barrister, no swimming ability necessary. You'd freeze to death way before you'd drown. Now, here is the town of St. Anthony at the very northern tip of Newfoundland. When we make landfall, we drive the vans up this coastal highway here, roads permitting, to

450

St. Anthony. We'll set up headquarters at The Moose Shack," Hunter calmly said.

"Am I the only one here who feels a tad sea sick?" said West.

"Pussy," countered Delilah.

"Pay attention team. Here is Belle Isle. We'll set up a base camp here. This will allow us to get to the Labrador coast faster and increase our search range. Tomorrow, Jim will teach arctic survival to those of you who need it."

"I thought we were going by helicopter to the floes," said West.

"We are. Two choppers arrive in St. Anthony tomorrow. Room enough inside for the pilot, one journalist, one crew member, and one barrel of fuel."

"That's why we need the base camp. We'll store fuel and supplies there. Closer for the choppers to refuel and take us to the hunt," explained Karma.

"Hence the tents and arctic gear," said a nervy West.

"You said we drive the vans to St. Anthony 'roads permitting.' What if we do not have permission of the roads?" asked Margaux.

"Nous devons improviser, oui?" said Hunter with a sly smile.

"Très bon, je aime improviser," she answered with a wink and a nod.

West watched with captivation as the bewitching Margaux removed a flask from her jacket. Taking a seductive swig she handed it off to a giddy Vanessa, who was thrilled to be having the time of her life. As Delilah watched West watch Margaux, the ferry boat

451

slammed down hard once again, knocking out the light above them. Hugh grabbed Hunter's arm, whilst under the table, Karma placed her hand on Delilah's thigh. Margaux took out one of her many cameras and fired away at her new shaky subjects. Forty-nine miles to go.

Those that thought the ferry ride was rough were unprepared for the "roads" that the vans had to navigate. Stopping, starting, circumnavigating, mud, debris, branches, wildlife, little or no visibility, pee breaks, jangled nerves, early nightfall, and finally St. Anthony and the Moose Shack. Grandma Martin was the longtime innkeeper and all-powerful proprietress of the house. When you stayed under her roof she made it abundantly clear that her Moose Shack was not a democratic establishment. If you were to look up 'autocrat' in a Newfie dictionary you would find an intimidating photo of Grandma Martin. No-nonsense, clear-headed, fair-minded, and sharp as a rose thorn, she made the rules, and it was understood that all were to follow in lockstep. The only landlord in town willing to house the "rabble-rousers," she liked and respected Hunter–considered him a friend– even though she disagreed with his annual reason for showing up on her doorstep. Secretly, she admired the gumption of the young, idealistic GreenPlanet eco-warriors. She thought they were, for the most part, "good kids."

When the scruffy contingent finally arrived in the dark of night, Grandma Martin had hot stew and biscuits waiting for them. Introductions were made, rules were laid down, food was devoured, and all headed to a warm, comfortable bed, and some much-needed sleep. All except for two.

In front of the blazing stone fireplace, West and Margaux were getting to know each other as they put a dent in Margaux's whiskey bottle. They didn't come all this way to sleep.

"Look, Hemingway, Miller, Elliot, Mailer, Shakespeare, whomever. Call them misogynistic if you want, but you can't say they're not great writers," said West.

"How can someone be called a great writer if they are so unevolved?" countered Margaux.

"What a piece of work is man? Great art is not about your approval of the artist. If Matisse were the biggest asshole on planet Earth, that wouldn't mean he wasn't a master painter."

"Oh, so now you want to inform me about French painters. And how much time have you spent in France?"

"Zero time. Never been there."

"Mon Dieu. Idiot."

"I have a problem. Maybe you can help me?" said West.

"I'm sure you have many problems," she said.

"So I've been told. Here's my problem. It's your problem too. You are very beautiful. Very beautiful. Obviously smart, sophisticated, and successful. But that giant stick up your ass is a huge turn off. It must cause you much pain and anguish, and now it causes me great distress. Is there any way that we can, as a team, try to dislodge that stick from your ass, so we can make the most of our time together in this Godforsaken place?" said West.

Margaux thoughtfully picked up the bottle sitting in front of her, and poured herself and West the remainder of the whiskey. Sipping hers, she looked into the fire, and contemplated his question. "Unpredictable, probably reckless," she thought.

"Oui, oui, il ya," she said to her new subject.

#

Seated around the long family table, the GreenPlanet delegation chowed down on a hot breakfast while Hunter reiterated the plan of attack. At daylight, an angry crowd of locals and seal hunters—a.k.a. swilers—had begun to gather outside the Moose Shack. They had grown into a large and boisterous mob. Some held up signs reading 'Mainlanders Not Welcome' 'None Of Your Damn Business' 'Seals Equal Jobs' 'Newfies-True Ecologists' 'Moose Shack Traitors' 'Go Back Home'.

Four brave men, helicopter pilot Peter Luddington, helicopter pilot Crispus Davis, NBC reporter Stephen Dietz, and Newsweek journalist Rob Hogan firmly, but politely made their way through the agitated crowd to the main entrance of the lodge. At the front door they were met by Grandma Martin's security men, and after adequately identifying themselves they were permitted entry. Once inside the Moose Shack, the four men found their way to the dining room where they were warmly welcomed by Hunter, et al.

"Pete, good to see you. Crispus, you're a sight for sore eyes," said Hunter shaking hands and slapping backs.

"Hunter, meet Stephen Dietz, NBC News, and Rob Hogan, Newsweek," said Captain Luddington.

"Glad you boys could make it. How's the welcoming committee out there?"

"Not exactly sure they're happy to see you again," said Captain Davis.

" That hurts. That hurts," said Hunter with a sad shake of the head.

"Would love to do a sit down ASAP," said Dietz.

"Roger that. You're staying at the Spinnaker, right? Get yourself situated, get something to eat, and then we'll do whatever you want this afternoon. I've got to get some of my people on a helicopter to Belle Isle while the weather permits."

Hunter stood on his chair for more a dramatic effect.

"West, Delilah, Karma, Margaux, fifteen minutes! Peter and Crispus will be flying you to Belle Isle. Jim, grab your camera. I want you along for the ride, too. Let's go before Mother Nature changes her mind!"

Uninhabited, covered in snow and ice, and located in the middle of an angry sea, Belle Isle was a most unpleasant slab of Mother Earth in the winter. The chopper ride wasn't bad, but now, on terra firma, with each passing minute, the weather deteriorated. West was pounding the final tent stake into the frozen ground, as Delilah and Karma built a protective ice wall around the front of their tent. Cameraman Jim Dunn planted a red signal flag into the ground, then grabbed his camera and commenced shooting film. Margaux was shooting still photos of West as he planted the GreenPlanet flag next to the red signal flag. The wind was gusting now, and snow began to blow. Captain Luddington rolled a barrel of fuel away from the clearing where the two choppers sat. It was go time. He jumped in and fired up the engine.

"Doesn't the word 'belle' mean beautiful?" West yelled at Margaux.

"Oui, stand still!"

"Let's roll Jim! Weather's getting nasty!" barked Luddington.

Jim gathered together the four stay-behinds for last-minute words of wisdom.

"Listen up team. Weather is getting serious. We've got to get the choppers back. Get yourselves into the tent and hunker down. Don't do anything stupid. Remember what we talked about. You can freeze to death in ten minutes out here. We'll be back tomorrow to pick you up. Your gear is excellent; you've got food and water. Good luck," he said giving each a quick hug.

Running through the blowing snow whipped up by the chopper blades, Jim hopped in and buckled up as both helicopters were already off the ground and in retreat. West followed him to wave farewell. As the helicopters moved swiftly out of site, West took a look around at their isolated and dangerous surroundings. An intangible shudder of cold came over him. This was no joke. He made a mad dash for the tent full of women.

The winds were strong and steady, but their shelter had been expertly secured, and once inside it gave the quartet a quasi-sense of well-being. It was snug; two battery operated lamps, arctic sleeping bags, sleeping pads, a hunting knife or two, flashlights, water bottles, and sandwiches. West had his borrowed copy of *Bury My Heart at Wounded Knee,* Delilah was equipped with journal and pen, Karma decided eighteen hours of sleep was the best course of inaction, and Margaux had her flask and cameras. It was only for one night, right?

When Captains Luddington and Davis, and cameraman Dunn walked back into the Moose Shack a feisty press conference was underway. Standing in front of the roaring fireplace were Hunter and Vanessa Gray Reynolds. They were answering questions from a handful of journalists. Invited to watch and listen were four chosen representatives from the mob of locals that continued to swarm the lodge.

"Canadian Fisheries are no help, just the opposite. They do the bidding of the government," said Hunter.

"Last year members of GreenPlanet sprayed the baby seals with a harmless green die to make their pelts worthless. This year, there is a laughable new law making it illegal to spray paint a baby seal," said Vanessa.

"What do you know about seals?" yelled a local swiler as his mate yelled "Go back to Hollywood!"

"Here's what we know about these seals and this seal hunt. It's a money-losing endeavor for everyone except the Canadian and Norwegian fur tradesmen. The good people of Newfoundland certainly don't make any money. As soon as the seal's head is bashed in and it's throat slit, the skinned carcass is thrown on the ice like garbage. The over-population argument is ludicrous. Thirty million Harp seals have been reduced to one million. I would think every single person in this room would be as outraged as we are. Instead, you do the bidding of a few wealthy businessmen and then suffer the wrath of world opinion," countered Hunter.

Stephen Dietz, the American reporter from NBC, wanted to know why Vanessa Gray Reynolds would be traveling to the ice floes? What did she think her value was? Would she be a help or a hindrance? Hogan from Newsweek followed by asking her if she was prepared to be arrested?

"Why not me? I can help provide a worldwide audience and use my celebrity for something important," she explained.

"I don't think the fine, upstanding members of the Fisheries Department would want to arrest Vanessa. Don't believe the Canadian public would want them to do that. Does she look very threatening to you?" Hunter mocked.

"You wouldn't be trying to put the fisheries officers in a no-win situation, would you? Condemned in the eyes of the public before anything illegal happens?" Hogan asked.

This inspired the four locals to explode. "Throw her in jail!" "Hollywood phony!" "No place for a hoser!" "Beau cave!" Hunter feigned innocence. Raising a hot cup of coffee to his lips, he contemplated Hogan's question before answering. "Absolutely not. Never crossed my mind," he said. "This coffee is good."

There was no hot coffee inside the lonely tent on Belle Isle. Surrounded by large snowdrifts, the protective ice wall was no longer visible. The temperature had dropped precipitously, darkness came

458

early, and out in the elements it was not a fit place for man nor woman. Inside the tent, West, Delilah, Karma, and Margaux were bundled up, stuffed into their arctic sleeping bags, and situated as close to each other as they could get. The battery-operated lamps were their only friends.

"Well, here we are. Just us girls," said West.

"Delilah, is it true? You were sa petit amie?" asked Margaux.

"No! Stop. You both promised. No speaking French. Not fair to Karma and I," demanded West.

"Shut the fuck up," Karma barked at West.

"He was never officially the boyfriend. He was given a trial run, but," answered Delilah.

"Susan says he acts without thinking," hissed Karma.

"You three do know that I'm right here, in the same tent, right?" asked West.

Karma was grouchy, grumpy, pissed, irritated, angry, and she had to pee. There was no going outside. Unsurvivable outside. Back at the Moose Shack, they were advised to take adult diapers with them for such an occasion. Delilah and Margaux were wearing theirs. West and Karma opted out. West figured he could simply stick his dick out the tent flap and pee. Not sure what Karma was thinking, but now she had to do something.

"I need you to look over there," said Karma guiding West's eyes away from her.

"Why?" asked West.

"I have to pee."

"Go ahead. You're in a sleeping bag. I can't see

anything."

"LOOK OVER THERE MOTHERFUCKER!"

West looked at Delilah and Margaux, rolled his eyes, and then stuck his head into his sleeping bag. It took some minutes before Karma was able to let it flow. When she was finally relieved of her burden the smell of warm urine filled the tent. A muffled laugh could be heard coming from inside West's sleeping bag. When he came back up for air he didn't dare make eye contact with Karma. Instead, he pretended to read his book in earnest.

"You're a fucking asshole," declared Karma.

Dealing with the seal hunters, West thought, will surely prove to be a more pleasant experience. The night passed without incident. Margaux shared her flask of whiskey with West and Delilah–Karma declining any further liquids, and all slept soundly. Mercifully, the next morning arrived, tent in tact, and with it the light of day. The yellowish sun was a sight for weary eyes, and although it didn't provide much warmth, it did lift the spirits of the tent-bound warriors. The winds had stopped, and the roar fell silent. Frosty tears of joy were born at the sight of the two incoming helicopters. Chopper doors opened upon landing, blades continuing to whirl. Karma ran as fast as her pee-stained legs would take her, straight into the chopper piloted by Captain Luddington and cameraman Jim Dunn. West, Delilah, and Margaux were waved over to the chopper piloted by Crispus Davis. All piled in and buckled up, deliriously happy to be lifting away from Hell Isle.

Vanessa, the pampered movie star that she was,

decided to make last minute Moose Shack arrangements for a third, luxurious corporate helicopter to escort herself, Hunter, and the two newsmen to the ice floes, fundamentally making the Belle Isle sleep over unnecessary. It turns out Karma didn't need to pee her pants, and the other three could have enjoyed a cozy night in front of the roaring fire. Oh, my. The posh chopper with Hunter, et al. was in the air, in the lead, and had already located the sealing ships.

"How was your night? You ready?" asked Captain Davis."

"Roger that. Where's Hunter?" asked an excited West.

"In the third chopper," said Davis.

"Third chopper?"

"Blood on the ice. Kill is in progress. We're minutes away."

With telephoto lens, Margaux took photos of the inhabitants in the other chopper. Peter, Jim, and Karma looked just as serious as Margaux's chopper mates. Below them, the Labrador coast came into view, and then two massive Norwegian sealing ships. As they descended in altitude, Chopper One–Hunter's chopper–could be seen resting safely on the ice floe. Red, blood-streaked patches of ice were in close proximity to the sealing ships.

Choppers Two and Three landed on a frozen patch of the Gulf of St. Lawrence next to Chopper One, and only a few hundred yards away from dozens of swilers in the act of slaughtering baby Harp seals. Hunter gathered everyone around him for last second

461

instructions.

"Listen to me very carefully. As you are aware, Hugh has stayed behind in St. Anthony. He'll be able to work faster and more effectively there, which means less jail time for us. The Seal Protection Act, passed in our honor, clearly states that no person other than a sealer is legally permitted to touch a seal. When we do, we'll be arrested. You've been filled in on our strategy. Please stick to the plan. I don't want to relive what happened last year with Jean-Paul going to the hospital. No improvisation. Got it? Any questions? These guys are violent. They are in killing mode. Don't provoke them. Don't touch them. Let's go!"

The GreenPlanet team along with the members of the media made their way through the bitter cold air, and hard packed ice toward the seals and seal killers. As they got closer, they walked past fresh and bloody baby seal carcasses. They could hear the men yelling, and the seals barking and screaming. They could see the ice covered in seal blood. Arriving at the scene of the crime they were met by several blood-covered swilers and two Canadian Fisheries officers. In the background was the giant ice-breaking factory ship. Jim and Margaux commenced documentation mode; 16mm film rolling and still photos clicking away. Both were focussed on a nearby swiler clubbing, then skinning a baby seal.

"Go no further. Interference with the government-sanctioned seal harvest is a violation of Canadian law, and you will be arrested and taken to jail," said one of the officers.

"Just out for a stroll, officers," said Hunter.

Delilah took two steps toward the swiler with the freshly skinned seal. He didn't allow her a third step. Snatching up the raw and bloody skinned carcass, he trotted it over and held it up inches in front of Delilah's face.

"How about that, eh?" he said with a laugh.

Delilah could feel the contents of her stomach contemplating escape.

"Go fuck yourself," she said refusing to vomit.

Hunter took his cue. Spying a baby seal yet to be 'harvested,' he walked past the two officers to the small animal, stood over it, then plopped down on top holding it's front flippers by its side. In protection mode, he sat there as the two officers and several furious swilers approached and surrounded him.

"You've been warned Mr. Mack. You are now in violation of Canadian Fisheries law," said the officer.

"I would like for this seal's life to be spared today," Hunter calmly requested.

Cameras were rolling. NBC and Newsweek were bearing witness and taking notes. The whole world would see what next transpired. One of the swilers angrily announced "I would like to kill that seal, officer."

"Mr. Mack. An authorized fisherman has made it known his desire to harvest that seal. Please remove yourself or be arrested."

Hunter nodded to Vanessa who then joined him. Rolling off of the baby seal, Hunter continued to hold the front flippers down allowing Vanessa to replace him atop the animal. Backing away, he allowed one of the biggest movie stars in the world to take the stage, something she was most expert at. Hunter held up his hands as if to say "I've done what you asked. No interference from me." The swilers were apoplectic. The officers were unsure.

"Miss Reynolds. We need you to make way for this man to kill this seal. If you do not, you will be arrested."

Vanessa said nothing. Instead, she hugged the baby seal putting her face next to its. Her eyes filled with tears as the cameras captured it all. Delilah and Karma sprung into action. Selecting two more baby seals, they proceeded to duplicate the actions of Hunter and Vanessa, straddling each pup to protect them from imminent death. The fisheries officers didn't know what to do. They didn't want to arrest the GreenPlanet women, it would look weak, and they were instructed by their superiors not to arrest the movie star if possible. They were frozen in place, pun intended.

Trailing Delilah was the swiler with the bloody seal carcass in hand. This time he shoved it smack into her face, covering one side of her face with seal blood and guts. She gagged.

"The pup you're sittin on will look just like this in two minutes," he growled.

Before he could finish his last word, he was tackled from behind and knocked to the ground. West pushed the swiler's face deep into the bloody seal carcass and began to swing wildly. From behind, a seal club violently cracked West across the back, causing him to go limp and helpless. Two swilers grabbed him by the arms and dragged West across the ice toward the

Norwegian factory ship where the ice was broken and the seawater exposed. A line of men swiftly positioned themselves between West and his compatriots preventing any intervention on their part. Holding him face down in front of an ice hole, the two men pinned his arms while a third shoved his head under the frigid water. Squirming and kicking, West fought hard not to drown. The swiler yanked West's head out of the water for a quick gasp of air, and then shoved it right back in again. This was repeated several times as the onlookers bellowed and screamed. Before it became deadly, the two fisheries officers took hold of the swiler and pulled him off of West. Hunter and Jim pushed through the army of men that surrounded them, and dragging West away from the ice hole they immediately covered his face and head with their arctic gloves and caps. While Hunter and Jim worked feverishly to prevent frostbite from taking hold of West's face, the two officers conferred with the swilers and then returned to the three women sitting atop their seal pups.

"Alright ladies, you may sit there on those seals for as long as you wish. No one will arrest you today. As you can see, the sky grows dark and the weather grows worse. I suggest you run for cover, but it's up to you," said the officer in charge.

Hunter and Jim helped West to his feet, dragging him back to the female-protected seal pups. Two red flares were visible next to the three helicopters. The signal to depart.

"We have to go," said Hunter.

Vanessa, Delilah, and Karma didn't move. They

knew what would occur the moment that they abandoned their pups. They also knew that the red flares meant the bad-weather-clock was ticking.

"You did great. I'm so proud of each of you. The world will see. The video. The photos. Everything changed today. Seal hunting suffered a mortal wound today. I'm sorry, but we have to go. Right now," said Hunter.

Hunter took Vanessa's hand and gently lifted her off of her baby seal as she sobbed uncontrollably. Jim helped Karma to her feet, and a limping West did the same with Delilah. He reached out a frostbitten hand, and wiped some of the seal blood off of her face. Delilah, stone-faced, knelt back down, and kissed the baby seal on top of its head. Standing defiant, she put one of West's arms around her neck, and assisted him in the return to the choppers. As the GreenPlanet team and members of the media gave ground, falling back to the waiting choppers, Delilah stopped to bear witness. The swiler that had rubbed her face in the freshly slaughtered seal guts was smashing the head of the seal pup that she had tried to protect. She refused to turn away. Tears froze on her face. Her knees buckled as she puked on the snow-white ice. West lifted her up, placed his arm around her neck, and looked into her eyes. Nothing was said. Time to fly away.

It took them two and a half days before they could depart St. Anthony and return to Halifax. The bad weather halted all sealing operations and all sealing protests. Out of respect, love, and concern for Grandma Martin, the GreenPlanet gang took their leave as soon as it was possible. The 16mm film footage would accompany Hunter back to London, and once in the lab, it would be developed, edited, and offered to international news outlets. Images of the slaughter had already appeared on some NBC news broadcasts. The story was being told.

West had superficial frostbite on parts of his face, the top of his head, and on one hand. His recovery would be one hundred percent, but he would look like a car accident victim for a couple of weeks. The Canadian government decided against prosecution in lieu of the protestors exiting the country posthaste, which they were happy to oblige.

After a drink or two at the Halifax airport, it was time for some emotional goodbyes. Inside the main terminal West, Delilah, Vanessa, Karma, Hunter, Hugh, Margaux, and Jim were about to head in opposite directions. Four would fly east to London, four would fly south to JFK, and three of the JFK four would continue on to California. Vanessa would be staying in New York to dine with Warren Beatty ostensibly to discuss an upcoming film project. Hmm. During an abundance of hugs and handshakes Margaux whispered in West's ear. There was a high probability that her work would take her to Los Angeles in the near future, and should she look him up? Yes. Sure. Formidable!

At JFK, Vanessa scurried off to her waiting limo while Karma was saying her farewells to West and Delilah.

"Well, well. I'm privileged to be flying off to the incredibly beautiful city of San Francisco, and sadly you two must head home to the less than desirable Los Angeles. I'm relieved and happy that this time around I was able to get closer to you and Delilah. We didn't connect last summer on the Maggie May, did we? But, I must say, we love having Susan in San Francisco, and now I can go back and tell them good things about you too," Karma said.

"Send our love and support to everyone in the San Francisco office," said Delilah with semi-enthusiasm.

"I know you'll miss me," said West.

"Let's talk soon about having a joint meeting. We could do it in San Francisco. It might be the right time to talk peace treaty," said the carefree Karma overjoyed to be getting the fuck out of Dodge and heading home to the city by the bay.

West and Delilah watched the bedraggled Karma lug her duffle bag through the airport terminal. They also watched as the 'normal' travelers parted like the proverbial Red Sea to make way for her and from her. It then became apparent to Delilah that she and West probably looked a tad like outcasts or outlaws themselves. Seal blood and guts, frostbite, adult diapers, and not enough booze could do that to a person.

"What do you say you and I go find us a couple of cocktails?" said Delilah taking West's hand into her own.

Delilah's hand in his, always, and without fail, stirred him to his core. He never wanted to let it go. Her hand was validation. Her hand always brought him back from some far off dreamland. Joni Mitchell lyrics from some mystical lockbox entered his head:

*There's a man who's been out sailing in a decade
full of dreams*

*And he takes her to a schooner and he treats her
like a queen*

*Bearing beads from California with their amber
stones and green*

*He has called her from the harbor; he has kissed
her with his freedom*

*He has heard her off to starboard in the breaking
and the breathing*

Of the water weeds while she was busy being free

#

It was as if they'd spent a lifetime together. As if they'd gone through fires, floods, hurricanes, feasts, famines, children, riches, wonderment, ups, downs, trials, tribulations, winds, rains, sunsets, and satori. Floating. They were both floating on the same day, at the same time, in each other's company. Drinks in the airport bar, soft-spoken turbulent-free conversation at thirty thousand feet, heads resting on shoulders, minds free of conflict, satisfaction from surviving the bloodshed and the horror, contentment without the thought of what was ahead. With every breath was the inhalation of rejuvenation. Maybe more time should be spent in each other's company? Not maybe, absolutely should be. That doublewide in Malibu would be the perfect spot to continue their re-bonding, their recovery, their renaissance. They had their entire lives ahead of them, right? Bob Dylan lyrics from some mystical lockbox entered Delilah's head.

*May God bless and keep you always, may your
wishes all come true*

*May you always do for others, and let others do for
you*

*May you build a ladder to the stars, and climb on
every rung*

May you stay forever young

West and Delilah hadn't taken ten steps into the
terminal at LAX before they recognized bright familiar
faces attached to familiar bodies with familiar arms
dramatically waving to capture their attention. Kate
and Salinger. There, at LAX, to intercept them. West
was oblivious; Delilah was alarmed.

"What are you two doing here?" asked Delilah.

Kate hugged Delilah, and suspiciously kissed West
on the cheek. Salinger gave both big hugs staying very
close to West.

"What happened to your face?" Kate asked West .

"Oh, uh, a bit of frostbite," answered West.

"Time is short. West, love, you and Salinger are off
to Japan in an hour. Here's your ticket. Give Delilah
your baggage claim. We'll take care of your luggage,"
said Kate.

"I'm what? Japan?"

"That's impossible. We've just been through hell.
He's exhausted," said Delilah.

"A suitcase with fresh clothes and toiletries has
been checked for you. Accommodations have been
arranged and paid for you and Salinger."

"It's a sixteen-hour flight to Nagasaki. Plenty of
time to sleep," said Salinger patting his hand.

"You're serious, aren't you?" said West.

"You're going to Iki Island. Thousands of dolphins are being corralled into a cove, then slaughtered by Japanese fishermen. They claim the dolphins are decimating their fish supply. Truth is they've overfished the waters and now consider the dolphins their enemy as well as their cash cow. The American public has caught wind of it and a great uproar is building. You will do live reports for KWOT and several national media outlets. Connor Kilkenny wants you to call him as soon as you get on the island. Salinger will be there to assist you with whatever you need. Your departure gate is at the opposite end of the airport, so you two have to get going now. You have your passport and your ticket. Salinger has your visa and plenty of money. Time for you to go."

When the Canadian swiler was holding his head under the arctic water, West eventually went stiff. Helpless to alter the moment, he became motionless. Just like now. Salinger, detecting his confused condition, found his hand, and interlocked her fingers with those very same fingers of his that belonged to Delilah. She tried to lead him away, but he wouldn't budge. Delilah, however, was not frozen. She was in motion. Gently reclaiming West's hand from Salinger, she said for all to hear "you don't have to do this if you don't want to." But she knew and he knew. He was going. Adventure was calling. Sleep and Delilah be damned.

West, the perennial deer in the headlights, kissed Delilah, gave a silly dazed look in Kate's direction, and found Salinger pointing toward their exodus.

"There's a key in the mailbox if you want to stay in

Malibu," said a sheepish West as he was whisked away by Salinger.

A stoic Kate and a disgruntled Delilah observed Salinger and West as they ran for their gate located at the opposite end of the terminal.

"You're trying to kill him," said Delilah.

"I'm making him a star," said Kate.

"Too much. Too fucking much."

"He's fine. He's young. He's loving every second of it. He didn't remotely consider not going," Kate said.

She was right. Delilah understood that Kate was absolutely correct. Delilah was well aware of whom she had picked up on the beach that day one year ago. She saw it then, she saw it now. Didn't make it suck any less. Linking her arm, in resignation, with Kate's, the two very different women traversed the challenging terrain that was LAX, onward to baggage claim, and subsequently to the yellow brick road that was the 405.

Sixteen more hours in the air; a two and a half hour open-ocean ferry ride from Fukuoka to Iki Island, and then straight to the cove where a flotilla of Japanese fishermen in small boats were corralling dolphins toward an army of waste-deep men wielding knives and spears. The water was blood red when West and Salinger arrived. Unlike the Harp seals, which were passive and mostly silent, the dolphins thrashed in the water, screaming until they perished at the hands of their killers. Onshore, the curious were passively observing the butchering of the dolphins as onlookers might take in a surfing competition.

So. They were now present at the scene of the

crime. West would take notes and bear witness in order to report back to the rest of the world. Salinger would commence with the still photography and the media coordination. But. At this precise moment. Something needed to happen. Action needed to be taken. No one was intervening. West didn't know what to do, and the clock was ticking.

Salinger was approached by two locals that spoke English. Thinking that she was from the American media, they were eager to explain to her the who, what, where, when, and whys of the blood red cove. This was, they said, only the second year of the "culling" of the dolphins. Before last year–1978–it was never necessary, but an unexpected combination of "unfortunate" factors had changed things. The ocean currents had mysteriously changed thus altering the route of the fish schools closer to the shores of the archipelago. The dolphins, thousands of them, naturally followed the fish that comprised their food source, and as a result, wiped out the fish close to shore, the same fish that the fishermen had depended on. Suddenly, there was no food for the people, and the fishermen could not earn a living. They wished that this action was not necessary, but alas. The explainers strategically left out two key elements of the story. The over-fishing of the local waters by the fishermen, and the appetite for dolphin meat by the Japanese people. Fish and dolphin meat equaled money. Lots and lots of money. Even though the dolphin meat was full of mercury and deadly toxins–thanks to us humans–it was widely sought after and consumed on the mainland of Japan. Dolphin meat brought in a pretty penny and a pretty yen.

West was studying the various elements that comprised the slaughter. The fishermen had dropped long metal poles into the water and were banging them aggressively. It was explained that the banging of the poles created a frightening and disorienting sound that rendered the dolphins passive, making it much easier for the men to corral them into the cove and into shallow water. West could see that nets were laid out across the lagoon to prevent the dolphins from escaping. There were scores of dolphins that had, as of yet, to be butchered. He had an idea.

Scanning the onlookers, West spied a fellow surfer with surfboard on the roof of his car. Hurriedly, he took off his shirt, kicked off his shoes, and dropped his jeans, under which he was wearing his Hang Ten board shorts. Waving at his Japanese surfing brother, he pointed to the stick on his car. Could he borrow his board? To go 'out there?' Seeing this, a frightened Salinger grabbed hold of West's arm.

"West, no!" she pleaded.

Breaking away, he bowed and shook hands with the Japanese surfer, who willingly handed over his board and his blessings. Running full speed, West hit the water, tossing the board in front of him, and then on he climbed. Paddling hard toward the nets that entrapped the dolphins, he yanked a spear out of the bloody hand of an unsuspecting fisherman. His mission: cut the nets.

Thrashing dolphins, angry fishermen, blood, guts, and mayhem defined his newest gauntlet. Successfully arriving at the nets, he was forced to straddle the surfboard while attempting to use the spear tip to cut through the netting. The water at the mouth of the lagoon was choppy and much colder which exacerbated his task at hand. The bloody spear proved frustratingly useless. Chucking it into the sea, West tried and failed to pull the netting apart with his hands. Placing his body weight on top of the net, he tried to push it down far enough for an escape route for the dolphins. Not happening. The netting could not be breached. His ideas and his time ran out.

Surrounded by Japanese fishermen, West and his surfboard were captured, and with firmness and force, guided back through the cove of slaughtered dolphins, onto the shore, and into the waiting arms of the law. Ruby red from head to toe, he was stained by dolphin blood and by abject failure. Thankfully, for him, Salinger was instantly by his side. Somehow she persuaded the local authorities to let West go free. The killing for that day was coming to an end, and she promised that they would depart the cove right away, and the island come morning. Giving them reason to believe that she was sympathetic to their local cause, she described West as an impulsive, passionate, lover of the sea, a good man, and the son of a fisherman, even though his father was indeed a rocket scientist. West, concerned for the fate of his fellow Japanese surfer, apologized to him in front of the local authority for "stealing" his surfboard, thus saving him from any legal repercussions.

Salinger, with West's discarded clothing under one arm, commenced embarrassed negotiations for a ride to their hotel with one of her dolphin slaughter explainers, while, unbeknownst to her, West had already sealed the deal with his new surfing pal. Under the watchful eyes of the keisatsu, West and Salinger took one last look at the grisly cove full of dead and dying dolphins, before climbing aboard the surf-mobile, and thus making a solemn retreat to what they considered to be the safety of their hotel.

It was only two or three days ago–time currently incomprehensible for West–that he was sipping some of Margaux's whiskey at Grandma Martin's Moose Shack, battered, bruised, and bundled up in front of the blazing fireplace. Here, at Hotel Iruka, on the opposite side of the world, he was still battered, still bruised, but now naked with no fireplace in sight. An Asahi beer had replaced the whiskey, and a bathtub full of hot, red water substituted for the fireplace. The hot water stung every part of him as he feebly tried to clean his skin and ring out his board shorts. The dolphin blood didn't want to exit either one, and he didn't have the energy or inspiration to try harder.

Salinger was in the outer room pacing back and forth. She had the phone to her ear, struggling to make a clear connection to Los Angeles.

"Yes, I'm still here. Go ahead. Hi Connor. This is Salinger Daniels. He is. Can you hear me? I'm going to hand the phone to him, hang on," she said as she was walking into the bathroom. Looking down at West soaking in the tub, she couldn't see anything but red water. She couldn't see his dick or anything, not that she cared. "Connor Kilkenny," she said handing him the phone.

"Kilkenny old friend. Que pasa? What's that? Sorry,

476

hard to hear you. Ah, there you go, much better. Yep. From the ice floes of Newfoundland to the Sea of Japan. Fuck yes. It's a horror story. I'm still kicking. My pleasure. That's why I'm here. OK, let's do it. Lead the way mi amigo," said West handing the bar of soap to Salinger.

As West commenced with his radio report, Salinger applied the soap to his shoulders and back. She had better luck, and the blood transferred from his skin to the water in the tub.

"Connor, I'm speaking to you from the Japanese island of Iki, in the south Sea of Japan. It's a bloodbath here," said West as Salinger rolled her eyes.

As he continued to relay his story back to Los Angeles, Salinger washed the blood from most of his body. Reliving the events of the day filled West with new emotion, and Salinger rubbed his shoulders to keep him grounded.

"They say that we have no right to tell them how to live their lives. They point out that Americans kill and eat cattle. No, no. I wasn't taken to jail. I was detained and released. The killing was done for the day. There are only a handful of us here, bearing witness and reporting to the world. I've been told today was the final day of killing. Me? I was, there was a Japanese surfer who let me use his board. I paddled out into the lagoon, through the dolphins and the fishermen. I tried to tear down the net, but I failed. They got me before I could save any of the dolphins. I failed. I'm so sorry," he said.

A clicking sound was heard, and then a dial tone. The line was dead. Burying his head in Salinger's chest, he wept.

"Turn around and let me get your other side," she said.

#

Salinger allowed West to drink his beer and wallow in dejection while she continued to wash the blood off of those parts of his body that were above the bath water. Unwilling to travel any further south, she handed him the red bar of soap, and left him to his own devices. The double bed was less than encouraging. Lumpy, trampled, and well worn. She had reserved and prepaid for a room with two twin beds, but upon arrival was told none were available, not to mention that their reception at the hotel front desk was downright chilly. Salinger guessed correctly that news from the cove had arrived before they did, and the undisguised animus from the hotel staff clearly screamed persona non grata.

So, one bed would not be an issue. There would be no extracurricular activities. They were bone tired. More than twenty-four hours had passed since either of them had a decent hour's sleep, plus Salinger was confident that West had fresh memories of her heightened reaction to his one night stand with Kate. She saw herself as a younger, wiser sister to West. One certainly cannot be picky when embedded in the trenches of warfare, and after all, they had just witnessed spirit-draining barbarity. They were in this thing together, on the battlefield and in bed.

Extracurricular activities didn't remotely enter West's head, well, okay, they did, but the nightmarish blur of the past days made it easy for him to embrace sleep instead of Salinger. In truth, he was worried that sleep would not come his way. Life had gotten way out of hand. Very fast, very furious, and very troubling. One moment all was thrilling and promising, and then the next moment was filled with darkness and dread. He didn't dare look into the speculative mirror. He knew that he wouldn't like what he saw.

They must have been asleep for hours, but it was hard to discern when the loud banging on the door shook them out of their respective comas. Salinger's head, at rest upon West's chest, shot up when she heard the loud, angry Japanese voices coming from the other side of the hotel room door.

"Anata ga koko ni kangei sa rete imasen!"

"Amerika ni modotte iku!"

"Doko ka ni itte!"

"Anata ga koko ni kangei sa rete imasen!"

"Usotsuki!"

You didn't need to know Japanese to understand the message: WE DON'T WANT YOU HERE! Salinger, with courage screwed to the sticking place, peeped through the peephole in the door and saw two middle-aged Japanese men. She recognized one from the hotel reception desk, and the other, unfamiliar, was wearing a similar hotel uniform. Out the window, the sky was beginning to lighten as day was about to begin. Hopping up and down as he pulled on his jeans, West waved Salinger away from the door. His plan was to throw open the door and confront the angry voices. Enough was enough. It was time to stop being a pacifistic punching bag, and to deliver some angry blows of his own. Silence. Everything was abruptly silent. Looking again through the peephole, Salinger saw no trace of the men. Were they gone? Were they coming back? How many? She looked to West for guidance.

"Let's get the fuck out of here," he said to her delight.

#

The taxicab was driving east on Sunset Blvd. Another twenty-four hours of restless travel; West and Salinger were delirious. West had gratefully accepted Salinger's offer to sleep at her place. He couldn't imagine making the drive to Malibu on this night.

"I'm ill. My jet lag has jet lag," whimpered West.

"I know. What day is it?" said an equally wounded Salinger.

As the taxi passed by the Cinerama Dome, West noticed the marquee: THE CHINA SYNDROME.

"Look at that. I never called that woman back," he said.

"What woman?"

"That movie woman. Remember?"

She had no idea what he was talking about, and couldn't care less. Putting her head on his shoulder, she closed her eyes and slept.

Late the next morning, West and Salinger, fully clothed atop her bed, were dead to the world when the phone on the bedside table rang, and rang, and rang. Eyes closed, Salinger put the phone to her ear. It was Kate.

"Hello? Yea, we made it back last night. Feel like

480

shit. No. What news? Where?" said a groggy Salinger? "Pennsylvania? You're joking. Uh, huh. Yea, he's here. Sleeping. Hang on. West. Wake up. West, Kate's on the phone. It's important. Come on. West? He's been through a lot. Dead tired. He needs to sleep. Yes, I can be at the office in an hour or so. Okay. Bye," said Salinger as she hung up the phone, placed her pillow over her head, and fell back into a deep sleep.

It was six o'clock in the evening when she opened her eyes. A piece of notebook paper was on the bed next to her. On it was written: DIDN'T WANT TO WAKE YOU. HAD TO GO HOME TO MY OWN BED. SEE YOU MONDAY. WEST. She remembered Kate's phone call. "Fuck me!" Falling out of bed, she flipped on the television to discover one seriously concerned Mr. Walter Cronkite reporting the nightly news. As he spoke, behind him were images of the Three Mile Island nuclear power plant. The initial stages of a nuclear meltdown that had begun the night before were well underway; the citizens of Middletown, Pennsylvania were in imminent danger. Video showed the cooling towers with a giant plume of steam rising above. Grasping the phone, she madly began to punch in numbers.

"Kate. It's me. I'm on my way."

The following morning, Friday, March 30th, Salinger was back in the office along with most of the principal players in the L.A. operation, including Susan, who had flown down from San Francisco. The empty seat at the conference table belonged to the runaway West. Kip and Kate were secretively whispering into each other's ears, while Susan was debriefed by Will and Delilah.

They wanted to know all of the gossip and goings on from within the San Francisco office. Salinger, at her desk, was on the phone trying and failing to reach West.

"He doesn't have a phone and he doesn't watch TV. He probably has no idea what's going on," Delilah hollered to Salinger.

"He hasn't responded to his pager," said Kate.

"He hates that thing," added Susan.

"You want me to drive out to his place?" Salinger volunteered.

"I'm here!" bellowed a manic West as he crashed through the door into the war room.

"Why didn't somebody call me? You let me sleep for two days! Do you have any idea what's going on? Three Mile Island is melting down! Holy fucking shit!" he proclaimed as he vaulted into his seat at the table. "Sorry I'm late. Do you need me to go to Pennsylvania? Asap? No problem. Hey Susan!"

"No, we don't. Take a big breath there tiger. Welcome back to the land of the living. You look wild and woolly. We'll get to Three Mile Island in a moment, but first, the spotlight is on Kip. Mr. Asher has been a busy lad these past few months, doing some rather important behind the scenes reconnaissance. Rumor has it things around here are about to radically change course. Kippy, the floor is yours."

Kip, eyes down, and his chin in his hands, carefully collected his thoughts before beginning. Looking around the table at each whale saver, he smiled a vulnerable smile.

"First off. Susan, thank you for dashing down here

from San Francisco on short notice. We didn't want you to miss this meeting. Important that you're here. Second. West and Delilah and Salinger. Tremendous work in Newfoundland and Japan. You have no idea what you've accomplished, you don't. Historic, meteoric change is right around the corner. West, trust me when I say that the frostbite will disappear and you'll look as cute as ever. I'll be brief. Thanks to years of relentless political and lobbying efforts, as well as our successful activist efforts to show the world the grim realities of modern-day whaling, it looks very likely that the IWC will grow from eighteen to twenty-three member countries when they convene in July. The five new members don't want whales to be killed. These new members will tilt the balance of power away from the ten whale-killing countries and toward the good guys. In short, Hunter, Kate, Will, and I are virtually certain that by the end of July there will be a worldwide ban on all commercial factory ship whaling. In other words, if we're correct, it's about to be over," he said eyes glistening.

There was a stunned silence. He paused so that his words could take hold. Did everyone correctly understand what Kip had just announced?

"You mean we did it? We won? No more whaling? asked West.

"Whaling won't be completely eradicated, but ninety percent, yes," said Kip.

"Jesus."

Kate chimed in with a note of caution.

"There still exists the possibility that some countries will succumb to the intense pressure that

483

Russia, Norway, and Japan will bring upon them, but we're fairly confident that when all is said and done it will go our way. Which means a change of direction for us, a change in strategy. If we are correct in our analysis, it means a 1979 'Save the Whales' voyage is not absolutely necessary. Even though the whaling fleets will be hunting whales this summer, the whale populations will no longer be in jeopardy, and the whalers will be on their way out. The anti-whaling voyages, as you know, are expensive, dangerous, and politically divisive within the organization. The end results can easily go wrong. This past summer we were very fortunate to find the Russian whaling fleet just before time, money, fuel, and morale ran out. Additionally, this breaking news eliminates a messy problem we weren't sure how to solve. It seems that the Sea Pirates, lead by our old friend Paul Revere, have every intention of doing battle with the whalers this summer, IWC decision or not. We very likely would have been in the odd position of peacekeeper. You're all very aware of Mr. Revere's love of the spotlight, and his love of extreme and dangerous measures. His plan was to track us at sea until the whalers were located, and then charge to the front and wreak havoc," explained Kate.

"So we stay home and let the Sea Pirates harass the whaling fleets for us," said Will.

"And if they fail to find the whaling fleets, their failure makes us their master in the public eye, and if they do engage with the whalers there's a high probability that it will be explosive, which also makes us their master in the public eye" Kate added.

"Impressive," gushed Delilah.

"And to add to that bit of revelation, we also believe that we've dealt a mortal financial and PR wound to the Canadian Harp seal slaughter as well as this latest incident involving the slaughter of dolphins by Japanese fishermen. Both appear to be on life support," said Kip nodding approval in the direction of his young pal West.

"Which brings us to the nuclear arena that, as of thirty-six hours ago, includes Three Mile Island," concluded Kate.

Whoa. Okay. Time out. Let's pause here for a moment of reflection. What just happened here? For five or six years, Hunter Mack, Kip Asher, and many, many others have dedicated their lives to saving the great whales from extinction. Saving them from needless and brutal slaughter. Exerting an all consuming, 24/7 commitment and sacrifice that have become synonymous with their individual identities. How do they process—if, in July, the IWC bans all commercial whaling—their victory? What happens if you join a cause and the cause disappears? What do you do? Where do you go? Who are you now? Yes, there are other important and noble causes, some within the same organization. Seals, dolphins, toxic waste, and nukes, for example. Some whale warriors will move onto the next item on the list and keep marching; some will not.

If my thesis is correct, that altruistic endeavors are messy, that altruism is not pure, rather, it is a mixture of sincerity, and selfishness, and neediness, then what happens when a rag-tag group of searchers temporarily come together under the auspices of an admirable cause and that cause goes away? What now? I once was lost, but now am found and now I'm lost again? Which "brings us to the nuclear arena and Three Mile Island," as Kate just said. Three Mile Island, Diablo Canyon, San Onofre, Indian Point, Rocky Flats, Hanford, Surry, Millstone, Farallon Islands, nuclear waste, atomic bomb testing, Chernobyl. Kate also said "things around here are about to radically change." Ah, yes, "The times, they are a changin.'" Who is this room will pivot?

#

Change was never a welcome guest in San Francisco. In their perfect GreenPlanet world there would be no office to the south, there would be no Hunter Mack, there would be no talk of abandoning the save-the-whale voyages, there would be no oversight, no questions asked. A return to the past was viewed as the only acceptable change, but it was April, the season was changing, and surely that couldn't be objectionable, right? Start small and build from there. Perhaps spring would prove a fertile catalyst for a new and harmonious way forward? Change is inevitable, right?

In the common area of the San Francisco headquarters Jonah, Kai, Karma, Catty, Sunset, Jade, and Susan were endeavoring to receive in earnest their invited guests from the south, West and Delilah. Upon her return from the ice floes of Newfoundland, Karma had submitted a mostly positive report with regards to the upstarts Delilah and West. To her fellow San

Franciscans, she proposed a friendly "sit down" with their tribesmen to the south. An "exploratory meeting of the minds," she said. Susan, after all, had come from L.A., and she was well liked, well respected, and her joint effort on the Farallon Island campaign was showing excellent results. She also reminded her northern colleagues of their stubborn, rebellious decision to forge ahead with their own plans to conduct another whale voyage in the upcoming summer. How would they pay for that? What about a boat? Maybe the L.A. people could arrange for the use of the Maggie May? How would they locate the whaling fleets now that Congressman Ryan had departed the planet? The unpopular pronouncement that came from London: No Whale Voyage in 1979. How would they get the approval of Hunter and International? Was a revolt absolutely necessary? Maybe the L.A. people, if they were on board with the plan, could prevent that drama? Worst-case scenario, they could cross-examine the Angelinos, reassert their perceived authority, and pressure them for money, hence, this peace summit.

Jonah, Kai, and Catty had zero interest or intention of playing nice with the scum from the south, or with Hunter, or with anyone else for that matter. Jonah's kingdom was under siege, and had been for some time now. He was keeping a close eye on the evolution of the rogue Sea Pirate organization. He concurrently admired and loathed Paul Revere for the revolutionary enterprise that had siphoned money and manpower away from his precious GreenPlanet. He worried that the Sea Pirates were about to steal their thunder. His other eye was perpetually glued to Hunter. Jonah's gut told him that something wicked this way comes. Hunter had been too quiet, too civil. So, for the moment, let's see what these L.A. people have to say.

"You two look a lot better than the last time I saw you," said Karma.

"What, you didn't like my black eyes and frostbitten nose?" West said.

"I hope we only see each other in beautiful San Francisco from this day forward," added Delilah.

"Maybe you L. A. people should close up shop down there and join us here? There's plenty of room," said Catty.

"That's an interesting thought. I'll bring it up at our next meeting," said Delilah.

"Susan loves it here. Don't you Susan?"

"Hard not to love San Francisco," answered Susan.

"We're serious. All of us under one roof, less overhead, more money for campaigns."

"Our adventure in Newfoundland was a wild ride, but Hunter says we made good progress," West said.

"Except for the money it brings in, I couldn't give a smelly shit about Harp seals. We're here for the whales, man," barked Jonah.

"No movie stars need apply," added Kai.

"Those are the only people that we know," said West.

"Jonah, shut the fuck up. Whales are not our sole mission. Right, Susan? Farallon Islands? But, since we're on the topic of whales, the summer's almost upon us. We're wondering if Captain Jones would be making the Maggie May available to us again?" asked a hopeful Karma in Delilah's direction.

"Only two people are able to persuade Captain Jones. Hunter and West," Delilah said.

Hunter and West? Jonah was done with this meeting.

"Fuck Hunter Mack. We don't need him or his permission. We're GreenPlanet. We're autonomous."

"Well, there you go," said West.

"We don't need you or your boat or your Captain Jones or your fucking Hollywood friends. What we do need is all the money that you've illegally drained from us," snapped Catty.

Jonah rose from his chair, and as he did, he let out a loud fart. Kai and Catty took his cue, and also stood to leave. Kai tried to fart, but failed.

"Okay! Time out! No, no. We invited West and Delilah to our house to talk about working together in harmony. They're our guests; we're all on the same team, so let's end the ugliness right now. I think a marriage of the two offices would be amazing, come on, we're just getting started" Karma pleaded as her three colleagues walked off in odorous defiance.

Susan remained silent throughout. She was the only one in the room that knew of the secret plan to create a new, consolidated GreenPlanet in the United States, an American entity that would be under the control of the international organization, Hunter's international organization. What she considered noteworthy was the recruitability of Karma and Jade. She also had firsthand knowledge of how money was spent in San Francisco. She observed the management, as well as the corps of volunteers. Did they sincerely care about the whales? Absolutely. Were they sincere in their efforts to create a healthier planet? They were. Were they equally as passionate about retaining the roof over their commune, the free food in their bellies, and the chemically altering substances in their brains? One hundred percent. Did they view the personal use of public donations as villainy? They did not. Susan was smart. She understood Hunter's master plan. No American-based whale voyage meant instantly tighter finances that would spring holes in the keel of the San Francisco vessel. She saw the big picture unfolding before her eyes and it was bloody fascinating.

West, Delilah, Susan, Karma, and Jade went to lunch at Hamburger Mary's before West and Delilah hopped on their PSA flight back to Burbank. Karma tried to reassure her new friends that Jonah would eventually "come around," and Susan assisted by making it clear that Jonah had completely rejected her when she first arrived on the scene in San Francisco, but had since acquiesced, allowing her to do her work without interference. It was agreed by all that they should not give up on the idea of joint endeavors between the two offices, Jonah be damned. Difficult as it was for Susan, with a bright smile on her face she soldiered on, waved goodbye to West and Delilah, and headed back to the circus that was her new home. It's been said that April is the cruelest month.

#

West and Susan were much more concerned about May, and for good reason. They were required to be back in the Jefferson County, Colorado courtroom where, the year before, they had been arraigned on charges of trespassing and obstruction of a public passageway at the nuclear weapons facility down the road. Last November, forty protestors that included West and Delilah had been found guilty of trespassing and not guilty of obstruction, and they now awaited the sentencing that had been delayed on appeal.

The courtroom was crowded; the atmosphere was tense. Last year, the lawyers for the defense had attempted and failed to apply the 'choice of evils' defense. Essentially, this defense argues that the defendants had no choice but to break the law in order for a greater offense to be avoided. The protestors blocked the train tracks in order to save the greater Denver population from any further cancer deaths. The judge wasn't buying it. He didn't see causality because he didn't see harm being done by the plant. During the trial, expert testimony from renowned nuclear scientists and health officials was kept from the jury. The judge wanted to hear the testimony behind closed doors before anything might be admitted in court, which, unsurprisingly, it was not.

The distinguished experts testified with regards to the effects of radioactive material on the human body, how trace amounts could cause a sharp rise in cancers. They testified to the high risk for plant workers and nearby residents. The plant's location was considered to be a poor choice due to its close proximity to the Denver metropolitan area. The water table was without a doubt contaminated. Cancer deaths were on the rise. The nuclear plant was a killer. The jury would hear none of this. They were instructed only to decide on trespassing and obstruction charges with no regard to what was being reported in the media. It was a clear, but uncomfortable decision for the jury—guilty of trespassing. The judge was seconds from announcing his sentencing decisions.

"Explain this to me one last time," said a very nervous West.

"Last November we were found guilty of criminal trespass, but the judge issued a stay of execution of sentence because we appealed," explained Susan.

"Which kept us out of jail?"

"Now we're waiting for him to come out and tell us our fate," she said.

"If he says we have to go to jail, does that mean today? We're not going to jail today, right?" said West.

"Don't know. It's different for you and me because we crossed state lines. The locals will probably get probation, but"

"Stop right there! I don't want to know, and why are you so calm? Jesus, I'm freaking out."

The doors of the judge's chambers opened, and the judge and several lawyers for both sides entered the courtroom. The judge didn't even bother to sit down.

"Ladies and gentlemen. Thank you for your patience and good behavior. The plaintiff and the state of Colorado have decided to drop all charges made against the specific defendants listed here. Counsel for both sides have discussed the particulars and are in agreement. This then brings the matter to a close and all are free to go. I know you've had a very long day. Thank you once again. This court is now adjourned," announced the judge to a dazed courtroom.

As the judge exited the courtroom, the congregation leaped to their feet, shaking hands, jumping up and down, and embracing with great relief and enthusiasm. Some broke into song, some into dance. The media scrambled. A nearby reporter overheard a woozy West ask Delilah for clarification.

"What just happened? asked West.

"The lawyers for the corporation that owns the plant dropped the charges because the federal court agreed to hear the appeal, and that meant that all of the disallowed testimony from the nuclear scientists and medical experts in this state courtroom would be allowed by the feds, and that would result in a white-hot national media spotlight that they wanted no part of. So they ran for cover, but as the saying goes, "you can run, but you cannot hide," said the reporter as he dashed to an empty payphone. And that was that, for this group, at least. They were free to go, but hundreds more protestors still awaited their fate. Most importantly, a half million Coloradans had some serious thinking to do. There was a killer on the loose in their neighborhood. What would they do about it?

Yesterday, before West flew to Denver to meet up with Susan, he and Delilah went to lunch at this little Mexican place in Hermosa Beach. It was on the way to LAX, and he wanted to have a long, hopefully not last, gaze at the Pacific, and gaze at Delilah. Not knowing what the fate of West and Susan would be, both offices, north and south, were on edge. The lawyers offered cautious optimism. They were fairly sure that the local protestors would receive probation and a modest monetary fine, but they were less confident with regards to those that came from out of state to intentionally commit a crime, which included Susan and West. The "crime," they instructed, was minor. Trespassers almost never go to jail, unless. It was that intangible, however small, that had West wriggling in his seat, paying more attention to his margarita than his chimichanga. Seeing this, Delilah applied an unworried face, and conducted herself as if it was just another beautiful day at the beach.

"I'm sure everything will turn out just fine," said West.

"No big deal. This tostada is muy bien," answered Delilah.

"Susan doesn't seem worried," he continued.

"Right."

"I mean, trespassing is not a jailable offense."

"Right."

"That's what the lawyer said."

"Pretty much."

"Do you think?"

"No. I don't think so."

"I gave you the keys to the trailer, right?"

"Got em."

"That tostada does look good."

"Yummy."

West downed the remainder of his tequila beverage, and put two drink fingers in the air. The uncomfortable lull in the chatter persuaded Delilah to reach over and take his hand into hers. There was that hand again.

"I wish Susan was a guy; we might be put in the

same jail cell."

Delilah remained silent, holding his hand until the margaritas mercifully arrived. She pictured West and Susan in the same jail cell.

"That wouldn't be good. This margarita is delish," she said.

As West and Susan were learning their fate in Colorado, Delilah was purposely preoccupied with work outside of the office. There was no way that she was going to sit around, clock watching, and waiting for the phone to ring with news from afar. What she needed was action as the antidote for her jangled nerves. She also needed a partner-in-crime for this particular endeavor, but no one was available except for Will, so he would have to do. She figured that she would have to pressure him, or beg him, or offer some future quid pro quo, but surprisingly, he not only agreed, but he jumped at the chance to be her co-conspirator. Go figure.

They were on San Onofre state beach pushing a Zodiac inflatable boat into the surf. Next door was the San Onofre Nuclear Power Plant. The state beach was fenced off from the beach that fronted the power plant, preventing the public from access to the restricted area. As the Zodiac entered waist-deep water, Delilah hopped in and moved to the front as Will climbed on to take the helm. He cranked up the outboard engine while, onshore, members of the invited media took still photos and shot TV video. Throttling up, he moved them out into deeper water, and then veered port side to the subdivision of ocean that lay directly in front of the nuclear power plant.

"You do remember that I can't swim, right?" said Delilah.

"Yep," said Will.

"Nothing to worry about, I know. If anything were to happen, you would jump in and save me. Right?"

"Jump in?"

"And save me."

"So, something I never told anyone last summer," said Will.

"What? No. Don't you fucking say it! How is it no one in this damn organization knows how to swim?"

Will handed her a life vest, which she gratefully donned, and as he steered the Zodiac closer to shore, Delilah removed the lids off of several plastic containers that were labeled SAN ONOFRE NUKE WATER. At the same time, they were looking for a disturbance on the surface of the water that would reveal the power plant intake and outtake pipes.

"There. Over there," shouted Delilah.

Will pointed the Zodiac in the direction of the churning water, and brought her to a position close enough for Delilah to take several samples. She continued to take intermittent samples as Will followed the pipes all the way to the beach in front of the power plant. Beaching the Zodiac onto the restricted beach was not part of the plan, but Will noticed that the media had made their way onto the non-public beach. Men in suits and hard hats appeared to be their escorts.

"Hold on!" Will yelled as he gunned the outboard and headed the Zodiac straight for the beach and the waiting media. The Zodiac, blaring loudly as it went from water to sand, came to an abrupt halt thirty yards in front of their captive audience.

"I don't think we're allowed to be here," said Delilah.

"You worry too much."

"It's Friday. You never want to get arrested on a Friday," she continued.

Once out of the Zodiac, they waited for the members of the media to surround them. Delilah noticed a dead fish on the sand and snatched it up. As the cameras rolled, she used the fish as a visual aid to make her points.

"We're here as concerned citizens. We've just taken water samples at different depths along the plant's outtake pipe. This water and this fish will be tested for radionuclides, including a battery of other tests for toxic waste, and radiation contamination. We fear the results will demonstrate radioactive contamination of the marine life and water surrounding this plant. We hope we're wrong," she said glancing at the men in suits.

Will had his eye on something else. A dark object on the sand, about fifty meters down the beach. He took off running. The carcass of a dead California sea lion, its side split open, its guts hanging out. The animal hadn't been dead for long, and Will was certain that the gash in its body was not the result of another creature. The cut was clean, as if opened by a zipper. A boat. It had to be a boat.

As members of the media and security from the nuclear plant caught up with him, he removed from his vest a radiation dosimeter and placed it at the tip of the sea lion's nose and mouth. Twenty-five microsieverts. Before security could intervene, he placed the dosimeter next to the spilled guts. Seventy-eight microsieverts! This animal was radioactive. Delilah tossed Will her dead fish prop. Twenty microsieverts! Radiation from the nuclear plant contaminated the fish; the sea lions ate the radioactive fish; the sea lions would eventually die from radiation poisoning unless they met an early demise from a boat ripping them in two. The cameras were rolling, and Delilah took the baton.

"Let me guess what these men in hard hats and suits will tell you. They'll disingenuously say that there are no problems here. That public safety is their number one priority. They'll say the water is safe, the air is safe, and those surfers out there are safe. All is well. Not to worry. People of Three Mile Island, what do you say?"

As the cameras clicked, and the video recorded, one of the security guys pointed at the abandoned Zodiac and then out to sea. Delilah understood that this was their one and only 'don't go to jail for the weekend' opportunity. She touched Will's shoulder.

"Time for us to go'" she said to everyone on the beach, and that meant Will too.

Backing away from the dead sea lion, the media, the suits, and the hard hats, Will and Delilah remounted their ocean-going chariot, throttled her all the way up, and sped off to friendlier environs, terra firma, and the arrest-free weekend!

As I mentioned earlier, both offices, north and south, were on edge this day, waiting to hear the verdict from Colorado. When the phones finally rang in both locations, and all concerned had learned the good news regarding Susan and West, sighs of relief, and weights lifted from shoulders were universally shared. In the spirit of ohana, Delilah called Karma in San Francisco to provide her with a report on their San Onofre experience. This unexpected courtesy pleased and inspired Karma so much that she and Jade decided they, too, could contribute something before this day was done. Arriving at Fisherman's Warf within the hour, they made a rush for the aisles of fresh fish. Carrying hastily hand-made signs under their arms, each one selected a large fish raising it high above her head. In the other hand, they held respective signs that read: CESIUM–PLUTONIUM–URANIUM, and FARALLON RADIATION. It didn't take long before a crowd of onlookers assembled followed by the arrival of a television news truck. Their impromptu street theatre was about to become the live backdrop for the evening news. Karma was beaming. Inspiration felt good. Collaboration felt good. Girl power felt good. West and Susan had escaped jail. Will and Delilah had escaped jail. Karma and Jade had temporarily escaped Jonah, and Hunter had escaped Davy Jones locker all on the same day.

Only hours ago, 5,300 miles east of the California coast, in the middle of the English Channel, Hunter was in the middle of his own escape trick. On this morning, an anonymous caller had contacted the London office with what he referred to as "inside information" concerning the use of a Belgian freighter hired by the British government to clandestinely dump nuclear waste in the southwest part of the channel—barrels of plutonium to be specific. The dumping, said the caller, was to begin within hours.

The UK Atomic Energy Authority (UKAEA) had been the recipient of intense public and political pressure for years to cease and desist it's irresponsible, unethical, and deadly poisoning of the northern seas. Spokespersons for UKAEA repeatedly stood before the cameras and assured the British public that past nuclear waste dumping was an unfortunate although innocent error of judgment never to be repeated again. Hunter and GreenPlanet knew better.

It only took the GreenPlanet ship Tempest four hours—from the port of London—to traverse the channel and find the Belgian freighter in the act of dumping their surreptitious toxic cargo. Barrel after two-hundred-litre metal barrel were hoisted on winches, steered over the side of the freighter, and callously deposited into the sea. Having prepared their inflatables en route to the channel, Hunter and his crew were ready to leap into action without delay. Upon discovery of the freighter, two two-man inflatables were promptly launched off of the stern deck of the Tempest. Hunter captained the lead Zodiac that would race alongside the freighter in the process of dumping the nuclear waste into the sea. Zodiac number two carried the cameraman who would document the illegal activity for the entire world to see.

The Belgians were not happy to have unexpected visitors intrude in their illegal operation. They were quite familiar with the GreenPlanet logo splashed across the side of the Tempest, and quite hostile towards the environmentalist's worldview. When Hunter instructed his mate to position their Zodiac under the winch dangling two heavy barrels of nuclear waste there were angry voices and venomous gestures from the crew of the freighter. Hunter made his refusal to move out of harm's way clear. They were there to make sure not one more barrel of plutonium would hit the water.

Fire hoses were employed, but failed to move Hunter and his co-pilot out of the drop zone. Wind speeds across the channel were on the rise as was the height of the swells that banged the Zodiac into the side of the freighter. Directly above their heads, the metal barrels swayed precariously back and forth. No matter, they refused to move. It became apparent that the chief officer had reached the end of his temperamental rope. Time was running out, and his mission was no longer under wraps. He was furious. He directed the winch operator to release the barrels, and before those watching on the Tempest could sound the alarm, the heavy metal barrels of atomic waste came smashing down onto Hunter's Zodiac flipping it upside-down, destroying it. The two barrels made a direct hit on the bow of the Zodiac seconds after Hunter had leaped into the sea. The crushing of the bow flung the back end of the inflatable high into the air ejecting his fellow GreenPlanet helmsman. The English Channel water was cold, dangerously cold. Hunter and Ian—his mates' name was Ian—surfaced from beneath the sea, and were promptly scooped out of the water by their mates in the camera Zodiac. No bones had been broken. Ian had a laceration on his head from smacking into the transom of the overturned Zodiac, and Hunter's arm was bleeding from contact with one of the metal barrels. It was a very close call, but they would, as fate would have it, live to fight another day. As the freighter fled the scene, the freezing eco-warriors watched helplessly as additional barrels of nuclear waste fell into the sea. One never knows who might be on the other end of a ringing phone. Maybe an anonymous caller with a hot tip?

#

Not all GreenPlanet days were that intense, that magnified. The normal organizational experience was more like living next to a volcano, or in the case of the Californians, a geological fault line. The days were typically dormant, devoted to conducting research, answering mail, fundraising, and lobbying change-makers. One went blithely to the office, be it in London, or Sydney, or San Francisco, or Seattle, or Los Angeles without the presumption of high drama, but the internal Richter scale was perpetually primed. Senses were acutely tuned to detect the slightest rumbling, the slightest shaking. When a day or a week passed by without turbulence, the GreenPlanet body politic autonomically exhaled, stretched, and feigned normalcy. The turmoil-free month was another thing altogether. Fewer and farther between, the sure and steady month caused more trepidation than an LAPD black-and-white in the rearview mirror.

The remainder of May, all of June, and the early

days of July were quiet everywhere within the organization. No rumblings of revolution. No arrests. No offices suddenly shut down, accounts closed, assets seized. No rogue actions or calls to arms. Quiet. A stark contrast to this same time one year ago when the troops were feverishly preparing to sail west to confront the Russian whaling fleet on the high seas. Not this year. No Maggie May this year. No seasickness, bad weather, stalling outboard motors, dead whales in the water, Russian voices on the radio, endless scrubbing of decks, no First Mate Lincoln's less than four-star pancakes. No harpoon guns pointed at your head. Quiet.

July 13th was a Friday, and it was just past noon on this seemingly lazy summer day. Curiously, all hands were on deck, but not much of anything was happening. The phones were quiet. The Telex was quiet. The whale savers were quiet. No sounds from radios or televisions, only the sound of a ticking clock. An uncomfortable quiet. An expectant quiet. A hospital waiting-room quiet. West, wearing tennis attire, was at his desk leafing through the latest issue of Surfer Magazine. Delilah was pretending to read the Nuclear Regulatory Commission Report lounging in front of her. Will and Kip were in Will's office unenthusiastically staring at opposite sides of a chessboard. The door to Kate's office was closed. Inside, she was methodically pacing back and forth while meditatively taking in, then expelling, deep breaths. Salinger was mind-numbingly reorganizing her giant Rolodex, throwing out expired cards and returning misplaced cards to their proper place. Susan was there, as if she had never left, as if they had all gone back in time. She had the chair at the Telex machine flipped around so that she could stare at the clock above the strategy board. She was wrestling with a disturbing thought. Maybe the Telex machine wasn't working? Maybe it accidentally became unplugged? Wheeling around to inspect the electrical connection to the machine, it looked good, looked normal. The power light was on. Susan was there.

Salinger, failing to remain unruffled, abandoned her Rolodex in order to smash down the full contents of her wastebasket. Stomping, she figured, would be therapeutic. As she was stomping her trash to death, phone line number one rang and everyone jumped. The door to Kate's office flew open, Kate scurrying to the doorway to watch and listen as Salinger answered the call. It was Hunter. The sleeping-giant Telex machine bolted upright, suddenly whirred back to life, scaring the shit out of Susan. Will and Kip came into the war room as the Telex clacked loudly, typing the news that all were waiting to hear. Line two rang, then three, then four. The entire phone bank lit up. Kate jumped on the call with Hunter, while the rest of the gang answered the blinking phone lines. The Telex was hurtling at racecar speed. As she read the ticker-tape news, the emotion on Susan's face was unforgettable.

"July 13, 1979. LONDON, ENGLAND. 8:00 PM GMT.

FOR IMMEDIATE RELEASE:

'IWC BANS FACTORY SHIP WHALING—ESTABLISHES SANCTUARY'

IN LONDON TODAY, SIXTEEN MEMBERS OF THE INTERNATIONAL WHALING COMMISSION VOTED TO

BAN ALL WORLDWIDE COMMERCIAL FACTORY SHIP
WHALING WITHIN FIVE YEARS, DECLARING THE
INDIAN OCEAN, THE RED SEA, THE ARABIAN SEA,
AND THE PERSIAN GULF WHALE SANCTUARIES. THIS
DECISION IS A GREAT VICTORY FOR
ENVIRONMENTALISTS, AND ALL OF THOSE AROUND
THE WORLD THAT HUNGERED TO SEE AN END TO THE
BRUTALITY OF THE SLAUGHTER OF THE LAST
WHALES. VOTING AGAINST THE BAN WERE IWC
MEMBER COUNTRIES RUSSIA, JAPAN, AND SOUTH
KOREA. FOR MORE INFORMATION CONTACT:
GREENPLANET: +44 20 5353 5352.

Tears flooded Susan's eyes as West crossed to the
strategy board, picked up a black marker, and wrote
SAVE THE WHALES placing a large check mark next to
it. The phone lines continued to explode, but they
would go unanswered for the next few minutes. A
circle was formed, hands were joined, and tears were
shed. A difference had been made. Victory had been
realized. West embraced a visibly overcome Kip. Kip
and Hunter and Kate had been doing this for a long
time. They had fought many bloody, unsuccessful, and
disappointing battles, and they had the battle scars to
prove it. What must it be like for Kip and Hunter? If
West felt this monumental wave of emotion, what were
they feeling? What was Kate feeling? She was the
woman behind the curtain, the mastermind of the
whole damn thing. Usually a rock, she was bawling
with the rest of them.

"Right then! Attention! Settle down folks. Listen.
Hear those phones? They need to be answered, and we
must all be on the same page with our replies, which

are the following: One: This is a great day for whales and whale lovers. Two: Much more work to be done. Hunter informed me that the proposal for a three-year moratorium on Sperm Whale hunting was two votes short of passing. The Japanese and Russians are in the south Pacific as we speak. Killing whales. The international consensus is the remaining Sperm Whale killing will be banned within two years. Three: Regarding this summers whale campaign, we continue to fight on behalf of the whales until one hundred percent of whaling is ended. We WILL NOT be sailing in the last half of this summer. Four: we extend our congratulations and gratitude to the members of the IWC who made possible this historic day. Extinction is now off the table. The whales have been protected. Any questions? The cameras are on their way. Let's set up an area for the press over there. West, please tell me that you have other clothes?" she said wiping her eyes.

"I've got a clean dress shirt and a jacket in my office," volunteered Will.

"Brilliant. Switch pants with him too. Kip, don't disappear. You're also doing interviews."

Delilah led the charge to answer phones as volunteers appeared out of nowhere. It was controlled chaos. Standing room only. TV reporters and cameras surrounded West in one corner, Kip in another, and Delilah in another. Connor Kilkenny was there, interviewing, and then flirting with Kate in her office. Volunteers manned the telephones and opened champagne bottles. Well-wishers arrived with flowers, food, booze, beer, and briefly, carefully concealed drugs. 'Save the Whale' t-shirts were autographed and passed around for one and all. Susan answered questions from an LA Times reporter, as Salinger had the delicate task of doing interviews for Japan's Nippon TV Network. Will, wearing West's too small tennis attire, poured more champagne for himself, movie star Vanessa Gray Reynolds, and television star Natalie Singer. Camera flashes abounded as the corps' official media duties morphed into party and celebration. More and more people crowded the already full office, spilling out into the hallway, and in front of the building. The party was on. West's memory was hazy as to what had happened between the transition from the office to the house in the Hollywood Hills. Did Delilah drive? Whose house was this? Champagne continued to flow, pot smoke wafted, and cocaine was in pure white abundance. Mountains of cocaine. In attendance were rock stars, movie stars, porn stars, record executives, radio DJ's, authors, and film directors. There were fully clothed, half-clothed, and no clothed revelers in the swimming pool. Whose house was this? Standing off to the side of the pool, champagne glasses in hand, looking out over the lights of L.A. were West and Delilah.

"Remember that first night? Standing by the pool?" said a drunken West.

"I do," she said.

"I couldn't take my eyes off of you."

"You still can't."

"Can you blame me?"

"Yes."

"You know what's crazy? You can succeed in

changing the world. What do you do then?"

"I had this same conversation with my friend Thurgood. He said 'They'll always be cracks in the foundation.' He also said 'Sometimes history takes things into its own hands' she said taking his hand into hers.

"I don't know what that means, I'm wasted," West said laughing.

A young starlet squealed with delight as two very familiar leading men tossed her into the pool. It occurred to West that maybe these Hollywood Hills parties were a regular thing and not just a special celebration of saving whales. A well-dressed young woman approached him handing him a calling card. The personal assistant of a very famous television star, she wanted to know if she could steal West away for a minute or two to meet the "most beautiful woman in the world?"

"Think I've got that covered," said West holding up Delilah's hand for her to see.

The party raged deep into the night. Delilah, wise woman that she was, celebrated a wee bit more, caught up with some old friends, and then shrewdly took her leave. West did not follow the same playbook. He was everywhere. The kitchen, the living room, the 'by invitation only' private study–home of the Peruvian cocaine mountain–the billiards room, more than one of the bathrooms, the back of the house, the front of the house, the pool cabana, and eventually into the pool itself. He caroused with everyone, Susan, Salinger, Will, and Kip. Connie! He remembers dancing with Connie. They might have shared an illegal cigarette.

He's pretty sure that they did. He's absolutely positive that he and Kate briefly made-out in the Peruvian cocaine mountain room, and then abruptly stopped, panicked and alarmed. He talked prog-rock with a famous author, books with a rock star, Scientology with a bewitching actress, free-form radio with a local politician, and string theory with a director of porn films. He drank a half case of beer and several whiskeys. He smoked some and snorted some, and he successfully avoided the thoughts of 'what next?' Catching his breath, out by the pool, the sparkling city in full view, he studied closely the lost tribe that defined his social circle. The voice of Shakespeare Jones was in his head. "On borrowed time club," is what he called it. "The shadow," is what he said. At this late time of night, it was lights out in brother Wyatt's Folsom prison cell. What would his reaction be? Would he be proud? Would he give a fuck? Would he even know? That motherfucker didn't even go to his own father's funeral. He was now in prison for some serious fucking shit. Why in the world would this even register on his radar? West grew embarrassed. Embarrassed to think that the minuscule part he played in protecting whales from decimation was noteworthy, was a thing to be celebrated, an accomplishment. He remembered when Roy quoted Nietzsche's "psychological egoism." "The altruistic person projects themselves onto the object of their compassion," so sayeth Nietzsche. Roy said, "you're trying to save yourself, feel good about yourself." Yea? So? Okay. Maybe I am? Is that bad? Look at where I am right now. Look at this ride I'm on. Wild.

509

Enthralling. Spellbinding. Seductive. Gratifying. Look at this house! This swimming pool! Those mesmerizing naked women! I'm twenty-six! About to enter my first Saturn Return. Next year I'm eligible for the 27 Club and I'm on borrowed time so sayeth Shakespeare Jones!

It was time to go home. Home to brother Wyatt's trailer in Malibu. Somehow–West couldn't piece it together–his VW bug was parked down the street. He must have followed Delilah when they left the office? He had no memory of driving there. Oh well. Instead of driving down Laurel Canyon to Sunset, then west to PCH, he drove north and found his way onto the Ventura Freeway heading west as fast as his little car could go. He visited every lane, the marching powder surging through his brain. 'Out of his mind' would be the fitting way to describe his condition. 'Out of body' is pretty good, too. Lord only knows how he didn't kill himself or any innocent late night travelers, but some mysterious act of providence placed him in front of his abode, house keys in hand, front door opening, bed calling. Gonzo-eyed and staring at the ceiling, he felt that his heart was about to come out of his chest. Panic set in. Was he about to die right here in Wyatt's trailer? Was he having a heart attack? Had his borrowed time run out? He rolled off of the bed and staggered to his feet. Pace, he thought. Back and forth. Use motion to counter the drug, to assist the heart. Back and forth. Back and forth. Heart pounding; chest heaving. The sun was streaming through the east-facing windows of the trailer when he finally collapsed on the bed in exhaustion. "Psychological egoism." "Trying to save yourself." "Like in 'Go west young man?" "You're a fucking asshole." "You see that shadow?" Back and forth. Back and forth. Forward march.

WHEN THE STUDENT IS READY

Within days after the Three Mile Island nuclear meltdown, some well-known musicians created the activist organization called MUSE–Musicians United for Safe Energy. Jackson Browne, Bonnie Raitt, Graham Nash, and John Hall were the founding brothers and sisters. Their intent was to do a series of concerts to raise awareness of the growing global threat of nuclear power. Record executive Danny Goldberg had departed Swan Song records and was in the process of creating Modern Records when he signed on to co-produce a film with Julian Schlossberg of Castle Hill Productions documenting the five nights at Madison Square Garden. The line-up of musicians was impressive: Jackson, Bonnie, Graham, and his pals David Crosby and Stephen Stills. James Taylor, Carly Simon, Tom Petty, Jessie Colin Young, and a young Bruce Springsteen making his first appearance in a film. An enormous team of supporting musicians included Mike Campbell, Leland Sklar, Waddy Wachtel, John Hall, David Lindley, Ry Cooder, and so many more. Five nights, September 19, 20, 21, 22, and 23, sold out on the blink of an eye. This was the perfect event for a Los Angeles GreenPlanet operation in transition from a heavy emphasis on marine life to a broader scope with particular attention being paid to all things nuclear.

The first night, September 19th, backstage was a beehive of activity. Lots of young, longhaired people were moving with urgency and purpose. The sounds of the growing concert audience steadily increased in

512

volume with each passing minute. West and Kate were carefully maneuvering their way through the backstage hustle and bustle when she grabbed West by the arm and pulled him out of traffic.

"Wait right here while I go find John Hall," said Kate.

" Look, that's James Taylor over there," said a wide-eyed West.

"You think you can stay out of trouble for fifteen minutes? You have to be on top of your game tonight. Arms up."

A baffled West raised his arms above his shoulders as Kate proceeded to pat him down for contraband.

"Turn around," she commanded as she removed a flask full of whiskey from his back pocket. She concluded her body search by patting down his crotch.

"Fifteen minutes. Don't move. Don't get inspired. Don't make any new friends."

"Was that crotch grab for me or for you?"

Kate scurried off into the bowels of the Garden, reluctantly leaving West to his own devices. Coming toward him he saw a guy with a camera on his shoulder and an attractive raven-haired young woman holding a microphone. Remember the last time West crossed paths with a beautiful raven-haired woman? They were about to pass him by when West decided–in direct opposition to Kate's instructions– to make some new friends.

"Hey! Microphone girl! Come here! Talk to me!" he bellowed.

The young woman and the cameraman stopped.

"I'm not a girl. I have a name. Barbara," she said

without malice.

"Hey Barbara. I'm West. GreenPlanet. You probably want to interview me."

"GreenPlanet, right, save the whales," she said.

"You can put a check mark next to that box. Whales saved. Now I'm here to save the planet."

"You're not wearing your Superman outfit."

"Let's do this. Let me know when the camera is rolling," he said brushing himself off, running his hands through his hair, then taking a couple of deep breaths.

Barbara discreetly gave a behind-the-back signal for the cameraman to roll film.

"I'm not interested, thanks anyway," she said.

"Barbara, c'mon! Let's do this!"

"Sorry, no time. Besides, light's no good here."

"Three months ago I stood on stage and addressed forty thousand people at the Diablo Canyon protest. I spoke with the Governor of California. Bonnie, and Graham, and Jackson were there. I'm here in New York to speak at the rally in Battery Park. I'm here for you. Right here. Right now. There's plenty of light! Non-radioactive light!" exclaimed West.

"I'm afraid the enormous shadow of your ego has you standing in the dark," she said recording everything.

"Barbara. You and I. All of these brilliant musicians. Fifty thousand people coming through those doors. We're all here for an important reason. A life and death call to arms. Three Mile Island, Rocky Flats, Seabrook, atomic weapons, nuclear waste disposal. The China Syndrome. Air and water. Air and water and the food chain. The genetic chain. At risk for short-term monetary profits. Individual and corporate greed. You and I and those fifty thousand voices, we don't matter to the corporations. For the powers that be, it's always money before people. It's time for us to stand up. It's time for us to fight. On the reservation, at Diablo Canyon, the Farallon Islands, in the South Pacific. I haven't even mentioned other countries. What about Russia? What if there was a nuclear meltdown in the Soviet Union? I'm here. Not going anywhere. No intention of being silent. No cowering in the shadows. Time to make some noise, some music. Time to be heard," West finally concluded.

Barbara snuck a look at the cameraman, who nodded his head 'yes,' just as Kate returned to the scene of the crime.

"We'll see how things go. Maybe we'll speak in a couple of days. Bye," said Barbara, as she and her partner walked off whispering to each other. Their motto: Film everything; you never know what you will use in post.

"You wanna meet up for a drink?" West yelled after her.

"What "speak?" What "we'll see?" I told you not to move," said Kate.

"Didn't move a muscle."

"Did you talk to, do you know who that is?" Kate sputtered.

"What? Yea. Barbara," said West.

Kate removed the flask of whiskey from her bag, removed the cap, and took a big swig.

"Barbara Kopple and Haskell Wexler. Academy Award-winning filmmakers. They're documenting these

515

concerts," she murmured between gulps of whiskey. "What did you say to them?"

"Nothing," West lied.

"Lord have mercy," she said taking him by the arm and marching him off to parts unknown.

"Hey, can I have my flask back? Please."

The Battery Square Park rally took place on the last day of concerts, Sunday, September 23rd. Two hundred and fifty thousand people attended. West got bumped from the line-up of speakers that day, and he was okay with that since he was still feeling foolish for his pay-attention-to-me encounter with Barbara Kopple. Kate arranged for him to do some live reports for KWOT radio in Los Angeles where, consciously, he never once used the pronoun 'I'. Although not a believer in a Supreme Being, he privately prayed in earnest that his speech to Barbara was not covertly recorded—as Kate suggested was a strong possibility—and if it was that it would end up on the cutting room floor, or better yet, accidentally dropped into the Hudson. His prayers, it seems, were answered.

Five days later West found himself on Higuera Street in sunny, downtown San Luis Obispo accompanied by his comrades-in-arms Delilah and Salinger. They were petitioning passersby and those taking their lunch break in the perfect California weather. The soon-to-be-online Diablo Canyon nuclear power plant was on their minds. Delilah blocked two young businessmen who were more than happy to make her attractive acquaintance.

"Hi guys. Do you have a moment? I could use your help," she said holding up a photo for the smiling guys to see.

"Do you know who this is? Take a good look. No? That's Diego Garcia. He owns the Mexican food place just up the block. Wonderful man. I'm sure you've eaten his yummy food. Look. Here's a picture of his family. Mr. Garcia's restaurant is exactly six miles from the two nuclear reactors at Diablo Canyon. If and when there is an accident, or an earthquake, or a meltdown, Mr. Garcia, his family, everyone working, eating lunch, and standing right here where we are standing, all of San Luis Obispo, will be radioactively poisoned, wiped off the map. It breaks my heart," she said.

Uncomfortable, disgruntled, and disappointed, the two businessmen took their leave without a word.

"Go have lunch at Garcia's! The food is so good!" Delilah yelled after them.

There was always a long line at 'Tommy's Fish and Chips' food truck, simply the best fish and chips on the entire California coast. The food truck line was the ideal captive audience for Salinger who spied two female college students and a young mother pushing a baby stroller.

"I'm visiting here. Long lines normally mean good food," she said to the college students.

"Tommy's is the best," said the redhead.

"The fish is fresh?" asked Salinger.

"Right off the boat at Avila Beach," said the brunette.

"I'm sold. Thanks for the hot tip. Did you hear that people? This fish is right off the boat at Avila Beach! Can't get any fresher than that!" Salinger loudly announced.

In a more discreet voice, she asked the young mother if Avila Beach was where the nuclear power plant was being built? The young mother nodded a sheepish 'yes.' Returning to her broadcast voice, she made sure the entire captive audience could clearly hear.

"That's an ocean water cooling system, right? Right? It is, people, it is. What will we do when radiation leaks into the water, people? What's Tommy going to do when the local fish are radioactive? This food truck is six miles from those two reactors! The little baby in this stroller is six miles from ground zero. Anybody see the video from Three Mile Island? Anyone want to go visit there? Call GreenPlanet. Call the Abalone Alliance. Get involved people! Get involved! Those fish and chips smell so, so good. It's making me hungry. Tommy's is six miles from ground zero!"

Half a block from Tommy's food truck, West had cornered a middle-aged businesswoman searching for her car keys. He approached with clipboard in hand, and a smile on his face.

"Two seconds, I promise. A few quick survey questions. You work downtown here? Yes? Okay, and you also live close to downtown? Great. Husband? Check. Kids? Check? Parents live nearby? No? Okay, so, what we're doing is compiling a comprehensive list of 'next of kin' for all of you that live in the San Luis Obispo area, that live in the shadow of the Diablo Canyon nuclear reactors. When the meltdown occurs, we want to be able to have some way of knowing the history, the stories, and the identities of the individuals who once lived here. Even though most of you will experience a slow death, we..."

Before he could continue she cut him off. Pointing across the street at a suit-wearing man walking towards a car adorned with the SO CAL POWER logo.

"Look, you're talking to the wrong person. I get it. I'm with you. You want to talk to him. He's the main man. That's the plant manager. He runs the whole show," she said.

Whipping around without hesitation, West flung his prop clipboard to the ground and made a manic dash toward the unsuspecting man. Before the plant manager could slip into his car, West lunged, then bear hugged him from behind, pinning him against the car.

"You sir, are under arrest. Do not try to resist," said West wrestling the terrified man to the ground, sitting on top of him. Delilah and Salinger witnessed this at the same time as most of the Higuera Street pedestrians. Sprinting, they got to West before the rest of the crowd.

"What the fuck are you doing?" screamed Delilah.

"He's lost his mind," followed Salinger.

"As a conscientious member of this world, this great country, and this great state of California, I hereby make this citizen's arrest. You, sir, are under arrest for the breach of peace, reckless and dangerous conduct, and greedy disregard for your fellow man," announced West to a smattering of applause and laughter from the developing crowd. Salinger, encouraged by the applause, seized the moment yelling "No nukes! No nukes! No nukes!" Delilah was not encouraged. She was furious.

"West, get off him and let's go. Now. You don't

want to get arrested on a Friday!"

"It's not I that will be arrested. He's the one committing crimes against humanity. We wait for the police!" said West in full street theatre mode.

As the crowd hooted and hollered, a police car arrived carrying two unfazed police officers. Exiting their patrol car, they observed West sitting atop the Diablo Canyon plant manager.

"Officers, I've made a necessary citizens arrest and would like to turn this man over to your custody," announced West to goading applause.

The officers knew the plant manager. They had been to the construction site at Diablo Canyon on more than one occasion. Straight-faced, they knew what to do.

"Absolutely. Well done. We'll take him off your hands," said the senior officer.

West knew his fate, knew he was about to go to jail, but he didn't break character. He continued to put on his show. The junior officer helped West up and off of the plant manager, then led him to the patrol car where they were joined by the senior officer who proceeded to cuff both of West's hands behind his back. The Diablo Canyon plant manager, now on his feet, was shaky, but unharmed. Brushing himself off, he bellowed at West.

"I just had this suit cleaned!" he roared.

"You all right Bernie?" asked the senior officer.

"I'm fine. I just had this suit cleaned."

"You want to press charges?"

"Let him sit in the can for the weekend. That'll do."

The officers placed West into the patrol car as the

crowd offered a final round of applause. Delilah was not happy.

"Jesus fucking Christ! We work with a complete idiot!" she howled.

"Maybe, maybe not. You see what he's doing? Breach of peace. Reckless conduct. He's a piece of work, that boy, but he's not an idiot," said Salinger.

Delilah was beside herself. West, she knew, would be spending the weekend in San Luis Obispo's blue roof motel. She was also aware of what he had just done; she knew what Salinger was implying. Breach of peace and reckless conduct. West was establishing a legal precedent for civil disobedience. He was designing a playbook for future protest. No matter, she was still furious with him. Walking away from Salinger in the direction of Tommy's food truck she said with exasperation "Fish and Chips?"

Monday arrived, and with it the first day of October. The office in L.A. was, yet again, an all-woman operation. Delilah, Kate, Salinger, and a few female volunteers were conducting the necessary duties that were required to keep the environmental ship afloat when West and Susan strolled through the door. On her drive down from San Francisco, Susan was kind enough to rescue West from his temporary home in the SLO jail, seeing that Delilah had refused to take any of West's numerous come-bail-me-out phone calls over the weekend, ordering Salinger to do the same. This morning he had been released from jail, but Delilah wasn't ready to release him from her displeasure.

"Look who I brought with me? Sprung him from jail

when they weren't looking," said a jovial Susan.

"My fault we're a bit late. I made Susan stop by my place so I could shower and change clothes," said West.

"He needed to shower, trust me," Susan added as she administered hugs to Salinger and Delilah.

Delilah didn't like this banter about Susan escorting West to his shower, and she certainly didn't like the fact that she didn't like it. While hugging Susan, she felt frightfully insecure. Was it the way Susan said "trust me?" Was that West's shampoo she smelled in Susan's hair? "Paranoia strikes deep; into your heart it will creep."

There was no reason for Delilah to be jealous, or to fear duplicity. Susan had simply waited patiently as West washed the jailhouse cooties off his stinking self, slipping into a clean pair of freedom jeans. Completely innocent. Right? Absolutely. Except for a harmless little indiscretion. Not even an indiscretion. More like an indulgence or a self-gratifying reward. You see, Susan, by now, had spent months in the San Francisco office, surrounded by 'friendly' women and unfriendly men, and it had been a bit too long since she had enjoyed the sight of an attractive naked man up close and personal, and so who could fault her for modestly nudging open the bathroom door just enough for her to watch as West freshened up? Nobody needed to know that benign detail. West didn't know she was watching, right? And since he was more like a bratty brother to her, there was no harm done, just a much-needed stirring of stifled emotions.

Delilah inhaled two psychological breaths,

meditatively exhaling in an attempt to let go of her irrational fear. Susan, after all, had made the trip down to L.A. to meet with she and Kate. Susan and Delilah would be comparing toxic waste dumping notes while plotting a future joint campaign to tackle the issue head-on, after which Susan would also be meeting with Kate to privately discuss the rudimentary steps necessary for the creation of GreenPlanet America–but Delilah didn't know about that. So everything was cool, above board, copacetic.

When she became aware of the materialization of West and Susan, Kate stuck her head into the war room.

"Your arrest was brilliant. Well done," she said to West.

"Excuse me? What time is it?" he asked Susan.

"One forty five."

"And what day is today?" he asked Salinger.

"October 1st, 1979."

"Would you kindly record this exact moment when Kate Blair paid me an unsolicited compliment?" he directed toward Delilah who ignored him.

"Using the citizens arrest to turn the tables on them makes them the trespassers and not us. Spot on. You've a bunch of phone calls to return. Have at it. Susan, love, come chat with me when you get a chance," said Kate.

West tried and failed to make eye contact with Delilah as he passed by her desk, which provided Salinger with an opening to ask the elephant-in-the-room question.

"How was jail?" she asked.

523

"Jail? Exceedingly unpleasant. Strange, but I wasn't able to reach any of my GreenPlanet friends to come bail me out," said West.

"So I guess you didn't take a shower with your new friends?"

"It was offered, but I graciously declined," he replied.

West was what is known in the world of incarceration as a "weekender." Self-explanatory; a guest of the facility for forty-eight hours or so, just enough time to perform menial tasks like mopping, scrubbing, hauling, dumping, and garbaging. Also, just enough time to get into some serious trouble if you're not smart about things. Often, but not always, a weekender is lodged with other weekenders, but not always. Be humble. Don't act superior to others. Silence is a good choice to make. Show no fear while exhibiting no bravado. Eat what's put in front of you. Don't ask your fellow inmates probing questions. Don't hog the pay phone or change the television channel. If possible, be invisible. Cease to exist. Meditate on your foolhardiness. If you are an atheist, pretend to pray anyway. Finally, stink it up. Don't shower. If possible, don't shit. Keep one eye open. Breathe a huge sigh of relief and gratitude when released.

"You have a date tonight," teased Salinger.

"Date?"

"Connor Kilkenny. Monday Night Football," she said with a chuckle.

"Impossible. The game is in Green Bay," said West.

"At the Playboy Mansion. Connor's coming here to

get you at five."

What? Did West hear her correctly? The Playboy
Mansion? Tonight? He looked in Delilah's direction, but
she had her head down pretending to read. Salinger
and Susan did not have their heads down. They were
watching closely to see West's reaction and ultimate
decision. The decision was a no-brainer. He had always
fantasized about attending a party at the Playboy
Mansion with Hef and the bunnies and the debauchery.
Never in his wildest imagination did he think it would
ever come to pass. By all means he was going! He
deserved this, didn't he? The last forty-eight hours
were spent as a wretched weekender, Delilah and
Salinger deliberately abandoning him to the horrors of
county jail. He could have been killed! Or raped! Or
made to wipe some miscreant's ass! The only ass he
wanted to come close to now was Miss October.

"Hmm. Okay, well, let me think about it. I have to
catch up on some work, but there might be some good
money connections to be made there," he said with a
perfectly straight face.

Delilah made a gagging noise as Salinger and
Susan laughed out loud. From her office, Kate yelled
out "You must go and pet the bunnies!" which made
Susan and Salinger laugh even harder. So, there it
was. He and Connor Kilkenny were off to the Playboy
Mansion. What could possibly go wrong?

#

Like a kid in a candy store, West didn't know
where to look or point at first. The dance floor was
packed with VIP friends of Hef, wanna be friends of

525

Hef, celebrities, those who knew the right people, the right people, and dozens and dozens of young, revealing women. 'Bad Girls' by Donna Summers was blaring through the speakers, as all of the beautiful people were disco dancing in their bell-bottoms and disco shoes under the sparkling disco ball. West didn't understand how it was he and Connor were allowed into this inner sanctum, especially himself, but...

"My pal Darla insisted we come and hang with her and her sister Marla," Connor made clear. "I figured it would be cool," he added.

Uh, yea. I guess it would be cool, but right at this moment West was feeling kind of hot under the collar, under the radar. He was having flashbacks to Carla and Sky; remember them? Also "pals" of Connor. Very nice pals of Connor. Was Carla related to Darla and Marla he wondered? Hope so.

West and Connor were shooting pool when the Playboy bunnies Darla and Marla found them. Darla was wearing an L A Rams football jersey with the number 6 in the middle of her chest and Marla was wearing an identical jersey with the number 9. Connor said that they often stood close to each other to create the number 69. West was spellbound as Marla relieved him of his pool cue, strategically positioned herself by bending over the pool table, and announced that she was about to stroke his balls. Darla, carrying two glasses of champagne, handed one to Connor, kept one for herself, and placed her free arm around his waist. Let the games begin.

West would come to learn that Darla and Marla were not related to Carla or Sky–Connor found that notion hilarious–rather, they were sisters who both attended the same Ivy League university in New Jersey. Playboy was doing an Ivy League edition of the magazine, and when Hef saw the nude photos of Darla and Marla he instantly knew who would adorn his November cover.

After a few humiliating games of sixty-nine ball– Darla and Marla severely kicking the boys' asses–the foursome found a couple of unoccupied cigar chairs in the main living room, affording them a front row seat to the greatest show on earth. With playboy bunnies firmly situated on their laps, West and Connor sipped on scotch whiskey and took in the hedonistic scene. There was James Caan chatting up Dorothy Stratton. Warren Beatty, Cheryl Tiegs, and Robert Culp were assuming dashing and voguish poses for all to ogle. Bill Cosby, smiling that devilish smile of his, had his arm around the waist of a tipsy-looking bunny. There were three pro-athletes that must, I'm sad to say, remain nameless, and there was the man. There he was. Hef. Hugh Hefner, king of the castle, builder of the empire, playboy of the western world, silk pajamas and bunnies on each arm. West couldn't take his eyes off of him. He was afraid that Hef might look their way, not recognize him, and arrange for their swift expulsion, but it didn't happen. What did happen blew his mind. Hef waved at him! What? Hugh Hefner spotted the foursome, smiled an approving smile in West's direction, and then waved at them! Holy shit, the pope's blessing! Anything, everything was now possible, probable! Hef! My man!

Darla whispered something devious into Marla's

ear, and unannounced they jumped up off of the boy's laps. For a brief moment West was crestfallen, assuming that his fantasy bunny-time was coming to an end. It was not. Not even close. With bunny hands extended toward the lads, Connor and West were playfully led to the pool a.k.a. the grotto a.k.a. the aquatic pleasure dome a.k.a. Xanadu. Lush, with plenty of private nooks and crannies, the sultry lighting discreetly revealed copious naked revelers making merry. Marla and Darla deftly exited their football jerseys soon to be followed by their football shorts, then, completely at home in the buff–and the Holmby Hills– they waded into the perfectly heated water of the grotto to choose the consummate spot to continue their evening of socializing with their two boys. When the hand-waves of permission came from the bunnies to join them, West and Connor were naked and wet in a New York minute, Darla snuggling with Connor, and Marla snuggling with West. Naked in the grotto of the Playboy mansion on a Monday night in October of 1979.

More scotch whiskey appeared from some mysterious source, as things tended to happen at the mansion. West couldn't make out what Connor and Darla were jawing about, but he could see that they were deep into conversation. His girl Marla was explaining to him about Marine eco-systems; the subtle differences between intertidal zones and estuaries, between lentic and lotic fresh water systems; between fringing, barrier, and atoll reefs. She was tutoring him in all things whiskey. Highland, Lowland, Islay, Speyside, peat, wood, vanilla,

528

everything. These Princeton girls, he thought, were pretty damn smart. It also occurred to him that he would love to, if given the opportunity, closely examine her intertidal zones.

Delilah. How was it possible that Delilah was part of his present consciousness? Here he was, au natural, next to a flawless naked specimen of womanhood. Wet and whiskeyed, and willing to be wild, and yet, part of his brain was occupied by Delilah. The pristine image of a naked and super-smart Delilah was in his head at the same time a spectacularly naked and super-smart Marla was at his side. Can I say underwater erection? How about 'go with the flow'? Which is what West did. He and Marla and Darla and Connor sipped whiskey, chatted about the universe, and bathed in each other's beautiful nakedness. It was nirvana. It was more than West could have conjured. Sixty hours in the hole followed by nine hours at Hef's mansion. This time, he would, without hesitation, accept the offer, if presented, to shower.

After an excellent night's sleep in his own bed, not to mention two showers on the same day, West was back at his desk getting caught up and reacclimated. Upon his arrival in the office there were the expected giggles and raised eyebrows; all in attendance dying to know what kind of mischief he and Connor got themselves into, but all of that died out in due course. Delilah, as you might have guessed, was not one of the gigglers. She was the chief ignorer, the anti-enabler, keeping her head down, and her focus on her work. West was relieved that he detected no super weird energy from her, and overall, everything seemed to be okay. He declined to inform Delilah about Marla, because, he reasoned, nothing except nakedness happened. Salinger passed along a message from Kip for West to meet him at the Chimney Sweep at 2p.m. She said he sounded "kind of heavy" and "pensive." Her budding reputation as a "drama queen" precluded any cause for concern by West, and he didn't give it another thought until he arrived at the bar where Connie, looking doomy and gloomy, had a cocktail waiting for him when he sat down at the bar next to Kip.

"To my brother and sister, and to the great journey that lies ahead," said Kip raising his Cuba Libre into the air.

"If I'm your sister, you've got some heavy duty incest issues to deal with, sugar," said Connie.

West didn't need to be a great detective to grasp that something was adrift, something was up. He also had a sneaking suspicion that the drink in Kip's hand was not his first.

"So, why the hush-hush meeting?" asked West.

"I'll get to that in a second, but first, I want to tell you how impressed I am with you, and how important you have become to the organization."

"Happy to be a part of it," replied West.

"Big things are around the corner and I want to be sure that you'll be here."

"I'm not going anywhere. Where would I go?"

Connie, drink in hand, was trying to make a get-away when Kip stopped her.

"Connie, stop. Come back here. You need to hear this too," said Kip.

"I don't want to hear this," she whimpered.

West watched as the two of them, awkward and serious looking, stared painfully into each other's eyes. He suddenly got a sick feeling.

"Oh, no."

"Mexico," said Kip.

"For good?"

"Yea."

"When?"

"Four days."

Connie poured three shots of tequila, and distributed them accordingly. Kip spelled it out. He was headed, temporarily, to Cabo San Lucas, before heading to his final destination, a remote stretch of beach on the Sinaloa side of the Sea of Cortez. He was, he said, done. The gas tank was empty, and the whales had been saved. It was time for him to ride off into the sunset for good.

West knew this day was coming. Everyone could see that Kip was spent, and West reckoned that Kip would be the first one of the lost tribe to exit the arena. It was a hard pill to swallow. He adored and worshipped Kip so much, but he accepted this as the right thing to do, and no one could dispute the fact that Kip had earned his empty gas tank.

"How's the surfing?" asked West.

"Almost as good as the tequila," said Kip.

"I'm there as soon as you are settled," West said with a gentle embrace.

Connie ran to answer the ringing phone, seizing the opportunity to wipe the tears from her eyes. For the longest time, she convinced herself that Kip was the one. During the early days, they would make plans for a future when Kip would settle down. There was talk of a house, and cats, maybe in the canyon, with a garden, and a fireplace. Maybe they would own a natural food place—with a bar? They would travel around the globe. Kip, you know, would be inheriting great wealth, and in his free time he could write a book about Jim Morrison. It would be a wonderful life if and when he settled down. But, sometimes, members of the lost tribe are never found. They never make it out of the dark tunnel. They claw and scratch and search until the gas tank is empty. Until it's too late. Connie, red-eyed, handed the phone to West.

"It's Delilah. She says it's important."

Connie held hands with Kip as West listened intently through the prehistoric receiver he held to his ear. When the news from the other end had concluded, West handed the phone back to Connie, and tested Kip one last time.

"I've got to go. Prairie Island nuclear plant in Minnesota is spewing radioactive steam into the air. The plant is being evacuated. You coming?" he asked knowing the answer.

"No, my brother. The wheel is firmly in your hands now," said Kip.

"One last big party before you go? Or two? Or three?" West said slapping him on the back.

"Far out, man. Far out," said Kip.

When West entered the office, phones were ringing and the Telex machine was clacking. As he passed by Salinger she handed him several phone messages. Delilah was talking on her phone, so he stopped to listen.

"It's too early for us to have an official statement. We're watching just like you are. We'll send out a press release as soon as we get a handle on things. Right, well, they also said there was no danger to the public at Three Mile Island," she said ending the call and picking up the next one.

West continued into Kate's office where she was watching a live broadcast from the Prairie Island Nuclear facility. Upon entering, she handed him an Associated Press report hot off of the Telex.

"Kip is leaving us," said West.

"Not now. Focus," she replied.

West spent a few minutes watching the television and reading the Telexes. The Nuclear Regulatory Commission was acknowledging that a steam generator tube had ruptured, and that radioactive steam had discharged into the atmosphere for "about twenty-seven minutes." The spokesperson for the NRC went on to say that the radioactive steam cloud "did not appear to be dangerous." "The total radiation exposure at the plant's site boundary has been estimated to be less than one-tenth of a millirem, well within permissible limits," he said straight-faced. One hundred plant workers had already been evacuated, and the State of Minnesota, as well as the power company, had radiation monitoring teams on site. Six miles away, in the town of Red Wing, residents gathered around televisions and spilled out into the street to see if they could pinpoint the poisonous steam cloud. In light of what occurred only six months prior at Three Mile Island, the residents of Minneapolis-

Saint Paul, forty-six miles away, were on notice, and on edge.

West spent the next two hours at his desk answering questions from the local media and the public, and in between phone calls he assisted Delilah with the drafting of a position paper regarding GreenPlanet's views and concerns with nuclear power plant safety around the globe. As he tackled his various tasks he tried to detect any negative energy coming from Delilah in his direction, but any feelings or emotions she might have had were veiled. He couldn't wipe the look of resignation on Kip's face, or Connie's palpable anguish out of his head. He needed to take a break.

"Are you hungry?" he asked Delilah.

"You have an hour before you go on the air with Connor Kilkenny," she said.

"I need some fresh air. Gonna walk across the street and get an Orange Julius," he said.

"Get me one, too," she said as he labored to get himself up and out the door.

Hypnotized, he watched the endless traffic stream by on Ventura Boulevard as he waited for the frothy orange drinks to arrive. The people occupying the passing cars confused him. They were strangers, alien and unfamiliar. He grew agitated, and took a quick peek at the corner street sign to verify his location. 13700 VENTURA BLVD? Across the street, he could see the building that housed the GreenPlanet office–the same office he had gone to every day for almost two years now–but he wasn't totally sure if that was indeed his place of work. The walk-up window opened, and the Orange Julius girl called out to him. In a fog he retrieved the cardboard tray of drinks from her, turning back toward the now unfamiliar street as she closed the window. Two steps were all he could manage before abruptly coming to a halt. Needing something to grab onto, feeling dizzy and faint, he dropped the tray of drinks and fell to the ground. Sweat poured down his face, his pulse was rapid, and he was overcome with extreme fear. Through the take-out window, the eighteen-year-old girl saw West collapse and came running out to assist him.

"Hey, you need help? You alright?" she asked in a panic.

West didn't respond. His breathing was heavy.

"Should I call for help?" she freaked.

"Give me a second," said West.

"You having a heart attack?"

"No, I'm good, I'm good. Sorry I made a mess here."

"I'll make you two more. No charge. You sure you're okay?"

"Yea, yea, just a little faint. Haven't eaten all day."

The unnerved damsel helped West to his feet and walked him–like a rickety old man– to an outside table where she carefully guided his ass onto one of the table benches. When she was semi-convinced that he wasn't going to die on her, she ran back into the fast-food joint to rustle him up some grub. West was shaking as he wiped the sweat off his face, struggling to regain his composure. Looking at the street sign again, he couldn't read it. It was a green blur. He checked his pulse. His heart was pounding. Orange

535

Julius girl returned with two more drinks, a burger and fries. She sat down next to him.

"Food," she said.

West, thinking he probably experienced a blood sugar crash, took a big gulp of his sugary orange drink, placing the frosty cup to his forehead. A blood sugar crash, yea, that explains things. Good, he rationalized, "be okay in a minute." Orange Julius girl, brushing the hair out of her face, up close and personal, made it possible for West to notice more of her features. She was striking, in an edgy non-conformist way. On her inner-upper right arm there was a tattoo of a seventeenth-century English dagger. She had his attention.

"Can I see your arm?" said a recovering West.

Facing him directly, she extended her arm out and across, allowing him to see even more of what she possessed.

"Girls don't get tattoos," he said. "What's your name?"

Looking at him like the almost-died-on-the-sidewalk pinhead that he was, Orange Julius girl detached herself from the table. She needed to get her ass back to work.

"My name is West. I work across the street. We should, you should, let me make it up to you sometime. Your kindness and your burgers," he said making absolutely no sense at all.

Grabbing the pen from behind her ear, without a moment's hesitation, she took his hand, scrawled some medieval-looking text, turned without a word, and reluctantly returned to the dead-end world of foamy orange drinks and deep-fried cuisine. For a brief moment West forgot his health crisis. Yes, he was reeling and spinning, but it wasn't his blood sugar. "What's happening to me? What am I thinking? How old is she?" are just a few of the questions that popped into his brain.

#

Panic attacks a.k.a. anxiety attacks a.k.a. freak-outs have nothing to do with blood sugar crashes, at least not in West's case. West didn't experience a blood sugar crash. His spinning world was of the existential variety. Cold sweats, shaking, heart palpitations, vertigo, high anxiety, blurred vision, dread, paranoia, agoraphobia, fear of failure, the quintessential identity crisis. The Orange Julius panic attack was his first 'recognizable' episode, but it would not be his last. As for now, he was back in the office doing his thing. Delilah was eating his untouched burger, and listening as West was being phone interviewed by Connor Kilkenny who was in the middle of his six o'clock newscast.

"We're still trying to gather all of the facts from Prairie Island. The truth, not the company line. As soon as we know something new, you and the KWOT listeners will too. And, as always, our volunteers are here to take your calls," West concluded.

West was fatigued. The clock on the wall displayed a fuzzy 6:15pm.

"That's it. You're done for the day. You look beat," said Delilah with mouth full of burger.

Line one was blinking and West picked it up before

Salinger noticed.

"Hey Connor. I didn't think I did that great. Cool. Tomorrow, same time. Roger that. Tonight? The bunnies? Oh man, I can't. Very tempting, but I, I'm fucking tired. I need to go fall into my bed. Yea. Yea. Yea. Deal. My apologies to Darla and Marla. Talk to you tomorrow."

"You don't have to pretend you're going home. Go. Play with your little bunnies. No one cares," said Delilah who cared.

On her way out, Kate stopped at West's desk.

"Good job. You sounded different. Not sure why. More sincere, vulnerable," she said.

"I don't like complimentary Kate. Could you please go back to being the mean, cold-hearted Kate?"

"Breaking news everyone. Jonah and Kai defected to the Sea Pirates. Took twenty thousand dollars with them. San Francisco office is in crisis mode. First item on our agenda tomorrow morning," Kate added making her exit.

"Whoa," said West.

"Good riddance," added Delilah.

"Go get some sleep. You look like shit," Kate declared on her way out the door.

"That's the Kate I like!" West yelled after her.

The instant that Kate's butt was out the door, Delilah and Salinger were on their feet, and closing up shop.

"Kip is leaving us," said West.

"We've already covered that ground. We're headed, right now, to the Chimney Sweep to wish them well. Stop by before you go see your bunnies," said Delilah.

"I'm not going to see any bunnies. What do you mean 'them'?"

"Will too. He's leaving the fold and returning to show business. Going to be Vanessa Gray Reynolds's manager."

West was blind. Delirious. Gobsmacked.

"You look tired. I think you should go home and rest. Friday night we're having the big official blowout at the Chimney Sweep. Susan is sticking around. Even Kate. Everyone will be there," said Salinger.

"What's tomorrow? Wednesday? See you all tomorrow morning," said a shell-shocked West.

Delilah and Salinger scooped up their possessions, and abandoned West in the now deathly quiet office. Slumping back in his chair, he stared at the ceiling. On his left hand, closest to his arrhythmic heart, he saw the inked name and digits of Orange Julius girl a.k.a. Myra. Included was the drawing of a dagger dripping blood. If it were up to me, if I was bestowed with the power, I would choose this particular moment as the perfect moment to implement panic attack number two; nobody around to save him; nothing in the world makes sense to him; the name and phone number of an eighteen-year-old delinquent staining his skin. If it were up to me.

He made it back to Malibu in time to watch the sun sink into the Pacific. A couple of fish tacos were consumed, and some gas was put in the car before inserting the key into the front door of his trailer. Heading straight for his couch, he flicked on the radio, snatched a bottle of bourbon from the kitchen counter,

539

and fell into a coma for the next hundred minutes. Two table lamps provided barely enough light for him to ponder the universe. Whiskey bottle in hand, he was slumped back on the couch, staring up at the ceiling when an outer voice shook him back to the present. The voice of Jim Ladd was suddenly penetrating the silent night. West sat up straight and listened to that familiar sound.

"Where you gonna go when the planet blows? Jackson Browne's 'Before the Deluge,' before that The Doors 'Ship of Fools.' We're talking about, we're discussing, the latest nuclear accident. If you just tuned in it was at Prairie Island. Very much like Three Mile Island we're getting the normal rhetoric from the government, everything's okay, don't worry about it, it's all under control. Just don't make the sheep panic is their philosophy, you know? I say we ain't sheep, we're living, breathing human beings, and we'd like to stay that way guys, and I say that it's time we take a long, critical look at the United States government and the Nuclear Regulatory Commission. It's not like these guys are batting a thousand. These are the people we're entrusting our lives to. Nuclear power is not a mystical, unfathomable problem. This is a man-made, self-inflicted, self-induced trauma that we're putting on ourselves. Some jerk in a bureaucratic position is telling you that nuclear power is necessary. Somebody who is making money, wants you to believe that, wants you to live under the risk, and is willing to risk your life and the environment of the planet to make money. It is as simple as that. Why do you think concerned people like Jackson Browne and Bonnie

Raitt and Linda Ronstadt and Tom Petty are doing concerts in New York and California? Not because they're getting paid for it. You ever think about that. The 'No Nuke' people don't get no money for it and they're working real hard. The people that are getting money for it are working real hard against the 'No Nuke' people. Does it start to compute? I want to leave you with a phone number. Our friends at GreenPlanet, very good people who are not buying the line. 986-2300, 986-2300. We are KWOT. We're known for taking a stand, opening our mouth way too big. Sitting here trying to get a little truth on the radio. I hope you're listening, as scared as you are. So. We'll end it this way. If we call GreenPlanet, if we think with our hearts as well as our minds, if we let them know that we don't want nukes in a non-violent, loving manner, then maybe you and I are on the road to meeting up with Pocahontas. One more time."

'Pocahontas' by Neil Young came through the speakers as West sprang to his feet. Why? What? He sat back down, and then he jumped back up again, pacing back and forth in the dim doublewide light. Returning to the couch, he lifted up a cushion and removed an old Skoal tin inside a plastic sandwich bag. On the coffee table were a mirror, straw, and razor blade. He opened the tin and carefully dumped some of its white powder onto the mirror. With great precision, he created three lines of coke. The right nostril was first up, then the left. Up he leaped, pacing back and forth, back and forth. Into the kitchen he sprinted, grabbing his money, wallet, keys, and jacket. On the way to the front door, he stopped and snorted

541

the third line. What? Where? He was scanning his abode with the wild eyes of suspicion. What? He wasn't sure. Jamming the Skoal tin back into the plastic bag, then back under the seat cushion, out the door he bolted.

It was late on a Tuesday night. The Chimney Sweep was empty. No Connie, no Delilah, no humans. Gil was behind the bar doing a crossword puzzle when West came speeding through the door.

"Gil, my man. Where is everybody?" said West.

"Long gone. Another nuke accident, huh?" replied a sedate Gil.

"Gone? Forever?" asked West.

"Want a drink? On me," offered Gil.

"Can't. I'm on borrowed time."

"Careful going home."

"Don't have a home," said West scrambling out the door.

West decided that the bar at "The Riot House" would provide him with the therapeutic action and adventure that he required at this moment in his life. His last visit to that fine establishment was a version of Mr. Toad's Wild Ride. Let's call it Ms. Morgana's Wild Ride. He hadn't had ass on barstool for five minutes before the bartender made him an offer he couldn't refuse. Placing a bottle of Irish whiskey in front of West, he proposed a business deal.

"I'll buy you a couple of drinks if you'll deliver this bottle to that guy sitting back there," said the bartender.

West turned to see a mopped-haired guy in his thirties sitting by himself at a back table, scribbling on a pile of bar napkins. Every now and then he would bark like a dog and pound his fist on the table. West was thinking that he recognized that face, but the drugs coursing through his brain made him unsure.

"Is he dangerous?" asked West.

"To himself," replied the bartender.

West came there looking for adventure–and free drinks were always welcome– so he tucked the bottle of whiskey under one arm and walked it back to the barker's table. Placing the bottle on the table in front of him, he turned to walk away.

"For God's sake, man. Come join me. You're all I've got," said the man pounding his fist on the table.

West considered the invitation for a fleeting moment, then cautiously joined him as his new friend arranged a couple of lines of coke on the table.

"You're going to do that right here, out in the open?" said West looking back at the bartender.

"No, we're going to do this. They don't give a fuck," said the barker.

The bartender had two drinks waiting for West who hopped up from his seat to retrieve them. He and the bartender watched as the barker retrieved, from his shirt pocket, a sterling-silver straw, and then snorted one of the lines of cocaine. When West looked to the bartender for guidance, he was met with a shrug of the shoulders, and a nod of approval. No fucks given. Returning to the back table, West took a long look at the familiar face.

"I'm West. And you are?" said West.

The second line of marching powder was snorted before West was granted his answer.

"Roland. Roland Thompson," said the man.

"You look like that songwriter, that Rocky Mountain High guy," said West eyeing the lines of cocaine.

"No!" he bellowed. "Jesus bloody Christ! Rocky Mountain High!"

"I guess not," West said.

West bellied up, and they drank some whiskey and snorted some coke and wondered aloud "what it all meant?" Neither one had anything to say about who they were, or what they did; instead, they were chemically altered brothers in purgatorial doom and gloom. Until Roland blew up.

"This is not doing it! This will not suffice! No, no, no, no, no!" he raged. "Echo Park. C'mon. You're driving," he commanded.

High up the hill, overlooking Los Angeles, the threshold of a well-kept, but worn house was guarded by three gangbangers who were sitting, arms crossed, on the front porch. It was graveyard quiet, and very late at night. Inside the house, dim red and blue lights revealed an old Latina woman, her daughter, West, and Roland. The old woman rested in a worn-out armchair while carefully supervising her daughter assist West and Roland, both in the process of smoking heroin. The scene was very peaceful and calm. It was obvious to West that Roland was well known and accepted in this home. Oddly, West was not afraid, of the gang members, of the strange surroundings, or the notorious drug that he was ingesting for the first time. West's euphoria was interrupted, not by fear or demons, but by internal combustion. Having lost any and all control, he dropped his head to vomit as the nimble daughter was already in motion with a plastic trashcan. Both Roland and West carried on with their opiate mission progressively dissolving into serene shambles. No words were spoken. Periodically, the daughter gently brushed back Roland's hair, providing cool water for he and West. On the wall was a velvet painting of Jesus watching over them, and bestowing on each of them all of his blessings. The old woman, now asleep in her chair, looked angelic as the faint light of day painted a supernatural halo upon her gray head. Outside, the lights of L.A. sparkled, but in a much different way than West had ever viewed them from the Hollywood Hills. A much more serious way. Far off, on the horizon, he could see the Pacific Ocean. He thought to himself "that's where I live; out there." On his left hand he saw a puddle of smeared blue ink, and the drawing of a dagger dripping blood. "Where did that come from?" he whispered to the velvet painting.

#

West didn't make it to the office Wednesday; rather, he communed with his bed and his swirling dreams. Change was not only in the air, it was now in his blood, too. The alchemical ball was picking up speed, and for those that did make it to the office, change was the primary topic of conversation.

In San Francisco, over the weekend, when all normally took their eye off of the ball, Jonah and Kai absconded with twenty thousand of the thirty thousand dollars that remained in the bank account of the Northern California GreenPlanet office. Off to the Sea

Pirates in Seattle they fled, leaving Karma, Catty, Jade, and the remnants of the motley groundlings to sink or swim. A cryptic note was left on Karma's desk that read: 1) Save the Whales! 2) Sea Pirates! 3) Revolution at all cost! 4) I copied the books!

Karma knew exactly what the message was intended to convey. Jonah was making it clear that he knew where all of the bodies were buried, and that if anyone from the San Francisco office made an issue of the missing twenty thousand dollars, he would provide the public with a detailed accounting of all monies raised and spent. Karma understood. Message received loud and clear. At least, she rationalized, he didn't wipe out the entire account.

In Los Angeles, Delilah, Kate, Susan, and Salinger were sorting it all out.

"They're ready to talk merger. Karma and Jade are on board. Catty doesn't want to, but now that Jonah and Kai are gone she can read the writing on the wall. Sunset defected to the Sea Pirates, too," said Susan.

"Superb. I spoke with Hunter. He has a plan ready to go," said Kate.

"We sure lost a bunch of men all at once," lamented Salinger.

"We've got West," said Delilah.

"And Rocky," followed Susan.

"And Hunter," added Kate.

"Also Will promises to help us from afar," said Delilah.

An uncomfortable pause ensued for all to reflect and resolve.

"Prairie Island looks worse than they initially

reported," Delilah said breaking the silence.

"They've evacuated the plant employees, but haven't said a word about those next door on the Indian reservation," said Susan.

"We saw what happened with Three Mile Island. It's early. Let's sit back, watch, and wait," Kate answered.

"We could tie this into the radiation deaths on the Pine Ridge reservation. That's a horror story that needs to be told," added Salinger.

Another silence elbowed its way into the room. Sadness and nervousness were palpable.

"Everything is changing; are you leaving us too?" Delilah said to Kate.

"Not for now," said Kate.

Each of them felt the powerful dark shadow of the unknown. It demanded their undivided attention. It had their stomachs churning. It wasn't going away any time soon.

The cloud of doubt lifted a bit on Thursday with the eagerly anticipated arrival of Rocky from San Francisco. West was back at his desk, and Will was at his, too. The extra bodies; the mix of male and female energies, provided, at least temporarily, a grounded confidence that had been missing from the office for some time. Rocky had plenty of San Francisco stories to tell. The northern office, as you might imagine, was reeling. Bills were unpaid, the rent was due, local media were sniffing around, and Hunter, rumor had it, was primed to pounce. Karma, Catty, and Jade were conducting many of their "meetings" in bars, as well as strategic café's that served adult beverages. The groundlings were becoming increasingly restless and emboldened. The foundation was on shaky ground.

Will announced the plans for his new endeavor: Stone Management. He had already signed his first two clients, Vanessa Gray Reynolds and Natalie Singer, and he was currently conducting covert discussions with Farrah Fawcett, trying to coax her into jumping ship and coming aboard with him. His clients, he explained, would not exclusively be actors and actresses. He would also be representing musicians and rock bands, and courting all of his rock-star friends and associates. Excited, thrilled, and re-energized, he promised to connect all of his people with GreenPlanet and their future fundraising efforts.

At the end of the day, Kate reminded everyone of the bon voyage party for Kip and Will to be held the following night at the Chimney Sweep. She also alluded to a pleasant "surprise or two." It was good, even if temporary, to have the gang back together again.

Friday night the Chimney Sweep was jumping. The music was loud, and there was an interesting mixture of smoke that filled the air. The GreenPlanet gang, including Connie and her sister Stephanie, commandeered a corner of the bar as all were in a festive Friday mood. Connie was doing her utmost to convince Will that her sister Stephanie was a great singer, someone that he should represent. She was a "star waiting to be discovered." Susan mischievously broached the name of Linda Paloma as a possible steal for Will, which unnerved West. He didn't realize that others besides he and Will might know about "that thing that happened with Linda Paloma." Did Susan know? Who else knew? He looked away from Delilah. Fortunately for West, three of Kate's surprises had managed to navigate their way through the crowded bar–diverting everyone's attention away from possibly embarrassing subject matters–to join the party. Hunter, Hugh, and Margaux des Jardin, straight off of an eleven-hour flight from London to LAX, were greeted with huzzahs and a hero's welcome. Hugs and handshakes all around, change was once again the elephant in the room.

"This is a nice surprise. You look great," said the Margaux-hugging West.

"Merci. Any way a girl can get a drink around here?" she said.

"Just happens I'm a close personal friend of the bartender."

"Vodka rocks. Double," she requested.

Hunter wrapped West from behind and tried to squeeze the life out of him.

"Hunter! Yes! What'll it be? I'm buying."

"I'll have what you're having," said the beaming Hunter as he threw his arm around West's neck.

Margaux squeezed in next to Delilah, and began to rifle through her very full travel bag.

"Bon soir, Delilah, content de te voir," she said with a kiss on the cheek.

"Hey girl, what brings you to L.A.?" queried Delilah.

"Chasing a story," answered Margaux handing Delilah a photo.

The photo showed Delilah, her face covered in

blood, sitting on top of a baby Harp seal on the bitterly cold ice floes of Newfoundland. It was a remarkable photo, jarring, filling Delilah's eyes with tears and memories.

"For you. Your face was all over Europe," said Margaux.

Bartender Gil placed Margaux's drink in front of her as he simultaneously freshened Delilah's. The second Hunter had drink in hand, he dragged West into a private corner away from the GreenPlanet revelry.

"It was very strange not being out there this summer," said West clinking glasses with Hunter.

"I know. Hard to replace a heightened experience like that," said Hunter.

"Whales are still being killed."

"Not for long. You know why I'm here?" asked Hunter.

West remained silent. The way in which Hunter asked the question gave him cause for concern.

"The time is right to take complete control of the U S operations," Hunter continued.

"Whenever I see Hugh on the scene, I know it's serious," West said.

"Precisely. Monday lunch. Just you and me. Don't look so apprehensive. All's well. Very well," Hunter said throwing back his drink with gusto. "Let's party."

And party they did. There was dancing and drinking; storytelling and fabrication. Hunter gave a minute-by-minute account of how things went down at the IWC meetings. He told of the grim and angry response from the Russian, Japanese, and Norwegian delegations as well as the backroom deals, and across-

the-table threats. Rod Stewart–an old friend of Kate's–
showed up with entourage in tow to have a few festive
pints before heading off to a variety of exclusive
parties, and though tempted to tag along, Kate
shrewdly remained a Chimney Sweep reveler for the
rest of the night. Knowing this might be the last time
he saw Kip, West stayed glued to his side, matching
him drink for drink. Impaired and impervious, he
listened as a drunken Kip served up a final offering.

"Hunter, you know, he's here to see you?" slurred
Kip.

"We're having lunch on Monday," confirmed West.

"He's here to see you! Understand?"

"No."

"Not supposed to say anything to you, or, say
anything, but, you, he's going to talk to you about, you
know he has one last dragon to slay before he, he's
got his eye on you."

"Can't believe you're leaving us tomorrow," said
West.

"Secret mission. He's going to sail into the blast
zone. No one knows. Don't say anything," said a
swaying Kip.

"The South Pacific? Mururoa?" said West.

"I didn't say anything."

West put his arm around the reeling Kip as they
stood for a few moments to watch the surrounding
circus.

"You, more than anyone. I can't say goodbye. See
you in Mexico," said West refusing to let go of his
fragile pal.

"Vaya con tequila," Kip said softly, raising two

drink fingers in the air.

#

When Monday arrived, West wasn't sure whether
he should be nervous or not, so he chose nervous.
There hadn't been a hint of a panic attack over the
weekend; he was able to catch up on his sleep, and as
a bonus he had done a bit of surfing with his 'platonic'
neighbor Dharma Blue. Delilah stopped by on Sunday
and they went for coffee and a long walk. It was a nice
weekend, but he was nervous nonetheless.

Alice's Restaurant was quiet on this mid-day
Monday. Partly cloudy, the surf rolling in under the pier
was flat and glassy. West and Hunter were able to
negotiate a prime window table with an inspirational
Pacific Ocean view. The Mexican food and margaritas
were ordered in Kip's honor as Hunter's 'raison de
visite' was underway.

"In the beginning, GreenPlanet America will consist
of two offices, L. A. and San Francisco, and we might
reopen a support group in Hawaii. Depends on how
cooperative everyone is," said Hunter with a mouthful
of guacamole.

"In the beginning?" asked West.

"Right. To appease and hoodwink any remaining
rebels in San Francisco. Maybe a year, maybe two,
then America will be consolidated into one office."

"San Francisco," said West.

"No."

"Oh."

"Washington, D.C.," said Hunter.

"What?" said West.

552

"It's not as bad as it sounds, very good in many ways. Access to power and money."

"No more GreenPlanet in L. A.?"

Hunter didn't answer him, instead, he pointed to a pod of California Gray whales that were passing by. Hunter liked drama. He was a master manipulator, a master persuader. Always five chess moves ahead of his opponents, he used the silence and the setting to assist him in his mission.

"I want you to run the entire operation. Executive Director. Everyone in Europe is well aware of your accomplishments, and all are in agreement with me. I won't have any problem at all convincing your fellow Americans, but I do need you to say yes," said Hunter.

West carefully put down his margarita, and waited to see if panic was about to join their table. Hunter pretended to concentrate on his huevos rancheros and the spouting whales. He pointed to West's empty margarita glass and nodded his head in the affirmative just as the waiter materialized with two fresh drinks.

"You've become media savvy. Your face is known here and abroad. You have an ever-growing activist track record. All signs point to you. I don't want you to answer me right now. You're caught off guard. It's a big decision. Think about it and we'll talk again after my trip to San Francisco. If you have any strategic thoughts or suggestions, I want to hear them. This organization needs someone smart, brave, and bulletproof. We want you. Any questions?" Hunter said raising his glass in victory.

What does one say to something like that? West was numb. Those words didn't make any sense. He wasn't sure what, exactly, he had just heard. The obvious answer was 'no thanks.'

"What do you think about protesting those atomic bomb tests in the South Pacific?" said West.

Hunter smiled a pained smile realizing that brother Kip was unable to keep his mouth shut. This, he concluded, would be a revealing first test for West.

"I trust that you won't mention that to anyone," said Hunter.

"You have my word. When you go, I want in," answered West.

Hunter downed his margarita in one gulp and tossed a guacamole-covered tortilla at West.

"How many kinds of tequila do you think they have here?" said Hunter.

Executive Director? Washington, D.C.? Run the whole show? What the fuck? This was unexpected. This was unsettling. This was unwanted. Once again pacing the limited square footage of his Malibu trailer, West was growing increasingly agitated. Why was this shit happening to him? What had he done to deserve this? It was all Lucinda's fault. If she hadn't been so stupid! Leaving him for no sound reason. His "drifter friends" she said. She wanted "more" she said. Look at what has happened! Look at what is happening! Fuck!

He stopped pacing long enough to check his pulse. Pulse checking was now a many-times-a-day occurrence for him. It seemed okay. Who cares? His heart could explode for all he cared. Delilah wasn't going to like this news one bit. West? Executive Director! Ha! Too immature. She was on the same page as Lucinda when it came to his maturity. Fuck it.

Why was he even thinking this over? The answer was 'No!' Absolutely not. No surfing in Washington, D.C. No Malibu sunsets in San Francisco. No Death Valley getaways with his buddy Roy. No! The answer is no. Passing by the couch, he slammed on the brakes, reached his hand under the seat cushion, and pulled out the plastic bag containing the Skoal tin, but before he could open it there was loud knocking on his front door. Freeze! Don't move, he instructed himself. At the sound of more knocking, he stealthily placed the contraband back under the seat cushion. Dharma! It's just Dharma. Relax dude.

"Dharma?" West yelled. "Hold on."

Fumbling with the doorknob, he opened the door to discover, not Dharma, but Margaux, champagne bottle in tow.

"Margaux!" exclaimed West.

"Who's Dharma?" she said walking past him into the luxury that was his trailer.

"Dharma? Oh, uh, neighbor. Old woman who lives across the way. She borrows things from time to time. You know, butter, and uh, tools and stuff," he lied.

Margaux took a very brief stroll and look around in case other humans might be on the premises. In the kitchen, she placed the bottle of champagne on the counter, snagged a dirty dishtowel, and proceeded to pop the top. Selecting the two 'best' water glasses– also dirty– from the cupboard, she filled them with bubbly, and rejoined West in the living room.

"Sit, s'il vous plait" she said handing him a glass.

Margaux was different. Not in a weird or bad way, just different. West had learned to resign himself to the improvisational nature of these days, and so he followed her orders, sat himself down on the old couch, and surreptitiously checked his pulse.

"Au drame," she said sipping a bit more champagne.

Placing her glass on the coffee table, she took a few steps backward, and then expertly proceeded to remove each article of her clothing until she was au naturel. She stood her ground for a moment, arms akimbo, so that West could absorb all that was about to take place. Approaching the couch, Margaux stopped to have another healthy sip of champagne, and then with aplomb, she straddled a submissive West.

"Butter and tools?" she said.

Butter and tools it was. I won't go into the specific details at this time, but it took the next three days before West was able to lie comfortably on his surfboard, and to lie comfortably to himself. As he always did in the past–when life needed explaining and the world spun out of control–he sought out the advice and companionship of his older, wiser, and best friend Roy. They would get out the camping gear–all of which belonged to Roy–fill the cooler with ice and beer, purchase three grocery bags full of comfort food, and drive out of the city limits into wide-open thinking country. On this last weekend in October, they found themselves in a deserted Death Valley, huddled by a roaring campfire, under a cold starry night sky, enjoying the Humboldt Gold that Roy was decent enough to provide.

"Don't have any rent. My brother's mobile home is

paid for. The Econoline is paid for. Not many expenses, student loan, food, electricity, gas, insurance. I don't get paid much by GreenPlanet, but I get by," West was explaining.

"Still getting paid to service Cassandra Eaton?" asked Roy.

"Haven't had time. Life's been muy insane."

"You don't have time to have paid sex?"

"Truth be told, I ended the whole Cassandra thing," said West.

West wanted to tell Roy about the panic attacks; wanted to tell him about the offer of Executive Director. He needed guidance and direction, but he said nothing.

"Saw Lucinda a couple of weeks ago. She came over for Sabrina's famous pot spaghetti. She asked about you," Roy continued.

"Next subject."

"Ever miss being one half of a couple?"

"I'm not relationship material. Damaged goods," West said.

"Not what I asked you," said Roy.

"I'm on this giant wave right now. Have to ride it to the end," said West.

"Giant waves are dangerous."

"Yep. But if you make it all the way in and survive, you have one hell of a story to tell for the rest of your days."

"She's looking good," Roy said as he fired up another joint.

"Sorry. I'm taken."

The two best friends spent the rest of the weekend

being desert rats. Life was always simple with Roy. It was healing. All about friends, food, nature, and recreation. These days, whenever West parted company with Roy, he always felt foolish. How could he have wandered so far off of the path? Why did he feel the need to pull the tiger's tail, kick up the dust, and push things to the limit? It wasn't that long ago when he was content to hit tennis balls, search for the perfect wave, and eat Sabrina's pot spaghetti. If Lucinda hadn't...he wondered what Delilah was up to? Delilah understood him. Right?

#

The time had finally come for the formal creation of GreenPlanet America. Hunter and Hugh had spent the last four weeks in San Francisco examining the books, meeting with lawyers and accountants, turning over any and all rocks, and taking oral histories from all willing staffers and volunteers. The picture that was uncovered wasn't good, but it wasn't all bad either. Yes, money had been consciously misappropriated. Yes, a disproportionate percentage of donations and membership money went to the housing, feeding, and entertaining of the Northern California tribe, especially the 'top dogs.' But. Campaigns were conducted, work was ongoing, press coverage was positive, and results had been achieved. Disdain for accountability, and shameful rationalization for the "proper usage" of funds were the primary factors that resulted in the misuse of the public's money. In the case of Jonah, it was outright theft. Karma, Catty, and others 'in the know' were guilty of looking the other way, not to mention, enjoying for themselves the spoils of petty cash. It was the classic case of a small operation that experienced explosive growth, notoriety, and cash flow, but didn't have the trained, educated, experienced, and ethical personnel to handle things properly. All of that was about to change.

In the L.A. office, luggage was piled high next to the front door as West, Delilah, and Salinger were about to depart for LAX on this 'Finally a Friday' in mid-November. Kate had some parting words for them before she let them go.

"If all goes according to plan, you'll be in meetings tomorrow and Sunday, finalize details Monday morning, and back on a plane to L.A. Monday evening. Next week is Thanksgiving, so let's plan on Tuesday in the office and the remainder of the week you will be free to run wild. A historic GreenPlanet weekend is about to begin. Nothing will be the same starting next week. Good luck and Godspeed," she said with a sparkle in her eye and a clap of her hands. "Very well. Off you go."

On the short flight from LAX to SFO West was subdued. Two voices were competing for his attention. Half of his brain had decided not to accept the Executive Directorship when offered while the other half was thinking crazy thoughts. His inner voice suggested that he graciously, wisely decline the offer, while his ego voice painted a picture of success, ambition, and status. He pretended not to know which voice had won him over.

Saturday was spent outlining the structure of the new organization. GreenPlanet San Francisco and

GreenPlanet L.A. would be under the umbrella of GreenPlanet America. GreenPlanet America would be under the umbrella of GreenPlanet International. If there were to be any American satellite offices—i.e. Hawaii— they would answer to GreenPlanet America. A predetermined percentage of funds raised by each office would go to GreenPlanet America for the operation of its separate office. Seventy-five percent of all monies raised would go toward campaigns approved by International. The Executive Director would be selected by the chosen members of the committee, and the staff of GreenPlanet America would be hired by the newly chosen Executive Director. It was a long, exhausting, grueling, but ultimately productive day. Drinking and carousing at the Buena Vista Café was determined, by unanimous vote, to be the order of the night.

When Sunday morning arrived, everyone was surprisingly on time; unsurprisingly hung over; bleary, weary, anxious, and excited. Today would be the day that a GreenPlanet America Executive Director would be chosen. Karma, as well as the others, didn't have a clue as to how this day would play out. She entertained serious thoughts of being 'the one' that would be considered the obvious, proper, most fitting person for the job, but she was also suffering the sting of aiding and abetting Jonah in the improper operation of the San Francisco office. She knew Hunter well, and fully expected him to have a handpicked candidate ready to roll. The fact that he had not pulled her aside for any clandestine chats gave her pause and doubt. Yesterday, it had been decided, that temporarily, the

GreenPlanet America office would "borrow" some of the vast and empty office space that was part and parcel of the San Francisco operation until they moved into their own space, presumably close by in San Francisco—not a word was mentioned about Washington, D.C. Who was this person that would invade their San Francisco space, and disrupt their routine? Would they come from outside the country? Would he or she be accepted by the group? West also didn't have a clue—although he thought that he did— as to the forthcoming events of the day. He was keyed up and jittery. His had made his decision. This day was circled on his calendar.

"I know everyone is tired. Change is happening fast, and that is always an ass kicker. The time has come for us to talk about the American office personnel, in particular, the selection of an Executive Director. I've spoken at length with someone that Hugh and I and the European members feel would be the best person to take on this challenge, someone who is well versed on all topics, an excellent communicator and motivator, someone that is trusted by staff and volunteers in both offices, someone that has continually performed at a high level," Hunter said.

Karma promptly ascertained that she was clearly not 'the one.' She had not, sadly, spoken "at length" with Hunter about anything like this. Dropping her head, she knowingly accepted defeat. West, on the other hand, had spoken with Hunter at length, and he, too, dropped his head, but not in defeat.

"After several days of careful thought, I'm pleased to report that this person has agreed to accept the

561

position of Executive Director if offered. I urge you all to seriously

consider, and then elect Susan Noble as the first Executive Director of GreenPlanet America," said a beaming Hunter.

Silence. Susan. Brilliant. Spot on. Everyone knew it then and there. No one knew what to say or do.

"I think we should have multiple choices. Karma should be on the ballot, " said Sunset.

"Multiple candidates are up to you, but International retains veto power if we feel that it is necessary," Hunter replied.

"Thank you Sunset, but I would prefer to continue running the San Francisco operation, and I agree with Hunter, Susan is the perfect choice," said Karma.

West was dizzy. Delilah could see him gripping the edge of the table for support.

"What's wrong?" she whispered to West.

"Not feeling well," whispered West.

"We hope you'll give our suggestion serious consideration. Susan is sitting right there. Tell her your concerns. Ask her questions. Talk it all out. You've got forty-eight hours. Good luck," concluded Hunter.

West, sweat pouring down his face, watched as Hunter gathered up his papers, grabbed Hugh by the arm, and without a look back in his direction, exited out of the building. Too weak to stand up, he watched as Susan was immediately surrounded by her friends and colleagues from both offices. There would be no other candidates. Susan was unanimously chosen by day's end. She was, as Karma said, the perfect choice. But, what just happened? That was the question currently tormenting West's brain and his equilibrium? What changed since his lunch four weeks ago with Hunter? Why did he feel sick? Betrayed? Ashamed? He was, after all of his self-denial, going to accept the predetermined offer that did not happen. Was Hunter angry that West butted into his secret Mururoa plans? Maybe he finally saw what West knew all along, that he was an imposter, a phony? It felt like a cruel joke intended to cause him pain and humiliation. What the fuck?

By the time he, Delilah, and Salinger boarded their flight back to Los Angeles, West had regained most of his composure. The shock had subsided, and in fact, as the hours passed, he was progressively relieved that the course of events had unfolded in the way that they did. He loved and adored Susan, and yes, she was the perfect person to captain the ship. He didn't want to relocate to San Francisco; eventually to Washington, D.C., Malibu suited him just fine. Delilah was in Los Angeles, as was Roy, and tennis courts, and surfboards, but he now struggled with two sources of pain: 1) Hunter's rejection and 2) his own swelling madness.

West was in awe of Hunter. His admiration and respect for that man was off the charts. It pained him to think that he had lost the approval and friendship of someone he so cherished. He racked his brain for a solution, for a way to get back into Hunter's good graces. The fact that he was prepared to say 'yes' if offered the Executive Director job, angered him. It made him feel weak, and blindly, foolishly ambitious. He was mortified. The world, and he it was clear, had

563

reached the heights of insanity. West was adrift at sea, and didn't know how to find his way back home. The seventies were coming to an end, and West had no idea who he was.

#

Monday and Tuesday in the L.A. office were short days. Everyone was buzzing about the new organizational structure, and all were ecstatic that Susan was chosen as the first Executive Director of GreenPlanet America. Everyone was also deliriously happy to have the following five days free to escape the never-ending GreenPlanet circus, and to reacquaint themselves with how the rest of the known world lived.

On the Wednesday night before Thanksgiving, West and Delilah had settled into their VIP seats– courtesy of Will– at the Santa Monica Civic Center in excited anticipation of Bob Dylan and his band. Both were huge Dylan fans, neither had ever seen him live in concert, and this was an impossible-to-get ticket. The energy in the Civic Center was an odd combination of restless and privileged. It was fifteen minutes past eight and there was no sign of Dylan.

"He's calling it his Gospel Tour. There was almost a riot last night. Newspaper said he refuses to play any of his old songs. Only new Christian tunes," said Delilah.

That explains the free tickets, thought West. What Christian tunes? He didn't know what Delilah was talking about. Bob Dylan and Christian tunes? Absurd. Finally, there was some activity on the stage. One of Dylan's backup singers walked out, stepped in front of a stage-center microphone and began to deliver a never-ending monologue on the merits of the Christian faith.

"When you accept Jesus Christ into your life, miraculous things begin to happen. He is the true savior, he is," blah, blah, blah, blah, blah.

"The whole world has gone stark raving mad. What the fuck is this?" West gasped.

"You and I have never had a God conversation," said Delilah.

"We've never had a moon-is-made-out-of-green-cheese conversation either."

"You've never been a believer?"

"We choose our beliefs."

"Meaning?"

"You're free to believe whatever you wish. If it works for you, makes your worldview comforting, helps you cope with the fact that no one here gets out alive, terrific, good for you."

"But."

"But it doesn't make it true."

"Your belief."

"Correct. Look around you. Thousands of people. The biggest threat to everyone here? Different worldviews. Different beliefs. Rattles the cage. Shakes the house of cards."

"So we try to convert the cage rattlers, and if that doesn't work we banish them from the kingdom."

"Or execute them," said West.

From offstage, Dylan and the rest of the band sauntered into sight. Wearing an all-white suit, Dylan made his way to center stage, arms extended, bestowing his blessings on each fortunate soul in the Santa Monica crowd. In no hurry to play music, he took over the microphone to launch into his own religious screed. The crowd was not happy. Booing, jeering, cries for "Rock-N-Roll," rang out. Stomping feet, and cries of "Judas," did not deter Mr. Dylan.

""Well. What a rude bunch tonight, huh? You all know how to be real rude. You know about the spirit of the anti-Christ? Does anybody here know about that? Well, it's clear the anti-Christ is loose right now. Turn the lights on in here. I want to see these people. Turn some lights on. Give them some light. Let them in the light. You want to rock-n-roll? Go see KISS if you want to rock-n-roll. There's only two kinds of people: There are saved people and there's lost people. Yeah. Now remember that I told you that. You may never see me again. I may not be through here again, you may not see me, sometime down the line you'll remember you heard it here. That Jesus is Lord. And every knee shall bow to him. There's certain men, you know, many of them who live right in this town who seek to lead you astray. You be careful now," Dylan concluded as he and the band finally assumed their positions.

As the first tune–'Gotta Serve Somebody'– began, Delilah looked at a horrified West.

"So, in conclusion, let people believe whatever they want," she said.

"Just don't insist that I must believe your bullshit too. That's when we have problems," answered West.

Pleased to learn that she and West were on the same very important page, Delilah gathered up her things.

"You okay?" she asked.

"Let's get the fuck out of here," said West.

West and Delilah readily vacated their VIP seats, clasped hands, and walked up the aisle toward the exit, and maybe some pizza.

"You learn something every day," she said smiling.

"Fucking unbelievable," said West.

December marked the final days of the decade. West achingly remembered when the sixties came to an end. He remembered how sad he was to see that magical, mystical decade ride off into the sunset, and now he was even sadder to see the end of the seventies. The 1970s turned out to be the roller coaster ride of all roller coaster rides. Turbulent, exciting, surprising, rewarding, painful, and ultimately defining. And ultimately inexplicable. The greatest music ever created had to fend off the temporarily insane appetite for disco "music," only to be assaulted on another flank by the growing popularity of 'glam metal' and 'new wave.' Cable television was growing, and there was a rumor that a music television network was being developed. Its concept was to combine songs with video. Music videos. What? How or why would The Allman Brothers or Led Zeppelin or Yes or Tom Petty or the Stones or every other great rock band be involved with that? Music videos? West thought it was preposterous.

As 1979 transitioned into 1980, fashion suggested a growing narcissism, an escape from the social politics of the day leading to a passion for material things. Money, cars, gadgets, credit, clothes, drugs. Me, me, me, me. Club drugs a.k.a. designer drugs

567

were replacing the mainstream substances. Ecstasy, poppers, methamphetamines, ludes, Ketamine, and DMT. Cocaine was king. Cocaine was everywhere. There was a rise in 'crack cocaine.'

Jimmy Carter was about to start the last year of his first term as President of the United States, and it became more and more clear that his Republican opponent in the 1980 election would be the former Governor of California Ronald Reagan. The same Ronald Reagan that, as a secret informant, turned in names of his fellow actors to the House Un-American Activities Committee, ruining lives and careers. The same Ronald Reagan that believed in little or no taxation, rewarding the rich, and arguing that the financial benefits of lower taxes to the top five percent would "trickle down" to the meek and hungry masses. Californians were already aware of the disaster that was Ronald Reagan. What if he became president? Jimmy Carter was struggling. Long lines at gas pumps around the country had become a frequent occurrence thanks to the Iranian Revolution that resulted in the decreased output of crude oil. Only four weeks ago fifty-two Americans were taken hostage after Iranian-Revolution-supporting students stormed the U.S. Embassy in Tehran. The hostage-takers demanded that the overthrown Shah be returned from the United States to Iran to stand trial. They also wanted Iran's frozen assets in the United States to be "unfrozen," and for the United States to butt-out of Iranian affairs. Carter was floundering and Reagan was on the rise.

As the door to the seventies was closing, West was as insecure about his way forward than ever before.

Where would his path lead him? Would he ever find his way out of the jungle? What did the fucking eighties have in store for him? Unlike last year when he and Connor ferociously rang in the new year, this December 31ˢᵗ would be a low-key Chimney Sweep affair with he and Delilah, Salinger, Connie and Gil, Will popping in briefly, nothing more than an enjoyable Monday night. West went home with Delilah, and upon waking the next morning it was 1980. No Malibu earthquakes; no unfamiliar naked women in his bed; no 1970s.

#

1980, for West, was mostly a fever dream. He struggled to correctly identify, much less connect, the formative, developmental dots that were actively composing his work-in-progress persona. Seemingly unrelated fragments of 1980 events swirled around his conscious and subconscious mind. Soviet tanks, ground troops, and helicopters invading Afghanistan, culminating in the assault and eventual occupation of the Tajbeg Presidential Palace. More than a million Time Square people huddled together on a freezing cold night to ring in the New Year. The U.S. embassy in Tehran surrounded by an angry mob of student revolutionaries. American hostages, handcuffed and blindfolded, being paraded in front of TV cameras. President Jimmy Carter giving the State of the Union address. Susan behind her desk as the new Executive Director with Jade, Rocky, and Salinger as her handpicked co-workers. Salinger was gone!

He often flashed back to St. Patrick's Day when he

and Connor Kilkenny went to Hollywood Park to drink and watch the horses run. It was a beautiful sunshiny day as the horses made their final turn toward the home stretch. West was jumping up and down as the crowd around him built into a frenzy. When the number-three horse crossed the finish line first, West lost his mind. At the cashier's window, he watched in awe as the cashier counted out two thousand dollars.

He regularly revisited the 1980 instances of Delilah playing the hero. First, a dozen Pilot Whales were stranded on the beach at Dana Point; she was in chest deep water leading a group of volunteers as they threw buckets of seawater on the thrashing, over-heating whales. With inflated pontoons, they fought, but failed to tow the whales back out to sea to the safety of the open ocean. On that day, Delilah was taken to the emergency room with a separated shoulder. On another occasion–down the road at Sea World– she led the charge to free a dying orca in captivity. Five hundred people blocked the highway. KWOT covered the protest as it happened. She went to jail on that day.

For reasons he didn't understand, he was haunted by the eruption of Mount St. Helens. In his recurring dreams a gigantic column of ash and debris would rise above the mountain, and then the entire north face of the volcano would explode into pieces, resulting in a massive landslide and lava flow. Snow, ice, and glaciers melted as people and animals ran for their lives. He would replay this dream over and over and over.

As the year progressed there were many other

ghosts that haunted him. During the summer, Paul Revere and his band of Sea Pirates intentionally rammed their boat Threshold Guardian into the Nisshin Maru, a Japanese factory ship that was processing dead whales. People on both vessels were injured. It was an international incident. Also during the summer, West traveled to the Pine Ridge reservation in South Dakota. He remembered signs posted at multiple locations along the Cheyenne River displaying the nuclear radiation symbol. In an old dilapidated shack, he sat beside a Native American woman near death. Her expressionless children were there. She was dying of radiation poisoning.

Will talked him into joining him at a porn house in the Valley. Drugs, ugliness, and nakedness abounded. People fucking in the open, people spiraling out of control. It was dark. It was depressing. He didn't participate. One afternoon he found himself sadly headed to Cassie Eaton's house, and not for a tennis lesson. Halfway there he stopped, threw her into reverse, and went home. On the night of June 1st, in a chemical fog, he and Myra a.k.a. Orange Julius girl with the dagger tattoo, found themselves on his shitty couch, drinking whiskey and watching with wonder the first night of a new cable television channel called CNN. They watched until the sun came up. Fortunately, he didn't make any naked regrettable decisions.

One might reasonably conclude from West's year of haunted fever dreams that 1980 was not kind to him, that for him it was zero steps forward and two steps back, but that was not the case. He performed fairly well. He assisted Susan as the architect of the GreenPlanet America playbook. He expertly kept GreenPlanet in the news via radio, television, and print interviews. He served as liaison with the American Indian Movement, the anti-nuclear movement, and all things marine mammal related. He may have been "on borrowed time," as Shakespeare Jones continually reminded him. He may not have been a 'man with a plan,' but he was trying to formulate one. He was trying to divine just how much time he would be allowed to borrow. He was trying to emerge from the jungle.

Without warning, West's fever broke on the evening of the autumnal equinox. September 22nd, 1980. It was a Monday. His restlessness and confusion disappeared like an impetuous September San Francisco fog. Within him was a feeling of lightness to the point of weightlessness. A great burden lifted from his neck and shoulders. It was a strange and unfamiliar tranquility.

Delilah's internal radar detected something unusual about West. He exuded a positive chi that she hadn't felt for a very long time. She took him to the Chimney Sweep that evening. Just for a few drinks. They hadn't seen Connie in a while and she wanted to say hello. On the television above the bar, patrons were ignoring a breaking news bulletin showing the invasion of Iran by Iraq, and Connie, savvy bartendress that she was, countered the buzz-killing television images by turning up the volume on the jukebox. When West and Delilah walked into the bar, Connie lit up like a Christmas tree. La familia! It would be a lovely reunion. Lots of laughs and stories; hugs and kisses.

On the walk back to their respective cars they held hands and made dinner plans for the end of the week. Since the beginning of the year, it had been a concerted effort on both their parts to spend time with each other on a regular basis, and West had tried, as best that he could, to explain to Delilah his quandary. He told her of the periodic panic attacks, which, over time, had become less frequent. He confessed to her his identity crisis dilemma. He showed his love for her as often as he was able. Delilah exercised patience. She had decided to wait and see. Would or could West grow up in time to make things work? Would he come to his senses? "We'll see," she thought. "But, the clock is running."

Monday, September 22nd was the autumnal equinox in North America and the spring equinox in New Zealand. In the tiny seaport of Russell–about two hundred and thirty kilometers north of Auckland– Hunter Mack was bellied up to the bar at the Duke of Marlborough Hotel. Strong drinks, hearty food, and a good night's sleep were the final items on his checklist of things to do before boarding his thirty-nine-foot sailboat come morning. He would be sailing solo on this trip, sailing anonymously, covertly, 4,700 kilometers due east across the South Pacific to the Mururoa atoll in French Polynesia. The French government was about to conduct more atmospheric nuclear weapons tests, and Hunter was determined to stop them. He, too, was feeling the weightlessness and serenity that often comes at the end of a long and difficult journey. He could detect a faint golden light at the end of his particular tunnel.

As his sailboat Synchrony sailed out of the Port of Russell into the South Pacific, the New Zealand morning light was a cobalt sailor's delight. Filled with pride and gratitude, Hunter raised the GreenPlanet flag up the mast, took a step back, and gave it a long look before returning to the helm. Weather permitting; it would take about ten days for him to reach his final destination. Questions remained to be answered. Would he be intercepted by the French military before he could get close enough to disrupt their atomic tests? If he made it all the way, how long would he be able to occupy the bomb zone? Would his sailboat be rammed? Would it be boarded? Would he fight if necessary? Would this be his last time unto the breach? As New Zealand faded from sight, and all that surrounded him was open ocean, Hunter breathed a heavy sigh. Filling his lungs with ocean air, he maneuvered the Synchrony in the best possible direction for the sails to fill with wind, and race him with the least effort toward the light at the end of the tunnel. Looking out over the majestic sea, he mumbled some last words to himself.

"I must down to the seas again, to the vagrant gypsy life, to the gull's way and the whale's way where the wind's like a whetted knife, and all I ask is a merry yarn from a laughing fellow-rover, and quiet sleep, and a sweet dream when the long trick is over."

It was a gray day as the Synchrony approached the twelve-mile bomb test exclusion zone. Hunter didn't sleep well the night before knowing what lay before him. Due to heavy fog, he could not see the atoll in the distance, nor could he see or detect on radar any military vessels heading his way. Proceeding with extreme caution into the direction of the blast zone, he checked and rechecked the documents in front of him. This was indeed the scheduled day of testing. Where were the bad guys? On the radar screen, he could see the atoll getting closer and closer. Into the captain's log, he made the following entry: "Arrived Mururoa mid-day. Visibility poor. No bad guys in sight. Bomb test rescheduled? Heading toward..."

Before he could finish the entry there was an enormous explosion. Bright white light flashed across the sky and water. Radio and radar were knocked out. The sailboat tossed like a toy in a bathtub. Hunter, temporarily blinded, scrambled, crawling his way to the main mast. With rope in hand, he proceeded to secure himself to the mast, praying that the Synchrony would remain upright. As the last knot was tied, he could partially see before him, a menacing tsunami wave created by the detonation of the bomb. Helpless, and realizing his fate, he hung on tight as the wave picked up the Synchrony and threw her across the sea like a football. The main mast, with Hunter tied to it, broke off from the now capsized boat to be tossed upon the heaving sea. Bleeding and semi-conscious, Hunter watched in horror as the Synchrony sank like a carrier anchor beneath the waves and out of sight. His right collarbone was poking through his shirt. A collapsed lung made it impossible for him to breathe. He could feel the life pouring out of his body. "This is how it ends," he whispered. He didn't try to untie himself from the floating piece of wreckage. He didn't call for help. He didn't pray for salvation. From below the water, the GreenPlanet flag floated to the surface not far from where Hunter lay dying. A weary smile replaced his painful grimace. "What a ride?" he concluded. "What a ride." Those were his final words, and with that, he took one last precious breath of ocean air, closed his eyes, rolled over, and let the sea take him.

#

Monday was the sixth day of October, and West—guessing that no one would give a shit—played hooky from work and went surfing with Dharma Blue. Dharma was cool. She made it clear from the get-go that she wasn't interested in anything more than being West's friendly neighbor who would pop by for the occasional beer, or, when time permitted, school him in the art of surfing. She'd met Delilah twice prior, and all was 'no problema.' They dug each other if truth be told, and this made life for West más fácil.

A sublime south swell made for the creation of tasty waves four to six feet high. At Malibu, this was a primo day. Dragging their boards and zonked asses out of the water after an excellent session of surfing, West and Dharma had just enough energy left to tease and taunt each other. A frisky Dharma reminded West of what "a pussy surfer" he was before throwing a wad of seaweed in his face, and West, unable to catch the fleeing Dharma, collapsed in exhaustion on the sand only to find Delilah waiting for him.

"Hey Dee, what's up?" said West breathing hard.

Dharma plopped her board down next to West. She could see that Delilah had been crying.

"Delilah? You okay sweetie?" said Dharma.

"Hunter," said Delilah.

West held his breath. Delilah's face told him everything. Tears filled his eyes. Soaking wet, and covered in sand, he wrapped his arms around Delilah, and didn't let go. No words were spoken. Delilah's sobs spoke volumes.

Hunter's body had been found, the day after the bomb blast, bobbing in the sea, still tied to the severed mast. After medical examiners released the body several days later, confident that it was radiation free, it was flown to Colorado Springs for funeral services and burial. West hadn't been back to Colorado since he and Susan escaped jail time in Jefferson County, and now there he was dressed all in black under a radiant blue October sky.

Hunter's mother spoke. She told tales of his childhood in Colorado Springs. She expressed her fear mixed with parental pride each time that she heard news of her son's dangerous escapades. She spoke of the pain that comes with burying a child. Several GreenPlanet people also addressed the congregation. Kip wasn't one of them. He wasn't in attendance. "Unbearable," figured West. "Unfathomable."

Ten days had passed since Hunter's funeral, and West found himself sitting across the conference table from Hugh Simon and Kate Blair. Hugh and West hadn't exchanged many words at the funeral, and West was caught off guard when Kate informed him that Hugh had made the trip to Los Angeles specifically to see him.

"Yes my heart is broken, but I'm angry that he lied to me," said West.

"That's incorrect," said Hugh.

"He lied to me twice. About becoming Executive Director and about going with him to Muroroa. I don't know what I did to make him turn on me."

"He never said that you could go with him to Muroroa. Never. You invited yourself, but that was not to be, fortunately, for you. And he meant what he said about becoming Executive Director," said Hugh.

"That so? Where oh where is Susan when we need her?"

"If you'll stop behaving like a child and think back to that October lunch."

"You weren't there!"

"He never said Executive Director of America," Hugh snapped.

West glanced at Kate who was staring lasers into him.

"He talked to you about 'running the show'," said Hugh. "International."

Panic attacks often appear when you least expect them. At the onset of this attack, West took three deep breaths, rolled his shoulders, and allowed it to pass through him.

"He was grooming you to take over for him. I think your ridiculous American expression is "the whole enchilada," said Kate.

"Impossible," said West.

"It's why I'm here. International has sent me here to persuade you to accept the position of Executive

Director," said Hugh.

West rose from his chair as if to leave. Five paces toward the door, five paces back. Four paces toward the Telex machine, four paces back. He had never liked that ugly orange vase on Salinger's desk. Slinging it against the strategy board felt good; orange shards flew in all directions. His desk was piled high with folders and paper. Clearing it off in one violent swipe was just what the doctor ordered. Much better. Sweat covered his forehead.

"He didn't disown me?" said West returning to his seat at the table.

"He loved you like a little brother," said Kate.

West placed his head into his hands and cried like a baby.

"I should have been with him on that boat," he sobbed. "I should have been there."

#

On Tuesday, November 4, 1980, the former Governor of California, Ronald Reagan, was elected as the 40th President of the United States, the same somber night that West and Delilah sat at an LAX departure gate waiting for West's London flight to begin boarding.

"You sure are quiet," said West.

"Nothing to say," Delilah mumbled.

"You mad or sad? Or glad?" he joked.

"You're an idiot."

"I'll take that as mad."

"You know in your gut that you don't want this, but your ego is putting you on that plane."

"This is a once in a lifetime opportunity."

"Idiot."

"You don't think I'll do a good job?"

"You belong here."

"I belong..."

"With me."

"I'm damaged goods."

"Fuck off."

The flight began to board, and West couldn't look at Delilah because he knew that she was right. He started to go.

"Please give me a kiss goodbye," she said.

With trepidation he returned to kiss her.

"Will you come visit me?" he asked.

"No," she said as she turned and walked away.

West watched her go. He glanced at the ticket in his hand, shook his head, and smiled an odd smile. It was time to board a plane.

#

Delilah was at her desk working when Kate emerged from her office.

"Just spoke with the London office," said Kate.

"How's our boy doing? Does he already have an English accent?" joked Salinger.

"He never showed up."

Delilah stopped what she was working on to give Kate her full attention.

"The weekend came and went, then Monday, then yesterday. They haven't seen or heard from him. He's dropped off the radar," said Kate.

Delilah had gathered her things. As she headed for

the door, she stopped to look in Kate and Salinger's direction.

"Want me to come with you?" said Kate.

Delilah shook her head 'no' and out the door she ran. Speeding up the hill to West's mobile home, she hit the brakes, jumped out of her car, and rummaged for the keys to his trailer. After several knocks went unanswered, she put the key in the door, opened it, and entered. It was dark inside. Opening the curtains allowed the natural light to reveal the same shitty trailer that she saw on that first day. No West in sight. On the table she saw an empty Skoal tin, an empty tortilla chip bag, and empty beer bottles. "His mess for me to clean up. Perfect," she thought. The bedroom and bathroom were unoccupied. There was no dead body in the kitchen. She concluded that he hadn't been there. Closing the curtains, she ran back out the door and into her car, but she had missed something. In the dark of the living room, on the shitty couch, stuck between the cushions, was an old tattered map of Baja, California.

Delilah was sprinting. Sprinting to their spot on the beach where they first met. Gasping for air, looking in all directions, she was devastated to find nothing. No West. No miracle. Winded, she collapsed onto the sand. The beach was empty. No humans except for Delilah. Staring sharply out to sea, a puff of white on the water caught her eye, and then a spout of water, and then two spouts, and then three. A pod of Gray whales was very close to the shore. The largest whale slowed in front of Delilah and stared her down. Not a confrontational stare, mind you, but more like the mutual recognition of an old friend. After a few unbroken moments, the whale disappeared below the surface of the water as Delilah observed the pod head south toward Mexico. Mexico! That's it! She should have known. In her mind, Delilah followed the pod of whales on their journey down the California coast, around the tip of Cabo San Lucas, and up into the Sea of Cortez. She pictured the whales slowing to a crawl as the largest whale stopped to make eye contact with a lone figure sitting on the Mexican sand. West and the whale locked on to each other's gaze, overjoyed to see each other once again. They understood that they were where they belonged, that they had made it out of the jungle, at least for the time being, until they all returned north, into the waiting arms of loved ones that waited patiently for their return.

A Note from the Author

Saving Whales is a work of eco-fiction inspired by my observations and adventures as a Greenpeace activist in late 1970's Hollywood. In a short four year period from 1977 to 1980, I would unexpectedly–some would also say undeservedly– skyrocket from part-time volunteer to become the very first National Director of Greenpeace USA. I saw things. I did things. Some things I regret, some things I survived, some fill me with pride, some leave me shaking my head, and some make me laugh out loud. I crossed paths with rock stars, movie stars, television stars, porn stars, politicians, criminals, millionaires, grifters, and gurus. Some of my time was spent in the company of beautiful women, some was spent in the company of illegal substances, some was spent staring down the barrel of a Russian harpoon gun, and some was spent in the Jefferson County jail. I spent time on the Pine Ridge reservation and at the bar at the Royal Hawaiian Hotel. I've been on stage, back stage, and upstaged. After all of these years, and these many roads traveled, I still find myself searching for a way out of the jungle.

DENNIS DELANEY is an American writer and actor, and former environmental activist who (in 1980) became the first National Director of Greenpeace USA.

In May of 1978 he was arrested with Daniel Ellsberg and twelve others at the Rocky Flats Nuclear Weapons Facility in Golden, Colorado. Their arrest for trespassing and civil disobedience resulted in a high-profile trial, and national media coverage of the life-threatening environmental disaster caused by the radioactive waste and plutonium contamination in the Denver, Colorado area.

Later that summer, he joined the crew of the Greenpeace ship M/V Peacock, as they non-violently confronted the Russian whaling fleet in the South Pacific.

While a Director of Greenpeace in Los Angeles, he joined forces in 1979 with The Alliance for Survival and the Abalone Alliance to protest the construction and opening of the Diablo Canyon Nuclear Power Plant in San Luis Obispo, California. In 1980 he would move north to San Francisco, recruited by the chairman of Greenpeace International, David McTaggart, to be selected as the first National Director of Greenpeace USA.